FLYING INTO THE FLAMES OF HELL

FLYING INTO THE FLAMES OF HELL

Dramatic first hand accounts of British and Commonwealth airmen in RAF Bomber Command in WW2

Martin W. Bowman

Pen & Sword
AVIATION

First published in
Great Britain in 2006
by Pen & Sword Aviation
an imprint of Pen & Sword Books Ltd
47 Church Street, Barnsley
South Yorkshire, S70 2AS

Copyright © Martin W. Bowman, 2006

ISBN 1 84415 389 4

A CIP catalogue record for this book is available from the
British Library.

Typeset by Concept, Huddersfield, West Yorkshire
Printed and bound in Great Britain by CPI UK

Pen & Sword Books Ltd incorporates the Imprints of Pen
& Sword Aviation, Pen & Sword Maritime, Pen & Sword
Military, Wharncliffe Local History, Pen & Sword Select,
Pen & Sword Military Classics and Leo Cooper.

For a complete list of Pen & Sword titles please contact
Pen & Sword Books Limited, 47 Church Street, Barnsley,
South Yorkshire, S70 2AS, England
E-mail: enquiries@pen-and-sword.co.uk
Website: www.pen-and-sword.co.uk

Contents

Phantom bombers on the old airfields
Where do you fly tonight
Are you off to visit Berlin, Hamburg, Nuremberg or Mannheim
Or somewhere in the Ruhr, east of the Rhine

Phantom bombers on the old airfields
Where do you fly tonight
Through a moonless or full moonlit sky
Giving battle as you fly
Returning shrouded, but with your spirits aces high

Ghostly engines, silenced by time
Outlined at dispersal by rings of rime
With ghostly guns of noiseless rattle
Patiently waiting the phantom hours of battle

Phantom bombers on the old airfields
Where do you fly tonight
If you will only wait for me to join you
In the air battles of long ago
It will be in the company of my old aircrew

The Bomber Airman's Lament (Tune of: *Empty Saddles in the Old Corral*), Louis Patrick Wooldridge DFC

Introduction

It was an article of faith in the pre-war RAF that modern twin-engined bombers like the Hampden, Wellington, Whitley and Blenheim, with revolving machine-gun turrets and flying in close formation to maximise defensive fire power against attacking fighter aircraft, were unbeatable: 'The Bomber Always Gets Through.' It was even assumed that these aircraft didn't need any form of fighter escort to reach and destroy their assigned targets. In the raw practice of war, however, this belief was rudely shattered. Bomber operations against elements of the German fleet at Brunsbüttel and Wilhelmshaven on 4 September 1939 were met with stiff opposition from both fighters and flak, two Wellingtons and five Blenheims being lost. The elderly Whitley squadrons in 4 Group were immediately employed in night leaflet-dropping operations, and made no appearance in daylight at all.

The 3 Group Wellingtons and 5 Group Hampdens kept searching for the German navy in daylight during the remainder of September 1939 but the serious losses inflicted on 29 September, when a complete formation of five 144 Squadron Hampdens were destroyed over the German Bight between Heligoland and Wangerooge Island by Bf 109 fighters, soon convinced the Air Staff that a profound change of its daylight policy was necessary. It was two major disasters in December 1939 that finally persuaded the Air Staff that a radical change in direction was necessary if future bombing operations were to stand any chance of success.

After April 1940 Bomber Command decided not to abandon completely the use of bombers in daylight. Although the Hampden and Wellington units largely shifted to night-time bombing, someone had to do the daylight offensive operations unless the RAF was prepared to admit that it had nothing for this most visible of its tasks. Thus the Bristol Blenheims and Fairey Battles in 2 Group and the AASF (Advanced Air Striking Force) stood forward as the best of a bad lot.

When Bomber Command took the decision in May 1940 to start strategic bombing of Germany by night, there was little the *Luftwaffe* could do to counter these early raids, as no specialised night-fighting arm existed. The creation of a true night air defence of the Third *Reich* was dramatically accelerated when Göring ordered General Kammhuber on 17 July 1940 to create a night-fighting arm. By the end of 1940 the infant *Nachtjagd* had matured into three searchlight batallions and five night-fighter *Gruppen*. At least nineteen Bomber Command aircraft were destroyed in the 'Kammhuber Line', as the continuous belt of searchlights and radar positions between Schleswig-Holstein and northern France were christened by the British bomber crews. A total of fifty-nine RAF bombers were shot down by *Nachtjagd* during May 1942, about half of which were claimed during the night of 30/31 May when the first Millenium or 1,000 Bomber Raid was made on Cologne. A force of 1,046 aircraft set out and forty bombers and two Intruders were lost – a 3.8 per cent loss rate. A further 116 aircraft were damaged, twelve so badly that they were written off. The fires burned for days and 59,100 people were made homeless. The second 1,000 Bomber Raid, against Essen, took place on the night of 1/2 June with a force of 956 bombers. Some bombers returned early with mechanical and engine problems. Thirty-one aircraft failed to return. A third 1,000 Bomber Raid took place on the night of 25/26 June when 1,006 aircraft, including 102 Wellingtons of Coastal Command, attacked Bremen. June 1942 saw a record 147 Bomber Command aircraft destroyed by *Nachtjagd*.

During September 1942 eighty-six Bomber Command aircraft were lost. With the coming of autumn weather and a decrease in Bomber Command activity, during October 1942, only thirty-eight bombers were destroyed. In January 1943, the acute U-boat danger that threatened to sever the vital lifelines between the UK and the US pulled Bomber Command away from the strategic area bombing campaign against German cities and it led to a series of raids against U-boat bases in France and Northern Germany, which would last until the start of the Battle of the Ruhr two months later. By early 1943, Kammhuber's defence line had been completed and *Lichtenstein* AI-radar equipped aircraft were now capable of exacting a maximum toll of 6 per cent bomber casualties on any deep penetration raid into the *Reich*. Thus, Bomber Command losses rose rapidly during the first few months of 1943.

The date 5/6 March has gone into history as the starting point of the Battle of the Ruhr, Bomber Command's spring offensive for 1943. Operational statistics for the period of the Battle of the Ruhr (5/6 March to 23/24 July 1943) reveal that a staggering 1,000 Bomber Command aircraft were lost from 23,401 sorties dispatched, or 4.3 per cent. Bomber Command introduced a series of new tactics during the Battle of Hamburg (24/25 July to 3 August 1943). The massed bomber stream, new target-finding radar (which permitted the bombers to find their targets individually through heavy cloud and in the moonless periods), new target finding and illuminating tactics that were concentrated in the élite Pathfinder Force (PFF), and last but not least, the (radar) jamming device code-named 'Window', all resulted in complete chaos in Germany. Unable to obtain a true picture of the air situation, and unable to control the night-fighters in the air, at a stroke the German air defence found itself reduced to the bare elementals of night-fighting. During the Battle of Hamburg Window prevented about 100 to 130 potential Bomber Command losses. Over four nights 3,000 bombers dropped 10,000 tons of HE (high explosive) and incendiary bombs to devastate totally half of the city and kill an estimated 42,000 of its inhabitants. After the fourth raid on the night of 2/3 August, a million inhabitants fled the city. Albert Speer, Minister of War Production, warned Hitler that Germany would have to surrender after another six of these bombing raids.

On the night of 30/31 March 1944, Bomber Command suffered its highest loss of the war on the Nürnburg raid when sixty-four Lancasters and thirty-one Halifaxes (11.9 per cent of the force dispatched) were lost (and ten bombers crash-landed in England). The famous Avro Lancaster was the most successful bomber used by the RAF in the Second World War and in 1944 it established its superiority over every other type. By March 1945 there were no fewer than fifty-six squadrons of Lancasters in first-line service with Bomber Command.

From April 1944 Bomber Command became engaged in the preparations of D-Day, mainly focussing on transportation targets in France. It is a popular belief that after the Battle of Berlin, Bomber Command crews had it relatively easy – less deep penetration raids into Germany, more shallow penetration trips into France to disrupt German communications in preparation for Operation *Overlord*, fewer losses to *Luftwaffe* night-fighters and smaller percentage losses as Bomber Command grew larger by the month during the spring and summer of 1944.

During the prelude to the invasion of Normandy, Bomber Command had been controlled by the Supreme Allied Commander. With the Allied armies advancing into France, in September 1944 the Chief of Air Staff once again gained control of the Command for a new precision bombing campaign aimed at oil and transportation targets, and for a resumed area bombing campaign. Devastating raids by over 1,000 bombers became fairly commonplace, whilst operational losses began to fall quite dramatically.

The early months of 1945 saw a tremendous increase in Bomber Command's operations, both in tempo and number, forty raids being mounted in February alone. Although it has gone down in history as one of the most controversial bombing raids of the war, for most of the participating aircrew at the time the Dresden raid of 13/14 February 1945 was simply another well executed and very efficient area bombing attack. In March 1945, Bomber Command flew a record fifty-three day and night operations. Bomber Command's last bombing operations in World War II were the obliteration of Wangerooge, a failed attempt at destroying Hitler's 'Eagle's Nest' at Berchtesgaden in daylight on 25 April 1945 and the oil storage depots at Tonsberg in Southern Norway on the following night. Yet, the war was not over for the weary bomber crews – four days later they were called in again, but this time to drop food, not bombs. With the Germans on the brink of defeat, thousands of people in the western and north-western provinces of the Netherlands, which were still in German hands, were left without food. Parts of that country had been under German blockade and some 20,000 men, women and children had died of starvation during a very short period, the survivors being in a desperate plight. To relieve the starving Dutch people, between 29 April and 8 May, 2,835 Lancasters delivered 6,672 tons of food supplies in dropping zones that were marked by 124 Mosquito sorties.

By the end of the war no fewer than 73,741 casualties were sustained by Bomber Command, of which 55,500 aircrew had been KIA (killed in action) or flying accidents, or died on the ground or while prisoners-of-war (PoWs). It is a casualty rate that compares with the worst slaughters in the First World War trenches. Operational bomber losses were 8,655 aircraft and another 1,600 were lost in accidents and write-offs. Approximately 125,000 aircrew served in the front line, OTUs (Operation Training Units) and OCUs (Operational Conversion Units) of the Command and nearly 60 per cent of them became casualties. In addition, almost 9,900 more were shot down and made PoWs to spend one, two or more years in squalid, desolate Oflags and Stalags in Axis-held territory. Over 8,000 more were wounded aboard aircraft on operational sorties. Bomber Command flew almost 390,000 sorties, the greatest percentage of them by Avro Lancasters, Handley Page Halifaxes and Wellingtons. Theirs of course were the highest casualties.

Acknowledgements

I am most grateful to the following people, many of whom related their wartime stories to me or, as in the case of Ron Read and Edwin Wheeler DFC, they very kindly allowed me to quote from their privately published books, '*If You Can't Take a Joke*' and '*Just to Get a Bed*', respectively. Equally, the late J. Ralph Wood DFC CD kindly made his unpublished manuscript, *My Lucky Number was 77*, available to me. My sincere thanks to the other unsung heroes, who are: John Aldridge; Jim Allen DFC; Theo 'Bluey' Arthurs; Harry Barker DFC; Ralph Barker; Theo Boiten; CONAM; Frank Diamond DFC AE; Dr Colin Dring, Mildenhall Museum; Colin 'Joe' Dudley; Malcolm Freegard; Ken Grantham; Audrey Grealy; Trevor A. 'Happy' Hampton; J. B. Hughes; John 'Jimmy' Anderson Hurst; Olive Hurst; George 'Ole' Olson RCAF; Ron Read DFC; Ernie Rodley; Leslie Sidwell; Derek Smith DFC; Steve C. Smith; Jim Sprackling DFC; Martin Staunton; Tom Tate; Arthur 'Spud' Taylor DFC; Marguerite Taylor; Edwin Wheeler DFC; Tom Wingham DFC; J. Ralph Wood DFC CD; Jack Woodrow; Louis Patrick Wooldridge DFC; Johnny Wynne DFC.

CHAPTER 1

Just to Get a Bed

Edwin Wheeler DFC

Well written verse, perpetuates a story
And these flyers are deserving of long fame
Thus Dear Lady? Well you may ensure their glory
(It matters not if all forget my name).
Those who commenced their war by bombing Kiel
In murderous daylight and got shot to Hell
Their Whitley losses now seem so unreal,
The Wellingtons took part and went as well;
Someone has to tell of Battles' slaughter
In gallant raids to halt the foe's advance;
Of shot-up Blenheims struggling o'er the water
From horrendous flights to Holland and to France.

'*Address To Calliopes*', Jasper Miles,
RAF Lancaster tail gunner

It was surely fate that destined my entry into this world on 5 November 1920 – a date traditionally celebrated as Guy Fawkes Day, following the Gunpowder Plot to blow up the Houses of Parliament. Twenty years later, I too, was to be involved realistically and dangerously with fires, explosives and the burning of my fellow men.

Home was a three-roomed tenement in the North London Borough of Islington. I had been preceded by two brothers and was to succeed another brother and two sisters. There was no doubt that the accommodation was totally inadequate for a family of that size, but sleeping three to a bed was considered acceptable in the dominantly poorer families of that time. My father was a fitter, luckily in regular employment but poorly paid, which seemed normal to us then. Life was pretty miserable and on reaching the ripe old age of 14 I decided to leave school. So in 1934 I started my working life as an office boy at Herbert & Sons Ltd in Goswell Road, London. In 1937–8 it was becoming evident that Adolf Hitler was intent on annexing territories adjacent to the *Reich* and the storm clouds over Europe were massing. My main concern now was that I was getting taller and outgrowing my fold-up bed in the tiny kitchen at home and this became more of a problem as time went on, when I began to get troublesome bouts of cramp. In the cinema one

1

evening I saw George Formby in *Something In the Air*. (In my short lifetime I had read with avid interest and I had marvelled at the heroism of men and women who had actually flown the Atlantic and had spanned continents to Australia and South Africa in frail aircraft. These courageous flyers were an inspiration to us all in years to come.) Immediately, I felt convinced that my salvation could lie in joining the RAF – if only to get a bed large enough to accommodate me without doubling my knees with cramp!

The war clouds were becoming more dominant in early 1939. Newspapers were announcing recruitment campaigns for the armed services, but Prime Minister Neville Chamberlain was telling everybody that there would be 'peace in our time'. A further bout of cramp convinced me that I should make my move. I ventured to Adastral House in Kingsway, where I announced that I was 18 years old and that I sought a career in the RAF. The Recruiting Officer said that there were vacancies for wireless operators on a six-year engagement. In April 1939 I underwent a rigorous examination but my excitement was so intense that I just could not pass water. I made a quick trip to the local J. Lyons Corner House at Holborn to down two cups of coffee, then went back to Adastral House – but still with no results. The Centre closed at midday for the weekend, so I was told to return on Monday morning to perform the final act. Waking on Monday morning, I decided not to pass water until I reached the Recruiting Centre. After much drinking of tea I filled three bottles and was harangued by the medical orderly who swore I was providing samples for the twenty applicants attending that morning.

An aptitude test followed but by this time I knew how not to put square blocks into round holes – so I passed the second stage. It was only then, when my mother was asked to produce my birth certificate that I discovered my surname was not Wheeler. What a shock when you find that you are a 'Scheidweiler' with a German heritage and a great grandfather from Hannover! Even the RAF flight lieutenant was somewhat taken aback at this revelation and after furtive glances and discussions in a back room with other officers, it was decided to visit Somerset House in Aldwych to trace the family tree. Somewhat bemused by all this, I sat in awe in Somerset House whilst the investigations were proceeding. Later I was told that I would be accepted, but that during my RAF career I would be known as Edwin Scheidweiler – alias Wheeler. My mother was of Irish descent and with the combination of my father's German ancestry, I imagined that the RAF had strong reservations about my entry.

I was elevated to the lofty rank of sergeant direct from AC2 (Aircraftman Second Class) on 25 May 1940. The decision to promote all non-commissioned aircrew to sergeant status was purportedly to provide certain privileges during a probable short life expectancy, coupled with the desire to prevent dissemination of information regarding operations and confidential matters to 'other ranks'. This promotion was not well received by the existing NCOs who had spent long years in the ranks as AC2/AC1/LAC1 and corporal before achieving those three stripes. The influx of large numbers of aircrew – mainly with only one year's service – was strongly resented and the hallowed Sergeants' Mess was never the same if you believed their arguments. In voting for Mess Committee Members, the dominance of aircrew ensured that they installed their favourites – much to the disgust and chagrin of the 'old sweats'. This attitude became tempered in time as operational casualties followed, with the resultant loss of familiar faces and appearances of replacements in the Mess. At this time, resplendent in a uniform bearing the insignia of a Wireless Operator's 'sparks' badge, Air Gunner 'flying bullet' and three stripes and of course enjoying all the hitherto unknown privileges of the Sergeants' Mess, one felt suddenly important. The ego was boosted dramatically but there was a pervasive feeling that it was to be short-lived; it was all too good to be true.

By July 1940 I had a total flying time of 62 hours and I left OTU to join 150 Squadron, my first operational squadron, in 1 Group Bomber Command.[1] Arriving at Newton in Nottinghamshire some hours late after difficulty in getting a train, I found the aerodrome almost deserted and devoid of aircraft. It was evident that the survivors of the Squadron were still finding their way back from France by whatever means they could, following the fall of France on 18 June. After seven days of waiting and complete inactivity, the surviving crews of 103 and 150 Squadrons from France started to dribble in with tales of the horrors they had experienced in those last weeks when they were endeavouring to stem the Nazi tide. They quoted the loss of five Fairey Battles out of five in an attack on the bridges at Maastricht.[2] With new crews arriving from OTU and aircraft (Fairey Battles) flying in daily, the semblance of a squadron was building up again and the crewing-up procedure was under way. It was my good fortune to be teamed up with Harry de Belleroche and Dil Thomas, pilot and navigator respectively, who were to become fondly known as Rocky and Ginger. After their experiences in France and the withdrawal, which in itself had presented such huge problems for them, they could not have been too enamoured with the idea of having a 'rookie' wireless operator/air gunner but of course they gave me great support and encouragement.

During our conversations in the Sergeants' Mess I was able to find out from Ginger Thomas details of their experiences in a fully operational squadron and the qualities and calibre of other squadron members. Young faces bore the marks of the hardships they had had to endure and they looked far older than their years, such were the rigours of their experiences in a comparatively short period of battle conditions, after that long period of non-activity known as the 'phoney war' from September 1939. Sitting in the comfort of the Mess, listening to the hair-raising experiences of Ginger Thomas, Bugs Burrows and Paddy Wildman, gave a clue of what was to come. In the confusion of the withdrawal from France, Ginger Thomas and a few other airmen and ground crews had lost contact with the Squadron. They were told to trek towards Brest on the west coast by whatever means they could, in the hope of reaching a ship uplifting survivors for return to the safety of the UK. Eventually reaching Nantes, they were informed that they should embark on the 20,000 ton Cunard White Star liner *Lancastria*, a converted troopship capable of evacuating 5,000 troops. Imagine their consternation when they found the liner full to the gills and they were refused permission to board. Little did Ginger know his luck, for on 17 June 1940 the *Lancastria* was bombed by

Junkers 87 dive-bombers and sunk within half an hour of the attack with the loss of over 3,000 soldiers, sailors and airmen. It was a date he would always remember. Further up the coast he was relieved to find a British destroyer still taking survivors and so was able to be evacuated safely. On 21 June 1940 the Franco-German Armistice was signed and the capitulation to Italy followed three days later.

The air attacks on Britain following the French capitulation were greatly intensified. There was great speculation on the probability of an airborne invasion of southern England, which could only be met by a depleted defence following the debacle in France. The RAF Fighter Command front-line aircraft were comparatively few in numbers and required time to build up strength. Bomber Command, similarly, was sadly lacking in numbers of front-line aircraft and consequently the effective contribution it could make was almost insignificant. We had to pray for time to build up an effective striking force, but how much time could we anticipate?

Three weeks after joining 150 Squadron, during which we had flown only 9 hours on crew familiarisation, came the day, 25 July 1940, when we were instructed to report to the Operations Room for briefing for our first operation. Our squadron effort was to be only three aircraft to attack an airfield near Antwerp. The total Command effort for the night was to be 166 aircraft to attack seven targets in the Ruhr and various airfields in Holland and Belgium. Our Fairey Battle L5510 was to carry four 250 lb GP (General Purpose) bombs, two under each wing, so we were told it was vital not to waste the effort, but it did really seem to be an insignificant effort. Briefing over, we returned to the Mess to contemplate our first mission. We reflected on our chances of being back in the Mess the following day. With take-off planned for 2350 hours, we experienced at 2100 hours the operational aircrew pre-flight meal of eggs and bacon, which was to be a feature of all future operations. One rarely saw eggs as part of the normal diet and it was therefore considered to be a special bonus for risking your head being blown off. What a super incentive! At 2315 hours we were transported to our aircraft to prepare for take-off. My pulse was racing and I was sweating more than a little. During the pre-flight checks, it was my job to ensure that the radio and intercom were working satisfactorily and that sufficient canisters of ammunition were stored safely. Initially, the warmth within the flying Sidcot, fur-lined boots and flying helmet, was rather overpowering, but the temperature fell drastically once in the air, especially with the cupola open at the rear of the Battle. The cupola had to be open to enable the Vickers Gas Operated (VGO) gun to be swivelled from port to starboard.

Ginger took up his position as navigator in the well of the aircraft – a most unenviable position – and sorted out his route maps. Rocky ran up the engine to full power, checked that we were all satisfactory and then said, 'Here we go chaps, good luck!' We bounced across the grass field and at 2355 hours took off for the first of our affrays against enemy-held Europe.

Of the three Squadron aircraft assigned to attack Hingene airfield near Antwerp one piloted by Sergeant Pay had to return to base within half an hour with engine trouble. This left ourselves and one aircraft piloted by Flight

Lieutenant Hugo Beall, a Canadian whose observer was Sergeant Ian Bishop and WOpAG [wireless opeator air gunner] Bugs Burrows – all ex-AASF (Advanced Air Striking Force) veterans at an early age. My brief was to keep a listening watch on the Command frequency at half-hourly intervals for possible recalls or diversions and at my position in the rear of the aircraft – with the cupola open – to man the VGO gun against possible fighter intervention. It was very cold, but at the same time sweat was very evident under my flying helmet. Many times I thought that I had sighted interceptors but then realised it was the shadow of our own plane on the cloud. It was a constant switch from 'safe' to 'fire' on the VGO gun, but I was determined not to be caught napping. The thoughts that went through my mind varied. 'Have the armourers correctly set the interrupter gear on the gun?' This enabled the gunner to sweep the area of fire to the rear and quarters without shooting off the tail of the aircraft. 'How near is my parachute in case I need it in a hurry?' Happily, the flight was uneventful and we dropped our four 250 lb bombs on target with 7/10ths cloud obscuring results. (The term 'uneventful' quoted against many of the sorties described during two tours of operational duty were deemed so only because of the fact that we did not encounter fighter attacks or sustain major damage from anti-aircraft (AA) fire from the ground defences. There were still many dangers from adverse weather conditions, severe icing, mechanical problems and navigational errors prior to the advent of radar aids, all of which constituted normally acceptable flying hazards.) We returned without incident and landed back at Newton at 0325 hours. Our first operation was over. I thought, 'one down and 29 to go'. If they were to be as easy as the first then perhaps I would see my twenty-first birthday! Ginger emerged with his maps and logs smothered in glycol. This was to be a persistent feature on all future flights; the Battle was notorious for its glycol leaks.[3]

Four nights later, on 29 July 1940, we were briefed to attack Waalhaven and took off at 2330 hours with our usual 'magnificent' load of four 250 lb GP bombs. In my anxiety to scour the sky for enemy fighters, I was guilty of missing the group broadcast, which had issued cancellation of the operation and instructed all aircraft to return to base. Eventually, I informed Rocky of the recall and back we went to good old Blighty. With 10/10ths cloud conditions it was necessary to obtain homing bearings from Newton and finally we landed and taxied to outside the control tower. Climbing down from Battle L5447, we were met by the CO, Wing Commander Hesketh who said, 'Do you realise that you were the only aircraft over enemy territory tonight?' Nevertheless, he was glad to see our safe return and he handed me my first pint of beer, which was to be the first of very, very many over the ensuing years.

In the next three weeks we were engaged in Army Affiliation Exercises and bombing and gunnery practice from Catfoss. On 15 August we carried out a North Sea Sweep, and whilst there was a risk of interception by enemy intruders this was not counted as an operational mission. A week later our base at Newton was attacked and nine bombs hit the airfield rendering it partly unserviceable, but we were able to continue our flights to Catfoss for bombing and gunnery. One of the bombs dropped by the low-flying Dornier had landed close to living quarters and failed to explode. The airmen were evacuated from the living block and were temporarily accommodated in tents pending the arrival of the bomb-disposal squad. By nightfall the Army disposal squad had not appeared. Two airmen affected by the evacuation had gone to town and returned to base rather the worse for liquor and decided that they would remove the unexploded bomb so that everybody could return to their normal living quarters. They acquired a wheelbarrow and proceeded to manhandle the bomb; apparently it fell out of the barrow several times. The offending weapon was eventually dumped without further mishap. In the sober light of day they reflected on the stupidity of their actions but no doubt were amused by the questions constantly asked, 'Where is our bomb?' Rumours abounded that they were to be court-martialled but we never did learn of any action against them.

A few days later we experienced more excitement. We had just completed a 'compass swing' to ensure its accuracy when we noticed a 103 Squadron Battle standing outside the main hangar, from which a flame seemed to envelop one wing. There was feverish activity by several airmen who were endeavouring to subdue the fire and to release the four 250 lb bombs suspended under the wings. An Australian pilot, Flight Lieutenant Blom, rushed forward to give a hand but the fire spread rapidly and the first bomb exploded with an ear-splitting noise, blowing out all the windows in the main hangar and killing the three persons on or near the aircraft, including Blom. As the plane was enveloped in flames, the ammunition exploded in all directions and we threw ourselves to the ground, where we stayed until the ammunition expended itself. The unfortunate incident was the subject of most of the conversation in the Mess that night.

With the threat of possible invasion, it was evident that we would use every device to prevent a landing on our shores, even the use of gas. We kitted ourselves out in anti-gas clothing, climbed into the aircraft, then proceeded to spray the surrounding areas, not with gas of course but with aniseed. On landing, we had to scrub down the fuselage and we rued the day we might have to use gas. Our girl friends in Nottingham were constantly asking us about the sweet sickly smells that were dominant after our aircraft passed over. We were tight-lipped and never revealed the sinister truth.

The army affiliation exercises were most realistic. Large numbers of army formations, including mechanised units, were 'attacked' at Guilsborough near Northampton and outside Kettering, then at Royston and Woburn. Attacks were made by diving from 7,000 feet to 500 feet to simulate German *Stuka* dive-bombing tactics. The pressure in diving had the effect of forcing me to the floor of the plane and it was impossible to reach the gun to carry out a strafing exercise. Furthermore, my breakfast came up at ten times the speed of consumption and I rued the day that we would be called upon to dive-bomb the enemy. Many valuable lessons were learned from this exercise.

It was evident to Bomber Command Headquarters that the operational days of Fairey Battles were coming to an end and we all sighed with relief. Whilst we awaited our fate with bated breath, some pilots were notified of their postings to Fighter Command to supplement the squadrons designated to meet the oncoming onslaught in the Battle of Britain. On 25 August 1940 we made our last flight in the Fairey Battle, just as far as Stradishall in Suffolk where we were to join 214 Squadron in 3 Group for a conversion course to Wellington ICs. Rocky (Harry de Belleroche) had been promoted to flight lieutenant and he was to be our captain, with Pilot Officer Paul Carlyon as second pilot, Ginger Thomas as observer, Sergeants Gutteridge and Bossom as front and rear gunners and myself, wireless operator/relief gunner. Cross-country exercises were the order of the day for the next two weeks and having not then flown in a Wellington at night we were surprised to learn that our first 'Wimpy' operation would be on the night of 17 September.

We were briefed to fly in Wellington L7859, take off at 2340 hours to attack invasion barge concentrations at Ostend. After the discomfort of flying in Battles, the Wimpy was luxury indeed. I had a reasonable seat and warmth to operate the TR1154/55 radio receiver/transmitter. The security of having two pilots and armament at the front and rear, and armour plate behind my seat, gave me much more confidence than I had felt before. Ginger had the luxury of a seat and table to consult his maps and his log was at last, glycol-free! We reached the target and sighted the rows of barges, but Rocky must have had a lapse of memory as he put the Wimpy into a dive – he must have thought he was still in a Fairey Battle. The reaction from the crew was immediate! 'What the bloody hell!' was yelled from each crew position. It is a wonder that the wings were not torn off – such was the angle of dive! However, we survived and there were fewer barges when we left. The operation was repeated on the nights of 23 and 24 September against Calais and Le Havre with great success. Paul Carlyon was proving to be a pilot of great ability and quickly gained the confidence of the crew. It was obvious that he would receive captaincy of his own aircraft in the very near future. Paul was a genial giant of a man and he had actually gone the full distance, ten rounds, with the great American Heavyweight Boxing Champion Jack Sharkey. With Rocky and Paul, we considered we had the best two pilots in the Squadron.

On 27 September 1940 came the call for 'ops' briefing at 1630 hours, which gave a clue to our next mission being of longer duration – possibly our first against *Reich* territory itself. Speculation became fact as we trooped into the briefing room in the ops block to find the large target and route map with the vivid red route tape leading to the Ruhr. The target was to be a railway marshalling yard at Hamm. The Intelligence Officer gave details of the importance of the target and the anticipated areas of flak and searchlight defences. The weatherman gave an optimistic view of conditions *en route*, over the target and on return to base. The more experienced crews made sly interjections that the weather reports were conjured up from gazing into a crystal ball, and later on we were to reach the conclusion that indeed this was near to the truth. Details of the bomb load, fuel and armament were outlined and after a few words of encouragement from the Squadron CO – the usual 'Hit 'em hard lads!' – we broke off for individual briefings on navigation, radio procedures and gunners' guidance.

The Wireless Leader issued the 'colours of the day' – to be fired off in the event of being fired at by our own anti-aircraft defences and/or fighters. The

Vickers Armstrong Wellington being bombed up at Mildenhall. The Wellington, Handley Page Hampden and the Armstrong Whitworth Whitley and Bristol Blenheim, all twin-engined bombers, were the mainstay of Bomber Command early in the war. The Wellington, affectionately known as the Wimpy (so called from the American Disney cartoon character 'J. Wellington Wimpy in 'Popeye') which had carried out the first RAF bombing raid of the war and suffered high losses by day, had been conceived by the brilliant British scientist, Dr Barnes Wallis using geodetic or lattice work structure. (RAF)

half-hourly broadcast by Group headquarters was to be logged and acted on accordingly and radio silence was to be maintained except in dire emergencies. All messages were to be in code for which we were issued SYKO machines for encoding and decoding purposes. Anticipated enemy radio beacons to enable position 'fixes' to be obtained were announced. Every aspect appeared to be covered and transport was arranged to take us to dispersal points at 1915 hours for a take-off at 2010 hours in Wellington IC L7856. The intervening hour and a half was spent in writing the odd letter, reading, playing cards, emptying pockets of all matter that could be construed as being helpful to the enemy in the event of our being shot down and captured. Boarding the lorry with all our kit to reach our aircraft 40 minutes before take-off, the nervous banter of the crews gave the impression that we were going to a party – a 'party' from which some of us were destined not to return. Standing outside the aircraft, last cigarettes were smoked, one or two lads had a final 'pee' over the tail wheel and then we climbed aboard.

Everybody took up their positions, made their usual pre-flight checks and then we heard the first aircraft starting engines. Our turn came and the engines burst into life. They were run to ensure no magneto drops and then 'chocks away' and we were taxiing out in a long line of both 150 and 214 Squadrons. In succession, with a green light from the Flying Control caravan the aircraft took off from Stradishall and we were on our way into the unknown. Once over the sea, the gunners tested their guns, taking care that no other friendly aircraft were endangered by doing so. We reached the enemy coast without event and set course for Hamm. It was not long before we entered belts of searchlights, which were blinding in their intensity and one felt that they were only looking for you and you were exposed to the world! At 15,000 feet we experienced heavy flak and saw the black puffs of smoke all round us and could hear the noise of the shell bursts over the sound of our engines in spite of wearing helmets with ear pads. It was, to say the least, unnerving but we pressed on with hope and a prayer. In the run up to the target area it seemed that all hell had broken loose. We seemed unable to lose the searchlight concentration, the sky was filled with bursting shells and lower down we could see the tracer trails of the flak.

Ginger in his capacity as observer, encompassing duties of navigator and bomb aimer, had taken up his position in the bomb-well. He proceeded to give his instructions to Rocky – 'Left, left, steady, right, steady'. If a small correction was required then directions were said quickly and for major corrections the instruction was drawn out. It was an eternity before we heard him say, 'Bombs away' with a cacophony of sound breaking out all around us. Paul shouted 'Let's get out of here'. Rocky proceeded to throw L7856 around the sky in an endeavour to escape the flak and searchlights. This was eventually achieved and unscathed we set course for home. As we looked back we saw the glow from incendiaries and the flashes of bombs bursting in the target area – giving us immense satisfaction. The gunners traversed their power turrets and kept up an incessant search for fighters. Once across the enemy coast we felt we could relax only slightly, but enjoyed the hot coffee from our flasks. All we had to do now was to get back to base and we were looking forward to our special aircrew ops breakfast – eggs and bacon![4]

Ginger shouted to me to join him on the floor and to brace myself for the inevitable crash. I did this, placing the logbook between my teeth. Then there was no further engine noise, just the whistling of air rushing past. Rocky and Paul were fighting to hold the aircraft in a level position. It seemed an eternity but my life flashed through my mind and I prayed that the end would be quick, hopefully not to be enveloped by flames within that geodetic mesh! Looking up from the floor I had a quick vision of trees flashing past and then we struck terra firma. The impact was terrific and Ginger and I were lifted as one, momentarily it seemed that we were suspended in mid-air and then we together crashed through the bulk-head doors, over the main spar and then down to the rear turret. Concussed but still aware of being alive, we tried to struggle to our feet, but earth and potatoes had penetrated to a depth of about two feet and progress to an escape hatch was difficult. Our means of escape was through the pilot's hatch over the cockpit. But then panic set in as I saw a red glow from the front of the aircraft and immediately thought 'We are on fire!' Falling down with every step I eventually reached the cockpit to find all other crew members gone; the supposed 'fire' was in fact the red light glow from the light left on over the radio set. I was still convinced that the plane was going to ignite and explode at any second – having seen such things with other crashed Wellingtons. I stood on the pilot's seat to gain exit through the hatch but fell back three times through sheer anxiety. Finally, I made it to the roof and couldn't see how far off the ground I was because of the intense darkness. I thought, 'Here goes, two broken legs would be better than a frizzled corpse', and jumped into the unknown. It was about 10 feet to the ground and once I realised I had still two legs, I started to try to break Olympic records in an attempt to get clear of a potential time bomb. The memory of that morning will remain with me for ever. It did do one thing for me, it gave me confidence just thinking that I had survived such a horrendous experience.

Running away from the site of the crash, which turned out to be at Barton Mills, Suffolk, just a few miles from base, I ran into an Army patrol of three men – one of whom turned out to be a near neighbour of mine when living in Islington. What an amazing coincidence! Shaking almost uncontrollably I was taken to join the other members of crew. Back at the Station, I was amazed that the CO's concern was not that we had safely survived the crash, but that we had lost an aircraft valued at thousands of pounds. (The subsequent Court of Inquiry blamed the radio problems on 'abnormal – possible atmospheric conditions, low height etc.')

Throughout November and December we underwent training flights with various captains and at this time further pilots were transferred to Fighter Command to replace pilots lost during the Battle of Britain. Instructors were urgently required and Rocky found himself *en route* to Rhodesia to pass on the benefit of his considerable experience to trainee pilots. We were then allocated to a crew under the captaincy of Flying Officer Dicky Morton with Flying Officer Freddy Savage as second pilot. At this point Sergeant Fred Denman joined the crew as front gunner replacing Sergeant Gutteridge. Denny, as he became known, came from a family of London taxi drivers based in Cricklewood, all members of the DOB (Done Our Bit) Club located in that borough. In December the CO, Wing Commander Hesketh departed to be replaced by Wing Commander C. J. C. Paul.

On 7 January 1941 we were once again re-united with Paul Carlyon, with Freddy Savage as 'second dickie'. We were delighted with this move. Two nights later, on 9/10 January, in Wellington IC R1042, we recommenced operations, this time against Rotterdam – a return flight of 3 hours 15 minutes. It was an uneventful trip, during which Paul Carlyon gained the confidence of the crew by his unflappable attitude. His ability was proven a week later, when on 15/16 January we set off to attack naval installations at Wilhelmshaven and found ourselves in cu-nimb cloud conditions, with huge formations of ice building up on the wings forcing us to descend rapidly. It was not unexpected when we were compelled to abandon the mission and return to base. Of the ninety-six aircraft operating that night, only one, a Whitley, was lost. The heating system in our aircraft failed and the cold was intense and numbing. We were to learn from later missions that the heater system was likely only to work to the extremes. i.e. nothing at all, giving freezing conditions, or the other extreme – baking almost to melting point! I don't know which of these extremes I preferred.

Weather conditions precluded our flying operationally again until 10/11 February when in *C-Charlie* we made our longest flight yet, to Hannover (6 hours 35 minutes). A total of 222 aircraft were committed to this target, of which four aircraft were lost and enemy intruders shot down three more over the UK. It was common when preparing to land that the flarepath would be switched off when enemy fighters were known to be in the area. We had to cruise round with our navigation lights extinguished, making it very hazardous with other returning bombers in the same circuit, all with trigger-nervous gunners anxious to strike before being struck down themselves.

The Blohm & Voss U-boat yards in Hamburg were our next target on 12/13 March and the force of eighty-eight aircraft included Manchesters and Halifaxes for the first time on a German territorial target.[5] Two nights later it was the turn of Gelsenkirchen to be attacked by 101 aircraft, of which 100 returned safely. In each of these raids on German territory, the anti-aircraft and searchlight defences were superb and caused much consternation among the aircrews – incredulous of their accuracy and no doubt they were responsible for many bombs being scattered.

On 19 March Sergeant Cliff Cooper went to Buckingham Palace and was presented with the DFM by the King for his excellent record as an air gunner in France whilst operating in Fairey Battles. A party to celebrate this well-earned award was held on his return; we needed no other excuse to get sloshed!

Seven squadron aircraft were detailed to attack the submarine base at Lorient on the French west coast and we were fifth away at 1810 hours, routed out over Lyme Regis and arriving over St Brieuc (France) still in daylight. The 10/10ths cloud *en route* disappeared over the target area and we bombed from 11,000 feet. The ground defences and searchlights were ineffective and caused us no trouble and we landed at Newton on the stroke of midnight. One of our aircraft, piloted by Flying Officer C. Elliott, had not returned to base. Whilst waiting into the early hours in the Mess, news came through that the overdue aircraft had evidently got lost in trying to find base and had crashed into a mountain at Blaenau Ffestiniog in North Wales. With the exception of the rear gunner Peter Martlew, all were killed including my good friend Barry Killen. We would miss Barry's fooling around on the piano when he returned after each sortie and his infectious laughter, which had always raised our spirits.

With continuing losses of dear friends, it was necessary to dispense with emotions and invariably this was helped through the Mess parties, which were arranged for no specific reason. The foolhardy endeavours to walk the length of the Mess with a pint of beer balanced on the head, and the battles between opposing sides armed with soda siphons created havoc for the staff.

Our fourteenth operation was on 30/31 March 1941, when six squadron aircraft were ordered to attack the two German battle cruisers, *Scharnhorst* and *Gneisenau* – nicknamed 'Salmon & Glukstein' (famous London store). These were lying in dock at Brest on the French coast. Intense flak and

11

searchlights were encountered in clear conditions, but the attack was pressed home. When we returned to base a 'red' warning was on with a suspected enemy intruder in the circuit and once again we were circling the 'drome awaiting clearance. Sergeant Vic Coleman attempted to land and was attacked by cannon and machine-gun fire, sustaining damage to a landing wheel and petrol tank. He promptly opened up the taps and weaving violently to ward off further attack; he diverted to Waddington and landed satisfactorily. We too went to Waddington, not wishing to risk being shot down over our own base. Our Flight Commander, Squadron Leader Hugo Beall, flew with us on this trip, replacing Freddy Savage who was preparing to receive his own captaincy.

Our next operation, on 8/9 April, was a return to Rotterdam to attack oil storage tanks. Only five of our squadron aircraft were involved. One of these, captained by Flight Lieutenant Frank, took a heavy flak battering over the target. The aircraft lost all of its hydraulics, but got back safely to base with its bomb doors still open and no undercarriage or flaps. To our delight Frank made a safe belly landing. Boy, did that crew beat the record in evacuating the wreck! We had, for the first time, Sergeant Sam Huggett as our second pilot. Sam was such a shy, reserved person, not reacting to all our usual crew banter, but he was a good pilot. A return to Brest was our next mission, on 12/13 April, and we found 10/10ths cloud over the target and the bombs were released through the cloud with unobserved results. We were getting sick of the sound of Brest and wondered how much longer those two battleships would survive. I suppose the Royal Navy were content to have them confined to port and not on the open seas to wreak their havoc. Three nights later, 15/16 April, five crews were detailed to attack Kiel, an important naval base on the north German coast and four to the Channel ports. We were airborne at 2040 hours in very good weather conditions; heading out over Skegness to Sylt and Flensburg, but on arrival at Kiel 8/10ths cloud covered the target. The town's batteries set up intense heavy anti-aircraft fire. Without radar we were obliged to bomb using dead reckoning. No results were observed so we scorched it back to base, landing at 0410 hours.

Three aircraft set out on 17/18 April for Mannheim. Weather conditions were foul and we were unable to locate the target. We were loathe to bring our bombs back so we decided to off-load them on an aerodrome near Brussels, encouraged by the sight of a resultant large fire. It was to be almost two weeks before we operated again. We did some cross-country exercises with Sam Huggett at the controls during daytime and in the evening sorties were made into Nottingham. The last days of the month [30 April/1 May] arrived and after a night-flying test in a strange aircraft (R1495) we found ourselves being briefed to attack Kiel again. One of eight aircraft assigned, we took off at 2055 hours, following the coastline down from Kappeln to the target where we found 10/10ths cloud at 10,000 feet. Bombing of any specific target was impossible, but the searchlight activity was intense. We decided to let the searchlight crews have the benefit of our considerable bomb load, following which there was an immediate extinguishing of all lights. It was the turn of Cologne on 3/4 May, but once again cloud came to the rescue of the *Reich* and the target was totally obscured. Nevertheless this raid counted towards our first tour and we had clocked up our twentieth operation – about halfway to the desired total before being 'screened' to take up instructional duty at an OTU (Operational Training Unit). An uneventful raid on 5/6 May was to Mannheim and yes, 10/10ths cloud again obscured the target area. Flak was of barrage form and only slight damage was experienced. We landed back at base at 0440 hours and were content to watch the dawn rise as we hungrily consumed our eggs and bacon.

On 7/8 May we were on our way to St Nazaire, the U-boat base. We were airborne at 0015 hours, one of ten squadron aircraft detailed. We had a daylight landing at 0610 hours, debriefing and the usual breakfast. We thought we might become egg-bound if we operated too frequently. The bad news was that R1374 captained by (Flight Lieutenant) Freddy Savage, who had previously flown with us as second pilot, had failed to return.[6] Replacement crews were to arrive in the next 48 hours. There was no respite for us as that same night we were despatched to Bremen, but this time the weather was excellent and the target objectives stood out with complete clarity. All crews were satisfied with their results and we landed unscathed at base at 0455 hours. It was so unusual to bomb in clear conditions, and the crews eagerly scanned the displayed photographs of our bomb plots later in the morning.

Some 48 hours later (10/11 May) we were off again, this time to Hamburg. The weather was perfect. Nine of our aircraft were involved and we crossed the coast at Cromer, then went on to Texel on the Dutch coast and then Hamburg, which was clearly seen, giving us ideal bombing conditions. We bombed from 15,000 feet and saw detonations in the target area. It was on this trip that we were concerned to find on entering the aircraft that a number of 25 lb GP bombs were lying loosely on the bed and immediately presumed they had been left there by armourers in error. The skipper, Paul Carlyon, scotched that idea, saying the bomb racks were full and the 25-pounders were to be released individually through the flare chute by the wireless operator when over the target. I couldn't believe my luck!

As we neared the target area, I took up my position near the flare chute, and pushed out the extension to allow the bombs to enter the slipstream under the tail section. At the height we were flying it was necessary to plug into the oxygen supply. If one had insufficient oxygen at that height, one was apt to do silly things and act irresponsibly. Having plugged into both oxygen and intercom, I awaited orders to proceed. At this point I found that my oxygen tube was too short to allow me to reach the bombs on the bed without disconnecting from the oxygen supply point over the flare chute. The flak was now becoming intense and accurate and I could hear distinctly the crump of the bursting shells over the noise of the engines. My priority now was to get rid of those loose bombs as quickly as possible. I disconnected from the oxygen point, moved over to the bed, cradled the first 25-pounder in my arms and moved back to the chute. I plugged back into the oxygen, took several deep breaths and loaded the bomb into chute. I pulled out the fuse pin and then released it quickly. This operation was to be repeated five times! After the second bomb was released I was becoming tired. The intercom lead was getting caught up in the geodetics and I wasn't sure if I was getting enough oxygen in short bursts. Generally, there was a state of confusion and we were constantly being urged by the Captain to 'get rid of those f***ing bombs' whilst being coned by searchlights and hammered by flak.

The procedure of fetching the bombs, loading them, pulling out the pins and then releasing was too laborious. The last three bombs went straight down the chute with the pins still in and I was glad to see the back of them. I expected that if they landed in one piece, the enemy would treat them with the utmost caution, so at least they would have a nuisance value if nothing else. My relief was such that I sat down on the catwalk and inhaled oxygen as deeply as possible. My fuzzy head cleared and I was then able to tell the skipper that it was a bloody crazy idea to contemplate that performance being a feature of future operations and bloody dangerous too!

I resumed my position at the radio set and listened for the Group half-hourly broadcast. The depth of the searchlight defences was incredible and it seemed that we were constantly illuminated in spite of continued evasive action. With the heavy flak around we at least thought we would be safe from fighter attacks. Denny Denman was in the front gun turret and Bill Bassom in the rear turret. I kept a lookout in the astrodome. We had just emerged from the searchlight activity when Denny said he had to go to the Elsan toilet located in the rear beyond the main spar. I was to relieve him in the front turret. Denny had passed me on his way and I was preparing to go forward to replace him when there was an almighty crack of exploding AA shells and I was convinced we had sustained a direct hit. My reluctance to enter the front turret in those circumstances kept me rooted to the spot. I heard a mumbling over the intercom from Denny and then nothing more. Calling him brought no response so Paul told me to investigate.

I clambered over the main spar and nearly fell over Den's body lying prostrate on the floor. In the darkness it was necessary to feel my way around and I was about to pull his helmet aside to shout in his ear to ask if he was alright and was horrified to find his face a mass of 'gooey' fluid. I thought that he had been hit in the face, which seemed a gory mess. I stayed with him until we were clear of flak and on our way home across that awful long stretch of the North Sea, of which I had a dreadful fear of having to ditch in. A little more composed and convinced that we had suffered our first casualty, no movement or sound coming from Denny, I knelt down beside him and was aware of this pungent smell, which certainly wasn't how I imagined blood to smell. I pulled off his helmet and in the process nearly strangled him with his intercom lead and oxygen tube. I shouted at what I thought was his ear and noticed that he was stirring. He whispered that he had been hit but that he could feel no pain. Yes, sometimes you could be so badly hurt that you were oblivious of pain and in a semi-coma! My hands had become wet with this 'goo' from his face, but it smelt like strong disinfectant. My eyes were beginning to focus in the darkness and suddenly I realised what had happened. The proximity of the bursting AA shell had been sufficient to dislodge the Elsan toilet from its mounting. It had hit the roof of the aircraft; it had struck Denny on the head, rendering him unconscious, and the Elsan contents had emptied over his face!

As he came round I explained my theory. He was unconvinced. We finally landed at base at 5.15 am and on emerging Denny looked as if he had been rehearsing for a minstrel show – he was covered in black disinfectant and smelled atrocious. We were still laughing hysterically during debriefing and when we sat down to our traditional eggs and bacon we asked him to sit at a separate table. It had been an eventful night and one from which Denny was to gain a lot of laughs when repeating his experience over a few jars of beer. Before we got to bed we learned that aircraft 'H' had failed to return with the loss of the crew captained by Flying Officer V. G. D. Spiller. His gunners were Sergeants Vickers and Patterson who were good friends of mine; we had spent some good times together. Three replacement crews arrived the next day, one of which under the captaincy of Pilot Officer C. Landreth was to be posted missing within ten weeks of joining the squadron.[7]

Our twenty-fifth operation was achieved on the night of 12/13 May 1941 when eight squadron aircraft were detailed to bomb Mannheim. Weather conditions were so adverse, which made Ginger's dead reckoning (DR) navigation vital, that we released our load through 10/10ths cloud on DR and no results were observed. The heavy flak barrage was the only thing of note on an uneventful trip, but I'm sure Denny welcomed that after his previous experience.

Three days later eight aircraft were ordered to Swanton Morley to operate against Hannover that night. Having been briefed and delivered to our aircraft, *C-Charlie*, we prepared for take-off but on running the engines one was found to have a serious magneto drop. Engine fitters were called but their efforts were to no avail and our trip had to be abandoned. At least, that was one more day to survive. Having reached twenty-five ops in our first tour, we began to wonder how much longer our luck would hold.

Whilst we stayed overnight at Swanton Morley, back at Newton three aircraft were taking off at 0140 hours for the 'considered' easier target of Boulogne. The Channel ports were the usual targets for new captains to 'blood' their crews. One of these captains, newly appointed, was Sergeant Sam Huggett who had flown with us as our second pilot on a number of raids and we had come to treat him as a special friend. A very competent pilot, we had visions of him completing his first tour of ops without mishap. Alas, he completed his attack as scheduled and was returning to base when he lost an engine and finally crashed near Leicester with the loss of five crew members, including himself. We all felt shattered at this news. Another crew on this 'Fresher' trip to Boulogne, newly arrived Pilot Officer Topp and crew, were to survive this operation but were fated not to return from Hamburg some seven weeks later. So many crews were not surviving to see ops in double figures. On returning to base from Swanton Morley we were detailed to make a search for a missing aircraft down in the North Sea. The chances of survival after ditching in the sea were minimal, but we scanned each dogleg thoroughly for sight of a dinghy or wreckage. Added dangers, of course, came from enemy intruder aircraft that would have welcomed the sight of an unescorted Wimpy over the sea. After 3 hours without result we reluctantly left the area and returned to the comfort of the Mess, pitying that unfortunate crew if they were still adrift somewhere in that hostile sea.

Two weeks of bad weather gave us a respite from operations and we were occupied with Lorenz Beam exercises at Waddington. On 2 June 1941 we were off again in a force of twenty-five Wellingtons against Duisburg in the Ruhr. The raid was uneventful and we landed back at base quite unscathed at 0440 hours. After debriefing and breakfast it was bed in daylight and sleep was difficult with all the usual camp noises. At 11 am I was up again to learn that my promotion to flight sergeant was through; another excuse for a celebration drink!

C-Charlie was detailed for return raids to Duisburg on successive nights on 16 and 17 June. While searchlights and flak were accurate and intensive, we were not hit and survived our twenty-seventh sortie. Our CO Wing Commander Paul was then posted to Bomber Command HQ and Wing Commander R. A. C. Carter assumed command of the squadron. A week later we attacked Cologne again without incident and we hit the sack again by 6 am.

On our nights off or when stood down, most aircrew departed for either Newark or Nottingham by the station transport that was laid on. If we were in Nottingham in the afternoon, then it was generally tea at the Kardomah followed by a visit to the cinema. If it was just on a squadron or crew 'bash', then it was into Nottingham and 'The Black Boy' or 'The Flying Horse' where a favourite sport was, as far as possible, to drink our way along one of the shelves! From there we would move on to 'The Trip' (The Trip To Jerusalem), which is reputed to be the oldest pub in Britain and is built in the rock below the Castle walls. If really slumming, 'The Dog' (The Dog and Partridge) was the place to go but that was to be put out of bounds to RAF personnel. We returned without mishap but with rather more 'fuel' than when we set out! The beer must have been heavily diluted, as we were easily able to consume eight pints during the opening hours of 6 pm to 10.30 pm and we were always first in and last out! Apart from the booze and the 'line-shooting' about operational experiences, girls of all ages, shapes and sizes were drawn there like magnets and many of the lads failed to reach the last bus back to camp, some trickling in at daybreak.

Walking into the crew room one morning, we spotted that the 'service-ability' board bore the names of girls in Nottingham, many of them familiar to us. There were details of their sexual prowess, dates when they should be overlooked, whether they were married or not and if overnight accommodation was available etc. This information was updated almost on a daily basis and it needed to be consulted before embarking on any blind dates. Mostly, the crews enjoyed their own company and were content to drink themselves silly and to join in the most bawdy of songs. There was always a piano player available – ready to accept the many drinks bought for him or her in return for hours of musical entertainment. The only difficulty was locating the bar through the thick fog of cigarette smoke. Everybody seemed to smoke. The luxury of dying from cancer never occurred to anybody. It was expected that death could only arrive by violent means.

When ops were scrubbed too late for going to the 'flesh-pots', which was not unusual, home-made entertainment in the Mess was the order of the day. High Cockalorum was a favourite sport, especially on two squadron stations, as most were and usually when sufficient anaesthetic had been consumed in the bar to deaden the pain! There were several versions, but it was usually one squadron against the other. There were various formats, but that which I remember best was where one team formed a pyramid in the corner of the ante-room with the trophy on top – sometimes a body and at others, something considered to be of value to the opposition. The object was for the attackers to capture the trophy and, of course, it resolved itself into a heaving mass of injured bodies! There were also numerous stories of motorcycles and horses being ridden around messes, which I have heard told at various stations but never actually witnessed. At Syerston, it was said that a motorcycle was ridden up the left-hand stairs, round the upper floor, down the right-hand stairs and out of the front door. It was also reported that the Padre's horse did a similar circuit, but this time, in the Officers' Mess. I have not the slightest doubt that these incidents happened but when, where and how many times, I cannot be sure. What is certain however, is that some lucky aircrew, like me, were in somewhat more danger of injury in the Mess than we ever were out of it!

It was the turn of Düsseldorf in the Ruhr on the night of 30 June. This being our twenty-ninth operation, we had reason to believe that we were an experienced crew now and with high hopes of thirty successful ops we could look forward to a 'rest' at an OTU. I was, however, destined to fly a further nine sorties before this happened. As we entered July, Pilot Officer Landreth, our second dickie was given his own crew captaincy and we took on Sergeant Griffiths as his replacement. One sortie against Bremen and two against Cologne were conducted satisfactorily, Cologne having its heaviest raid so far with extensive damage in the centre and east of the city. The success achieved was due to a spell of good weather and clearer conditions. Bomber Command in this era were totally dependent on visual target sightings; there still being no radar navigational aids that were to dictate the course of the air war in later months.

On the morning of 11 July 1941 we got to bed at 6 am after returning from Cologne, only to be roused at noon with the news that 150 Squadron was moving out of Newton that day to Snaith, near Goole. We weren't very happy with this news, our stay at Newton being one of comfortable accommodation and messing, with easy access to Nottingham where female company had been very receptive to the glamour 'boys in blue' and where we had built up a good relationship with the licensees. It was time also to say goodbye to the flying Banana Morris Car, so called because it was painted bright yellow. This vehicle was devoid of doors and did sterling service on its excursions into Nottingham. Ginger and Ian Bishop were the joint owners, having paid £5 for it. With the lack of private use petrol, it ran on a mixture of aviation spirit, paraffin and oil, clouds of smoke issuing on each of its runs. I can't recall any bother with the Service Police and the CO took a low profile. He was surely aware of the notoriety of the Flying Banana, but perhaps thought it was an outlet for his crews from the tensions of operational flying. I can still hear the loud cheers from bystanders in the streets of Nottingham as it passed on its way. The Banana didn't bear a tax disc, Ginger always retaining postal orders to the value thereof for the possible eventuality of being challenged, at which stage he would say: 'It's in the post, Officer.' This happened at Ratcliffe, Nottinghamshire. When confronted by the law and the pet answer was offered, but one of the twelve occupants of the car shouted, 'Get some Berlin time in, Copper!' The irony was that none of us had yet been to Berlin, but the remark obviously riled the Constable and consequently cost Ginger and Bish a week's wages. Ginger recalled that he took it to a race meeting one day and that it went faster than the horses he backed that day.

We arrived at Snaith at 3 pm and were horrified to find a newly constructed airfield with Nissen hut accommodation and clouds of dust blowing everywhere. The whole place was in violent contrast to the peacetime set up at Newton and we were all shattered with the conditions and at the thought of having Goole, the nearest town, as our social activity base. We hardly had time to settle in when we were briefed to attack Bremen, taking off at 2235 hours into thick cloud. Reaching operational height, we found ourselves icing up; it was forming up in layers on the wings and it was most uncomfortable. We finally reached the target area and released our bombs with intense relief on Vegesack near Bremen. Some 7 hours and 10 minutes after take-off we landed at Mildenhall, to where we had been diverted because of fog at Snaith. After all the uneventful flights from Newton, we visualised that probably our luck would change after having moved to a new base.

The next operation on 21/22 July 1941 was to be our most hair-raising experience. Entering the briefing room, we looked expectantly at the operations map and saw the red route ribbon targeting to Frankfurt, our first raid on that city. We were airborne at 2210 hours and wondered if we were destined to return to Snaith in the early hours of next morning. The usual searchlight and flak activity was experienced near and over the target. Once our considerable bomb load was released we felt relief and thought it was just a matter of getting home now, hopefully without incident. Not long after leaving the target, it was apparent that our starboard engine was not functioning satisfactorily. Paul was concerned that the engine was sounding like a bag of old bones and said that the oil was obviously not getting through to it. We gradually lost height and Paul directed Denny and myself to operate the manual oil pump located behind the main spar, in an effort to get oil through to the engine. We found, in turns, that the manual pump was almost inoperable; it took immense effort to force it one way and then the other. It was intensely cold and our fingers became numb and we experienced cramp in our legs whilst in the crouching position. It was obvious that our efforts were not working; we could hear tremendous grinding noises coming from the engine and the strain was causing the plane to fly crab-like. Sparks and fire were spitting out from the engine cowling and we were losing more height. I had visions of having to ditch in the North Sea and cursed the possibility of our coming to the end of our luck on our thirty-fourth operation.

The noises were becoming more pronounced and Paul was having great difficulty in maintaining course and height. Something drastic was obviously going to happen and it did. With flames and sparks and tremendous grinding within the engine, the propeller, with an accompanying section of engine, suddenly tore itself free and spun forward and upwards, fortunately, to disappear over the tail and downwards to the North Sea. If, in its final torment it had spun into the fuselage then without doubt I wouldn't have been around to pen this report! As it happened, the aircraft flew much better without it, although we were still losing height and we were concerned at the risk of not reaching the mainland. I was instructed to send out 'Mayday' SOS signals – breaking the usual radio silence because of our dire circumstances. We aimed for the nearest coastal point and it seemed an eternity before we made landfall and made a successful one-engine landing on the grass field at Marham in Norfolk.

We ran to a halt, and clambered out to gaze at the gaping great hole in the engine nacelle and the surrounding ground crew stood there mouthing their amazement. It was not until very much later that Ginger informed us that we had a 1,000 lb bomb hang-up still in the bomb-bay and that we had un-knowingly made a fairly heavy one-engine landing on the bumpy grass 'drome, which might easily have dislodged the bomb. Ginger's character was such that he would have carried a guilt-complex over this incident, but the crew immediately dismissed this notion out of hand by reason of his wonderful dedication to the job in hand. Hadn't he always navigated us to and from the target so expertly and got us back to friendly territory time and time again in spite of the many hazards and diversions? So, we thought, 'Well, we have got charmed lives, haven't we?' Furthermore, we had taken off from Snaith on two operations and not yet been able to land back there! Was this to be a feature of future operations from there?

Two days later, on 24 July, we just couldn't believe our ears when the CO said that six crews were to participate in a daylight operation against the German battleships *Scharnhorst* and *Gneisenau* lying at anchor in the French port of Brest. A total of 150 aircraft were planned to make the attack in formation, but at the last moment this had to be changed because of the departure of the *Scharnhorst* to La Pallice. The force to Brest was then to be composed of 100 aircraft, of which three were to be Flying Fortresses flying at 30,000 feet in the hope of attracting German fighters prematurely. Then eighteen Hampdens escorted by three squadrons of Spitfires with long-range fuel tanks were to attack in anticipation of drawing off more enemy fighters. Finally, the main force of seventy-nine unescorted Wellingtons from Nos 1 and 3 Groups were to attack in the final wave. This was to be our first daylight operation and without fighter escort, and in the knowledge that our formation flying technique was far from efficient and enemy fighter prowess was widely known, we did not give much for our chances. As a diversion for this raid thirty-six Blenheims all escorted by Spitfires were to attack Cherbourg docks in the hope of drawing German fighters from the main raid. Very apprehen-sive, we took off at 1050 hours and it took quite some time before our six aircraft could take up some semblance of a formation and set course. The weather was good and visibility excellent, there being no cloud in which to hide in the event of attack.

The German fighter opposition was stronger and more prolonged than anticipated by Group HQ, but the crews involved had not shared their view. We were struggling to maintain formation and then found that our oxygen supply failed. With the target area sighted ahead with the bursting flak our engine-driven generator failed and discussion followed on the situation pertaining. With the generator out of action, so many of our electrics would not function and, more importantly, our bombs would not release. Having come so far, naturally we were disappointed but had to abandon our mission and turn for base. The remainder of the force pushed home their attack but they were badly mauled by the German fighter attacks. Ten Wellingtons were shot down, 12.5 per cent of the total force, but six hits were claimed on the *Gneisenau*. Of the fifteen Halifaxes attacking La Pallice, five were shot down and all the remainder damaged, but five direct hits were registered on the *Scharnhorst*, putting her out of action for four months. Two of the eighteen Hampdens were lost to fighter attacks. It was considered a highly successful operation but with heavy losses. We landed back at base at 4 pm, somewhat disappointed but comforted in the knowledge that we had survived our thirty-fifth mission. Each operation now was tempting fate – how much longer could we survive when so many crews were coming to grief before reaching double figures of ops completed? The strain was telling on each crewmember and each flight seemed so much harder than ever before.

This was to prove Ginger's last operation of his first tour. He was to go on seven days' leave before going to Canada for his prestigious Specialist Navigation Course. Sadly, we were to lose a super navigator and friend. I think we wished that the rest of us could say '*finis*' to our first tour of operations but this was not to be. Paul was promoted to flight lieutenant and we celebrated this fine captain's new rank and thanked our lucky stars that we had been fortunate to be crewed with such a competent pilot and skipper. Still anticipating news from Group HQ that our first tour of ops was over, we found ourselves briefed again for yet another raid on Cologne. Thunderstorms and severe icing were experienced again and we could not locate the target through 10/10ths cloud. We turned for home with our bomb load still intact and then a partial cloud clearance enabled us to see the outline of Courtrai airfield and down went our full load. They must have wondered why a lone aircraft singled them out. There was still no news from Group HQ and we were airborne again, this time to Frankfurt, which had bad memories for us with our previous raid on this target. Very good bombing results were obtained by the sixty-five Wellingtons and thirty-three Hampdens involved and only three aircraft were lost. One of the crashing bombers went straight into a rubber factory employing over 2,000 people.

On 8 August we were assembled in the CO's office to be told at long last that our operation that night was to be our last and that we were then to be 'rested' at an OTU. The target was Hamburg, not the easiest of targets for our last excursion and we all wished each other good luck and promised ourselves a party if we were fortunate enough to return. We had come to rely on each other so much over a period of one year and had become the staunchest of friends. We almost regretted the necessary split-up to various stations after this last flight together. We reached the enemy coast and experienced flak for the last time and as one engine was not functioning we were forced to abandon our task at Groningen. However disappointing this last sortie was, we had survived where so many crews had not. When we taxied to our dispersal we climbed out of *C-Charlie* and all kissed the ground in thankfulness, embraced our faithful ground crew and invited them to a final party to show our appreciation of their marvellous service and dedication. The rivalry between the respected ground crews was great and they would all uphold the merits and achievements of their aircrews. While we were fully engaged on flying operations, the ground crews invariably had to hang around, sometimes in the coldest of weathers, awaiting our return. Their smiles on our return were indicative of their delight that we had brought their aircraft home safely, although sometimes with varying degrees of damage. We were saddened to learn that Pilot Officer Landreth and crew were lost in the Frankfurt raid (6/7 August), which meant that we had lost all the earlier second pilots on our crew when they had received their captaincies.

Some three weeks elapsed at Snaith before our postings came through, but we had finished our flying commitment with 150 Squadron. Finally, on 28 August 1941, we left Snaith and I found that Denny and I were to be 'Screens' (instructors) at 27 OTU Lichfield in the Midlands. We all expressed the hope that the war would be over before we had to undertake a second tour of ops, but that seemed highly unlikely as the war had gone badly for Britain – virtually on her own but for the gallant help of the Commonwealth. However, against all odds we had survived Dunkirk, the Battle of Britain and in a smallish way were hitting back at the *Reich* with limited bomber forces, which compelled the enemy to retain forces in defence that could have been so usefully employed in other theatres of war. I was now 21 years old, had completed thirty-eight operations, was still fit and unscathed and furthermore was in love with Mollie who had been a colleague when we were employed at Herbert & Sons Ltd at Edmonton in North London.

Rocky (Harry de Belleroche) had gone to Upavon prior to posting to Rhodesia for instructional duties. He returned to carry out his further tour of operations with 97 Squadron at Bourn. Rocky was over Darmstadt when his Lancaster sustained a direct hit and the aircraft broke up. He found himself alone in the cockpit section of the plane, finally freed himself and baled out. He damaged his back on landing in a garden with his 'chute draped over a wall. The inhabitants were evidently in an air-raid shelter. Because of his injuries he was unable to evade capture and spent the rest of the war in a PoW camp, finally overrun by the Russians. Ginger Thomas completed his second tour, reaching sixty operations in total. He received a DSO in addition to his DFM and was then posted to HQ Bomber Command, where he worked under Air Chief Marshal 'Bomber' Harris. The three of us could say that we had earned our keep since those days back in 1939–40. And we lived to meet up again over forty years after the war! Fred Denman (Denny) completed a second tour on Wellingtons in the Middle East and was awarded the DFM.

Paul Carlyon was posted to 214 Squadron and had to say goodbye to his faithful bulldog Pickwick. This animal didn't show a lot of affection, but was always awaiting Paul's return from flying, sitting outside the control tower until satisfied his 'guvnor' was safe, and then waddling back to the Mess to await his breakfast. Paul was shot down and killed over the Bay of Biscay in a raid on Lorient in 1943.

Notes

1. 150 Squadron had returned from the Advanced Air Striking Force in France in June 1940 and was posted to 1 Group to continue flying Battles until it was re-equipped with Wellingtons.
2. By Battles of 12 Squadron on 12.5.40. Four crews were killed or captured. Flying Officer D. E. Garland and his observer, Sergeant D. Gray, were awarded posthumous VCs. LAC L. R. Reynolds, the gunner, received no award.
3. Three Hampdens, two Blenheims and two Wellingtons were lost on 25/26 July 1940.
4. L7856 was destined never to reach base, however. Cloud base was low and problems with the radio conspired against them, until finally, almost out of fuel and with one engine out, Rocky said they would have to make a crash-landing.
5. No aircraft were l although two Wellingtons and a Blenheim FTR from a raid by eighty-six aircraft on Bremen and three aircraft were lost on the raid on Berlin by seventy-two bombers.
6. All six crew were killed when the aircraft was shot down by flak near Nantes.
7. KIA 6/7 August 1941, Frankfurt.

CHAPTER 2

M for Mother

Trevor A. 'Happy' Hampton

Five jolly bomber boys, flying over Germany,
Up came the fighters, one, two, three,
And the rear gunner cried as he buckled on his parachute,
Who'll come on Ops in a Wimpy with me.

(Sung to the tune of '*Waltzing Matilda*')

As a trained bomber crew, we were posted to 149 Squadron, Mildenhall, in February 1941. This was the squadron that featured in the well-known wartime film *Target For Tonight* and for a short time our station was like a film set. After a few days in the Officers' Mess I seemed to detect a subtle sort of deference being bestowed upon me by other junior officers. Nothing was said but everyone was so 'very nice'. At first I thought it might be that I had arrived as a fully fledged flying officer, with 600 flying hours in my logbook, rather than the more usual humble pilot officer straight from training school. For a day or two I basked in my fool's paradise.

We had been assigned a brand new Wellington IC [Rl474], which should have made me a little suspicious. My ground crew painted on it our squadron letters 'OJ' and our identification letter 'M'. For radio telephony purposes, each letter of the alphabet has an associated word and the code in those days was 'A' Apple, 'B' Baker etc. and for 'M' it was 'Mother'. Secretly, I was delighted. I had a good mother and she would look after me – it was an omen.

Apart from myself, my own crew consisted of a front gunner, second pilot, navigator, radio operator and I had arranged for an old friend to be my rear gunner, a Sergeant George Gray, but to me he was 'Junior', he was so very young. Junior had been a commissioned pilot. He was an excellent officer, much better than I, and knew his King's Regulations – but as a pilot he was accident-prone. He also clashed with his flight commander, who did not rest until Junior had lost his commission. I was there and saw it all and it was most unfair. But these things happen in the services and the RAF nearly lost a good man. But not so. Junior promptly rejoined in the ranks as an aircrew gunner and didn't put up his pilot's wings, which he was fully entitled to, but *M-Mother* finished up with three qualified pilots in the crew.

I began to notice that my crew, also, were being treated with a touching courtesy quite alien to the wartime RAF. I mentioned the phenomenon to

Junior. He looked at me incredulously. 'Don't you know Skipper? There have been eleven *M-Mothers* since Christmas!'

I was a bit shaken but I soon consoled myself – I still had faith in Mother. Out of our squadron of eighteen aircraft, they must have been losing one *M-Mother* every week.

It was usual to do several trips as a second pilot before getting a command, but in view of my flying experience, although mostly on fighter types, and my seniority, I had been given command immediately. However, just to show me the ropes and to demonstrate how 'easy' it was (his words), my flight commander, Squadron Leader Sawry Cookson (Cooky), decided to accompany us on our first trip. He naturally assumed command and we left my second pilot behind.

The first trip was, more or less, a 'blitz' on Cologne. The Germans had had a go at Coventry in November 1940, which I had seen burning from my own aircraft, so I didn't feel too badly about it – but really, at heart, I was no bomber pilot.

With an inferno below we steamed over the city at 140 knots, at 8,000 feet, the ceiling for a Wellington with a bomb load. Having done two runs over the target area, we were chased off by ground fire and searchlights, diving into the protective cloak of darkness clear of the city and levelling out at 2,000 feet. Cooky let me take over and he went aft for a word with the crew. When he returned to the cockpit I was climbing but he stopped me – 2,000 feet would be OK.

We cruised along quietly and eventually came across an enemy airfield, all lit up for night flying. 'Go down and stir them up a bit,' said Cooky, so down we went. Once round the circuit and they realised there was a cat among the pigeons, and let us have some flak and light tracer fire. I looked at Cooky and he nodded towards home. I set course and started to climb, but again he told me to stay at 2,000 feet. It didn't seem right to me – but he should know.

We stooged along for some time and I was beginning to feel confident. I noticed that when I looked straight down immediately beneath I could see intermittent flickering lights immediately beneath the aircraft. So much for blackout precautions – I was looking straight down the chimneys of a large city, probably Rotterdam but I didn't get the chance to confirm with the navigator, Sergeant Cymbalist. At that moment there was a blinding flash and *M-Mother* was on the instant the focal point of countless searchlights and we seemed to be trapped in a cage of golden rods. I was petrified into immobility, but it did slowly dawn on me that the air was composed of vicious tracer shells and bullets. The crack of exploding shells could be heard above the noise of our engines – that meant they were close and then a much louder one rocked the aircraft. The starboard wing went down, followed by the nose. I had the stick right back and the wheel hard over to port, but *M-Mother* was diving out of the sky and I was quite helpless. The altimeter was unwinding like a mad thing, I watched it go past 500 feet in numb despair and I knew we were 'going in' – this was it, and on our first trip. Oh, Mother!

Under such circumstances, imminent death brings with it no acute agony of mind, as one would expect but a hopeless numb realisation of the end. I knew

A Wimpy crew with their mascot – one of Disney's Seven Dwarfs – and a bomb in 1941. (via Dr Colin Dring, Mildenhall Museum)

it was no good struggling anymore and I was just about to let go of the controls and cover my face for the final blinding crash when Cooky's voice came over the intercom, 'Come on, hold it!' We might have been on a training exercise. I hung on, with Cooky leaning across me, helping to take some of the weight and we eventually levelled off at 200 feet, the searchlights and flak losing us as we dived earthwards.

Our speed was down to 85 knots and we were flying in a semi-stalled condition, tail down and nose up. Our two Bristol Pegasus engines were at full boost, but we couldn't gain speed or height and I dared not let our nose or wing go down the slightest degree. We staggered home across the North Sea, every moment expecting the aircraft to drop a wing and spin in, but as we burnt up our fuel, inch by inch we made a little height and crossed the English coast at 500 feet. Cooky could see that I was exhausted and he managed to slide underneath me into the pilot's seat. Cooky saved *M-Mother* that night. He was a remarkable person who just did not acknowledge danger and was quite fearless. This was proved time and time again and some of the stories I was told of his exploits made me decide that I would prefer to be on my own, thank you. He was awarded a DSO later and he had a DFC. What became of him I do not know. I hope he made it – but I doubt it. I felt I had the edge on him as a 'safe' pilot, but who wanted 'safe' pilots in 1941? We could not possibly have made the usual circuit round the airfield but luckily, with the light of dawn, we managed to make a straight approach from the east right on to the grass runway. I expected Cooky to make a full power approach and do a wheel landing, but too late I realised he was holding off to do a 'three pointer'. The starboard wing naturally stalled first, a great chunk of it was missing and down we came into Mildenhall, a shaken crew.

At dawn the ground crew pushed off for breakfast, having written us off as one more *M-Mother*. However, they were soon out on 'M' site again and seemed genuinely pleased to see us back, although it meant the fitting of a new wing.

I was rather looking forward to the interrogation by our Intelligence Officer, one John Cobb, of water and land speed record fame. 'Everything OK?' asked John. 'Yes, bombs on target,' said Cooky. 'Come on, let's get some breakfast.' I was learning fast

After some sleep, to my surprise, I found that the night's experience had improved my morale and my faith in *M-Mother* had been justified. My crew was not convinced and Junior privately expressed the hope that he would be re-commissioned before he got the 'chop'.

A new wing was fitted and I carried out an air test. On reporting the aircraft serviceable again, Cooky informed me that he was lending my *M-Mother* to

The aircrew and part of the ground crew of Wellington IC M-Mother *of 149 Squadron at Mildenhall in 1941. Pilot, Trevor A. 'Happy' Hampton is third from right. (via Dr. Colin Dring, Mildenhall Museum)*

'A' Flight for the coming night's operation. I could stand down with all my crew except for my second pilot, Sergeant Evan Roy Cooke, who they wanted to borrow.

During the afternoon of 17 March Sergeant Ronald Warren, the captain of the unserviceable 'A' Flight aircraft, sought me out in the 'B' Flight crewroom.[1] He was in a dreadful state and made little effort to hide it. 'I'm told I have to take your aircraft tonight, Sir – and it's *M-Mother*.'

I said, 'Yes, look after her; she's flying nicely with the new wing.'

The poor boy was nearly speechless but in a rambling disjointed manner he told me he had done some twenty-eight operations, had only two more to do of his present tour and now fate had dealt him *M-Mother*. (In 1941 twenty-eight ops was really something for in those days we didn't make one dive for the target, let everything go and then race for home – no. We were instructed to drop half our bomb load, fly away and then make a second attack, having stirred up a hornet's nest and let the rest go. The idea, I presume, being to let the enemy think we had twice the number of aircraft. And we did it one at a time, not hundreds at a time as they did later, to keep them up all night.) In 149 Squadron she really was the 'end'. I felt a little piqued. I didn't like to think of my aircraft as a leper. In truth, there was little expressed sympathy wasted in the wartime RAF and none was expected. This expression of fear to an officer he hadn't even spoken to before was unprecedented in my experience. It was more than just a premonition to the boy. He had made up his mind they were for the 'chop'. Instead of trying to laugh him out of it, I found myself comforting him and my last words were, 'I guarantee *M-Mother* will bring you right back'.

I lived out of camp in a caravan at Barton Mills, deep in the woods, and I was woken up by the sound of firing. The following morning, 18 March, driving along the road from Barton Mills to the airfield, I saw the tail end of a Wellington bomber sticking up out of the roof of a house. Just clear of the slates I read 'M-OJ'.[2]

A new Wellington (R1587) was towed out to 'M' site and yet another *M-Mother* was prepared for operations. In this one we completed a few operations and to everyone's surprise, returned intact. One night, intent on blasting Hitler's three pocket battleships lying in Brest harbour, we were being shaken up by the combined defensive fire of the three battleships and all the Brest Peninsular flak. The navigator was chanting over his bombsight for my benefit 'Left. Left. Steady. Right. Steady', when I heard Junior shout something about a fighter.

Without any conscious intention on my part I had *M-Mother* in a vertical diving turn to starboard. The navigator shouted, 'Bombs gone' but added that he didn't know where. From the rear turret Junior howled, 'Hell, Skipper. What are you doing? You frightened the daylights out of the Jerry fighter. You turned right across his bows.'

It wasn't only the Jerry who was shaken.

Back at base Junior took me on one side; the others had delegated him. 'Skip, you really must see Doc about your ears.' I did and was grounded for further examination. To my surprise the news caused consternation in the crew. Squadron Leader Anthony W. J. Clark, just posted to the squadron, took over 'B' Flight from Cooky, who was promoted, to Squadron Commander. Clark also took over *M-Mother* and my crew for the time being and decided on a daylight training flight to get to know the aircraft and the boys. He had only been on the camp a few hours and could not have known *M-Mother*'s reputation. Being a senior officer and on such short acquaintance, my crew wouldn't have presumed to mention such a subject and I didn't say anything; what good could it have done?

I watched *M-Mother* climb away with mixed feelings on 17 May. It is not nice being grounded, even temporarily, and I had a guilty sense of having let my crew down. I wandered into the crewroom, wondering what I should do until their return, but hearing the commotion of the fire engine and the ambulance getting underway, I went outside to see what was up. Someone shouted across to me, 'Your aircraft has gone in. A Hurricane flew smack through her'. I jumped into my car and headed for the distant column of black oily smoke that marked the end of one more *M-Mother*.

In the middle of a potato field I stumbled amongst the still smouldering remains of my aeroplane and friends, until the station doctor walked me away. 'You shouldn't be here. You can't do any good.' It was of course bad for morale, my morale. One of the fire crew came up and told me that the tail and rear gun turret were in the next field, unburnt. My unspoken question was answered before I dare ask it. 'The rear gunner didn't have time to get out. They were only at 2,000 feet.' I walked over to a stretcher on which was the only body they had recovered. From beneath army blankets protruded two beautifully polished boots. It was the last I was to see of Junior – the 'tail end' captain of *M-Mother*.

To the others around, it might have seemed that I was staring morbidly at my dead friend, but they didn't know I was trying to get a final message through to him and the intercom was worse than usual. 'You very nearly made it Junior – your commission had been approved.'[3]

I had a talk with Cooky, who laughed at me at first, but once he realised I was dead serious he agreed to drop *M-Mother* from the squadron aircraft board and replace it with *P-Peter*. I was posted away for training as a test pilot and lost touch with my Bomber Command friends, but I hope the trick worked. However, *M-Mother* had looked after me. I felt she would – I had a good mother.

Notes

1. Warren had had a close shave flying another *M-Mother*, on 11 February. Returning from an attack on Hannover at 8,000 feet they could not land back Mildenhall and went to Digby where they crash-landed with the undercarriage up and the second pilot, Sergeant Early, was killed and the rest of the crew injured.
2. *M-Mother* had returned safely from the raid on Bremen but had been jumped by a Ju 88C night intruder flown by *Leutnant* Rolf Pfeiffer of I/NJG2 from Gilze-Rijn, Holland, as it was coming into land near Beck Row. Sergeant Ronald Warren, the pilot, and the five other crew were killed in the attack. The Wellington took the top off a garage and flattened a row of conifer trees before ploughing into the side of a bungalow, demolishing the

lounge, kitchen, hall and bathroom and back bedroom. Ellis Titchmarsh, an insurance agent and his wife, Irene, escaped unhurt as they had taken refuge under their bed when they heard machine-gun fire. Their bedroom was the only room left standing and it took six men to lift the debris of a wall off the bed that saved the occupants' lives. Mr and Mrs Titchmarsh had to take separate lodgings with different people and did not live together again for nearly a year. Pfeiffer was lost on the night of 17/18 August 1941 when his Ju 88C-2 R4+HM of IV/NJG2 crashed into the North Sea. A Royal Navy vessel found the body of his navigator *Gefreiter* Otto Schierling in the North Sea on 26 August. Nothing was ever found of Pfeiffer or *Unteroffizier* Alfred Ranke, the gunner/engineer.

3. Hurricane I V7225 of 1401 Meteorological Flight at Mildenhall piloted by Flying Officer Iain Robertson MacDiarmid DFC had hurtled out of thick cloud towards the formation of four Wellingtons and had torn right through the fuselage of the leading Wellington, R1587, flown by Squadron Leader Clarke. The Hurricane impacted upside down on Lark Farm, Soham Fen near Ely killing MacDiarmid.

CHAPTER 3

The Nursery Slopes

Ernie Rodley

Where are the Poles with their gaiety and sadness,
All with the most unpronounceable names,
Silently, ruthlessly flying in vengeance
Remembering their homes and their country in flames?

'*Lancasters*', Audrey Grealy

I was one of the lucky ones. Joining the RAFVR in 1937, I already had instructing experience when war broke out. Consequently, I graced the first 'War Instructors' Course' at CFS in October 1939, after which I spent an exhausting and unrewarding year and a half in Training Command. Hence, by June 1941, I had over 1,000 hours in my logbook, but all spent in the vicinity of an airfield, so I was quite unprepared for any wider aspects of the art.

A strange set of circumstances rescued me from the thraldom of instructing. One of the new generation bombers, the Manchester, had been suffering from a plague of engine failures. It could maintain height on one engine as long as the oil-cooler flap remained closed, but the straining good engine would gradually overheat and the flap had to be inched open. This was followed by a slow loss of height, which continued until the crew had to bale out or ditch. The Manchester was grounded to give Rolls-Royce time to develop the Vulture engine to a more reliable state. By mid 1941, this had been achieved but to play safe it was decided that 97 Squadron should be re-formed, equipped with Manchesters, but all pilots had to have at least 1,000 hours under their belts. Hence my good fortune.

Posted to Finningley OTU, I was delighted to see many familiar faces on the course. Most of these had been with me at Upavon in 1939 and, as each grinning face entered the Mess, a fresh roar of welcome went up. It was a major turning point in my life to be on that course. The boredom of circuits and bumps fell away. The high morale of the staff, headed by Babe Learoyd VC, lifted our depressed spirits, whilst a new keenness replaced the tedium of instructing.

For that period of the war, the course was good but, apart from the basics, such as practice bombing and night beacon crawls around the countryside, I remember very little advice on the art of staying alive in flak or fighter attack.

This was probably due to the fact that very little operational experience had been collated by then and crews just had to find out for themselves what it was like 'over there'.

We tried to make up for this shortcoming by hanging on the words of those who had survived a tour. As these respected individuals sank the pints readily supplied by the sprogs, we stored away their words of wisdom. Usually this advice was contradicted by the next guru, but we hoped to distil something useful out of those alcoholic evenings.

The flying was carried out on Wellington Xs – and very clapped out ones they were. Nobody actually suffered an engine failure, I am glad to say, because, having tried to make practice single-engined circuits, I am convinced that a pilot would have had to be very skilful – or lucky – to get away with one at night.

I cannot remember making a good landing on one of these machines. Apart from a shocking cockpit layout, the Wimpy was blessed with flap interconnected elevator trim. The idea of automatically offsetting any change of aircraft trim caused by lowering or raising flap was ingenious. It probably worked on younger aircraft, but these were so spavined that it was a gamble which way the trim would go – and when – after one selected full flap when crossing the boundary lights. Anyhow, these landings filled me with great admiration for the strength of Barnes Wallis's geodetic structure.

The final exercise on the Wimpy was a night cross-country across the North Sea to 3 degrees east. To this day I am convinced that the purpose of this route was to provide us with the experience of light flak – all at the expense of the Royal Navy. The track passed neatly over one of the east coast convoys.

We had turned back from 3 degrees east and were bumbling along towards base. Ahead of me a short distance – although I was unaware of it at the time – was another Wimpy, piloted by a chum of mine, Jock Keir. His was the honour of receiving the first naval salute, in the form of streams of light flak, whilst we, just behind, had a grandstand view.

What seemed to be a succession of roman candles rose from the blackness beneath, lazily at first but accelerating rapidly as they curved towards us, to whizz by seemingly only yards away. We immediately tapped out the letter-of-the-night on the downward recognition light, but the only result was to improve the unseen gunners' aim. We relied on leaving the vicinity after that.

Meanwhile, as Jock told me later, the aircraft ahead was dealing with the trouble in a very original way. Startled by the sudden eruption of flak, Jock dropped his cup of coffee and began to weave desperately. He shouted for his W/Op to fire off the colours-of-the-night and this worthy grabbed the Very pistol from its stowage and, with difficulty due to the evasive action, managed to insert the cartridge into the breech. He was not quite so successful getting the muzzle back into the firing aperture before his agitated finger had pulled the trigger.

Two glaring, glowing red balls ricocheted down the latticed interior of the fuselage, emitting dense smoke as they went. Only Dante could have done justice to the hellish scene, as Sidcotted figures staggered after the incandescent balls, kicking them whenever they came to rest to prevent the aircraft's fabric from catching fire. It was only after the panting crew was resting after the fireworks had fizzled out that they remembered the fuel overload tank resting on its chocks in the middle of the fuselage. It was a scorched Wimpy and crew that eventually made it back to base.

Later, we reached the last phase of the course, which was to convert on to the Manchester. Somewhat awed by the size of this monster, I found it a delight to fly. Everything worked – after all, they were nearly new – and I was relieved to find that I had not completely lost the art of landing. Actually, the Manchester was even nicer to fly than the Lancaster was. With 12 feet less in the wing span and with a closer engine-mass, it had a rate of roll like a fighter. The landing, with a trickle of engine to offset the high wing loading, was like that of the Anson. Then, once on the ground, the huge 16-feet props bit into the air, decelerating the machine like wheel-brakes. The Vulture was now very dependable. The big-end trouble had been overcome and one only has to remember how the Manchester took the brunt of the work at the Lancaster Conversion Units to realise what a good job Rolls-Royce had done.

The re-equipped 97 Squadron was based at Coningsby, a grass field near Boston and happily boasting peacetime quarters. We shared the Station with 106 Squadron, flying Hampdens. One of their pilots was a press-on type by the name of [Guy] Gibson.[1] After posting to 97 Squadron, we had to spend some time working up to operational fitness and we spent a lot of time wistfully watching 106 Squadron being bombed up and – need I say – bearing their wisecracks in the Mess.

The big day came at last and the new boys assembled in the Briefing Room. Our first raid was to be against the masses of sea-going barges, which were being collected in the Channel ports for use in the projected invasion of England. These targets were referred to as Nursery Slopes, being considered not too demanding for the new boys. I have no doubt those squadron commanders always tried to give their new crews as easy a target as possible for their first operation. Despite this, it is probable that a high percentage of our losses, especially in the early years of the war, were attributable to sheer inexperience on the part of the crews.

Our instructions were to take ten 500 lb bombs and hit the craft sheltering in the docks at Boulogne. Only if the target could be identified visually were the bombs to be dropped, otherwise we had to bring them back. The purpose of this was to prevent damage or casualties to our French allies.

It was pointed out that recently the enemy had been interfering with our W/T and R/T traffic and it was believed that several aircraft had been led astray. All messages and replies to calls for assistance must be treated with suspicion in future. This information was to have a traumatic effect on me later that night.

However, cheered by the report of minimal defences at the target we left the briefing room and went to collect our gear. It was a lovely night as we bounced across the soft turf, cleared the far hedge and throttled back to climb power. Passing across a blacked-out East Anglia, we climbed to 12,000 feet and I could soon see the glint of the moon on the waters of the Channel. There was not a cloud in sight as we droned on, the matt black of the English coast on the starboard and, ahead, the loom of the French coast. This was a piece of cake!

Directly on the nose a gaggle of searchlights on the enemy coast confirmed our navigation. The few gun flashes were not enough to intimidate us as we pressed cheerfully on knowing that everything was going our way. Just then, the lights and flashes took on an unfocussed appearance. They became more and more hazy until only a soft glow showed where they had been. From overhead I could see the dim mass of sea fog that had drifted over the target a few minutes too soon.

After flying around for a while, I decided to make a timed run from Dungeness, which was still clearly discernible. This run brought us to the same point on the coast, but still there was no break in the fog. After several more attempts to find the target, I had to make the dread decision to carry all those lovely bombs back to base.

I switched on my mike and informed the rest of the crew that I was returning to base and would steer north. Unfortunately, I think that the navigator must have been off the intercom at the critical moment. Quite some time later, after ruminating about the events of the night and wondering if I could have done any better, I decided that the time had come for a rather more scientific course. Putting down my coffee, I set the aircraft descending slowly and called:

'Navigator, have you got that course yet?'

'What course is that, Skip?'

'Back to base, where else?'

'Have we left the target then?'

'Dammit, I told you when we left.'

'How long ago was that then, Skip?'

For the life of me, I could not make a worthwhile guess and I let panic take the place of reason. The thought of failure was terrifying. My first reaction was to get inland and try to find a light beacon. That would give us a fix to start from again.

I turned towards the dark mass of the land. I was now at 2,000 feet and ahead was a large thee-pronged river mouth, much bigger than anything I could remember seeing on the east coast. Forgetting that the scale of everything had increased with the loss of height, I goggled at this huge waterway. Where on earth? What had happened? Had the compass gone haywire?

I grabbed my map and with the navigator's help tried to match what we could see with the map.

Then we studied the next map, then the next. It was just no good; this place resembled nothing between Brest and Stavanger.

There was nothing for it but to go inland, so I steered for the river, confident that we would find something to help. Suddenly, the well remembered light flak began to hose up, just ahead of us. A smart rate four-turn soon had us on the reciprocal course, heading for the safety of the sea. This confirmed that wherever we were, it was over enemy territory! Heart in my flying boots, I racked my brains as to what to do next. Then the cool voice of my W/Op, Bob Merrals, came over the intercom.

'Would you like a WIT fix, Skipper?'

Kicking myself for not thinking of this, I asked him to go ahead. A few minutes later his voice came again – not so languid this time. 'Skipper, there's something fishy here. They have given me a fix but the co-ordinates are not even on my flimsy'.

Remembering the warning at briefing, I realised that everything fell into place. We were up the creek, *sans* paddle. The un-English river, the flak, the attempt to give us a false position, all proved that we were not only lost but also lost over enemy territory!

My brain was a cold, useless lump as we flew uncertainly up the coast. There was only one emergency aid left and that would certainly be of little use. All military units in the UK monitored an R/T frequency for use in emergency, but obviously this would have only a short range. It would not reach friendly ears from our forlorn position. However, the firing had stopped, so what had we to lose by closing the coast and trying out the system?

'Hello, Darky, Hello, Darky,' I called, 'This is Lifebuoy A-Apple, Lifebuoy A-Apple, do you read?'

'Hello, Lifebuoy A-Abble,' came a distinctly Teutonic voice, 'Ziss iss Strradishall, vill you landt pliss.'

Aghast at being in actual communication with one of the *Herrenvolk*, I croaked: 'No, I'm bloody well not landing!' and turned away defeated. Well, that was that!

I measured by eye the course from Stradishall to Coningsby. About 350 degrees and not too far. What a pity it was not really the duty pilot at Stradishall talking. Then the thought struck me. What would our false friend say if we asked him for a course to steer for Coningsby? Put him in a bit of a quandary. He would possibly give us directions 180 degrees out so that we would go deeper into enemy held territory.

Deciding to give it a whirl, I called: 'Stradishall, this is Lifebuoy A-Apple, do you read?'

'Hello, Lifebuoy A-Abble, ziss iss Strradishall, vill you landt pliss?'

'Negative, will you give me a course to Coningsby, please?'

'Stand by pliss.'

With dry throats we awaited the reply that would seal our doom.

'Lifebuoy A-Abble, vill you steer 355 degrees pliss.'

A surge of hope. With tentative words of thanks to Stradishall we set off to see if things would work out. Within about 10 minutes we had found a beacon and the lightheartedness of relief from tension coloured our intercom chat until we were on the ground.

This euphoria soon left me when I was wheeled into the CO's office. He obviously had not taken kindly to being kept up all night, after everyone else had landed. After some terse introductory remarks, he went on: But when did you first realise you were lost?'

'Well, I didn't recognise the big waterway and they even fired at us.'

'That was Harwich. Obviously it looked so big because you were low. In any case, they have been on the phone complaining about you trying to fly through their balloon-barrage. They had to fire ahead of you to make you turn back.'

'But what about the W/T fix, Sir, that was not even on our flimsy.'

'Well,' he said graciously, 'We must take some of the blame for that, somehow we gave you the wrong flimsy at briefing.'

'It was definitely a Teutonic accent on the R/T,' I said, in a last attempt at self-justification. He waved this aside contemptuously, 'Everyone knows there's a Polish squadron at Stradishall!'

Note

1. Guy Penrose Gibson, born in Simla, India in 1918, joined the RAF in 1936 after leaving St Edward's School, Oxford. At the outbreak of war he held the rank of Flying Officer and in August 1940 he completed his first tour as a Hampden bomber pilot on 83 Squadron. He was promoted to Flight Lieutenant and won his first DFC (he was awarded a bar the following year). He was posted to instruct at an OTU before transferring to Fighter Command and a posting to 29 Squadron equipped with Beaufighters. In 99 operational sorties he claimed three enemy aircraft destroyed and was promoted to Squadron Leader with a bar to his DFC on completion of his second tour in December 1941. In March 1942 he returned to Bomber Command, was promoted Wing Commander and posted to take command of 106 Squadron. He was awarded the DSO with bar in 1943.

CHAPTER 4

One Wing

J. Ralph Wood DFC CD

Where are the fliers from Canada's prairies,
From cities and forests, determined to win,
Thumbing their noses at Göring's Luftwaffe
And busily dropping their bombs on Berlin?

'*Lancasters*', Audrey Grealy

On the Sunday during the long weekend of Labour Day, September 1939, I drove from Moncton in a car rented from a friend to Woodstock, New Brunswick, to visit the home and parents of my girlfriend, Phyllis Carter. As we left morning church services the newsboys were selling *St John Telegraph* newspapers on the street and on a Sunday at that. We were at War. Although war was not entirely unexpected, it still came as a bit of a shock. I had been in the COTC (Canadian Officers' Training Corp) the previous year while attending the University of New Brunswick, but I was a free agent and could join whichever service I wished. I had fear of being labelled a coward or yellow if I didn't volunteer my services to my country. I also had fear of losing my life if I did volunteer. There was no contest. The Royal Canadian Air Force was more appealing than either the Army or the Navy. The hour of decision was at hand, but it didn't take me an hour to decide on the RCAF. Being a fatalist, I was pretty sure my number would come up and in the air it would be swift and definite. As it turned out, they only signed up university graduates for training at this time. The rest of us were put on hold until June 1940 when the British Commonwealth Air Training Plan commenced.

In time I became an air observer – a one-winged wonder, or as we affectionately called ourselves, 'a flying asshole'. Sure, we were occasionally asked when we would finish our training and get the other half of our wings. There was an amazing amount of ignorance at this time, about the air observer. In April 1941 it was Farewell to Canada – next stop England. After 10 OCU at Abingdon, Berkshire, I moved up into the big leagues. No. 102 Squadron, RAF Station, Topcliffe, Yorkshire, was to be my new home for a while. I was to now operate and complete my first tour in No. 4 Group, Bomber Command. At this time we were all on loan to the RAF as the RCAF Bomber Command had not yet been established. Later, when it became active as

J. Ralph Wood DFC CD (Ralph Wood)

6 Group, some of the Canadians transferred to the Canadian squadrons. Several others and myself preferred to stay with the RAF. We got along fine with the Limeys and, besides, we thought that where we were on loan, we might get away with a little more murder and less discipline. I'll never forget my introduction to this first operational squadron. Arriving around midday, the officer commanding informed me that I would be on tonight's raid. Who? Me? Why, I hadn't even unpacked my kit bag. The flight's chief navigator suggested that he go in my place and I could watch him go through his routine preparing for the flight. I watched him prepare his flight plan, get the meteorology report, go to the intelligence office for his secret coded information, on rice paper so you could eat it if necessary, and other pertinent things to do before going off into that treacherous-looking sky. That navigator and crew never returned. This was a hell of an introduction, especially when stories were circulating about washing out the remains of a tail gunner with a hose, there was so little left of him.

I was on for the next night, 25 July 1941. The target was Hannover. Thirteen months after joining the RCAF I found myself in the briefing room nervously preparing my charts for the raid. I was trying to appear calm and nonchalant, this being my first op and not wanting to appear to be too much of a greenhorn. After the briefing, the navigators gathered around the huge plotting table in the operations room and worked out our DR (dead reckoning) courses to get us to the target and far more important, home again. Our dead reckoning was based on the predicted winds as supplied by the met section, the airspeed, the ground speed and the drift, as well as other information so important in our navigation. Many corrections and adjustments were made during our trip from new information obtained in flight. Our only navigational aids in these early days were from fixes obtained from our wireless operator and good only up to a limited number of miles from the English coast. I soon learned jokingly to call my navigation guesstimation! So here we were a crew of five: two pilots, a navigator/bomb aimer (observer), a wireless operator and a tail gunner. I never used a bomb aimer during my tours. They appeared later on in the war and there weren't always enough to go around. I felt that if I could get us to the target I should have the pleasure of bombing it.

My navigator's table was behind the pilot's seat in the cockpit. As we neared the target I unplugged my oxygen lead and my intercom, and dragging my parachute with me, made my way to the bombsight in the nose of our flying coffin. It was a long crawl in the darkness and without oxygen the going was tough. Reaching the bombsight and front-gunner compartment, I

J. Ralph Wood DFC CD (Ralph Wood)   *Pilot Officer Wood DFC CD (Ralph Wood)*

searched frantically for the oxygen connection to restore my strength. With the aid of a flashlight, partly covered so as not to attract any wandering enemy fighters, I found my connection and began breathing easier. I was now lining up the target with the bombsight as I directed the pilot on our bombing run – Left, Left – Steady – R-I-G-H-T – Steady – Left 14 – Steady – Bombs Gone. Our aircraft leapt about 200 feet with the release of tons of high explosives. Now we fly straight and level for 30 seconds, the longest 30 seconds anyone will ever know, so that we can get the required photo of the drop for the Intelligence Officer back at base. Picture taken. Let's get the hell out of here. With the flak bursting around us and the searchlights trying in vain to catch us, I crawled back to my plotting table in a cold sweat. The pilot was still taking evasive action as I gave him the course for home. The black blobs of 'smoke' surrounding the aircraft were flak. When you could smell the cordite it meant they were bursting too damn close. Arriving back at our base without incident gave me a great feeling of relief and satisfaction. It was hard to believe that I'd been over Germany, but harder to believe that I was back in England. Next came our debriefing by the intelligence officers, accompanied by a cup of coffee laced with overproof rum. I was tired but happy, after our seven-and-one-half hour trip. I guess I had that blissful first op behind-me-look written all over my face. I kept thinking, 'I've made it'. It was the first op I'd been dreaming about and working toward for thirteen months.

As I settled into squadron life at Topcliffe, I found that the best way to keep your sanity was to separate your pleasures from your work. I didn't want to become one of those casualties found walking around the airfield talking to himself. There was the odd one who cracked up mentally and you really couldn't blame him. Our CO was a queer one. We called him 'Curly' but not to his face. He was RAF permanent force and had been stationed in India too long. We thought he'd gotten too much sun out there. He was baldish and had a remarkably long, red handlebar moustache, which he took great pride in. I noticed during my stay there that anytime he put himself down to fly, the operation would be a comparatively easy one. How unlike Pilot Officer Cheshire, who was later to become Group Captain Cheshire, winning the VC and other decorations. He was described as a mad man who always picked the dangerous targets like Berlin for himself. Some said this was partly because his brother was shot down over Berlin.[1]

My second op, on 6 August, was Frankfurt – 7 hours of misery accompanied by engine failure. We were very glad to arrive back safely at base. Hannover was my third op, on 14 August, and proved as exciting as the first two. While over Europe we would drop thousands of propaganda leaflets down the flare chute. We also dropped flares out this chute as we approached the target area, enabling us to pinpoint the target itself. Before taking off we usually had a nervous pee beside the aircraft. This was much easier than trying to manipulate in the air. On our homeward journey we would get into our thermos of coffee and spam sandwiches. Of course, our real treat was the flying breakfast of bacon and eggs back at the base and our discussions of the attack with the other crews on the raid. Bacon and eggs were otherwise scarce as hen's teeth. At the ritual breakfast after every mission, there were empty tables, chairs, dishes and silverware aligned – for the men who weren't coming back.

For relaxation we would frequent the pubs in the village of Topcliffe and Thirsk, Ripon and Harrogate. Weldon MacMurray, a school friend of mine from Moncton, was stationed at RAF Dishforth. This was about 2 miles from Topcliffe, as the crow flies. We'd get together once in a while and exchange news from home. The nearest meeting place was the Black Swan pub, or as we called it, the Mucky Duck, in the village of Topcliffe. On one such meeting he informed me that Johnny Humphrey had bought it. Another time I was told that Graham Roger's number had come up. This was followed by news that Brian Filliter was missing in action. One day at lunchtime I answered the phone in the Sergeants' Mess and it was Weldon inquiring about me. He'd heard that I'd bought it the previous night. A few weeks later, friends of Weldon phoned me from Dishforth to say that he had failed to return from a trip. I found out later that he was a prisoner-of-war. Boy! Was I getting demoralised! Would I be next?

Frankfurt on 29 August represented about 9 hours' flying time. I was getting to have a healthy respect for those searchlights. When they had you coned they would shoot tons of crap up those beams at you. After a bit they'd quit, leaving us to the fighters for target practice. The Whitley was a tough old bastard in spite of its ugly appearance. The damn thing always flew with its nose down, slowly at that, but it could take a hell of a beating, nonetheless.

Op number five on 31 August was Essen. This was a comparatively short trip over enemy territory, but still consumed 6 hours and provided us with plenty of activity. Our tail gunner decided to put his steel helmet, used for air raids, to some practical use. He'd take it on ops with him and when things got hot over the target area, he'd sit on his steel helmet. He said no way was he going to get flak up his ass! Frankfurt on 2 September presented us with an engine failure and we were unable to complete the operation. If you carried the attack far enough you were given credit for an op. An op behind you was one closer to a tour, no matter how you looked at it.

A rubber factory just north of Essen was next on our list on 6 September. This raid saw us with a rear-gun-turret malfunction and an early and uneventful return to base. One of my compatriots from Moncton, a navigator, missed Great Britain altogether when returning from a raid. He landed in southern Ireland, which was neutral, and remained there in internment for the rest of the war, enjoying good food and drink while his pay and promotion continued. I still haven't decided whether he was a stupid navigator or a smart operator.

Op eight on 7 September was to Berlin. *Berlin* in a Whitley? I didn't believe it! Well, 10 hours later as we were being debriefed at interrogation, I felt quite elated. We had actually bombed the capital of Germany, but the trip wasn't that pleasant. I thought about that goddam 'Butcher Harris'. (Bert) Butcher was the deserved nickname of the RAF chief of Bomber Command. He didn't give a damn how many men he lost as long as he was pounding the shit out of the Germans. He was just as willing to sacrifice Englishmen as Canadians. I became involved in a heated discussion with my flight commander one night while partaking of some cheer at a favourite watering hole in Harrogate. I was complaining about not flying often enough and he came back with some derogatory remarks about my navigational ability. I told him that if that wasn't a yellow streak down his back, he'd put me down to fly with him. Sure enough, the next morning saw me listed as his navigator for that night A little under the weather that morning, I made sure that afternoon, during our air test, to take a few good whiffs of oxygen to clear the head. This was a tried and proven method of aiding your recovery.

Op nine, on 29 September, was to Stettin, north-east of Berlin. It turned out to be the best trip I'd made to date. We threw out our flares, which lit up the target directly beneath us. We made two separate bombing runs, dropping one stick of bombs on each run. We never reached our base that night as we were running short of fuel. My flight commander was particularly pleased with this 11 hour trip and my navigational abilities were never questioned again. My tenth op on 12 October was to Nuremberg, but we ended up dropping our load on Frankfurt as the alternate target. This turned out to be a 9½ hour trip. Our exactors, whatever they might be, were u/s (unserviceable) and we had to land at Pocklington, returning to base later that day. At this stage of the game we didn't fly as a set crew. The members were interchangeable for various reasons. For my part, I always made a quick appraisal of the pilot I was to fly with. How much confidence could I place in him? For that matter, how much would he have in me? We all had to depend on each and every crewmember. We were a team – each relying on the other to do his job to the best of his ability. On this and the following two ops, we had another Sergeant Wood as a crewmember. He was a Scotsman. During my stay overseas, my nickname was usually 'Timber', or 'Chips', or just plain 'Woodie'.

Op eleven to Duisburg on 16 October was one of the easier trips, in that 6 hours saw the operation completed and to our satisfaction. Making a good landfall on the English coast on our homeward journey always boosted the navigator's morale. By a good landfall I mean approaching the coast and hitting it just about where you were supposed to – right on track. I recall my pilot asking occasionally 'Where are we?' I'd shove a map or chart in front of him, pointing wildly to any spot over the North Sea or Germany depending on the occasion. This having satisfied him, I returned to my plotting table to work out our actual position undisturbed.

Operation twelve was to Wilhelmshaven on 20 October 1941 and again we were forced to bomb the alternate target, Emden. This was an 8 hour trip, but we managed to return to our own home base. The meteorology reports were very important to the success of our operations. The met section, at times, was about as accurate as it is today, leaving a lot to be desired. We called the meteorology information, 'met gen', which usually turned out to be one of the following: 'pukka gen', meaning 'good information', or 'duff gen', meaning 'bad information'. There was a story going around about a Whitley crew becoming lost and running out of fuel. The pilot set the automatic pilot and told his crew to bale out. This they did, with the exception of the tail gunner whose intercom had become disconnected and he failed to hear the order. A short time later the aircraft made a remarkably good landing on a sloping hill in Scotland. The tail gunner, upon vacating his turret, commented loudly on the pilot's smooth landing. You could almost see him passing out when he discovered he was the only occupant of the aircraft.

Joyce Shaw of Harrogate and I became acquainted while I was operating out of Topcliffe. I would visit her home and parents for a meal and an overnight stay once in a while. Joyce was later to become a member of the WAAF (Women's Auxiliary Air Force). The inconvenience of having their toilet facilities in a separate brick building at the rear of their terrace house located in the centre of this large city never ceased to amaze me. This arrangement, after an evening at the pubs, left a lot to be desired. And speaking of pubs, after the familiar 'time gentlemen please' was heard, one usually headed for a fish and chip shop. They were easily found as one could usually smell their tantalising aroma for blocks and we were always hungry. They were most often served in a paper cone made out of newspaper and liberally sprinkled with salt and vinegar. I still felt that good taste was due in part to the newsprint on the paper. It gave them that extra element of refinement!

Hannover on 30 November was my thirteenth op and destined to be my last in a Whitley. No. 13 – lucky or unlucky? I guess one had to call it lucky as we had a malfunction with our rear turret and we were forced to return to base.

The next five months were occupied converting to the Halifax bomber. This was done at Dalton, a satellite station near Topcliffe. This conversion course and some temporary duty at Lossiemouth in northern Scotland gave us a nice change of pace, including a rest from those bombing raids over Germany. Our Handley Page bomber was a beautiful four-engined bird with three gun turrets, front, mid-upper and rear. She carried a 5½-ton bomb load, cruised at 300 mph and had a 3,000 mile range. Our Hallybag, as it was fondly called, had a crew of seven, six in our case as I still acted as bomb aimer, navigator and front-gunner. The crew included a pilot, a wireless operator, a flight engineer, a mid-upper gunner and a tail gunner. The dinky little navigator's compartment was below and in front of the pilot's cockpit. You went down a few steps and entered a small section with a navigator's metal table down one side, ahead and below the pilot's feet. A curtain in the nose end hid the even smaller compartment where I would huddle with my Mk 14 bombsight and other instruments when we got reasonably close to the target. The gun I was supposed to operate when called upon was a Vickers gas-operated .303 machine-gun mounted on a swivel and stuck out through the Perspex nose, high above the bombsight. I recalled the short introduction lecture on the VGO; the RAF sergeant told us the gun was famous for jamming. All you had to do was look at it the wrong way and it would plug up on you. I hadn't fired a machine-gun since Bombing and Gunnery School at Mossbank late in 1940. That had been a Browning, not a relic like this. If a Junkers should suddenly make a pass, I really couldn't tell how I'd make out at all. But I was sure to give it my best try.

We transferred to 76 Squadron and operated out of Middleton St George, Durham. On 8 May I completed my fourteenth op, the first in a Hallybag, with Pilot Officer McIntosh as my pilot. Our target was Warnemünde and it was successfully attacked. There were many times a navigator had to remove his gloves to work at his charts and at this height it was C-O-L-D. Of course a Hallybag was always a deep-freeze proposition, even at the best of times. There were supposed to be pipes giving off heat throughout the aircraft, but this was a laugh. I found my hands and feet were always cold by the time an op was half over. You simply had to learn to live with it. It was around this period that I was listed to fly with a Canadian pilot by the name of Flight Sergeant Bellows. We were all at least flight sergeants by now! Well, due to a rash on the inside of my thigh, the medical officer took me off the flying list that night. He figured wearing the parachute harness would only irritate the rash, making it worse. So it was an application of medication instead. Flight Sergeant Bellows and crew, which included my replacement, bought it over the city of York, when their aircraft exploded on the way to Germany. Someone must have been looking after me that night or I would have crapped out as well.

Op fifteen was to Mannheim on 19 May. Sergeant Tackley was my RAF pilot. Our aircraft became unserviceable so we had to cut our trip short. On op sixteen on 22 May we raided St Nazaire, the only French target of my so-called 'career' in the air force. It was a quiet op but one more toward that ultimate goal – a tour. By now we were flying as a regular crew and getting to know each other fairly well. Off duty we would frequent the pubs and dance halls in Darlington and York. A few memories of these places come to mind, like the night we stole the stuffed ram's head from the Fleece, a pub in Darlington, with which to decorate our Sergeants' Mess. And how we 'sheepishly' had to return it the following day after a complaint was made to our CO. I recall the old walls around the city of York where the Minster Cathedral was visible from almost anywhere. I also remember Betty's Bar with its long mirror behind the bar, on which dozens and dozens of signatures had been scrawled. It would be interesting to know how many of these signatures belonged to men no longer in this world. Also, I think of The Shambles, where the upper storeys of the houses bulged out over the road. These and other fond memories are deeply cherished.

On 30 May we took part in the first three 1,000 bomber raids, the first being on Cologne. This was my seventeenth op and we really pranged the target, leaving it looking like the red-hot embers of a huge bonfire. Within an hour and a half 1,445 tons of bombs were unloaded – two-thirds of them incendiaries – and 600 acres of the city were devastated. With all these aircraft over the target during a short period of time, one wonders how many may have collided! Bomber Command had gathered up every bomber that could fly, even the Whitleys, some of which had been retired to submarine patrol over the bays in southern England. As a matter of fact the Jerry submarines soon learned that it was wiser for them to stay on the surface and shoot it out with the slow-moving Whitleys than to submerge and risk damage from the aircraft's depth-charges. On op eighteen, on 1 June, Flight Sergeant Tackley and crew took part in the second 1,000 bomber raid, on Essen. This was another spectacular raid, reminding one of paintings of the Great Fire of London. It was a vision of hell, a vision I would never forget. There was plenty of opposition over this target, which was part of the industrial centre of Germany. Those long cold hours sweating it out in the navigator's and bomb aimer's compartment always chilled you through, even with heavy flying boots, extra socks thick gloves and your flying suit. The usual 'cold sweat' didn't help much either.

Op nineteen was to Bremen on 3 June, a long haul over the North Sea. Every time we beetled down the runway I wondered if we were going to make it back. I guess I'd seen too many guys go for a Burton in the past year. 'Gone for a Burton' meant, in barrack-room language, 'Gone for a shit'. A Burton was a strong English ale, which caused one's bowels to move rather freely, necessitating a quick trip to the can. On 5 June I completed my twentieth op and took part in the third 1,000 bomber raid, on Essen. It was a hot one and they were ready for us. The damn flak was like lightning flashing in daylight. All about us the searchlights grabbed us over the target. The shell bursts made a squeaky, gritty noise. The smell of cordite was strong and you had the feeling that someone was underneath kicking your undercarriage, keeping time with the bunts. We were glad to get back without too much damage. A night on the town would sure look good even though we sometimes missed the last bus back to our base. But then there was always the air-raid shelter or a convenient haystack as sleeping accommodation. We were young and the first early morning transportation back to the squadron would suffice.

Op twenty-one, on 8 June, was Essen again. You began to wonder how much more it could take. Our crew consisted of two Englishmen, a Scotsman, an Irishman, a Welshman and myself as the Canadian. A very mixed crew and all nervous as hell. It must be remembered that each bomber was really a flying 25-ton bomb just looking for an excuse to blow up. The five tons or so of high-explosives and magnesium flares, plus another three or four tons of high-octane fuel, provided the ideal mixture for a violent explosion when hit in the right place by an explosive bullet or shell. We were losing too many of our friends. It was not very pleasant, when you awoke in the morning, to see them gathering up the personal effects of those who failed to return from last night's raid. The normal crew of a Hallybag being seven, three aircraft missing meant twenty-one wouldn't be around any more. New replacements would soon arrive and fill these empty beds. And so the war goes on!

Op twenty-two was to Emden on 19 June. As we crossed the enemy coast we threw out many bundles of Window by way of the flare chute. Window packages consisted of hundreds of metal strips, which fluttered down over enemy territory. A few aircraft could completely confuse the German radar detectors with the use of Window. Occasionally, we would take along a bag of beer bottles to drop out the chute, bottom first, over enemy built-up areas on our way to the target. We understood that these empty bottles with open tops would create a whistling sound similar to that of a bomb dropping. We felt better thinking that our little effort may have caused someone on the ground to change his underwear. This trip was no better than the rest. You'd think that by now we'd be used to it. We were all getting the 'twitch' as we experienced one 'shaky do' after another. A rough translation of 'shaky do' is 'a very frightening affair'. I must admit, I was absolutely petrified on many occasions. You had to live with it, control it. But I was lucky. Once the danger was over, I got over it fairly fast, until the next op. One of our Hallybags crashed on landing back at the base. The crew and aircraft were a mixture of broken bodies and metal. My morale was sure taking a beating.

Op twenty-three the following night was Emden again. It was another 'shaky do' but a little closer to the end of our tour. The target was burning like hell but the bombers were going down like flies.[2] One poor bastard got it right over the top of the target. Two guys got out and they held him in the searchlights all the way down. I heard in the Cracker's pub in London one day, what the Jerries do with our guys that get down. They threw them into the fire. One of our warning aids against enemy fighters was a light on the pilot's instrument panel, which flashed when they were approaching. This was called IFF (Information Friend or Foe) and was not to be confused with the familiar medical inspection term, FFI (Free From Infection). We usually called it 'Short Arm Inspection'. Sometimes, one had to urinate on these long trips in spite of having a nervous one on the ground before take-off. This was accomplished by using a funnel and tube arrangement conveniently placed at various locations in the aircraft. The pilot had his own funnel and tube, as he wasn't supposed to go wandering around the aircraft, even though he had the automatic pilot at his disposal. Well, this night he had to use it and the damn thing was plugged. Guess which navigator, sitting at his table, below and slightly in front of him, received this addition to his plotting charts! Having it freeze before I could figure out what was happening just made further plotting very difficult. As we had to land at Linton on our return, we did not witness yet another complete write-off of crew and aircraft as they attempted a landing at our base. Lately there were many rumours of sabotage as crews discussed the raids and allied events. On a cross-country practice trip we lost an engine (the engine had seized). The machine-gun-like noise and vibrations in the aircraft startled the hell out of us. It was so scary to our sensitive nerves that we nearly baled out. As a matter of fact, the flight engineer had already kicked out the door of the escape hatch in my compartment and away it went toward the English countryside. Who said we weren't nervous?

Op twenty-four to Bremen on 25 June was a pretty spectacular raid, but it was overshadowed by the incident I was to witness on our return to base. It was another total loss of an aircraft and its crew. They crashed and burned on landing. I'll never forget the spectacle of bodies trapped in the aircraft, the reek of smoke and the fumes of death. Not a pretty sight! It was all I could do to keep from throwing up. It's no wonder my nerves were wearing pretty thin. Again the word 'sabotage' was on everyone's lips. The rum and coffee was sure needed at interrogation on this night.

On the afternoon of 28 June 1942 our crew was detailed to do a cross-country exercise over the southern part of England. The purpose of this exercise was to give a newly arrived navigator to our squadron some more practice. I went along in case he ran into difficulties with his navigation. We also took along one of our ground-crew men for the ride. Halfway through the exercise as I was lying on the bench in the crash or rest position, midway in the aircraft, a sudden loud machine-gun-like noise was heard. This was accompanied by tremors and vibrations throughout our Hallybag and scared the living hell out of us. One of our starboard engines had seized and Tackley had to feather the blade in order to regain control of the aircraft. We were later to learn that oil leads to the engines in the Halifax would sometimes break due to the vibration and cause the engine to seize.

As we continued on our journey and nearing our base, the tail gunner asked me to sit in his turret for the landing. It was required to have someone in the tail for proper distribution of weight when landing and taking off. I declined, so he asked our ground-crew passenger to go back in the turret. While he went back to the tail, I took up my favourite position when landing in daylight. This was in the mid-upper turret with my heels on the ladder facing the front of the aircraft. This gave one a great view of what was going on, through the blister. We were about 1,000 feet off the runway when the other starboard engine seized, making that same terrible noise. With two engines on one side and none on the other we swung sharply to the right, plunging toward a farmer's field. Tackley never had a chance to feather the blade of this second engine. Viewing through the blister what looked like impending disaster, I frantically dropped to the floor and hung on to the bottom of the mid-upper turret ladder. I kept thinking, 'I'm going to look pretty foolish if nothing happens'.

The next thing I knew I was bouncing back and forth together with the target flares that had become dislodged from their usual position on the walls of the aircraft. When everything stopped rocking I immediately made for the door at the rear. After those three recent fatal accidents at our base, I was more than determined that I wasn't going to burn. Reaching the rear door, in what must have been record time, I found it to be jammed. I turned in a panic to the wall opposite the door where an axe was usually kept. Maybe I could chop the door open! As I turned I saw daylight where the aircraft had broken apart and quickly made my exit. My legs were so shaky I fell to my knees.

As I looked around I noticed Tackley on his back with his clothing smouldering lightly. I rubbed out the embers, thinking how fortunate it was that we didn't have a full fuel load at this time. I had no idea whether he was alive or not. I later learned that he hadn't made it. The flight engineer and wireless operator were both pretty badly gouged but eventually recovered. The ground-crew laddie, who filled in for the tail gunner, was found in the next field. The aircraft hitting first on one wing had slung him out of the turret like a clay pigeon from a catapult. His injuries consisted of a broken neck, a broken leg, a broken arm and a great many bruises. When I visited him in the hospital later, he told me he was recovering quite well, but didn't think he'd do any more flying. Apart from a few bruises and one hell of a scare, I was uninjured. Our Hallybag was literally in pieces. The fuselage was broken into at least two sections. The wings were torn off and the engines distributed around us. The meat wagon (ambulance) and fire engines from our base were soon tearing across the fields and took us to the station hospital. We were given a large belt of overproof rum and a quick medical, then dismissed. That is, those of us who were still mobile.

I thought, as we made our way to the Mess for tea, this has got to be a dream. I shook for 2 hours, as this dream became a startling reality. I came damn close to cashing it in. Twenty-four ops and we had to crap out on a lousy training trip. That night I went to the dance in Darlington where Tackley had a date with his girlfriend. I had to give her the bad news. I had never heard a girl scream before. As soon as possible I returned to my barracks and tried to sleep. It was an experience I will never forget, ever. These four crashes around our airfield, ours being the fourth, was playing havoc with my nervous system. I requested sick leave from the squadron medical officer who was reluctant to recommend it. Instead, he sent me to a Canadian medical centre in East Anglia where I found the reception room filled with other nervous aircrew. Most of them were there to go LMF (Lack of Moral Fibre). This meant that they would be stripped of all rank and placed on general duties. They would be in disgrace but they would remain alive. I thought to myself, 'There but for the Grace of God go I'. The most unlikely people, people like myself, could usually rise to the occasion. Just as big, tough guys fold under pressure. You never knew. I was interviewed by a Jewish Canadian medical officer whose first question was, 'Do you want to quit flying?' I think he was a little surprised when I assured him that all I wanted was a little time off to get away and put things together again before continuing my tour.

Armed with his recommendation for two weeks' sick leave, I returned to our base, packed my kit bag and headed for Dunoon, Scotland, where I was to meet Jim Wilson's fine family. While Jim was in Canada training to be a pilot, he had to pass through the No. 31 Embarkation Depot at Moncton. It was here that he met my parents and insisted that they pass on an invitation for me to visit his home whenever I could. Having just recently finished a leave in London and being rather broke, I readily accepted this kind invitation. Needless to say, my stay with the Wilsons was a real tonic and a lasting friendship was made. I also visited Edinburgh during this leave. It was here that a new experience was added to my assortment of nightmares. I'd wake up in the middle of the night to find myself standing on my bed and trying to push my way through the wall. I presume I must have been trying desperately to get out of an aircraft. Another version of this antic was a leap out of bed and finding myself standing beside it, wondering what the hell was going on. It was several years after the war before I was able to rid myself of that annoying performance.

Another English airman who visited my home in Moncton, while training in Canada, came from Ferryhill, not far from Darlington. On his invitation, through my parents, I visited his family one weekend. His father, a coal miner, took me to the miners' pub as his guest. These men were hard workers physically and were allowed a much stronger beer than you would find in the usual public house. I enjoyed meeting these people and my weekend with them.

When I returned to base I learned why our squadron medical officer had been reluctant to allow me a sick leave after our crash. All experienced aircrew were needed as most of the squadron was moved to the Middle East. From the reports that I received later, I guess I didn't miss anything and the living conditions there were far from enjoyable. On the other side of the ledger, I was faced with the prospect of becoming a member of a novice crew. My new pilot was Pilot Officer Campbell, who, on a scale of one to ten, rated a weak five in my nervous estimation.

On 28 August it was back to business, as we bombed Saarbrücken. It was not a very exciting twenty-fifth op and we had to land at Pocklington, returning to our base the following day. Our squadron had now moved to Linton to make room for a RCAF squadron of 6 Group Bomber Command. Our new Commanding Officer was Wing Commander Cheshire. He was a pilot officer when I was attached to 102 Squadron on Whitleys at Topcliffe. Norman Ross, a Moncton school friend of mine, was with a plane load of personnel being transported, bag and baggage, from one station to another, when it crashed soon after take-off. It appears that some of the baggage became fouled up in the cables and controls causing the accident. Everyone on board was killed and Norman is buried in the Dishforth cemetery.

Op twenty-six was to Saarbrücken on 1 September. We no longer had to drop flares to pinpoint our target. The Pathfinder Squadrons went in ahead of us and with their sophisticated navigational equipment, located and marked the target with their various coloured flares. We bombed these target markers and headed for home. As we crossed the English coast near Hull, all hell broke loose. Our own anti-aircraft guns opened fire on us and this didn't make us very happy. We quickly fired the colours of the day with our Very pistol and the shelling stopped. We were supposed to give this 'out of bounds' area over and around Hull a wide berth. But, as usual, we cheated a bit, cutting a few corners in order to get home earlier. Normally, this would go unnoticed but tonight, while we were over Germany, the *Luftwaffe* had bombed the hell out of Hull and the gunners below were not only nervous but trigger-happy as well.

Op twenty-seven on 4 September was Bremen. It turned out to be a hazardous experience, magnified by my state of nervousness. On our return to base I said, 'This is it' and approached the commanding officer who agreed to retire me from ops, crediting me with a full tour. In the heavies, a tour consisted of anywhere from twenty-five to thirty ops. I had twenty-seven to my credit. In October 1942 I was posted to 19 OTU Kinloss, in northern Scotland. This station seemed to be miles from nowhere and I was more than pleased to receive a new posting to my old haunts at 10 OTU in Abingdon.

I had been called in before my superiors and asked if I was interested in a commission and why hadn't I applied for one before? I explained that I was waiting for my warrant officer's promotion to come through first. A week later they informed me that they had enough officers on the unit at this time. I guess the RAF was looking after its own first. This didn't satisfy me, so on my next leave in London, I visited the RCAF headquarters to enquire about my promotions, or rather, lack of promotions. The officer in charge said they had been looking for me and with that, picked up my commission papers off his desk. I told him I didn't think he had looked very thoroughly, as I had been stationed at Abingdon for quite some time now and that was not very far from London.

Armed now with clothing coupons, a credit authorisation and a new regimental number, I headed for Moss Brothers. At this military clothing store I became fully clothed as a pilot officer from top to bottom. So on 13 July 1943 I became Pilot Officer Wood and returned to my OTU station, which was also a Group Headquarters, lousy with senior staff officers. Talk about being 'commissioned in the field'! I had my gear transferred from the sergeants' quarters to the officers' quarters, then went to the Officers' Mess for tea. It soon appeared that most of the 'brass' wanted to see me first thing in the morning. They were quite puzzled as to how Flight Sergeant Wood could go on a leave and return as Pilot Officer Wood. It really had them baffled. The next morning I had a great time explaining that I was tired of being a flight sergeant and wanting my promotion, did something about it. They looked at me in disbelief and I was relishing every moment of it.

We Canadians were supposed to do a tour of ops and a tour of instruction, then receive a month's furlough back home in Canada. After fifteen months of instructional duties I was getting horribly bored and very frustrated. This leave in Canada seemed to be just political talk that made good reading in the newspapers. I knew that another safely completed tour would see me back in Canada for good. Now, completely cheesed off, I forfeited my leave and applied for another tour. This was granted and I was posted to 1653 Conversion Unit on Hallybags. My pilot was a wing commander who had done a tour in the Middle East and would now be taking over a squadron when our conversion course was completed. Soon after our training began, I took a day off. When I returned, my skipper told me that the Air Ministry was looking for me. Right away I began wondering what mischief I'd been in that had now caught up with me. My skipper told me that they wanted to know why I had forfeited my leave to Canada and if I still wanted to go home. They also said I would be on a ship in one week. My pilot and I had a short discussion about this, as I didn't want to leave him and the rest of the crew in a lurch. He said it would be nearly a month before I got home, a month for my leave and a month or more to return to active flying and by that time the bloody war should be over. He urged me to accept the offer. I didn't need any urging. The next thing I knew, I was on the *Queen Mary*, which was docked at Liverpool. While waiting to sail, some mail arrived from Canada. One piece of mail from Phyl was an airgraph letter. It depicted Phyl holding a minister by the hand and a bridal bouquet in her other hand, standing on the dock, suitcase beside her, as the ship was approaching. The caption under this picture said, 'But really, Miss Carter, isn't this a bit unusual?' Little did she, or anyone else in Canada, realise that I was actually on my way home.

What a treat to sit down to a real meal again. The *Queen Mary* was provided with American rations. White bread, rolls, bacon and eggs, milk, porridge, steaks, etc., etc. It was like a dream world and our crossing the Atlantic, comparatively short. The most disturbing news as read on the ship's bulletins, was that we were losing over ninety heavy bombers almost nightly. It was not a very pleasant situation to return to after my leave. After docking at New York we boarded a troop train for Montreal. From here I phoned my brother in Montreal (who dashed down to the station to see me), my girlfriend, Phyl, in Saint John, and my parents in Moncton. They all found it difficult to believe that I was back in Canada and that they were actually talking to me. It must have been my new English accent! After a few days at home, Phyl and I were married in Woodstock, New Brunswick, on 4 March 1944. After a short honeymoon in the Laurentians, Montreal and St John, we returned to Moncton where I could see my parents and those friends still around. Three years overseas was quite an absence. My month's furlough soon came to an end and Phyl and I boarded the train for Montreal. After a night at my brother's, it was farewell again as I reported to the embarkation depot not far from his home. On the way to our ship in Halifax we passed through Moncton shortly after midnight. Mother and Dad had received word from friends in the CNR that the train would be passing through at this time and were down to meet me at the station for another tearful goodbye. I was surprised to see Weldon MacMurray's parents there as well, cheerfully lending their moral support. Weldon had now been a prisoner-of-war for almost three years.

During my leave in Canada, Bomber Command suffered its worst defeat of the war. This was the Nuremberg raid on the night of 30/31 March 1944, with the loss of more aircrew than were lost in the entire Battle of Britain. Over 800 experienced aircrew were dead, wounded, missing or prisoners-of-war.[3] Bomber Command's maximum acceptable rate of loss was considered to be

200 four-engined bombers with their seven-man crews a month. It was not much to look forward to on my return.

My return trip to the war zone was in the *Louis Pasteur*. There were no frills on this journey as we ate British rations, trying gamely to keep it down. We were jammed into cabins like sardines on this return trip. What a blessing it was when we arrived at Gourock, Scotland, and then by train to Bournemouth in southern England. Here we were sorted out and we operational types were sent to an Army camp in Yorkshire. They put us through an escape course that was nearly as bad as ops. They would take us miles from the camp in a lorry, then drop us, telling us not to get caught by the Army who would be looking for us. If the brown jobs caught you, they would transport you still further afield each time and so on. It was fun in a way but hunger made you a little careless as you raided someone's garden or tried to scrounge a beer in some isolated country pub. The obstacle course was something else. You had to climb over, under or through so many obstacles in a given time. We operational types, who had been 'under fire' sort of resented taking orders from the Army NCOs who were in charge. We did, however, finish our course and the majority was posted back to the various heavy bomber squadrons. From the time I arrived at Bournemouth and at every opportunity thereafter, I asked to be posted to a light aircraft squadron. The Mosquito bomber squadrons were now being formed and in order to get on one of these it was necessary for me to wait around and endure the agonies of this escape course for a second time.[4]

Coming home through a violent storm one night we were flying up and down like a bird in a chimney. The storm pitched us all over the place. At one time there were big circles of electricity around the tips of the propellers as we made our way through the clouds. It was an eerie sight. As we left this electrical field there was a very loud explosion. I was certain we had blown up and started looking frantically for my parachute. On our return to base we found it completely socked in with fog. Our station was equipped with FIDO,[5] a device for burning fuel oil on either side of the runway. The heat from this burning fuel would raise the fog enough for us to land in safety. We sure as hell appreciated this invention, as we had nowhere else to go.

Some nights at our debriefing Andy Lockhart and I would use up the rum ration of those who preferred their coffee without this additional fortification. This on top of our own ration had the effect of making everything seem great. The only difficulty was bicycling from the ops room to our barracks without going in the ditch. The only time we had bacon and eggs was for a flying breakfast when we went on ops. I used to think they used this as bait to get us to fly. Once in a while we would bicycle around the countryside looking for farmers to sell us some eggs. We would then have the cook at our Mess prepare them for a snack at night after visiting the pub. The eggs kept getting a little tougher and eventually we realised that the farmers were passing off duck eggs on us.

We usually slept until the last minute, then made a mad dash for the Mess before the doors closed. Most of us had this timed pretty well. So well that Andy and I decided to upset the pattern by piling as many bicycles as possible on top of the latrine building. Of course, a great many missed their breakfast that morning, including the CO, whose bicycle was also included. Our billets were huge tin cans, which we tried to keep heated with toy stoves and a niggardly ration of coal. These were called Nissen huts and were situated some distance from the Mess.

One unusual return from enemy territory, and most satisfying, included a dive beginning at the French coast from 32,000 feet to 10,000 feet reached at Southwold on the English coast. This 88-mile journey was completed in 11 minutes, which was fast, even for a Mosquito. With our 'Cookie' bomb gone, our two 50-gallon drop tanks discarded and our fuel load pretty well depleted, it wasn't too too hard to accomplish this feat. On one occasion Andy and I were at 25,000 feet completing our air test in preparation for the night's operation, when I happened to look up from my lap table. There was Andy, out cold and slumped over the controls. We were dropping like a lead weight – straight for the ground. My blood drained into my shoes as I managed to place my oxygen mask over his face in time for him to revive and pull the plane out of the dive. Thirty years after the war Andy reminded me of this long-forgotten incident. He told me that afterwards all I said was 'Do you always take a turn that steeply?'

Mining the Kiel Canal one moonlit night proved to be one of our more interesting ops. For our part in this operation Andy and I received an immediate award of the DFC. This award by the RAF to a Canadian I think added to the appreciation.

Nearing the end of my second tour I slept fairly well, ate badly, drank and smoked a lot, keeping my weight at 135 lb without trying. There was still always the chance of the fatal mistake. Experience helped but it wasn't everything. You had to be lucky, too. Guys often bought it long before this. My main objective was to finish my tour; then I'd have a free ticket back to Canada and my new bride. Believe me, once I got there you'd have to drag me away the next time. I never thought I'd miss Moncton that much, but I now dreamed about it all the time. I'd decided it was a pretty good town after all.

Notes

1. One of the flak victims was Flight Lieutenant Christopher C. Cheshire and his crew of Halifax I L9530 MP-L of 76 Squadron who were shot down on 12/13 August 1941. Cheshire and 4 crew PoW. 2 KIA.
2. Eight bombers were lost and only part of the bomber force identified the target.
3. Of the 795 RAF heavy bombers and thirty-eight Mosquitoes despatched, sixty-four Lancasters and thirty-one Halifaxes (11.9 per cent of the force despatched) were lost (and ten bombers crash-landed in England); it was the worst Bomber Command loss of the war.
4. Ralph Wood was successful. He teamed up with Andy Lockhart AFC, an old school chum from Moncton who was about to fly his first tour after instructing in Canada and they flew fifty ops in 692 Squadron. See *The Men Who Flew the Mosquito* by the author, Pen & Sword (2003).
5. Fog Investigation and Dispersal Operation.

CHAPTER 5

The Concealing Cloth

Edwin Wheeler DFC

Well, we hit the bloody target
Bombs made quite a lovely sight,
On another German stronghold
Burning dully in the night.
And we beat that Nazi fighter
When he jumped us near Cologne,
Climbing steep to port and firing
But he died a death alone.
Then the flak just south of Essen
Starting blazing in the sky,
And they hit the upper turret
What a lousy way to die.

'*Grey Dawn*', Robert S. Nielsen

Denny Denman and I, now instructors, thought 27 OTU Lichfield would be a 'rest' period, but it was in fact far from restful having to fly with pupil crews, which we considered at times to be far more dangerous than flying over enemy territory. For twenty months we were to train men from all parts of the Commonwealth. They came from Canada, Australia, New Zealand, South Africa *et al.* Life on OTU was just bearable after all the excitement of being a part of an operational squadron, the constant circuits and landings and the monotonous cross-country flights by day and by night almost driving one to distraction. There were the odd compensating factors, of course, and on the occasion of non-flying due to inclement weather, the powers-that-be were hard put to know how to occupy our time. The usual routines were continued into May 1942 but on 29 May it was apparent that something out of the ordinary was about to happen. The ground crews were being pressed like mad to ensure the full serviceability of all the aircraft and air testing was more prevalent. Parachutes had to be taken for closer examination and leave passes were cancelled, so something 'big' was happening. At 10 am the next morning we were formed into crews, mostly composed of instructors with a sprinkling of the more advanced pupils, and then allocated aircraft. I was assigned to Wellington IC 1645 under the captaincy of Flying Officer Temperley, with whom I had flown on some training exercises. Shortly after, we were in the air for an hour's formation flying and air-testing. Our formation had to be seen to be believed and with rumours of a daylight raid to be carried out in these clapped out Wellingtons, which had seen better days, we weren't too happy.

At 1830 hours on 30 May we were summoned to the briefing room in the Operations Block. A cloth covered the wall chart and the crews sat there fidgeting, awaiting the CO's arrival to announce what was in store for us. Finally, from the back of the room came the order 'Attention' and all personnel leapt to their feet as Wing Commander Jarman entered with Squadron Leaders Bamford and Burberry. We were greeted with the news that the C-in-C Bomber Command –'Butch' Harris was mounting the first raid in which over 1,000 bombers were to be unleashed on the *Reich*. This could only be achieved by supplementing the operational squadrons with aircraft from OTUs Coastal and Training Commands.

The concealing cloth was removed and revealed that our target was Cologne. It was announced that only 90 minutes would be allowed for 1,000 plus aircraft to pass through the target area. The dramatic figure of 1,000 planes was something like two and a half times the usual complement of aircraft available for night operations. The main danger was the prospect of collision. This was, however, an acceptable risk to get the bomber stream through the night-fighter boxes as quickly as possible and swamp the anti-aircraft defences. Such a concentration of HE (High Explosive) and incendiaries put down in a short period would overwhelm the fire services and the fires would consume large areas. The OTU groups were providing 365 aircraft, including Wellingtons, Hampdens and Whitleys. It was suggested that the loss factor of 10 per cent or about 100 aircraft would be acceptable for this size of operation. With the late withdrawal of the Coastal Command contribution it was necessary to make up numbers with totally trainee crews. The total despatched was 1,047 aircraft.

The days of specific targets had gone and with such a concentration of bombers in so short a space of time there would be no question of evasive action from flak or fighters, due to the greatly higher risk of collision with devastating effect on probably many friendly aircraft. Sitting in the Mess prior to take-off, the topic of conversation centred on the question of the adequacy of our aircraft, used day in and day out on training by various crews.

We took off at 2230 hours and it seemed as if the sky was full of black shapes, gun testing had been disallowed because of the density of the formations. We staggered up to 11,000 feet in our weary IC but with the bomb and fuel load it just wouldn't go any higher. This would make us a target for the accurate light flak. We were not alone. Some old Whitleys were below us and a lot slower and this was a slight encouragement for us.

Crossing the enemy coast, we were soon illuminated by searchlight batteries and we felt totally exposed. Aircraft were above and below and on all sides, making it impossible to take weaving action. Approaching the target area, all hell broke loose and there was no question of overshooting and going round for a second run. In running up, I was located in the astrodome and I could never recall having been so scared. Many aircraft above us with their bomb doors open revealed stocks of bombs, which when released were more than likely to land on the aircraft below. At the point of release, there were showers and showers of incendiaries and HEs passing us on all sides. These obviously accounted for the many explosions around us with many planes ploughing and plunging in big balls of flame into the target area. It seemed like one sea of flame on the ground and I felt sick for the poor devils below and the terrors they must have been experiencing.

We sighed with relief after our bomb load had gone down and wondered whether Cologne's wonderful cathedral had been obliterated. The return flight was mainly uneventful and we eventually landed at base at 4.30 am. Debriefing and breakfast occupied the next 2 hours and we climbed into our beds thankfully at 7 am. It was announced that the raid had been a success, Cologne Cathedral had survived, amazingly, and losses totalled forty-one aircraft – 3.9 per cent of the total force operating. We thought how glad we were to get this 'one-off' operation over and we could get back to our usual mundane but safer task of training. It was not to be, for two nights later the effort was to be repeated, this time against Essen in the Ruhr and we were to suffer all the same agonies again. This flight duration was 5¼ hours, but due to the considerable haze over the target it was not as successful as the Cologne raid and bombs were well scattered. Thirty-one of our aircraft were lost out of a total of 956 dispatched (3.2 per cent), which was lower than expected.

It seemed to us that if we were to fly operations we may as well be back on a fully operational squadron with the best available aircraft and not lumbered with clapped-out training types with a lesser survival potential. As it transpired, we were soon back to our normal instructional routine and the thought of further ops had disappeared. That is, until 31 July, when we were detailed once again, this time to Düsseldorf, and I was assigned to Flight Sergeant Chidgey, an exceptionally good pilot who originated from the West Country. We took off just before midnight and landed back just after 5 am. Our OTU contribution to the raid totalled 105 aircraft and our losses were heavy (over 10.5 per cent). We now resigned ourselves to being called for ops at any time in the future. There was no guarantee that being on a training station would relieve us of this likelihood.

In October 1942 at 27 OTU we converted to Mk III Wellingtons, which were a considerable improvement on the old ICs. By now the operational squadrons were being equipped with four-engined aircraft, although the Wellingtons were still operating in strength. 1943 arrived with no signs of an end to the war. My instructional duties continued into March 1943, by which time I was becoming bored with OTU life and thinking about a second tour on operations. On 27 March my old friend and Gunnery Leader, Flight Lieutenant Jackie Blair DFM said that he wanted to introduce me to a Flight Lieutenant Johnny Sauvage. He was looking for an experienced wireless operator/air gunner to fly with him on a night-bombing exercise at Cannock, a range widely used by OTUs in the Midlands. We were both impressed with each other and Johnny was a debonair but competent pilot who hailed from the Seychelles. Two days later Johnny approached me with the idea of under-taking a second tour of operations, his idea being to form a crew of experienced instructors who had already completed one tour. I asked myself if this would be fair to my wife Mollie and at the same time I weighed up the possibility of being returned to operations with an unknown crew, probably one with no previous operational experience. Johnny wanted a quick answer and I decided to throw in my lot with him. Jackie Blair, too, opted to become our rear gunner and I suddenly felt safer with such in-built experience. Johnny chose a very competent navigator and so I met 'Hitch' Hitchcock, another Londoner with considerable experience. We now had the nucleus of a crew so it was left to Johnny to approach the CFI to request a return to an operational squadron. Mollie did not know I had volunteered; she just thought it was a routine posting after a long stint on instructional duties.

The CFI reluctantly agreed to our request and the next day we were posted to Barkston in 5 Group where we were to form a complete crew, picking up a flight engineer and bomb aimer, thus confirming that we were to fly in a four-engined aircraft. On 5 April 1943 we found ourselves at Wigsley on 1654 CU (Conversion Unit), where we saw our first twin-engined Manchesters. The reports of the Manchester were far from complimentary; they were said to be under-powered and did diabolical things in flight. However, we had to convert to Manchesters before graduating to its four-engined counterpart, the Lancaster. At this point, we met Flight Sergeant Bill Waller who hailed from Romford and was to be our flight engineer and Pilot Officer Peter Burbridge our new bomb aimer. This was to be their first tour of operational duty. Both were jovial characters, married and had good OTU performances. So, our crew was now almost complete. A mid-upper gunner would be recruited on the squadron.

After two flights in Manchester L7491, an initial 4 hours on 'circuits and bumps' (landings), we did a 5-hour cross-country flights, including bombing at Bassingham Fen. We were unimpressed with the Manchester and thanked our luck that after only 9 hours of conversion we were transferred to Lancasters. What a different experience this was. The Lancaster was a beautiful aircraft in all respects and we immediately fell in love with her. Johnny said her handling was superb and it was great to have four engines, knowing that it would fly equally well on only two. After only 4 hours of acclimatisation on 'circuits and bumps' we were ready to undertake cross-country exercises, high- and low-level bombing and gunnery and bullseye exercises with the defence forces. We had completed 16 hours' day flying and 12 hours at night when we were pronounced 'ready' to join an operational squadron. Imagine our delight and excitement when, on 2 May 1943, we were posted to 97 (Straits Settlement) Squadron in 8 Pathfinder Group based at Bourn near Cambridge, with Mark III Lancasters, under the command of Wing Commander R. C. Alabaster DFC, a superb navigator. Apart from being an efficient CO, he was an absolute gentleman and was most caring for the crews under his command. Our living quarters at Bourn were pretty spartan but we enjoyed the atmosphere of life on the squadron.

Two days after arriving, we were called for our first operational briefing at Bourn and the adrenaline started flowing again. We had during that morning undergone fighter affiliation with Thunderbolts based at Debden and we were amazed at the manoeuvrability of the Lancaster, and with the fire power of the rear, mid-upper and front turrets we considered that we could face an adversary with greater confidence than ever before. We filed into briefing at 1700 hours and saw that our target was Dortmund. We drew a gasp when we saw our bomb load totalled 12,000 lb, comprising a 4,000 lb 'Cookie', four 1,000 lb and eight 500 lb GP bombs. The all-up weight with our considerable fuel load was staggering and we wondered how we were going to get airborne on the comparatively short runway.

At 2130 hours we were aboard Lanc ED862 doing our pre-flight checks and then the four engines burst into life. The sense of power as twenty aircraft taxied in line from dispersal points to the take-off runway was frightening. When one thought of 240,000 lb of explosive power, line astern and in close proximity, it needed only one aircraft to spark off a major disaster. At 2210 hours, the brakes were released and with all available power we surged down the runway. It seemed we would never lift off before we ran out of runway. At long last we were up – just! It appeared as if we were brushing the treetops and the ascent was painfully slow but sure. Hitch called out a course to steer to reach our coastal *rendezvous* with the main force. I tuned the radio to the Group frequency ready to receive the Command half-hourly broadcasts, which, in code, would transmit any relevant information as to target alterations, recalls etc. It was vitally important to listen to and log these transmissions as we were committed to radio silence except in the direst emergency. Transmissions from the aircraft would be picked up immediately by the German listening posts and we would give them ample opportunity to have a 'reception' party waiting for us.

Over the sea, the gunners tested their guns after making a careful search for other friendly aircraft. This procedure had to be terminated after a time in view of the danger when forces became so concentrated. The gunners were always apprehensive at the thought that their guns would freeze up after flying at 20,000 plus feet. One normally had only a split second to act if attacked by an enemy fighter. The warmth of the cabin and the constant droning of the four engines had the effect of introducing drowsiness. To keep myself alert in between broadcasts I took a walk, positioning myself in the astrodome and peering into the blackness of the night, sometimes to see the red-hot exhausts of nearby aircraft or the tell-tale vapour trails.

Crossing the enemy coast brought the inevitable deep lines of searchlights and accompanying flak – that aspect had not changed after two and a half years. I remembered it well! We got to the target and the Ruhr was solidly defended. It was a new experience for Peter as he took his position in front of his bombsight. After an initial 'Bloody hell' he directed Johnny on to the aiming point with his directions of 'Left, left, steady' and it seemed an interminable period before he said 'Bombs gone'. The uplift after the release of our full load was very dramatic. After the photo of our bomb plot was taken, Johnny said, 'Let's get the hell out of here'. He promptly threw the Lanc around the sky to escape the accurate anti-aircraft fire. Standing in the astrodome, the sight below was incredible – it looked like a sea of fire and I could imagine the hell being experienced by those poor unfortunates down there.

The return flight was uneventful until we switched on our IFF equipment, which identified us as a 'friendly' to UK defences. Listening in to the broadcast, it was evident that the weather was deteriorating. A landing at base was considered out of the question and we were directed to divert to High Ercall. A landing at a strange aerodrome after 6 hours of tension was not good for morale – we just wanted to get back to our beds and relax. Not so, we had to wait our turn for debriefing, then to follow the Duty Officer to find available sleeping accommodation here, there and everywhere. But at least we had survived the first trip of our second tour safely. As it was Bill Waller and Peter Burbridge's first operation ever I don't think they could sleep at all. They both had done their job competently and we were confident that they would prove to be valuable crewmembers. We flew back to Bourn the next day and found that there was a stand-down from ops, so we all went into Cambridge to celebrate, which we did in fine style. Eventually, when the pubs closed we found ourselves in the Dorothy Ballroom, a seething mass of dancers in many and varied uniforms. The girls appeared to drift towards the aircrew personnel, which didn't always please the Army chaps and there was isolated unpleasantness. There was never time to sit out between dances. One was always grabbed by discerning females. What a lovely life!

A week elapsed after our first operation with 97 Squadron before we were briefed to attack Duisburg in the Ruhr on 12/13 May. As our rear gunner, we recruited Sergeant Geoff Wood who had left the comfort and security of his farm in South America to help the country of his birth. A very shy person, Geoff stood about 5 feet 4 inches and was on the tubby side with bowed legs. One could imagine him in the saddle of a horse ranging his farm. More so as he always wore a lariat around his waist and we pictured him trying to lasso enemy fighters if they came too near. Jackie Blair reverted to the mid-upper gun position.

The flight was in bright moon with no cloud and excellent visibility. The target was clearly identified visually, which was a rarity. Our total bomb load of 11,000 lb went down at 2 am and the glow of the fires was seen from 40 miles away. As usual, the flak was intense and accurate but we came away unscathed and landed at base without incident at 0406 hours. We were awakened at 11 am with news that ops were on again that night [13/14 May] and an earlier briefing gave the hint of a longer target. Our flight engineer Bill Waller had to withdraw with a real stinker of a cold, flying at 20,000 feet on oxygen would do him no good at all. His deputy had to be Sergeant Ken Fairlie. When we saw that the target was Pilsen in Czechoslovakia, we wished that we all had bad colds! We took off at 2140 hours and we were not due back at base until approximately 5 am next morning.

In the bomb-bays we carried a 4,000 lb 'Cookie' and six 500 lb GP bombs, not inconsiderable for the distance involved. It was bright moonlight again. The visibility was very good but there was considerable ground haze. With such conditions, the gunners and lookouts had to be right on their mettle, we must have been so clearly visible to marauding fighters. A cluster of five red

57

TIs (target indicators) went down as we did our bombing run at 13,000 feet
and Peter saw our bombs going through the centre of the cluster. A vague
glow was seen through the haze as we turned for home. Around 7½ hours
after take-off we saw the welcome sight of Cambridge and landed safely at
Bourn at 0510 hours. By the time we had been debriefed and devoured our
eggs and bacon breakfast it was 9 am and tired as we were, it was difficult to
get a satisfactory sleep. Up again to lunch, we were delighted to learn that we
were not required for ops and many 'cat-naps' were taken in the Mess before
embarking on another affray in Cambridge.

We were allocated another aircraft, ED940 N-Nan and this letter was to see
us through the remainder of our operations. Ten days elapsed during which
time we did cross-country flights to get acclimatised to the new aircraft and
then we were back to blitzing the Ruhr once again. These trips of between only
4 and 5 hours duration suited us, even if the Ruhr was just about the most
heavily defended area of the *Reich*. We had 'clobbered' Dortmund, Wuppertal
and Düsseldorf by 11 June when we were called by the CO, Wing Commander

R. C. Alabaster and told that we were to make our first sortie as a Pathfinder Marker. The importance of accuracy in marking the target was emphasised and hundreds of main force aircraft following would be depositing their loads on our marker flares. The target [on 12/13 June] was Bochum. We attacked from 20,000 feet with 5/10ths cloud and at 1.21 am we witnessed one terrific explosion among the many bursts, and fires were taking a good hold. Our first marking raid had been a success and we were elated that our comprehensive training had paid off.

Three days later, we were, together with Flight Lieutenant Ernie Rodley's crew,[1] detailed to RAF Scampton, apparently for a special operation. Arriving on 16 June 1943 we found ourselves with detachments of other crews who had been formed into 617 Squadron and had carried out the daring raid [16/17 May 1943] on the Möhne and Eder Dams with such devastating success but with high losses. We had to undergo low-level night flying and bombing and after the dams raid rumours were rife that we would be assigned something similar. We were confined to camp, correspondence and telephone calls being forbidden. There was an air of secrecy about all we did. On 20 June we were called to briefing and looked at each other and said: 'Well, this is it. Good luck chaps!'

The target route board was uncovered and we caught our breath as we followed the red route tape down to the bottom of the map and saw no return tape. Then we saw the target – Friedrichshafen Zeppelin hangars and workshops, which apparently were housing important rocket and radar devices. Straining ourselves to fathom out what was to happen after bombing the target, someone said 'We're then flying on to Algiers in North Africa'. The crews hushed as the Station CO entered and the Operations Officer started the briefing. Take-off was to be 2145 hours and the total force was to take up loose formation at low level to keep under the enemy radar to create surprise. Crossing the enemy coast, low level was to be maintained until approaching the target area, where height was to be increased to 10,000 feet for bombing. In view of the distance involved, it would be impossible to return to the UK before daylight and the tired force would be easy prey for the fighters that would be amassed and waiting for them. For this reason, the whole formation would then fly on across the Mediterranean to Algiers – landing at Blida or Maison Blanche – subject, of course, to non-interception by Italian fighters based in Corsica or Sardinia. Return to the UK would be via a target in Italy – probably Milan or Turin – a night or two later.

The excitement amongst the crews was intense but certainly it looked a hazardous trip, lasting about 10 or 11 hours. Our aircraft was to carry mostly target indicators and flares, as was Flight Lieutenant Ernie Rodley's aircraft, only two 500 lb bombs being carried additionally. This was to be a real test of our marking ability. We lounged in the Mess, writing our last letters to be handed to the Chaplain for forwarding if we did not return. There was an air of nervousness among the crews, who were anxious to get on their way.

The buses arrived to take us to our dispersal points. Hitch, our navigator, turned to me and said: 'Ed, I don't bloody fancy this one at all!' I couldn't have agreed more with him. Jackie Blair as usual exuded complete confidence and was already comforting the crew with his anticipations of exploring the Casbah in Algiers. The engines were started and we joined the long procession of aircraft waiting to take off. Ground staff personnel were at the end of the runway to wave us good luck, not knowing the target but anticipating something special – in the wake of the Dam-busting raid. The noise on the ground must have been ear-splitting with so many aircraft at such low height. The eyes of the pilots and flight engineers had to be very keen, lifting over trees and high tension wires. As we crossed the enemy coast, it was just like daylight and as we hugged as close to the ground as possible we clearly saw doors of houses thrown open and the occupants waving furiously.

It was an immense feeling of power as we surged on, seeing dozens of aircraft all around us. There had been no flak so far, we were obviously too low and too fast for the light ack-ack but no doubt we were now being plotted even though we had achieved an element of surprise. As we approached Lake Constance for the run-up to Friedrichshafen we climbed to 9,000 feet. Ernie Rodley was at 10,000 feet with the main force above us. We clearly identified the target and made our run as the light ack-ack fire came piping up. Peter said how clearly everything stood out and we just beat Ernie to dropping our markers on the factory roof. Direct hits were observed as we turned to make a further observation and re-mark as necessary. We then ran into the flak, which was becoming more intense and suffered hits, which affected our hydraulics, one landing wheel dropped slightly with damage thereto. It was time to go and Hitch gave a course to Johnny for the next leg across the Med. We purposely lost height. The last thing we wanted now was to encounter fighters, even if they were Italian.

Daylight broke and we saw Ernie Rodley's aircraft above and on our starboard beam. As he reduced height to about 15,000 feet there was a blinding flash beneath Ernie's fuselage. Then his bomb doors opened and a flaming mass dropped out into the sea below. Unknowingly, he had a hung-up marker flare that had failed to release over the target and as it was fitted with a barometric fuse it automatically ignited below 2,000 feet. Fortunately, the flaming mass had dropped out and the fire in the bomb-bay became extinguished. Initially, it had been a shock to us witnessing the scene, but we were relieved to see him continue on his way. The gunners were more alert than ever now, searching the sky for expected interceptors who no doubt would welcome the sight of such big targets with their tired crews.

To cheers from the whole crew and congratulations to Hitch for good navigation we crossed the North African coast and sighted Algiers. We headed for the airfield at Blida and were redirected to Maison Blanche, where we saw masses of aircraft circling and waiting landing directions. All the planes were now perilously low on fuel, their crews tired and just anxious to land. The Flying Controller was an American who must have been nonplussed at the sight of so many Lancasters – all calling for permission to land. The first time we heard him he said 'The next baby on the circuit come in and land!' whereupon several anxious pilots headed their aircraft down, and it was only too evident that this was a dangerous procedure with more than a likelihood of collisions. The airfield was of sand and stone so clouds of dust rose as an aircraft landed. In spite of exhaustion after being in the air for over 10 hours, the sequence of landings took a reasonable course. Bill Waller called to Johnny 'Fuel almost gone Skipper. We must get down!' Calling the Flying Controller, Johnny reported: 'Fuel very low and we have no hydraulics – shot away, landing gear and flaps and brakes inoperative.' We were ordered to wait until all other aircraft were down before attempting our landing, lest we littered the airfield before others could get in. Stooging around when fuel gauges were reading nil is no fun and Johnny said, 'We're coming in!'

We could not establish if our landing speed was going to be excessive and with no brakes we had no idea where we would finish up. Not knowing to what extent one landing wheel was damaged, Johnny touched down virtually on one wheel and throttled back and hoped for the best. Eventually, the undercarriage collapsed and we spun round in clouds of dust – and we were all out of the plane in a flash. We had made it and we felt great! Air Chief Marshal Tedder greeted us and congratulated everybody on the first 'shuttle' flight. All crews were safe and the only aircraft lost was ours – a complete write-off!

The bulk of the shuttle force, with the exception of Johnny and Ernie Rodley, was called to briefing, the aircraft having been refuelled and bombed up. The force was to return to the UK via Italy and the Alps, bombing Turin on the way. Our crew was given the option of splitting up and flying individually within the other returning aircraft, or waiting at Algiers for some other solution. We did not relish the idea of flying as passengers with unknown crews so we opted to stay. We were flown home via Gibraltar in a Lanc and landed at Scampton after a 9¼-hour flight. As we emerged from the Lanc the Station CO greeted us and when he saw my branch of bananas he said how nice it was that I should think to bring them back. He peeled off six and handed them to me and said the rest would be sent to the children in the local hospital. I never did taste one banana as mine were entered as prizes in a raffle!

After six days we resumed marking operations, this time against poor old Cologne again. We were allocated Lanc III EE176, another *N-Nan*. With no cloud and excellent visibility we bombed at 0140 hours from 20,000 feet, releasing our markers and 10,000 lb bomb load, which resulted in a huge explosion at 0143 hours. Landing at 0340 hours, we decided on another thrash to Cambridge that evening. I had now completed my fiftieth operational sortie, which was as good a reason as any to celebrate.

On 11 July we made our first sortie against an Italian target, Turin. Everybody was saying how much easier the 'Eyetie' trips would be after the Ruhr. But of course we had to negotiate the Swiss Alps in each direction. Whilst passing through the Alps, the Swiss no doubt wishing to make a point of their neutrality, opened up with their AA fire, which although far from accurate, was strange since it came down toward us instead of upwards! The visibility was good and the Alps was an awesome sight. Over Turin we came down to 13,000 feet as the flak was haphazard and didn't present the problems we had become used to over Germany. With no cloud and clear visibility the target was defined and we took our time to ensure accuracy of bombing. Bomb aimer Peter Burbridge's words were: 'Piece of cake!' On our return the

Group broadcast gave us directions to divert to St Eval in Cornwall, no reason for the diversion being given. After 9½ hours flying, it was 8 am when we landed. By the time debriefing was over and we had finished breakfast it was 10 am and we sprawled in armchairs in the Mess until it was time to return to Bourn. Being called to the Adjutant's office, I wondered what I had done wrong but was pleasantly surprised to hear that I had been promoted to warrant officer with effect from 1 May 1943.

After a welcome pause of two weeks, my fifty-second operation came up, this time to Hamburg on 24 July. Our established crew was now working well together and we had complete understanding and confidence in each other. We resisted the temptation to go sick on the occasions that we were feeling under the weather lest we should lose our position in this crew. The target at Hamburg did not present too many difficulties in that most of the flight was over the sea and therefore we escaped the attentions of the flak that was experienced during overland trips to places like the Ruhr. We took off at 2200 hours with 8,000 lb of bombs plus our target indicators. There was very little cloud but hazy visibility and at 17,000 feet we ran into the inevitable heavy flak and released our load at 0105 hours. Two minutes later there was the most violent explosion near the aiming point, followed by a glow lasting for 40 seconds. This was confirmed later by all the squadron crews at de-briefing. Many large fires and a pall of smoke were visible as we turned away for that journey back across the dreaded North Sea. Around 6 hours after take-off, we touched down at Bourn at 4 am, another satisfactory night's work over. On this raid, the first use was made of Window, the metallic strips that were to cause such havoc with the German radar devices. The effect was noticeable because searchlights wandered all over the sky and the flak was haphazard.

On return from leave we found that new Lancaster IIIs had arrived fitted with *H2S*, the latest radar device, which enabled a picture of ground detail to be illustrated on a screen sited at the navigator's position. This latest device was to be the greatest advance in radar navigation and bombing technique. It meant that regardless of weather conditions, 10/10ths cloud, the ground detail could be identified – and therefore no targets could escape our attention. What a dramatic change from the early days of 1939–41 when everything was based on 'dead reckoning' navigation and so hopelessly out on many occasions.

Our new aircraft JA908, another *N-Nan*, took us off on a series of cross-country exercises for training with our H2S equipment. We were agreeably surprised with the results of our training in the new aircraft and we looked forward to our next operation to put the training into effect. Imagine our delight to learn that we were on our way this time to another Italian target, Milan. As markers for the following main force we carried only one 4,000 lb 'Cookie' in addition to our target indicators. At 1.20 am we attacked at only 12,000 feet with no moon or cloud and good visibility. Many fires were seen and one column of smoke rose to 5,000 feet – still visible from the Alps on the return journey. After 8 hours' flying, we landed safely at Bourn at 0530.

The next night we were stood down but two aircraft were detailed to attack Mannheim and our navigator Hitch was somewhat dismayed to find himself allocated to a crew captained by Flight Lieutenant Eaton-Clarke for this trip. We urged him not to get lost as we now had got used to him and didn't relish the thought of having to pick up a new navigator for the remainder of this operational tour. Fortunately, Hitch survived this one, arriving back at 0440 hours, getting to bed at 0700 hours, to be awakened with the news that we were all operating again that night.

Johnny Sauvage arrived at briefing with the news that he had been promoted to squadron leader – another excuse for a party 'thrash'. Only five aircraft had been allocated for the raid on Nuremberg, including a new crew under the captaincy of Pilot Officer L. Baker. It was nearly 2200 hours when we took off for this 7½ hour flight and we waved to Mollie and Ada (Bill's wife) who were standing on the road at the end of the take-off runway. (We were all staying at a windmill near Bourn on a living-out basis and thoroughly enjoying our social side of life. The remainder of our crew did not consider it wise to have wives living near the base, knowing when we were away on ops of the anxiety they experienced awaiting our return.) At 16,000 feet in 10/10ths cloud conditions, the *H2S* was proving a most valuable asset to our navigation and we bombed on a timed run, but all we saw was a red glow below the cloud. Unfortunately, Pilot Officer Baker and his crew did not return from their first mission.

Two nights later we were off again. It was a return visit to Milan and Geoff Wood had to cry off this one with a heavy cold and sore throat, so we had a Squadron Leader McKinson as our rear gunner. After bombing from 12,000 feet we had an uneventful return and at 0530 after over 8 hours in the air Bill and I were anxious to get debriefing over so that we could get back to the windmill before the girls were out of bed!

On 17 August we were warned that a special target was to be attacked that night, that we would not be allowed off camp during the day and no outside telephone calls would be allowed. Briefing for only three crews was at 1800 hours under a great veil of secrecy. Entering the Operations Room, we anxiously scoured the room for a hint of this 'special' target. A sheet obscured the route map until the CO arrived. When the unveiling revealed the target, we were none the wiser as it identified Peenemünde. It meant absolutely nothing to any of us – we had never heard of it! The Intelligence Officer rose to give his briefing and said that the target on the Baltic coast was probably the most important target ever to be attacked. Whilst not revealing it was a site for the development and production of V-1 flying bombs and V-2 rockets, he said that advanced radar equipment was its main function. Three aiming points, including scientist and production worker billets had to be destroyed totally – if not tonight, then tomorrow night and the night after if necessary. We were told that Peenemünde could alter the whole course of the war and had to be destroyed regardless of losses. This did nothing to encourage us, especially when we learnt that there would be no cloud and a full moon, and the attack would be from as low as 12,000 feet or lower. These conditions would be ideal for the German night-fighters so the RAF would adopt spoof tactics by sending a small number of Mosquitoes to Berlin, giving the impression that that was the night's target for the main force. Much publicity had been given to the fact that Berlin was high on the RAF priority list and the Germans were very sensitive to attacks on their capital city. It was hoped that their fighters would be concentrated nearer to Berlin and that by the time it was established that Peenemünde was to be the main target, the first two waves of bombers would have completed their task and been on the way home. The third wave, provided by 5 Group, could, however, expect to have a hot time.

We took off at 2108 hours and climbed to 18,000 feet. Our primary target was the scientists' quarters. The whole force would be directed by a Master Bomber. Group Captain John Searby of 83 Squadron based at Wyton was selected for this task and he was to fly over the target for the whole attack, giving a commentary and shifting the attack as necessary. Around 40 minutes could elapse from first to last aircraft on target. Some aircraft were fitted with *Oboe* ground-controlled radar – and other *PFF* aircraft with *H2S* but the conditions would allow for full visual attacks, providing smoke did not obscure the aiming points. From 08E we started to throw out Window.

We began to lose height as we approached Rugen Island and saw many aircraft around us in the almost daylight conditions. Fortunately, none were hostile so hopefully the Mosquitoes who had preceded us by an hour had lured the night-fighters to the Berlin area. We sighted the target clearly at 11,700 feet and already the enemy in the hope of thwarting the attacking forces had started a smoke screen. Light flak started piping up from the target zone as we went in with our green TIs and 7,500 lb bomb load. Peter reported direct hits on the living quarters and just then we suffered a direct hit from flak. Johnny shouted that we were going round in circles and could not fly straight and level. If the state of affairs could not be rectified we would have to consider baling out. It was a prospect that did not appeal one bit. To jump with the possibility of either landing in the sea or amid a hail of bombs just wasn't on. Bill beckoned me to follow him down the fuselage and with great trepidation I did so, regretting the fact that I was putting distance between me and my parachute. Bill indicated the trimming and aileron cables that had been severed by the impact. He busied himself with lengths of nylon cord and then Johnny said that he had recovered control of the aircraft. By now the target was a sea of flames and high explosions and we were intent on returning from whence we came with all speed.

The German defences were well alerted by now and fighters would be re-deployed from the Berlin area without delay. We felt sorry for the last wave of bombers entering the scene that would have to take the full brunt of attacks in ideal night-flying conditions. Several aircraft were seen going down in flames. Some 7 hours after take-off we had the welcoming sight of Bourn and we hoped that the target had been well and truly plastered and that it would not be necessary to return again the next night, when the *Luftwaffe* would be ready and waiting to wreak their revenge. Initial reports that morning indicated that the raid had been a complete success achieved through the element of surprise, the decoy raid on Berlin and the sheer audacity of operating under a full moon and clear skies. Out of the total of 606 aircraft assigned, forty four-engined bombers and one Mosquito were lost (6.7 per cent) and thirty-two suffered damage. In the daylight reconnaissance 12 hours after the attack, photographs revealed twenty-seven buildings in the northern manufacturing area destroyed and forty huts in the living and sleeping quarters completely flattened. The foreign labour camp to the south suffered worst of all. The whole target area was covered in craters. It was inconceivable that the site could ever operate again and at least we had gained valuable time against V-1 and V-2 attacks on London and our impending second front assault forces. This raid probably gave us our most satisfaction against all other targets attacked.[2]

On 23 August 1943 we made our first assault against the capital city. Berlin was always considered to be the 'big one'. It meant a long trip over heavily defended enemy territory and the Berlin defences were savage in the protection of the great city, which the Nazis swore would never be subjected to air bombardment. What a long way I had come since those dark days in 1940 when there appeared to be no salvation from the gloom. Here we were attacking the German capital in strength and talking more and more of an invasion of Europe. This was to be my fifty-seventh operation. Could I survive to see my sixtieth operation? It did seem to be inviting the inevitable with each further raid. So many crews had not even reached double figures and with so many more aircraft involved, losses mounted so that the likelihood of aircrews surviving twelve raids was still minimal. For this trip, we had an additional crewmember, Flight Sergeant Penny, who came as second pilot for the experience. Apart from the heavy flak and searchlight activity, the flight was uneventful, far less frightening than any trip to the Ruhr, and after bombing from 18,000 feet we were back at base in 6 hours 35 minutes.

Four nights later we were back to Nuremberg with another 7,000 lb of 'goodies'. These were placed on workshops and marshalling yards, bombing with the aid of *H2S*. On our return we were coned by searchlights and suddenly the heavy flak stopped, which indicated fighter activity could be expected. Jackie in the mid-upper turret spotted a fighter attacking from the starboard quarter and gave Johnny instructions to 'corkscrew' and he and Geoff in the rear turret gave a burst of fire, which made *N-Nan* shudder and the smell of cordite in the cabin was pungent. I was sitting at my radio listening to the Group broadcast and as I looked up I saw that there was a clean hole through the crystal monitor about 18 inches above and to the right of my head. A cannon shell had pierced it and gone straight out through the front of the aircraft. I was rigid, not daring to move an inch. The contact was brief and the fighter sheered off, much to our relief. One of the crews, captained by Flight Lieutenant C. B. Robertson, did not return from this operation.

On 31 August our hearts dropped when we saw that the target was again Berlin. It seemed that the targets were becoming so much harder these days and I gained the impression that time was running out for me and the odds were ever-increasing. It was at this stage that I was becoming more nervous then ever and was looking forward to finishing my tour of ops. Although we had a satisfactory trip we were upset to hear that Wing Commander [K. H.] Burns [DFC] had been shot down, it being subsequently established that the crew had been taken prisoner-of-war, except for Pilot Officer [E. G.] Dolby [DFC RCAF] who had been killed.[3] The raids on Berlin were becoming monotonous when we found ourselves in flight again on 3 September against the 'Big City'. The 7½-hour return trip was carried out without too much trouble. There was no moon, no cloud and good visibility and our bombs released from 19,000 feet were seen to burst in a built up area. The flak as usual was intense and accurate but we escaped damage. From the frequency of raids on the capital city, it was only too evident that the 'Battle of Berlin' had started in earnest and we were repaying ten-fold the attacks on London in 1940/41. All our crews returned from this operation, one having to return early after 2 hours when Sergeant Miller's mid-upper gunner Sergeant Williams was rendered unconscious at 20,000 feet after his electrically heated suit and oxygen supply failed.

The next night was a stand down for the squadron but then two nights running, on 5 and 6 September, we were to attack Mannheim and Munich. On the Mannheim trip a crew had to abandon this mission for the second consecutive night, this time as a result of the rear turret elevation and depression being unserviceable. I cannot recall seeing that crew again at subsequent briefings.

My sixty-third operation on 22/23 September was against Hannover, the birthplace of my great-grandfather. The following night [23/24] it was Mannheim and it was on this operation that we lost Flight Lieutenant [R. A.] Fletcher and crew, including Pilot Officer [W. H.] Layne, the wireless operator, who was on his second tour of ops and who never learned of his award of the DFC for earlier raids. The loss of this most experienced crew made me wonder how much longer our luck could hold out. I had exceeded sixty ops and wondered how soon I could be relieved. It was to be just one more week before my operational career was to come to an end but in that week I was to fly to Mannheim, again, to Brunswick and finally to Munich. On the Mannheim raid, we were coned by searchlights for a whole 6 minutes; it seemed as if every flak battery was concentrating on us and I thought it would be only a matter of seconds before they scored a direct hit. After a battering during this interminable period during which I had virtually given up any hope of escaping, Johnny finally gave them the slip by violent evasive action and we were away and on the return flight. If ever I prayed, it was never more earnestly than on that night.

Setting out for Munich on the night of 2/3 October 1943, we had no prior knowledge that this would be our final operation together. Perhaps it was just as well as we might have been even more nervous in our anxiety to survive. As it was, the trip was largely uneventful, except that we coaxed Hitch our navigator to leave his seat and take up position in the astrodome to see what was going on over the target area. His remarks over the intercom brought smiles to our faces when he said, 'Christ! Does this sort of thing go on every night?' Seeing the target area a mass of fires, he considered it was 'sheer bloody murder'. Ginger Thomas, too, was on this raid and he was to be involved in five further operations against Berlin.

Our crew was stood down for a few days after this until Johnny called us together and said, 'Well lads, do we want to go on, or for some of us at least, shall we call it a day?' Johnny, Hitch, Jackie Blair and myself had done our quota and we would ask to be relieved of further operational duty. For the other chaps, Bill, the flight engineer, Peter, the air bomber, and Geoff, the rear gunner, they had no option but to continue. Peter anxiously cleaned his pipe, Bill kept shuffling his feet and Geoff nervously fingered his lanyard whilst the rest of us tried to reach a decision. If we old-stagers decided to finish, then Bill, Peter and Geoff would be assigned to a new crew to finish their first tour. Whilst they were hopeful that the crew would not split up, they recognised that we had done our fair share of ops over a long period and in similar circumstances they would say 'enough is enough'. Johnny posed the question to us again and there seemed a reluctance to reply. Finally, I said that the last half dozen trips had been a nightmare for me and I had been getting progressively more nervous, so I was going to call it a day. Hitch, too, said he agreed with me and so it was decided to tell the CO, Wing Commander Alabaster, we had made up our minds. Naturally, the other three lads were disappointed, but they thanked us for the happy times we had enjoyed at Bourn and we wished them all the luck that was going. Bill Waller and Peter Burbridge entered a new crew after our departure from 97 Squadron at Bourn and had completed only four more operations when they were reported missing after a raid on Berlin. It subsequently transpired that their aircraft had received a direct hit on their bombing run and had exploded with its full bomb load. They wouldn't have known anything about it. Peter's wife had only recently given birth to twins and Bill's wife Ada would have been devastated, as she was totally devoted to him. I felt sick for days after that news, thinking perhaps that they might have lived if our original crew had continued. On the other hand, we too may have died on that fateful Berlin raid. Who knows?

We were to remain at Bourn for a further three weeks before learning of our postings but two of these were spent on leave. It was whilst I was at home on leave that I learned from the *Islington Gazette* that I was awarded the DFC. It had been announced in the *London Gazette* on 19 October 1943. My joy was complete. I had survived sixty-six operations.

Notes

1. See Chapter 3.
2. The raid is adjudged to have set back the V-2 experimental programme by at least two months and to have reduced the scale of the eventual rocket attack on Britain.
3. sic – Warrant Officer O. Lambert DFM was KIA also. Wing Commander Burns lost a hand.

CHAPTER 6

My War

Malcolm Freegard

Come the dawn, we'll be returning –
If we're lucky to survive!
Tired and weary – bent and battered,
Only glad that we're alive.
Then, around us you will gather,
Shaking heads in disbelief;
What has happened to your aircraft
Overwhelms your heart with grief.

'*To the Ground Crews*', Ken Grantham (35 Squadron)

Though crammed with incident, my war could by no stretch of the imagination be described as heroic; I was scared stiff most of the time. Militarily speaking, it began among the sand dunes, or 'burrows', as they were known, close to Westward Ho! in north Devon. I spent the first few months of the war there, together with some 300 or 400 fellow pupils evacuated from our school in London. During those months a number of masters and senior boys formed a platoon of the Local Defence Volunteers, later known as the Home Guard, later still as 'Dad's Army'.

Our duties consisted mainly of patrolling by night the length of those sandy acres in search of German paratroopers, who, it was confidently believed, would be disguised as nuns. How the presence of a battalion of ungainly Sisters of Mercy armed to the teeth and speaking German, could be expected to avoid public scrutiny and comment, was never adequately explained. The only incident from those early days that remains in the mind took place very early one morning while it was still dark. Our mild-mannered, scholarly, much revered, history master was suddenly and quite unexpectedly immersed in a ditch fill of brackish water. Us pupils were profoundly impressed by the fluency and inventiveness with which he employed words of a kind we had previously supposed to be unknown to him. He even included one or two quite new to my innocent 17-year-old ears.

Three months later I was an Aircraftman Second Class (AC2) in His Majesty's Royal Air Force. A brief period of illness prevented my leaving for Canada with my comrades to be trained under the recently established Empire Training Scheme, so I learned to fly in England, at Peterborough, North

Luffenham and Grantham. I was an average pilot. Indeed, I was assessed as above average but remained quite useless as a navigator. Once, I landed my Tiger Moth in a field near Corby to ask the way. It was a Sunday morning: the field was small and near the church. By the time I managed to land, at the third attempt, Mattins was in ruins and the Home Guard had turned out. With thinly disguised disappointment at my not being a representative of the *Luftwaffe*, they pointed me in the direction of the aerodrome, all of 5 miles away, and drove the inquisitive cows to one side so that I could take off again.

After that, things got more serious. While I was landing an Airspeed Oxford, a twin-engined trainer, one of the engines cut out, much too near the ground to do anything more useful than retract the undercarriage and plough through six large greenhouses that skirted the aerodrome at Grantham. I retain a vivid memory of a man standing by the nearest greenhouse, who, fortunately, realised just in time that the aircraft wasn't going to go over the top. Then there was broken glass, hundreds of tomatoes and bits of my aeroplane flying in all directions. What was left of the Oxford, minus its wings, ended up on its nose, leaving me to extricate myself from the straps in which I was hanging, conscious all the time of the sound of petrol gushing from a broken tank. Fortunately, I wasn't hurt and later that afternoon was sent off in another aircraft to practise formation flying.

There followed a brief period of flying boats at Invergordon in Scotland. This was enjoyable in a way but it entailed submarine patrols lasting 12 hours and more. Moreover, that uneventful part of Coastal Command regarded itself as the aristocracy of the RAF and it took many hours to graduate from third to second pilot and finally, to captain. I applied to train as a night-fighter pilot and in the strange manner in which these things were decided – perhaps as a kind of punishment – I was posted to Bomber Command to fly Wellingtons, those twin-engined warhorses that continued to operate well into 1942 alongside Halifaxes and Lancasters.

I was eventually posted to 115 Squadron at Marham and so returned to Norfolk, which even in those days I had long acknowledged to be the hub of the universe. My flight path to various targets in Germany and occupied Europe in the summer of 1942 frequently took me over Holt and Gresham's [public school] and sometimes over Sheringham, the scene of some of the happiest hours of a sunlit childhood. My first op was to St Nazaire on 17 June, followed by a minelaying operation on 18 June. Two days later we went to the port of Emden in north Germany and again on the night of 22/23 June when my aircraft [X3555] was damaged over the target. We came back on one engine and I struggled to reach home. Then the second engine went and I was obliged to ditch in the sea some 70 miles due east of Cromer. After 12 hours in a dinghy, my crew and I – five of us in all – were picked up by an ASR [Air Sea Rescue] squadron [278] operating from Coltishall. The rescue aircraft was an amphibian, the Walrus [L2238], which saved the lives of hundreds of aircrew during the war. The ASR crew[1] was pleased, as we were the first crew they had rescued. After patching us up we were taken back to Marham, where all except one of us recovered to go back on ops.

I returned to ops on 11 July, with a minelaying trip, and then it was off to Duisburg on 13 June. Minelaying trips were fairly cushy unless you saw a flak ship and people could, and did, get shot down. Duisburg was particularly well defended. It put the wind up you to see the old night-fighters creeping around. I hated bombing cities, I really did. I was happier when I was given military targets. Saturation bombing of German cities was awful. Waging war on children and old people and historic cities is not what I wanted to do. I was 20 years old. I had wanted to be a fighter pilot, where the war was one on one. When I joined 115 Squadron I was as patriotic as the next man. Then I began to think about all the energy and human ingenuity used to wage war that could have been employed in better ways. This war was 'an expensive spirit and a waste of shame'.

My seventh op on the night of 21/22 July was less lucky. Having set out at 2349 hours to bomb Duisburg again, shortly after bombing we were attacked from underneath by an Me 110 night-fighter close to Düsseldorf and my faithful Wellington [Mk III X3561 KO-X, flying at 14,000 feet] caught fire and was damaged beyond any hope of recovery. Fortunately, I was again carrying no second pilot that night. As it was, three of the five crew were killed in the aircraft (one of the lads had been married only three months).[2] After checking them to make sure they were dead, Sergeant Bill Rogers, the front gunner, and I escaped with some difficulty. I had been wounded slightly in the thigh by an exploding cannon shell and I had a hell of a job getting out through the front hatch. When I finally opened my parachute I was well under a 1,000 feet from the ground. I thought, this is it – I've had it. It's what I joined up for. But to my great relief, the chute opened and I landed in open countryside in a sodden wet field, breaking an ankle in the process. Guns were going off in the distance. Aircraft continued to fly overhead. I went to sleep wrapped up in my chute. When it started getting light I began walking along a road but I did not get far. A car with three *Luftwaffe* officers in it drew up and I was captured. Eventually, I ended up at the *Dulag Luft* interrogation centre in Frankfurt. There, the *kommandant* came to see me. He showed me a book and pointed out a photo of a group of people. One of them was my father! The book was about the Chiswick Convention, which my father and apparently the *kommandant* had attended every year. The *kommandant* was genuinely pleased that my father was his friend.

I was to be put on a train under guard for PoW camp. While we waited at Frankfurt railway station, a tiny, wizened, old lady, who was almost certainly Jewish, approached me. She was so small her head reached only as a far as my waist. She said to me, 'Got bless you.' I patted her gently on the cheek. There was uproar all around me. I was put on a train and finally taken away to captivity. 'For you the war is over' the Germans would say. Some of them said it crowingly. Others said it with envy in their voice. They must have thought, 'Ruddy war. Sodding Hitler. We're all in the same boat.' To them, 'For you the war is over' meant 'you lucky bugger'. They thought that for me the war *was* over. It wasn't, you know. The next three years were spent in *Stalag Luft III*, notorious as the setting of the Great Escape, following which, fifty Allied officers were executed on the orders of the *Führer* himself. I was one of those responsible for getting rid of soil from the tunnels. I was in the same hut as Tom Lees and two of the officers who were among the fifty who were executed. It was terrible. There were even one or two Germans who were as upset by the murders as we were.

Now I look back on the whole experience like it was a book you read about someone else. Sometimes, suddenly, I am there again. An expensive spirit, a waste of shame . . . .

Notes

1. Pilot Officer S. A. Trevallion – later Squadron Leader Trevallion DFC, 278 Squadron CO – and Sergeant T. Templeton, who had been guided to their dinghy by a Wellington and a Hudson and which took three attempts to take-off.
2. Warrant Officer II George Vincent Booth RCAF (USA), observer, Flight Sergeant Warnford Francis Victor Pink, WOP RAFVR and Sergeant John Munro, rear gunner, were buried in Nijmegen (Jonkerbos) War Cemetery. KO-X crashed 7 km SE of Roermond.

CHAPTER 7

The Last Op

Leslie R. Sidwell

*See them come home, sliding and roaring by. The bright, beloved marauders
of the sky. Stern and serene, young profiles and strong hands that have dealt
death and sorrow.*

*Over lands once fair with peace and wine, young love and song, they flew
impersonal elate and strong. See them come in to land, their smiles, their eyes.
The triumph in their step. But strangely lies pain in this mouth, pale horror on
that brow, that went unruffled, candid, gay, just now. They have returned, fierce
kinsmen of the wind. Brought back their lives but left their youth behind.*

Roy F. A. Yallop[1]

For 28/29 July 1942. The target named at briefing for 7 Squadron at
Oakington was Hamburg again but on a far bigger scale than two
nights ago. A note I made at the time said it was another 'Thousand
Raid'.[2] This was in the full moon period. Presumably the number was again
being made up with OTU crews. It was our usual crew in Stirling W7565,
B-Beer, except that Sergeant Paddy Leathem, the mid-upper gunner, wasn't
flying. He'd reported sick late on. Sergeant Albert H. C. Bates RAAF replaced
him. Our skipper was 23 year old Flight Lieutenant Douglas W. Whiteman. I
was a pilot officer rear-turret gunner. Sergeant A. L. Crockford, a new
sergeant-pilot arrival on the Squadron joined us late on that night to fly as
'second dickey' for experience. The rest of the crew consisted of Sergeants
Frank McIntyre, WOp/AG and John Boyle, navigator, both Australians, and
Warrant Officer C. F. Carter, flight engineer.

Out at dispersal we got everything finally checked and ready in the
sweltering heat inside the aircraft before climbing out into the oh-so-welcome
cool night air. It was lovely to relax outside on the grass and smoke casually
before reluctantly putting on the flying kit, which I knew would be badly
needed for the cold later on, after the muck-sweat had gone. I donned my
flying kit regretfully, knowing full well it would be freezing at height, and was
soon in another sweat in the aircraft.

We took off at 2229 hours. The weather was good. We passed over Cromer
and out over the North Sea. I spent the time taking the usual sightings from
my rear turret on flame-floats we'd dropped to check drift for the navigator.
We'd been briefed to cross the German coast north of the Elbe estuary, then to

*Stirling I W7444 MG-G of 7 Squadron being bombed up with 250 lb bombs at Oakington, Cambridgeshire. On 31 October 1941 Pilot Officer N. E. Winch and his crew took off in W7444 at 1752 hours for the raid on Bremen but they had to return early due to oxygen failure and the aircraft crashed while trying to land. There were no serious injuries to the crew of the forty Wellingtons and eight Stirlings that set off for Bremen. Only thirteen crews claimed to have found their target and one Welling-ton was shot down. (*Flight*)*

turn south some 20 miles north of Hamburg to run up to the target. There was heavy flak and we were hit just before the run up. Just after we'd bombed, someone on the intercom reported tracer coming up from below and we were hit by night-fighter attack from underneath. I reported a decoy headlight out on the starboard quarter and searched around for other fighters. I reported one coming in from above on the port side and told the skipper to turn to port. I think I hit him with a burst before my power went off. A fighter came in again from the rear and continued firing. My turret was shattered and we seemed to be in a steady dive. The skipper gave the emergency bale out order, quickly followed by what sounded like his cries of pain. Then the intercom abruptly cut off and we were on fire.

When my turret power had failed, I'd been left partly on the beam. I started to operate the dead man's handle (emergency winding gear) to centralise my turret so that I could get back into the fuselage to grab my parachute and bale out. (Chutes could not be stored in the rear turret as one did in earlier two-engined jobs, which were dead easy for rear gunners to quit in a hurry.) I

73

wound away like mad at the hand-winding gear behind me, very conscious that we were losing precious height. As if in a dream, I saw an Me 110 closing in from astern with his guns blazing away. I wound away as I watched him through the shattered Perspex. My painfully slow progress was like a nightmare. I was conscious of the EBO order given in what seemed some time ago ... Would I be in time? He was extremely close to me when he eventually broke away and I finally managed to move the turret sufficiently to fall back hurriedly into the fuselage. I grabbed my chute from the stowage outside the turret doors, forced open the nearby emergency exit door and as quickly as I could, jumped out into space. In those seconds I was conscious of flames and smoke up front in the fuselage. I gave no thought at all to any dangers of baling out, or that I'd had no practice in jumping. I just concentrated in getting out of a doomed aircraft. In my haste to get out I banged my head on something as I quit poor old *B-Beer*, partly knocking myself out. I pulled the ripcord without counting as you were normally told to do. I must have done the right thing because I came to swinging in the air. I could see the waters of the Elbe shining below, with the full moon bright towards the south.

After all the turmoil I was now swinging gently in a strangely contrasting silence, floating down and rather higher than I'd expected. This peace was suddenly interrupted by a dazzling searchlight, which probed around as if looking for me. It held me in its blinding beam. I felt naked, vulnerable and powerless hanging there, not knowing what to expect. I raised my arms and wondered, 'Is this it?' But it soon switched off as if satisfied that I'd been located and I was left to watch the Elbe more clearly as I lost height and to worry about landing in the wide waters. I'd never fancied coming down in the water and I pulled the rigging lines as instructed, hoping to spill air from the chute to alter my course. Probably more by luck than anything else, the Elbe disappeared and I braced myself for a landing, south of the river.

The ground seemed to loom up very quickly in the moonlight and it wasn't possible to judge my first parachute landing expertly. I landed rather clumsily and hurt my right ankle on the hard ground but tall growing crops helped to cushion me. I remembered that my first duty was to hide my chute. As I struggled to gather it all up I thought I'd have a good view of a big 'Thousand Raid' but I was surprised. Little was seen or heard and I wondered, 'Where are they?' My watch showed 0110 hours just after landing.

The sheer bulk of the parachute amazed me, first in trying to gather it together and then finding a hiding place for it. I seemed to be in the midst of waist-high wheat or barley. Loaded up with the parachute bulk I set out to find a hiding place, but I couldn't make much progress through the waist-high crops. I found a few bushes and scrabbled away with my hands on the parched ground to hide everything. In addition to my life-saving parachute (how I offered grateful thanks up to the trusty WAAF who'd packed it properly so that it functioned when needed), my Mae West, Irvin suit and parachute harness all had to be disposed of. It was an impossible job with the baked ground. My fingers and nails were damaged and torn. I did the best I could, then set out SW by my little compass. I was dazed with the bang on my head and there was blood on my left leg. On inspection, it was only a graze on the shin – probably caused when the turret was first shattered. My clothing seemed to have bullet holes in it from this and I realised how lucky I was to be alive. It seemed as if the others had 'bought it'.

I had to keep resting and every time I did so I heard constant swishing sounds and would jump up in alarm. Remembering the significance of the searchlight picking me up in its beam and switching off, I felt that my tracks through the crops were being followed and I tried to push on harder. After some time the truth dawned on me. The swishing noises were not pursuers; it was the breeze rustling the crops and I could relax a bit.

I knew I was south of the Elbe and tried to continue SW, thinking my best bet was Holland, over 100 miles away. I probably travelled in circles as my head reeled, my ankle was painful, my shin was bleeding and my fingertips were raw. Then I must have passed out. I woke up in sunlight with civilians bending over me, talking excitedly. They motioned me to follow them towards a nearby village. The atmosphere was quite amicable and after exchanging family snapshots with each other, I was locked in a barn.

Although pretty exhausted I awoke from a short doze to check my position and I soon forced a window and tiptoed quietly round the farm buildings, but the alarm was raised and I ran straight into a group of men as I rounded a corner. I was put into the barn again and this time I was told that troops would soon arrive for me and searched. Everything continued to be pretty friendly. I was given some black bread and a sort of sausage to eat, which I found quite unpalatable, but I gratefully drank from a jug of water.

About midday a *Luftwaffe oberleutnant* arrived with three guards. I had to strip for a more thorough search than the cursory frisk for weapons I'd had before. In the search they'd taken my 'escape pack' and had rumbled my tiny escape compass concealed very cunningly in my short stud, but they hadn't discovered that my pipe held another tiny compass and that my tobacco-pouch contained silk escape maps in the lining.

I was taken by truck towards the direction of Hamburg. I tried to keep a watch on the journey for anything interesting and after a shortish time we passed close to an aerodrome on our left where much activity was going on. I saw Me 110s and Do 217s. I think one of the guards tried to indicate to me by gestures that night-fighters from this airfield had finished us off and I sought some way of identifying this place. Our road was running alongside a railway line on the aerodrome side and as a small station came up, I managed to read the name 'Agathenburg'.

Somewhere along the road towards Hamburg we entered a camp. I was escorted upstairs into an office where a middle-aged *hauptmann* sat at a desk. He spoke briefly to my escorting officer, then the latter departed. The *hauptmann* motioned me to a camp bed at the far end of the office. He completely ignored my presence as he went on with his deskwork. I stretched out and fell asleep while I was trying to recall all the German words I thought I knew. I woke up later and a row was going on. The officer was playing merry hell with three scruffy-looking rankers who were obviously in some trouble. He continued to shout loudly at them before curtly dismissing them. Then he became aware that I'd been watching. In excellent English, smiling, he said,

'You've got to keep these bloody swine down!' Then he asked if I was hungry and a tray soon followed. The coffee tasted bitter but I drank it. There was a plate of some kind of biscuits and these went down well, but more black bread with margarine made me think. I could never take to it.

Afterwards the officer beckoned me to his desk and I sat down facing him. He asked me how I was and got a medical orderly in to dress the slight wound on my left leg, which had continued bleeding. They examined the bullet holes in my trouser legs. The *hauptmann* then started a mild interrogation, but nothing was pressed home when I replied that I could only give my name, rank and serial number. I think I was quite amazed (although I tried not to show it) that this didn't seem to surprise or perturb him at all. He said something about my friends, which I didn't understand properly. After a pause, he said that some of my comrades had been captured and would be joining me soon. I wondered who'd survived from *B-Beer*.

I slept again and woke up when two RAF aircrew walked in. They were Carter, our flight engineer and Crockford, the last minute 'second dickey'. Crockford was slightly wounded and both had lost flying boots in the process of baling out. Carter told me that the skipper and the three Australians had been killed and that no one else had got out. It confirmed the death cries I thought I'd heard just before the intercom had failed.

Transport arrived and we went south to Frankfurt, travelling through Buxtehude to Harburg railway station under charge of a *leutnant* and guards for our rail journey. It was cooler now after the heat of the day, but I was hardly aware of things like the passing of time. I was dazedly wondering about things back in England. Had my wife heard anything yet? I thought of the inevitable 'Missing' telegram she'd get. Had the Committee of Adjustment sealed off my room and possessions at Oakington yet? It was the usual routine for missing blokes. *B-Beer* must have made an awful mess when it crashed.

Harburg station was big and very busy. Our entrance caused some attention, mostly mild in the crowds. I learnt we were going to the interrogation camp near Frankfurt. No more details. There was an hour or two to wait for our train. The officer said in good English that we must not converse with each other. We had nevertheless managed to discuss escape possibilities. The *leutnant* and guards seemed pretty decent and we sat down in a refreshment room where the guards fetched us some soup, with glasses of rather weak beer. They only spoke a few odd words of English. We all exchanged family photos and things were quite friendly. A few onlookers made rude comments and were a bit hostile about the RAF, but the *leutnant* kept a grip on things and sometimes snapped back sharply. I couldn't help thinking back to the pictures of captured *Luftwaffe* types that appeared in our papers in 1940. Perhaps our very grubby and unshaven faces would be splashed in German papers to sustain civilian morale?

In the early hours of 30 July we entrained and left Harburg. Although well south of Hamburg, I thought and hoped that we'd see more signs of bomb damage but it was disappointing. Our route was via Bremen, Diepholz, Osnabrück and Münster. I half dozed but was always hopeful that our escorts might nod off when we slowed down or stopped, but no chance of escape arose. The many lavatory requests were always closely accompanied and they took it in turns to sleep. We tried to spot bomb damage whenever we stopped anywhere in the night, but little could be seen in the dark. It was a slow journey, with many hold-ups. I roused the others specially when we passed through the Ruhr. The visibility was bad. As we crawled through the murk we saw little of Essen. Our escorts shared their rations with us and the guards got out at stations to fetch us hot drinks. We saw bomb damage around the Essen area but it was depressing to see much of the city remaining untouched.

We had time to stretch our legs briefly at Düsseldorf before we ran into Cologne, where we had a long wait in the station. It was time for more food and drinks. Life in the station seemed busy in the night. Some damage to Cologne station had been patched up and I thought back to my first op, which had been to Cologne. I thought that this route down to Frankfurt was a real 'Cook's Tour' for RAF targets that had become so well known. When I peeped outside the station all I got was a view of mainly undamaged property around the cathedral nearby. I tried to draw the *leutnant* out about RAF bombing damage, but he just shrugged his shoulders. I don't think he was really interested in local problems. He lived in Berlin. We followed the Rhine with stops, some of them lengthy, at Bonn, Koblenz and Mainz. We left the train at Frankfurt-am-Main and walked through the crowds out of the station to a nearby tram-stop, where we joined the queue for Oberusel, our destination. The light was going when we left the tram. We struck off along a well-worn track to the left. Lights became visible and the wire of my first PoW camp appeared: *Dulag Luft* Interrogation Centre, before movement to *Stalag Luft III*, Sagan.

Notes

1 Poem in the back of a raid spotter's note book, owned by Roy F. A. Yallop, rear gunner of Lancaster PB366, which crashed on take-off from RAF Graveley (35 PFF Squadron) 24.12.44 with the loss of all the crew.
2 In all, 256 aircraft – 165 from 3 Group and 91 OTU aircraft, were due to be despatched but bad weather over the bases of 1, 4 and 5 Groups prevented their participation. Ultimately, 161 Wellingtons, seventy-one Stirlings and twenty-four Whitleys were despatched. Sixteen Wellingtons and nine Stirlings were lost and four OTU Wellingtons were lost and a Whitley crashed into the sea.

CHAPTER 8

A Canadian in Bomber Command

Jack Woodrow

They served in Canada and many far countries
Battling on the oceans, on land, in the sky
Where for years they engaged in a conflict
To ensure that liberty would never die

'*In Their Country's Service*', from *No Place To Hide*
by Sergeant George 'Ole' Olson RCAF, air gunner

I quit school in Windsor, Ontario, after grade 12 in June 1940 and went to work for Hiram Walkers in the mailroom at $40 a month. After turning 18 on 17 January 1941 I scouted out the RCAF Recruiting Centre in Windsor. In the meantime, I had been moved up to the Accounting department at $60 a month. I approached my boss and told him that those doing identical work at the Ford Motor Company down the road were making $80 a month. I said I wanted the same or I was quitting. His answer was that there would be no raise. I promptly went down to the recruiting centre, passed my medical, joined up and then gave my resignation. On 30 May 1941 I started aircrew training at No. 1 Initial Training School in Toronto where all future pilots and navigators attended. I passed with the rank of Leading Aircraftman and went on to No. 10 Elementary Flying School at Mount Hope in July but I didn't last long. We were flying the Fleet Finch biplane trainer. I had about 12 hours when my instructor let me go solo. On landing I ground looped the aircraft. After a couple of check rides, they decided to wash me out. This was a tremendous disappointment at the time but, who knows, it was best in the long run.

I was sent to KTS (Composite Training School) at Trenton, Ontario, where I re-mustered to observer and waited for a posting. I was very happy when my posting to AOS (Air Observer School) at London finally came through. We flew in the Avro Anson. On my first cross-country flight I got very airsick. That turned out to be the only time. I was never airsick again. At bombing and gunnery school at Fingal we flew in Fairey Battles and did both the bombing and gunnery in them. On 28 February 1942 I received my Observer wing and sergeant's stripes. After Astro Navigation School at Pennfield Ridge I was given Embarkation leave and then it was off to Moncton and Halifax, where I loaded up on canned hams and other suitable food for my relatives in England.

We had good accommodation on the 6-hour voyage to Scotland and after landing at Glasgow we were immediately loaded on a troop train for No. 3 Personnel Reception Centre at Bournemouth. I can truthfully say that the meal on the train was the worst that I had during my stay in the UK. Our meals and accommodation in Bournemouth were in former resort hotels, which had been commandeered by the government. It was pretty nice. However, with nothing much happening, it got very boring. One day we had some excitement when three Me 109s came in and strafed the cliff tops. A Spitfire got one after he had turned for home.

At 23 OTU Pershore, Worcestershire, we flew the Wellington for our operational training. Earlier that year the observer had been responsible for both navigation and bomb aiming. This had caused difficulties of concentration over the target (there was just too much to do and from different crew positions) so the old observer job was divided into navigator and bomb aimer or air bomber. At the same time, the requirement for a second pilot was dropped. Some other member of the crew would be given enough training to fly the aircraft in an emergency. So all of us observers had to decide what new job we wanted. I chose air bomber as I thought this would be the easier of the two jobs. In a way this turned out to be only partially right. The navigator jobs filled up faster and consequently some that wanted to be navigators became bomb aimers. The size of the crew remained at five. Crewing up was an interesting experience. The RAF method was very hit-or-miss but it seemed to work. You were all put into a room and told to crew up. After not too long our all-sergeant crew comprised John Michaud, pilot, from Montreal, Frank Rowan from Orilla, Ontario, was WOP/AG and M. T. 'Mac' McMillan from Vancouver was rear gunner. Our navigator was a sergeant from Alberta. I was promoted to flight sergeant on 28 August 1942.

The food at Pershore was miserable, monotonous servings of stringy mutton and Brussels sprouts. There was one day I still remember. The whole unit was formed into a hollow square on the parade square. The object of attention was a rear gunner who had fallen asleep on operations. He was stripped of his wings and rank badges in a slow impressive ceremony – which was the whole idea I guess. The parade had been dismissed and the young sergeant continued to stand there, alone in the middle of the square, head bowed, eyes averted, absently picking at the strands of thread where his NCO stripes had been. No one approached to offer him comfort. It was very sad.

On 7 October 1942 our crew was posted to 425 *Les Alouettes*, the French-Canadian Squadron flying Wellington IIIs at Dishforth, Yorkshire. The Wellington was the only two-engined bomber still flying on operations. I had been hoping for a four-engine squadron. I think we got posted to 425 Squadron because of our pilot, Johnny Michaud, who was French-Canadian. At that time the ground crew had a high percentage of French-Canadians and the aircrew were about 40 per cent with a majority of the pilots being French-Canadian. Our ground crews were, for the most part, top-notch. Those out at the flights had to service their aircraft for months on end in foul, bitter weather. In any case they did a tremendous job. For the aircraft they were assigned to, they treated it like a member of the family. Dishforth was a permanent RAF station but the airfield had grass runways. We shared the station with 426 'Thunderbird' Squadron. Our squadron CO was Wing Commander Joe St Pierre.

The Vickers Wellington III had two Bristol Hercules engines. It had a maximum speed of 235 mph at 15,000 feet, with a service ceiling of 18,000 feet and a range of 1,275 miles. It had a 1,000 lb load and a 600-mile range with a maximum load of 4,500 lb. That load was more than the B-17 Flying Fortresses could carry but, of course, at a much lower altitude. The Wimpy was not of stressed-skin metal construction. It was built instead on the 'geodetic' principle of countless strips of metal in a basket weave pattern, then fabric-covered. It could take lots of punishment. In fact, it was said that it was built like the proverbial 'brick shithouse'. Because of the Wellington's limited range compared with the four-engine Lancasters and Halifaxes, our targets were limited to the Ruhr, Frankfurt, Kiel and other targets in that area. The .303 calibre machine-guns were as useless as peashooters against the four 20 mm cannons on the attacking Me 110s or Focke-Wulf 190s. The only navigation aid on the Wellington was *Gee*. We sometimes used Astro navigation but only in special circumstances. *Gee* was an instrument that allowed a navigator to calculate the bomber's location by receiving pulse signals from a trio of widely spread out stations in Britain. *Gee* calculated the difference between the signals, giving the navigator an immediate fix of his own position. The range was about 400 miles, which meant it couldn't be used much beyond the Ruhr Valley and a few northern ports. However, *Gee* was pretty well jammed by the time we reached the enemy coast.

The Lancasters and Halifaxes had *H2S*. It was self-contained and thus independent of any transmitting stations on the ground. *H2S* sent a directional beam of high energy directly toward the earth, the beam rotating with its antenna approximately once per second. The aircraft's antenna picked up reflections from these beams. These reflections appeared on a cathode-ray tube. Each signal received registered as a spot on the screen. The various reflections created the necessary contrast to 'paint a picture' of the terrain below. It sounds simple but it wasn't. Operators had to practise to interpret the screen accurately. Also, at its early stage it had a terrible record of serviceability.

There was lots of squadron training to be done before we were ready for operations. New crews were often put on minelaying trips to help them get experience. This was especially true for Wellington crews because of its shorter range. A favourite target was the Friesian Islands off the coast of Holland and Germany. There was a lot of enemy coastal shipping and the mines caused a lot of damage. The normal load was two 1,500 lb mines, which were also called 'Vegetables'. Our first trip was cancelled twice because of weather and we finally went on the third night, on 16/17 November. However, our station did not have the capability of loading the mines, so we were sent to Middleton St George to be loaded up.[1]

Right after planting our two 1,500 lb mines, the captain asked me to take over the navigator's job. I ended up navigating the aircraft home. It was a satisfactory and a very memorable trip but ended in a blaze of ignominy. Each day as part of our flying rations we were given two chocolate bars. So when we finally went on our trip, I had six chocolate bars. Anyway, through normal excitement and nervousness from it being our first trip and a problem with our navigator, I ate all six bars on the way home. Then I started to feel pretty sick. Right after landing, I jumped out of the aircraft and immediately upchucked on the dispersal pad. Very embarrassing.

I don't really know what happened, but it seems our navigator got into a 'blue-funk' and was not capable of doing the job. We returned to Dishforth and I never saw him again. Later on we heard he was accused of LMF and whisked off the station. I heard from him several months later. He told he had been returned to Canada, discharged and then drafted into the Army. I never heard from him again and I feel very sorry that I did not make a greater effort to keep in touch. I have always felt disgusted with what the Air Force did with him. I think they should have been more understanding and compassionate instead of sending him home in disgrace as LMF. No rehabilitation was attempted. Maybe that first trip was an anomaly and he would have been OK with some help from the rest of us. But he never got the chance. I've always had the niggling thought that but for the grace of God, there go I. It was the saddest episode of my Air Force career.

I heard very little talk about LMF while I was on operations and never had any connection with it other than our navigator. I think there is a fine line between battle fatigue and being a coward. There are, of course, two sides to the argument. The Air Force had to fight it because if you could get out of flying just by saying you didn't want to fly anymore, where would it all end. I think they had to have a strict policy, but it should have been conducted with more compassion.

We now had to get a replacement navigator. He turned out to be Flying Officer Don LaRiviera from Brockville. I think he had about ten or eleven trips. I don't know why he was available but it was our good fortune. He was top-notch.

Typically, after taking off the first part of the trip was usually uneventful. After a short time the navigator would give the pilot a course that would take us over the coast at the proper point. He would then spend time trying to determine the true winds. I would ensure everything was right with the bomb-sight and the bomb fusing. The wireless operator would check his equipment and the gunner would check his guns after crossing the coast. We would continue climbing over the North Sea. On crossing the enemy coast we would usually be at our desired altitude. Flying at 18,000 feet in mid-winter could be a bone-chilling experience. This was especially true for the rear gunner who sat in his partially open turret. We had available thick socks, warm sweaters, long underwear, electrically heated inner suits, fleece-lined outer jackets and lined flying boots.

The whole aircraft rattled and vibrated from the piston engines. Oxygen masks were mandatory and we wore microphones and earphones to be able to converse. The aircraft seemed to roll and yaw constantly. The degree of stability depended as much on the pilot's strength as upon his skill because the controls were not power-assisted and it required all his energy to heave the aircraft around. And all the time the constant vibration hammered at you so that even a relatively uneventful trip seemed to get you into a very fatigued condition.

After leaving the target area, you had to be very aware of the fighters that would be following the bomber stream home. The German fighter defence was strong and well organised. Their radar-directed 'sector defence' was very effective at picking up individual incoming or homebound bombers. The .303 calibre machine-guns of Bomber Command were as useless as peashooters against the four 20 mm cannons on the attacking Me 110s or Focke-Wulf 190s. Consequently, the rear gunner's main job was to keep a sharp lookout for enemy fighters. In fact, seeing them first was the key to survival. The gunner would continually move his guns across, up and down, making quick reversals whenever he thought he saw something in the dark. He used a control column to turn the guns since movement was powered by hydraulics. The triggers for his four machine-guns were also on that control column. The area directly in front of him had no glass for better visibility. When he looked into the gunsight he saw an illuminated ring with an illuminated dot in the centre of the ring.

You really didn't relax until you were halfway across the North Sea. At that point I would start to think that we had another op under our belt. Every trip seemed to be filled with tension, which was unrelieved until the aircraft finally came to a halt at our dispersal pad.

My main job on ops, of course, was to drop the bombs as accurately as possible over the target. However, during a trip I had several other duties. I was the front gunner if the need ever arose. This did not happen very often. Near the end the front turret was faired in to decrease the drag on the aircraft. On 425 Squadron, one of the bomb aimer's jobs was to act as second pilot. This involved learning the aircraft's various systems and also practising certain manoeuvres so you could take over the aircraft in an emergency. We often had to cross the coast on the way home at a certain point. This was made much simpler if the North Star was visible. With my astro navigation training, reading it with the sextant was easy. The sextant's reading gave the latitude directly, so it ensured that we were crossing the coast at the right point. From the co-pilot's position, I would map-read and pinpoint identifying landmarks. Finally, from the astrodome I would help the rear gunner watch for enemy aircraft. So you can see that I was kept busy most of the time.

For the dropping of the bombs, as we neared the target, I ensured the bombs were fused and the bomb doors open. With the aiming point or the PFF markers in sight, the run-up began. I took command of the direction of the aircraft with 'Right' or 'Left, Left' or 'Steady' commands to the pilot. You could feel the aircraft being buffeted by the turbulence caused by the bomber stream and the flak. I had to try to keep the centre line of the bombsight on the target. Long fingers of light would sweep past as they tried to cone us. Sometimes a brilliant flash would blind me for a moment. Then finally,

'Bombs Gone'. The lightened Wellington seemed to leap up. The skipper had to struggle to keep it straight and level for a few more seconds to let the cameras record the bomb-bursts if possible. Then I would take a quick look to make sure all the bombs had released, close the bomb-bay doors and shut off the cameras. Then we turned for home.

Our trip to drop mines in Brest harbour on 2/3 January 1943 was our first trip in the New Year but the mines were not dropped due to bad visibility preventing pinpointing and the *Gee* pulses also faded. We landed at Middle Wallop in southern England and returned to base on 3 January. Our next trip on 9/10 January was to drop mines off the Friesians again. We planted two 1,500 lb mines from 800 feet and saw both parachutes open. On trip number five on 14/15 January we dropped mines using *Gee* from 800 feet at Brest harbour. Visibility was good and the rear gunner saw the parachutes open. We landed at Harwell in southern England because of range difficulties. We took off from Harwell for our sixth trip and bombed Lorient from 15,000 feet with seven 500 lb bombs. Fires were observed. We landed back at Dishforth.

For the first time on 26/27 January when we went to Lorient, we carried the 'Cookie', which the squadron had just started to receive. This was the first of the so-called 'light case' bombs, a mild steel tube into which molten RDX explosive was poured. This resulted in a bomb weighing 4,000 lb. It became a major weapon in Bomber Command's arsenal – a bomb noted for its tremendous blast. Bigger and more powerful 'Cookies' would appear later in the war carried by the Lancasters and the Halifaxes. They were ideal weapons for area bombing and were perfect partners for the incendiaries. These were 4 lb bombs packed into containers that broke open when dropped. There was also a 30-pound phosphorus-filled incendiary bomb. Our bomb loads could vary considerably depending on what was being bombed. It could vary from one 'Cookie' to different combinations of 250, 500, and 1,000 lb bombs mixed with incendiaries.

We bombed from 15,000 feet with the 'Cookie'. There was no cloud but it was hazy. We had good visibility. We saw our bombs burst in the southern part of town. There were plenty of fires on both sides of the river. Defences were negligible over the target, but there was much more flak when crossing the coast. I noted in my log, 'A successful trip'.[2]

According to the Intelligence Officer the purpose of the trip to Oldenburg on 30 January was 'to create despondency and despair among the refugees from Cologne'. There was supposed to be low cloud cover that we could hop into if required. We had bad weather but we didn't have our low cloud cover. I noted in my log, 'Another Met cock-up. Who thought up this operation must have had rocks in his head. Pretty stupid'. Under these conditions we were allowed to turn back without bombing Oldenburg. I had some fun on this trip. I was in the front turret and shot at anything that moved – livestock, dogs, etc. Didn't see any people.[3]

Trip nine was to Lorient again on 4/5 February. We carried a full load of incendiaries on this trip. Visibility was good and the bombs fell in the target area. There was intense and accurate light and heavy flak and the searchlights were numerous. We saw large fires all over the area. On 8 February I was commissioned as a pilot officer and I moved into the Officers' Quarters. My room-mate was Pilot Officer Bill Maxwell from Detroit, who was a rear gunner on 426 Squadron.

We led strange lives, residing in reasonably comfortable civilised surroundings. This was especially true at Dishforth, which was a permanent RAF station. We had lots of free time when we weren't required to fly. The nearest town to Dishforth was Boroughbridge. We would visit the neighbouring pubs and maybe a little further afield to go to dance halls. There were lots of nice-looking girls. We also spent a lot of time in the Mess. The food on the squadron was good. The only complaint would be the Brussels sprouts. They must have grown in profusion in England because there never seemed to be a shortage. We got so many that it was quite a few years after the war before I could eat one again. Many stations had four meals a day. Tea was roughly from 3:30 to 4:30 and supper from 7 to 8. As a sergeant I was billeted in a two-bedroom Permanent Married Quarters row house with three other Senior NCOs. We slept one in each bedroom and two in the living room. All eating and entertaining was done in the Sergeants' Mess.

Our days had a familiar routine. We got out of bed when we woke up. At the Mess, a quick look at the Battle Order would show who was on operations that night. If you were on, it usually meant a flight test had to be done to make sure the aircraft was ready. The briefings were usually in the late afternoon. The navigators and the wireless operators were briefed ahead of the rest of us because they had more information to absorb. At the briefing, the Intelligence Officer would talk about the defences. The weatherman would tell us what to expect in the way of weather. In both cases, there was a lot of guesswork. The Navigation Leader would discuss the route and the Bombing Leader would describe the target and the bomb load. These would be followed by short 'pep' talks from the squadron and station commanders. From this moment until the end of the operation everyone in that briefing room was incommunicado to the outside world.

Then we went to supper. After that we picked up our parachutes. Pilot chutes were fixed to the harness so that they formed a seat, which he sat on. The other crewmembers carried their chutes as a separate brown-canvas parcel, which before use had to be fixed to their chest by metal clips. Each crewman would carry the chute with him wherever he moved. The pilots didn't have to remember their parachute but, on the other hand, moving around in the aircraft's cramped interior with a pilot-style chute was difficult. We picked up our flying gear in the crew locker rooms and put it on. We then went out and got into trucks and drove across the airfield to be deposited beside our aircraft, usually just as dusk was falling.

After any necessary consultations with the ground crew, we climbed aboard and took up our various crew stations. The pilot proceeded with the engine start-up. This pumped life into the hydraulic systems and the gunners tested turret rotation and gun controls. Each crewman did their pre-flight drill and tested oxygen supplies and intercom connections. When it was time to go, our fully laden aircraft moved slowly from its parking pad and took its place in the line-up on the perimeter track as the line moved slowly toward the end of the runway in use. Then you waited for the green light from the Aldis lamp from the control van located beside the end of the runway, before turning onto the run-up place.

The run-up procedure did not take very long and we were soon turning onto the end of the runway. With Dishforth being a short length field, the brakes have to hold the aircraft until the tail is up. Then the brakes are released. There is a gradual surge as the skipper applies full power. The Wellington rapidly gains speed as it goes down the runway. The skipper compensates for torque swing with the throttle. Soon we are airborne. Then the pilot retracts the landing gear and then the flaps as we start our long climb to operational height. Ops were often scrubbed at the last minute. I think this happened close to half the time.

On 19/20 February we bombed Wilhelmshaven on PFF markers with a mixed bomb load. The PFF was the elite group in Bomber Command. It had the best crews and the latest and best equipment. Their mission was to mark the target with flares, either ground or air. Then the rest of the force bombed on those flares. This was to improve the bombing accuracy and it did. However, there were still many problems – most of them caused by our constant enemy, the weather. There was 8/10ths cloud and smoke over the target. Intense heavy and light flak was encountered but it was a very successful trip.[4]

A trip to the Friesians to drop mines followed on 20/21 February. Our pilot made a very rough landing. I was standing at the astrodome watching for other aircraft when this happened. The jolt pitched me over the main spar through the flimsy folding doors into the navigator's compartment. I was partially stunned but we were all in one piece. This bad landing strained the main spar and earned Johnny an endorsement in his logbook. I thought that this was very unfair since he landed under very difficult conditions.

On 24/25 February we used an overload tank to bomb Wilhelmshaven on PFF markers again. Our load was three 500 lb bombs plus six cans of incendiaries. Our thirteenth trip followed on 26/27 February 1943 to Cologne. Any target in the Ruhr Valley struck a chill into any aircrew. It had flak guns by the thousands and radar-controlled searchlights and endless miles of factories spewing out a permanent layer of haze. Along with the often lousy weather, it presented very difficult targets. The sight of a city under heavy attack was a totally new experience and like nothing you had seen before. It was like a huge fireworks display with the sound turned off. The sound you heard was the monotonous roar of the engines interspersed by the thuds of near misses and the clatter of bits of shrapnel hitting the skin of the aircraft. When you saw a target under attack for the first time, you were convinced that no aircraft could fly through the flak unscathed. Then you would see a bomber blow up and go falling out of the sky. You felt a twinge of guilt because a disaster suffered by another crew helped tip the scales of chance a bit in your favour. The other problem was the congestion over the target.[5] The RAF system was to concentrate their attack into a few minutes in an attempt to overwhelm the defences. You had to keep your eyes open to avoid collisions. You just strained all the time looking for the silhouettes of other aircraft with no lights on. We bombed on a good concentration of PFF markers. There were lots of both light and heavy flak and some searchlights. Searchlights could be as unsettling as being shot at. If an aircraft got nailed by one, others would quickly get you and form a cone. Then the aircraft became the centre of fire for the flak. This could be very bad. Immediate and harsh evasive action was required to escape.[6]

On the trip to St Nazaire on 28 February the PFF markers were good. Flak was heavy over the target and fires were seen for 70 miles after we left. We didn't fly another op for a while. While on operations I took advantage of the Nuffield Leave Scheme several times. The Foundation paid for your accommodation at many nice hotels in England. This usually included breakfast. On one occasion I stayed at the Queen's Hotel in Torquay. On my first evening there I struck up an acquaintance with an Aussie and a New Zealander. They were just finishing their week's leave. They offered to show me all the best drinking spots in Torquay. To celebrate their final night, they persuaded me to join them in a down-under drink. It was a pint of stout with some lemon juice to alleviate the heavy taste of stout. I found it enjoyable and drank it all night. The next morning I woke up with a dandy hangover. When the little lady came around with the morning cup of tea, my hand was shaking so bad I couldn't hold the cup. The little lady commiserated with me, thinking that I was suffering from some kind of operational 'shakes'.

Bomber Command losses were heavy. According to records 125,000 flew in Bomber Command. Fatal casualties, including those who died as PoWs, were 55,000. When you add the other PoWs and those wounded on operations or in accidents, the total casualty rate was nearly 74,000. It is a casualty rate that compares with the worst slaughters in First World War trenches. To undertake a tour of thirty operations, which was the requirement for a tour with Bomber Command in the central period of the war of 1941–3 and the first half of 1944, was to have only about a 50 per cent chance of surviving. The stats seemed to show that the chances of a crew surviving a first tour got much better if it could survive the first five or six operations. After all our training, the deciding factor for survival seemed to be experience. When we started, we had no idea of what we were getting into. Well into the tour, you started to count up the crews that had not returned since you had started. Then you began to realise the lousy odds you were fighting.

Having said all that, perhaps the most remarkable fact is that despite the cold, the dark, the lousy weather conditions, the flak, fighters and searchlights, the loss of comrades, the constant strain and fear, the general morale remained solid. I think most of us handled the strain well. We knew that ops were dangerous and stressful and that some crews would be lost, but we also knew the trip was necessary. In my experience, the number of aircrew who from loss of nerve were unable to continue operating was near zero on our squadron. Statistics show that it was less than one in 200 for the whole command. For my crew, I think we went through stages. During the first few trips we realised that we had got ourselves into something very dangerous. I think our morale sagged a bit. Then we entered a stage of confidence. The enemy had done his best and we were still around. I think we all felt we had the measure of the job. Then came a stage of discouragement. We realised how

Body of an RAF airman shot down over the Reich. (via CONAM)

lucky we had been so far and it was going to be tough to complete our tour. Then came the point when we might just complete the tour. By this time we had become highly experienced. We worked together as a highly efficient team. We each knew what to do and when.

To my knowledge the main effect of the stress from operations was over-drinking – whether in the Mess, in the local pub or when on leave. It could have a long-term effect. I know a couple of squadron mates who turned into alcoholics stretching into the post-war years. I don't know what finally happened to them. I certainly drank too much, but luckily I suffered no long-term consequences. I think we all developed an attitude of fatalism. You always thought it would happen to someone else. Deaths were cases of bad luck or bad timing. I think our age helped. I was 19 when I started on operations and finished by age 21. A doctor told me that when you are on ops, your system is all keyed up and the op is your release. When you are off flying your system is still keyed up but there is no release. So most of us used drinking as the release. It made sense to me. I did notice some changes in a few of the guys. The odd one who was normally noisy became very quiet while a shy one would become boisterous.

Of 125,000 men who flew in Bomber Command, fatal casualties, including those who died as PoWs, were 55,000. (via CONAM)

Over the North Sea on 29/30 March *en route* to Bochum we had engine trouble and had to abort the trip and on 4/5 April we could not attack the target at Kiel due to bad weather and 10/10ths clouds. No markers were seen. Our bomb load of incendiaries was jettisoned at the north end of Sylt Island because we could have run out of gas to take them back. We landed at Acklington in northern England. It was a very disappointing trip.[7]

Trip sixteen was to Duisburg on 8/9 April. We had 10/10ths cloud to 19,000 feet. No PFF flares were seen and we bombed on ETA. The flak was heavy. Of course, bombing results could not be observed. It was certainly very poor weather for operations. Weather predicting over Europe was far from a science. They were sometimes 180 degrees off. This unpredictable weather cut down on our effectiveness greatly. Sometimes, if there were no PFF flare or markers, we had to bomb blind. Sometimes we brought the bombs back. It was all very discouraging. The other effect of the weather was trying to return to base. Sometimes it would be socked in with fog and the only clear airfields

The dead crew of a Lancaster. To undertake a tour of thirty operations, which was the requirement for a tour with RAF Bomber Command in 1941–43 and the first half of 1944, was to have only about a 50 per cent chance of surviving. (via CONAM)

would be too far away as you could be running low on fuel. You stacked up over your own or some other field and hoped for the best. Preference, of course, was given to those with wounded on board or those about to run out of fuel. All in all, it was very nerve wracking.

Trip seventeen to Frankfurt on 10/11 April was fraught with 10/10ths cloud at 8,000 feet. We bombed from 17,000 feet. The flak was heavy and increased during the attack. There were no sky markers. A twin-engined fighter attacked us 40 miles west of the target. Corkscrew action was taken and the fighter was lost. The major defence for a bomber's survival lay in evasive action or 'corkscrewing', which had been developed by the RAF. It was practised over England with cameras instead of guns in both the bombers and the attacking Spitfires and Hurricanes. The gunner had to be alert to spot the faster-moving enemy fighters flying around the bomber stream. Then when sighted, he gave the warning 'Fighter attack, prepare to corkscrew'. Then at around 600 yards, which was the point when the fighter would open fire, the gunner would give the command 'Corkscrew port, go' or 'Corkscrew starboard go', depending on the side from which the attack was being made. If a port attack, the pilot would then commence the corkscrew by applying violent port rudder, port aileron and diving elevators, which had the effect of instantly removing the bomber from the fighter's gunsight. After diving about 1,000 feet, the pilot would recover from the descent by climbing in the opposite direction to recover his height and course to the target or home. Hopefully, we had lost the fighter. We had an advantage in this struggle. Our pilot, Johnny Michaud, was extremely strong and could carry out this evasive manoeuvre without tiring.

In the latter part of April we were informed that the squadron was being sent to North Africa [with tropicalised Mk X Wellingtons] to be part of 331 Wing along with 424 'Tiger' and 427 'Lion' Squadrons RCAF. May 1943 was a busy month. We got our new tropicalised Mk X Wellingtons and we were outfitted with tropical clothing. We went to many lectures on what to expect in our new theatre of operations. As it turned out, we had several crew changes and I was the only member of the crew who would do the whole tour with the pilot, Johnny Michaud.

Criticism of the Bomber Command bombing campaign surfaced after the war. The two main criticisms were the lack of effectiveness and the lack of morality of the campaign. Certainly, Bomber Command's effectiveness was reduced by the terrible weather conditions and lack of certain equipment. However, in the early part of the war, Bomber Command was quite literally the only force that could carry the war to the Germans and do damage to the German homeland. The defensive effort forced on the Germans justified it. According to Speer, the *Reich*'s Munitions Minister, it tied up many thousands of Germans defending Germany and repairing bomb damage. As for morality, we were told what the targets were. With area bombing, we knew civilians were being killed. But killing people did not enter your mind. From the air, the human factor does not mean what it would to an Army soldier. When you are in a bomber you don't see people, you see things – buildings, bridges, docks.

Like most aircrew I don't remember feeling any particular emotion toward the Germans. I had ended up as a bomb aimer and it was my duty to drop the bombs as accurately as possible. It was all sort of remote and impersonal. Our operations encouraged the British who had suffered so much and seen so much damage to their country. I had relatives living in the East End of London, which suffered greatly. I was staying with them once in 1944 when a V-1 buzz bomb came over and hit not very far away. On leave in London, I was always being thanked by the Londoners for giving it back to the Germans. I've never lost a moment's sleep from feeling guilty about bombing German civilians. They started it.

Notes

1. Sixty-five aircraft carried out minelaying to various places from Lorient to the Friesian Islands. Two Wellingtons and one Stirling were lost.
2. 157 aircraft were despatched. Two Wellingtons and one Lancaster were lost.
3. Of the nineteen Wellingtons of 4 Group and seventeen Bostons, which went to many places in Germany and Holland, only two Wellingtons and one Boston found targets to bomb. Four Wellingtons were lost.

4. Some 338 aircraft were despatched. Twelve bombers FTR (failed to return). Though Woodrow believed it was a very successful trip the Pathfinder marking caused the Main Force to bomb north of Wilhelmshaven. Following the raid it was discovered that the Pathfinders had been issued with out-of-date maps that did not show up-to-date town developments.
5. Some 427 aircraft were despatched to Cologne this night.
6. Ten aircraft – four Wellingtons, three Lancasters, two Halifaxes and one Stirling – were lost. Most of the bombs dropped fell to the SW of Cologne.
7. Some 577 aircraft were despatched. Twelve aircraft were lost. Thick cloud and strong winds made marking very difficult over the target.

CHAPTER 9

'If We Could Survive That, We Could Survive Anything!'

Derek Smith DFC

Eastward they climb, black shapes against the grey
Of falling dusk, gone with the nodding day
From English fields.
Not theirs the sudden glow
Of triumph that their fighter-brothers know;
Only to fly through the cloud, through storm, through night
Unerring and to keep their purpose bright,
Nor turn until, their dreadful duty done,
Westward they climb to race the awakened sun.

'*Night Bombers*', Anon

Approaching the middle of 1942, the Bomber Command Operational Training Units (OTUs) of 91 and 92 Groups were mainly equipped with time-expired operational squadron Wellingtons, Whitleys and Hampdens, with the Wellingtons or 'Wimpys' in the vast majority. Consequently, the C-in-C, Air Marshal Arthur Harris, wishing to put the numbers up towards the magical 'one thousand' put 365[1] of these into the air with an assortment of instructor and pupil crews for the operation against Cologne on 30/31 May 1942. Presumably, a similar number were dispatched for the second such major effort against Essen on 1/2 June,[2] during which there was no repeat of the success on Cologne due to haze and low cloud. In both cases the loss rates were acceptably low, being 3.9 per cent and 3.2 per cent. Losses among the trainee crews were not outside the norm,[3] probably because the German defences were not prepared for the magnitude of the efforts. Thus encouraged, these ancient aircraft were used again on 25/26 June against Bremen. The overall loss rate was 5 per cent, but 91 Group lost twenty-three of the 198 Wellingtons and Whitleys dispatched (a loss rate of 11.6 per cent). On 28/29 July 91 Group aircraft made up part of the force briefed for Hamburg, but only three bombed because of a bad weather recall – four Wellingtons were lost plus one Whitley, which crashed in the sea, and the overall loss rate was 15.2 per cent. On July 31/1 August 92 Group aircraft were part of the force dispatched to Düsseldorf with a loss rate of 4.6 per cent, but 92 Group lost eleven of its aircraft – 10.5 per cent.

During this time I had arrived at 25 OTU Finningley on 16 June, together with Eric 'Sammy' Sampson (aged 23). Sammy was a fellow sergeant observer with whom I had become friendly while sharing a cabin on the troopship *Orcades* on return from training in Canada and a room at the Bournemouth Aircrew Receiving Centre. By further good fortune, this was the era of the introduction of bomb aimers on heavy bombers to relieve the increasing load on the navigation side. Sammy opted to re-muster so that we could crew together. After further intensive training in our respective fields, our group were shut in a conference room on 10 July and by the RAF's tried and trusted method, instructed to 'Sort yourselves out and get yourselves crewed up!' This we did and emerged, some time later, as an all-sergeant crew. Sammy was the observer/bomb aimer. Gordon Oldham, a Rhodesian (22), a part-time store-keeper in partnership with his father and a taxidermist in his spare time, was our pilot. He was a great guy, very generous but with a good head for money. His girl friend was a ferry pilot in Africa and she had the George Medal. John (Ginger) Lees, our wireless operator, was a Lancastrian from Ashton-under-Lyne and the Old Father Time at 28. Maurice (Doc) Root-Reid, our gunner, was a newly qualified doctor in civvy street. He was a born humourist and it was impossible to feel cheesed off when he was around. He was a trainee observer, but while training on Bothas crashed and had to re-muster as an air gunner. He was miles above the usual run of air gunners and was 27. At 20 I was the baby of the crew and the observer/navigator. The training continued while we got to know each other on the ground and we eventually flew together as a crew for the first time on 15 August 1942. This flight marked the end of our supervised training in the air and we moved over to the Finningley satellite at Bircotes on 18 August to complete our basic operational training. We were beginning to regard ourselves as a proper crew, itching to get into the action but blissfully ignorant of the losses incurred by those who had come before us.

We enjoyed the happy, relaxed atmosphere of the station, which was largely due to being under the amiable command of Squadron Leader Roderick A. B. 'Babe' Learoyd VC of Dortmund-Ems Canal fame.[4] For the nineteen days following, we must have worked fairly hard. We carried out nine cross-country flights of ever-increasing length to the last three, all at night, two in excess of 6 hours and on the third we had to abort after four hours flying time due to a radio failure. Now, with our fifty-plus hours together we thought ourselves to be something of the first class crew we would eventually become but, really, we were very wet behind the ears and our Wimpy ICs were hardly in the first flush of youth! It was in this condition that we were destined to go to war for our baptism of fire in pursuance of the continuing policy of using half-trained crews in clapped out aircraft, to boost numbers.

On 10 September we were roused with the news that we were to operate as a crew that night and in my diary I wrote, 'Bags of panic on the whole station as soon as it was known that we were operating 18 aircraft detailed for the operation against Düsseldorf. Pukka briefing in true OTU style. We were briefed to cruise at a speed of 130 knots (149 mph) at a height of 14,000 ft with a bomb load of 4×500 lb'. My next diary note was 'Take off at 2000 hours watched by a good percentage of the station but only ten of the 18 aircraft got off the deck! Climbed to 10,500 feet over the North Sea but could get no higher with an IAS [indicated airspeed] of 100 knots! Were understandably north of target on ETA but were not entirely sure as none of us had ever seen a target before!'

The met winds must have been good because I had got no sort of reliable fix after leaving base but here we were, faced by what was obviously the target but still at some distance. In a letter to my father I said we were faced with four cones of searchlights so we headed towards what appeared to be the widest gap, but being well below the rest of the force, we were sitting ducks. Just as we were at a point midway between the two cones, a blue master beam swung on to us followed by about thirty others, holding us for what seemed to be a lifetime but was about 5 minutes.

Gordon was doing everything he knew with our ancient craft, losing more of what little height we had with what appeared to be most of the defences firing at us. We could hear the flak bursting while weaving violently through the smoke of the bursts and then, by some miracle, we were out of the searchlights and shell-bursts but down to 7,000 feet with a maximum IAS of just over 100 knots. The gods were certainly on our side as, by a further miracle, we found ourselves perfectly positioned for a quick bombing run on the target indicators followed by an untroubled run south-west from the target.

We now took stock, expecting to find considerable damage, but all we appeared to have sustained were two holes in the fuselage. My diary records 'We set course for home and seemed to be all on our lonesome'. This was not surprising at our 7,000 feet, which the aircraft refused to improve on. Over the Dutch coast an enemy fighter was sighted, but fortunately he didn't spot us and over the sea we picked up a J-beam and flew along it. The fighter pilot was probably looking up rather than down and J-beams were homing beams for the benefit of returning aircraft. I would imagine our landfall should have been between Southwold and Cromer but the next thing we heard, on the R/T, was 'Unidentified aircraft, unidentified aircraft, do you hear me? You are approaching the London balloon barrage – steer course 045 degrees'.

We assumed it was us and Gordon replied, 'Thank you. Steering 045' and we heard no more. Whoever it was that called was certainly our guardian angel. All in all, the Gods were with us that night because by steering 045 with a duff compass, we found a good pin point. We got an uncertain view of the Thames Estuary but then started to pick up airfield beacons and arrived back at Bircotes at 02.45 – about an hour after the next last and they were just about giving up on us. It transpired that only six of our ten had reached the target and two of those were missing which was 20 per cent of those who took off or 33 per cent of those who got there. The raid was a considerable success but the loss rate was 7.1 per cent of the force. There are no inclusive figures for OTU

Pilot Officer Gordon Oldham, pilot of Lancaster I QR-K W4236 K-King. Oldham was KIA on his second tour on 61 Squadron (Derek Smith)

aircraft but Upper Heyford lost five out of thirteen (38 per cent) so I expect ours was a fair average. To the best of my knowledge, OTU aircraft were only used once more on Main Force German targets and that was a week later on Essen when the loss rate was an unacceptable 10.6 per cent. It would seem that the message had got home. The cost of training a crew plus the loss of an aircraft, however ancient, delivering just four 500 lb bombs just did not make sense or counterbalance the small propaganda of numbers.

For ourselves, the miracle was confirmed. We had only the two holes already discovered but on inspection the next day it was found that the aircraft had a considerable oil leak with consequent loss of oil pressure plus faults in boost control, petrol gauges, cylinder head temperatures and a fault in the compass. In our predicament of height and speed a more experienced crew would have aborted but I suppose we were very green and determined to prove ourselves. Obviously, when we saw a fighter over the Dutch coast we must have been far south of that, towards France. Apparently, the enemy had bent the J-beam as we had theirs and *Darkie* turned out to be Manston!

In a letter to my father at the War Office in London where he was an mechanical engineer (the contents would have worried my mother), I said:

> If we could survive that, we could survive anything! Last night we were taking our bow over Germany at Düsseldorf. As you will have heard from the radio it was a large-scale show. We flew as a crew, which was a good thing as none of us had ever been under fire before and I must say the boys put up a grand show. We had an oil leak, which was not discovered, until our return. The Wimpy is supposed to cruise at 130 indicated air speed but owing to the leak we could only get 110. We were supposed to attack at 14,000 feet but could only get 10,000. It was very quiet all the way to the target, although I must say Jerry has very elaborate dummy fires and decoy towns. Anyway, we reached the target at 10,000 feet down below everybody else and then the fun and games began. We had to get through four cones of searchlights to get to the target so we aimed for the widest gap. We were just in the middle, weaving like hell when the purple master searchlight swung smack on to us followed by about thirty others. I think we must have been coned for about 5 minutes but it seemed a lifetime with, what seemed every gun in

The all sergeant crew of Wellington IC X9930 PP-B at Bircotes, the satellite of 25 OTU Finningley, after their first op, on 10/11 September 1942 as one of eighteen crews of 25 OTU for the raid on Düsseldorf. L–R: Gordon Oldham (22), pilot; Derek Smith, observer/navigator; Eric 'Sammy' Sampson, bomb aimer; Maurice 'Doc' Root-Reid, gunner and John 'Ginger' Lees, WOp/AG. Their op to Düsseldorf ended their OTU course and after leave and a posting to 1660 Heavy Conversion Unit at Swinderby in 5 Group, Oldham's crew gained two additional members before flying Lancasters on 61 Squadron at Syerston. Gordon Oldham was KIA on his second tour on 26/27 April 1944 when Lancaster I ME679 DX-K of 57 Squadron flown by Squadron Leader M. I. Boyle DFC was involved in a collision with Lancaster I of 44 Rhodesian Squadron piloted by Flying Officer G. W. Oldham DFC. There was only one survivor from Boyle's crew. All seven of Oldham's crew died (Derek Smith)

Germany firing at us. We could hear the flak bursting and were flying through the smoke of it but we were only holed twice. Gordon did some wonderful piloting and we were down to 7,000 feet before we finally lost them. One good thing was that there was not the least sign of panic and the boys regarded it as a free Brocks Benefit [How naïve we were. We obviously had much to learn.] Anyway, we got out of it and made our run over the target to drop our four 500 pounders. We then made off at the terrific speed of 100 knots!

Over Holland Doc saw a fighter but we managed to evade it and reached base having had trouble with petrol gauges, boost control, cylinder head temperatures and the compass. She certainly was a ropey kite but we made it although we arrived back an hour after the others because of these faults. According to the radio it was one of the heaviest barrages ever, well if we never get worse we will be OK. We have a great crew and will come through every time. We lost two kites last night, both crews off our course, including a good friend of mine, Stan Southgate.[5]

My father had asked me to tell him the truth of how it was, so hence this fairly graphic description of the experience. It is an example of how silly it was to send OTU crews to heavily defended targets in OTU aircraft.[6] I was never again to be in such close proximity to shot and shell. In fact, the total of hearing shell bursts in all the operations to follow did not add up to that experienced in that first 5 minutes of our baptism on 10/11 September 1942. It was one of the last times that OTU crews were sent to German targets because the losses of new crews in poor aircraft were too high. I did not tell my father that on our return, because of the duff compass, we had completely lost our bearings, as we had no *Gee*. We knew we had crossed a stretch of water but quite where was a mystery.

The Düsseldorf operation ended our OTU course and after a seven days' leave we were posted to 1660 Heavy Conversion Unit at Swinderby in 5 Group for conversion first to the dreaded Manchester and then on to Lancasters. These both carried crews of seven so we acquired David 'Woody' Attwood, an amiable individual from Tewkesbury, as flight engineer and Frank Emerson, a TT rider and aspiring Wimbledon speedway rider, as mid upper gunner. Both fitted the team of all sergeants very well and we became a very happy crew.

We arrived at 61 (Lancaster) Squadron, 5 Group Bomber Command, at Syerston to find that it was a pre-war permanent station on the Fosse Way with two Lancaster squadrons (the other was 106 and commanded by Wing Commander Guy Gibson DSO* DFC*). The Station Commander was Gus Walker, at the age of 26 the youngest Group Captain in the RAF. We found we had joined a crack squadron, which considered itself to be among the cream of 5 Group which, in its turn, considered itself to be superior to all other groups, although 8 (Pathfinder) Group had just come into being. In fact, it still rankled that two squadrons had been removed to form the nucleus of 8 Group, but these were to be later reclaimed when 5 Group launched itself as the 'Independent Air Force' for attacking small, specialised targets (Butch Harris's most important concession to the 'panacea target theory'). This was not to come about until 1944 but, in that mode, they proved that, within certain range limitations, small targets could be taken out by Bomber Command at night, more effectively than in the day by the USAAF, mainly because of the vastly superior bomb load carried. As for the 'crack squadron' theory, it may have been just luck or careful selection and training of crews, but it will be seen that 61 Squadron's losses in the Battle of the Ruhr were much the lowest in 5 Group. The Group always did the same ops together but our sister squadron at Syerston, 106 Squadron, suffered significantly higher losses than we did. Probably, this was just the luck of the draw, which was to play such an important part in our survival, but the morale of the squadron was very high during our time there.

Initially, we were accommodated in a barrack block next to the Sergeants' Mess, which was full, but we moved over within a matter of days, as rooms became available quite quickly, I regret to say. Sammy and I moved into a corner room on the ground floor in the front of the Mess and that was to be our comfortable home for almost six months. Being a peace time permanent station, these quarters were of the highest order and vastly superior to anything enjoyed by commissioned officers on the stations built in wartime.

It was just after we got to Syerston that I wrote a letter home dated 8 December in which I said, 'There was a nasty accident here tonight. An ops kite caught fire on the ground, with its bombs on. The Group Captain went out to it on the fire tender and the kite blew up killing two men and blowing the Group Captain's arm off'. Gus Walker was an extremely popular Commanding Officer. I seem to remember that he came back after his recovery. He certainly served again as a Station Commander because I saw him mentioned as Sir Gus Walker when CO at Pocklington and he went on to become an Air Marshal.

We considered ourselves to be a fully trained crew when we arrived but I was soon to realise just how wrong we were. I had heard mention of radar navigational aids coming on stream, but had never heard of the name *Gee*. However, soon after our arrival, the Navigation Leader, a very amiable Australian by the name of Flight Lieutenant Cliff Giles took me to the '*Gee* Room'. He introduced me to a *Gee* Chart, which was a normal Mercator's chart with diagonal crossing lines and the magic box called *Gee*. This had a cathode-ray tube on its face with two lines of signals, which were transmitted from stations in this country, one far south and the other far north. From this the operator obtained readings that corresponded to the lines on the chart and at their intersection, the position of the aircraft over the ground with very little error. Consequently, by taking three such fixes at 3-minute intervals, one immediately found the track made good over the ground and the speed over the ground (ground speed) by measuring the distance from first to third fix and multiplying by ten. The technique of operation was logical to someone with my sort of mind, something that could be assimilated quickly, and I required only a short spell of practice. However, this was not so for everyone as quite a lot made very heavy weather of it. Why this was left to be taught on the squadron I never quite understood as navigators had so much spare time on Conversion Units. Perhaps it was just that there were not enough sets to spare at that time.

By 21 December 1942 we were fit to make our debut over Germany in a Lancaster *D-Dog* and were briefed for one of the longest German trips, Munich, with Cliff Giles along as Flight Engineer. I was rather nervous, not because, we were going to Germany but because Cliff was alongside in the event, he left me to my own devices and he told me afterwards I had done an excellent job. We climbed to 20,000 feet and crossed the coast at Dungeness. A fighter was sighted off French coast but we evaded safely. The mountains were beautiful in the moonlight but the target was obscured by cloud and was badly marked. The flak was weak but there was some near Mannheim on the return. There was 10/10ths cloud from Brussels to base. We were first back at Syerston in 7 hours 10 minutes, having flown 1,400 miles over England, France, Germany, Luxembourg, Belgium and Holland. Some 137 aircraft were sent on the operation, with a loss rate of 8.8 per cent.

On Christmas Eve we were briefed to go to Turin but that was scrubbed for no apparent reason – we could only think that the festive spirit overcame our hard-headed boss! That was to be our only chance of going to Italy for one of their easy targets but an awful long stooge, although I believe the Alps were worth seeing on moonlit nights. However, there were no objections raised at our end and I wrote home that we had a most enjoyable Christmas and also, to thank my mother for the cake, which was much enjoyed by all the crew. On New Year's Eve we took a dim view when we were sent off at 1755 hours on a *Bullseye* and cross-country. The *Bullseye* was anti-aircraft cooperation and the cross-country entailed coming in off the North Sea via Oxford, Taunton, Winchester and King's Lynn to attack Sheffield. We got back to Syerston at 2215 and lost no time in joining the New Year's Eve party being held in the Mess. We next flew on 3 January for High Level Bombing and practice Air Firing at Wainfleet and then not until 8 January, when we were on the Battle Order to fly for the first time in *K-King*, which was to figure largely in our operational success. My record reads:

> On 8 January 1943 we did a *Gardening* (Mining) trip to the Friesians between Heligoland and the coast. I pinpointed on Nordeney by search-lights and flak from the airfield and our gunners returned fire. We dropped mines by a timed run. Coming home we were diverted to Tangmere because Syerston was closed down by fog. Our hydraulics were u/s so we had to get the gear down using emergency air pressure. We had to leave the aircraft and were collected by Squadron Leader Parker in another Lancaster the next day. There were 73 on minelaying. 3.2% lost. Airborne 5.30 hours.
>
> 3 February 1943. Ops. Hamburg. Good trip. Lot of inaccurate flak. Did target recce to observe results. Very scattered. 263 on, 6.1% lost. Wanganui.[7] On 6 February we had a further boost to our morale when we were entrusted with a brand new Lancaster II fitted with Hercules engines which we were asked to test fly for a couple of hours and report on its performance. Our impressions were favourable but we considered it to be somewhat lacking in comparison with our Lancaster Mark Is. Having done that pleasant duty we departed on leave for eight days from 9 February.

When we returned we were soon put back to work and our next trip was on 19 February 1943, to Wilhelmshaven, in *K-King*. In my diary I noted 'Bomb load $1 \times 4,000$ lb + 12 Small Bomb Containers (30 lb incendiaries). Good trip. Full moon and target was clearly visible. Bombed at 16,000. Flak heavy but below us. Greatest danger was of collision with our own aircraft. Flew away from target alongside a Halifax. Lot of bombing well off target. 195 on, 2% lost. Back at 2255 in 5 hours flat'.

I have described the bomb load as being fairly typical and will only mention in future if there are great variations. The bomb load described would have been almost 10,000 lb – about treble that of a Flying Fortress! The next day I said how much the lads had enjoyed the eggs, which I must have brought back with me. Aircrew did well for eggs as bacon and egg was the usual meal on

Five of the crew of Lancaster I W4236 K-King, which had been accepted by 61 Squadron on 19 September 1942. Gordon Oldham, far left; Eric 'Sammy' Sampson, bomb aimer; Frank Emerson, mid upper gunner; David 'Woody' Attwood, flight engineer and Derek Smith, far right. (Leutnant Norbert Pietrek of II./NJG4 shot W4236 down en route to Mannheim on the night of 9/10 August 1943. Sergeant J. C. Whitley and three of his crew evaded capture and three were killed). Flight Sergeant Frank Emerson returned for a second tour on 61 Squadron with Flight Lieutenant Bill Reid and was with him on the night of 3/4 November 1943 when Reid earned his VC and Frank was awarded a DFM. (Derek Smith)

return from our long treks over Northern Europe, but some extra was always appreciated.

I have only mentioned, in passing, the ever-prevailing hazard of being hit by bombs dropped by 'friendly aircraft'. We lucky ones in Lancasters suffered from it less than those below in Stirlings, Halifaxes and Wellingtons, but we had our fair share from higher flying fellows. One occasion I recall most vividly was on one of the all-5 Group, all-Lancaster trips to Essen early in the Battle of the Ruhr, when the attack would have been very concentrated. We were in the middle of our bombing run and as usual, I had gone out of 'the Office' to watch the fireworks. Unfortunately, as I emerged, I looked up and there, about 50 feet above was one of our 'friends' with, like us, bomb doors open, presenting a sight I had never seen before and, thankfully, was never to see again! It was our fortune that he was on a slightly different heading and as he released at the same time as us, the bombs just avoided being a direct hit. It seemed an age but it was all over in a matter of seconds; there was no time for me to do anything more than pray and the rest of the crew were quite unaware of the danger we had been in until I told them afterwards.

The weather was not too good at this time as we only flew on 21 February for 1½ hours doing some low-level formation and bombing and then an NFT (Night Flying Test) prior to 25 February 1943, when it was an op to Nürnburg. I noted, 'Quite a boring trip. Defences were swamped. On the 400-mile leg from Mannheim we saw no flak or searchlights. *Paramatta*.[8] 337 on, 2.7% lost. 9 hours! Our longest trip'.

After a day off on 27 February we did an hour NFT for 28 February 1943 op to St Nazaire in *K-King*. It was one of our only two non-German trips and we used *Paramatta*. The trip was a piece of cake and we had no trouble at all. The opposition consisted of five searchlights and a few guns. It was very much different from German targets. Some 437 aircraft were on, with 1.1 per cent lost. We were back at 0035 in 6.30 hours.

On 1 March 1943 we had an op to Berlin in *K-King*. The Big One! We arrived bang on time to the minute after being 15 minutes late taking off. There were about 100 searchlights but flak was poor. Were the fighters operating? The port outer engine went on fire over the centre of target area. Gordon warned we might have to bale out but the Graviner engine fire extinguisher was operated and the fire was extinguished. We set course for home on three engines, on which the Lanc could maintain normal airspeed with a few extra revs. Just to make matters worse, this was where we suffered our only failure of communication, which could have proved fatal and taught us a very valuable lesson. I gave Gordon the course to steer, which he repeated back to me as usual, but either he repeated the right course back to me and put the wrong one on the compass or I misheard him. Anyway, when we got back to extreme *Gee* range I was shocked to find that I was getting fixes about 30 miles south of track. Upon checking with Gordon, I found we were steering a course 10 degrees out and on three fans! Our Guardian Angel was certainly working overtime as we had an extremely quiet return and with the good old Lanc's great performance, we were back with the others. It was a case of least said soonest mended, but we had learned our lesson and Woody checked with

Gordon and me from then on. It was certainly no easy stooge as of the 302 aircraft on, 5.6 per cent were lost. We were back in 7.40 hours at 0250.

By this time we developed a theory of our own that, unless coned by searchlights, weaving in the target area was of little use as it could just as well lead into flak as away from it. In our view, speed was of greater value so, having got our photograph, Gordon turned on to the new course with the nose down to lose 2,000–3,000 feet while gaining a great deal of speed out of the danger area. Of course, this showed by the straight lines on our photographs and debriefing officers questioned our policy but accepted that, if we preferred it that way, then it was up to us. We rarely weaved but preferred to use variations of height if our equipment warned us of radar-controlled tracking in our vicinity and our survival proved it worked for us. From a navigation point of view I preferred it, although it gave me more work in obtaining a mean ground speed. The German night-fighter's favourite method of attack was to come up at a steep angle under the unprotected belly of the bomber until nearing stalling speed, fire a burst aimed just behind the wings and fall away, raking the cockpit and inner tanks with shells. To overcome this, we combined our method with dropping our wings alternately on a quick, sharp change of course to give our gunners the opportunity to spot a stalking fighter. At very least, this would indicate to the enemy pilot that here was a crew on their toes and he would probably look elsewhere for easier prey. *K-King* was due a major service and a complete engine change so we did an NFT in *H-Harry* for 30 minutes on 3 March and started a run of six operations in ten days without any other flights.

We aircrew of the heavy bomber squadrons of Bomber Command lived very strange lives, especially those, like us, who occupied a very comfortable, pre-war station. In good weather, we could operate two or three times a week. The chances of surviving a thirty-operation tour were about two to one against. On the other hand, we returned to very comfortable living quarters, had extremely good food and performed no arduous duties of any sort. Just so long as we were there to fly, as and when required, nobody bothered us very much. I was a sergeant for practically the whole of the tour and shared the comfortable room in the Mess with Sammy. Being built pre-war, the Sergeant's Mess was superior to all the Officer's Messes I encountered later on wartime stations. In addition, the catering was of a higher standard than that provided for officers on those dispersed establishments. The general facilities such as dining room, ante-room, bar and billiard room were of the highest order and it was somewhat like living in a three star hotel and going out to war as and when required. In addition, we had generous leaves which, at Syerston, were nine or ten days every eight weeks so we kept in constant contact with our families and sweethearts – that is, those of us lucky enough to survive from one trip to the next! Against that, I should point out that in between, we were on duty seven days a week and were only stood down when not required for flying.

It is probably appropriate that I try to give a picture of a day in the life of operational aircrew on a heavy bomber squadron. Time of rising would depend largely upon whether operating the night before and if so, time of return. If it had been a non-operational night, then we would get up just in time for breakfast, which ended around 09.00, wander down to the 'Flights' for a general natter and probably a game of cards. The NAAFI van would come round, so out for a cup of char and a wad (NAAFI cake). Then it was back to the Crew Room, by which time it would probably be known if ops were on, who was on the Battle Order and in which aircraft. If we were 'on', it was out to the aircraft for a chat with ground crew and an NFT if required. This latter usually took between 20 minutes and an hour, largely depending upon the weather and the inclination of the crew about sight seeing, although the work for the ground crew was always taken into account. Then it was off to the Mess for lunch and, probably, a game of snooker or billiards before the briefing for pilots, navigators and bomb aimers.

At this briefing, navigators would be the only ones working hard, getting route and timings on chart and log sheet and completing a full flight plan on the basis of forecast winds and temperatures. Then it was back to the Mess to fill in time and have a meal, depending much upon the time of take-off. We then went back to the ops room for the main briefing of all the crew and then in to the locker room to don flying clothing and collect our gear. We emerged having assumed heavyweight proportions, especially the rear and mid-upper gunners. Those of us up in the front had the benefit of a heated cabin so were attired in white, heavy, crew neck sweaters under our battledress tops with Mae Wests and parachute harnesses on top of that. The gunners, who occupied the unheated mid-upper and rear turrets, had the addition of electrically heated suits and flying suits between battledress and Mae Wests. All wore flying boots with leather lined shoes, with a suede lined upper attached by stitching around the ankle. This was to help evasion if shot down over enemy territory. The stitching could be cut and the upper disposed of, so leaving what appeared to be a normal black shoe.

In addition to this, we all carried additional luggage. The pilot had a seat-type parachute while the rest of us had the clip on chest type. All of us had two Perspex-encased escape outfits made of a size to fit in the battledress pockets. These contained a shaving outfit in kit form, a small compass in a waterproof container, a water bottle, needle and cotton for adapting a uniform, comb, small penknife, pills to purify water and to keep awake, chewing gum, Horlicks tablets and hard tack rations. We also had another waterproof container in which was a silk map of Northern Europe to be worn as a scarf and small amounts of European currency. We had various other escape aids. There was a tobacco pipe with a small compass in the stem, a comb with a magnetic strip as its body and an RAF button with a compass inside. This was revealed by using the reverse thread and a magnetised pencil clip, which, if balanced on a pencil point, turned to indicate magnetic North. We had had our photographs taken, unsmiling, in civilian pin-striped suits, which made us look like Mafia thugs on the small, passport type prints. We all carried these for use on false identity papers to be provided by escape organisations.

The navigator was the most heavily loaded. I had the regulation green canvas Nav Bag to carry all the navigator's 'gubbins' I required to ply my craft. This included bubble sextant, planisphere, Dalton computer, set-square,

Derek Smith DFC. (Derek Smith)

parallel rule, dividers in a box, pencils topped by erasers, maps, charts and aerodrome beacon letter flimsies. I also carried a .45 Colt revolver with six rounds of ammunition, a Commando knife (my own provided by my father), a flask of coffee and whatever flying rations I might be taking. Flying rations for each trip were generally a bar of chocolate, barley sugar sweets, chewing gum and a tin of pure orange juice. Most of us did not take much of this but kept it until we went home on leave.

The wireless operator would have his various code books and was in charge of the homing pigeon, which he would have collected from the pigeon loft in its little box, about half an hour before take-off. Pigeons were carried on all operational heavy Bomber Command and Coastal Command aircraft. Every station where these heavy aircraft were located had its pigeon loft, usually in the charge of a Corporal Pigeon Fancier. The purpose of carrying the birds was in case of ditching 'in the drink'; it could be released with a message of position on its leg and many aircrew were to owe their lives to these birds. Many crews liked to have a particular bird and some carried it to the extreme of believing it to be unlucky to have a different one.

Lugging all this gear, we clambered aboard 5-ton, 15 cwt and 30 cwt vehicles to be decanted at our various aircraft. We would chat to the ground crew while the pilot and flight engineer did their eternal checks and the pilot signed the Form 700. About 20 minutes before take-off the Wingco and/or Groupie came around in their Vauxhall to wish us well before we climbed aboard. This was up a five- or six-rung ladder towards the end of the aircraft, just in front of the Elsan portable toilet, which was only used in emergency, but 9 hours plus could be a very long time in our particular circumstances! Everyone except Doc, the rear gunner who went left into his lonely four-gun turret at the back end, went right. Frank soon left us to climb up into his two-gun mid-upper turret. We continued past the 'rest bed' on the left, which was really so that anyone wounded could be dealt with, and over the main spar and into the forward section, which was screened off to retain the benefit of the heater. Ginger, the wireless operator, took his place on the left in front of the radio equipment and just to the left of the astrodome above. My turn came next on the left facing port in front of the large navigation table, directly in front of the R/T set with the *Gee* set to my left. Gordon climbed into his armour-backed seat to my right while Sammy carried on down into the nose above his bombsight and below the two-gun front turret. Woody, the flight engineer, took his place alongside Gordon on a collapsible canvas seat and beside the fuel gauges. In daylight this area was open, but when it got dark a curtain separated me from the front so that I could have light to work. We now stowed our parachutes in their stowages, did our ground checks, plugged in to the intercom, connected up to oxygen and reported to Gordon in turn that all was well for take-off.

Gordon would be in contact with the control tower for any mundane things, but said nothing to indicate we were operating as the Germans had a very efficient monitoring system. Engines were started on a signal from the control tower and after a run-up, we would taxi out on signals from the caravan at the end of the runway and line up for take-off on a green Aldis lamp. It was at this point that we realised just how much support we had from the ground staff of the station as, if the hour and weather were reasonable, there would be quite a crowd of well wishers to see us on our way. Although we never gave it a great deal of consideration, this was one of the danger points of the operation. We were sitting on top of a 4,000 lb bomb and fourteen Small Bomb Containers – about four tons in all – with a slightly greater weight of 100 octane aviation fuel in the wing tanks, close to the 5,000 horsepower of the four Rolls-Royce Merlin engines. Gordon would lower slight flap and assisted by Woody slowly open the throttles while I stood behind them calling the speed from the airspeed indicator. Carrying our great load, it required most of the 2,000-yard runway to come unstuck and here at Syerston we were fortunate that the ground to the west fell away by about 150 feet to the River Trent so we reached 200 feet very quickly. The wheels and the slight flap were now retracted and we were on our way climbing slowly to our operational height of 20,000–22,000 feet, which could take up to an hour. Ginger would now wind out our 60 feet trailing aerial, which would enable him to pick up the half-hourly broadcasts at extreme range and heaven help him if he forgot to wind it in before we landed. Outgoing radio silence was strictly observed, but he had to keep a continual watch for any incoming instructions, although these were mainly passed at the normal scheduled times. If it had been an early take-off we would have seen hundreds of aircraft all heading in the same direction. If it had been after dark we usually showed our navigation lights until over the North Sea to avoid risk of collision.

We were now heading out into the great unknown. When we reached 10,000 feet, just after crossing the English coast, oxygen masks would have gone on for a period of up to 7½ hours. This was the exchange of one special aircraft smell for another – from that peculiar smell of petrol, oil, glycol and hydraulic fluid to that of rubber and oxygen. The enemy coast would be coming up, a danger period when we were coming out of the lighter sky of the west into the darkness of the east, which could conceal the lurking enemy fighters. Scattered bursts of flak would come up along the coast but, usually, nothing very serious. Then the long haul over unfriendly territory with the night broken by bursts of flak for those whose navigators had let them stray off course over heavily defended areas. We would have bursts of tracer from fighters and the turrets of attacking bombers and, occasionally, the brighter flash of exploding and crashing aircraft. Press on! It would never be us but some other poor 'so and so'. Then would come the strings of parasol flares dropped to light up the bomber stream and on the ground, brightly lit decoy targets. Because we got on so well together we were a chatty crew, which served to keep the gunners from feeling too isolated.

I was not expected to contribute too much outward, which was always understood, but I became more involved later. This chat also served to keep Ginger and me in touch with the great outside so that we could take a look at matters of particular interest. So, it was into the target, well lit by Pathfinder red and green TIs (Target Indicators), bursts of flak at all heights up to 25,000 feet, searchlights, exploding bombs and aircraft. Sammy, down over his bomb-sight, took over, directing Gordon straight and level on the bombing run. Numerous other bombers were doing exactly the same thing and danger of collision and being hit by falling bombs was as great a danger as the defences below. The call of 'Bombs gone' from Sammy and the Lanc would give a perceptible jump as we continued straight and level for the photograph by photoflash. I would have already given Gordon the course to steer out, which he set on the compass so I would have been up between him and Woody to take in the picture of burning streets and general mayhem below. Gordon would turn on to the new course while gaining speed by losing a couple of thousand feet. I probably had a cup of coffee and passed one to Ginger or *vice versa*. However, there could be no relaxing; this was a very dangerous period when fighters were waiting for the unwary 'sprogs'. We would head for home, hoping the fighters had landed to refuel or had been caught by our 100 Group intruders[9] who covered the stream. Ginger would give the odd blast of the AFN (American Forces Network) over the intercom or wander over and mouth, 'Where are we'? It was impossible to hear without the intercom over the racket of four Merlins within 20 feet and through a flying helmet. I would point to a spot on the track – he would think what a great navigator I was. If we had been out of *Gee* range for a couple of hours I would not tell him it was more hope than certainty!

If we were on the long trek back over the northern North Sea, Gordon would let 'George' (automatic pilot) take over for a spell. Exhaustion was a danger. On one occasion, over this area at about 0500, after being airborne for 6½ hours, with 'George' 'in', we hit a patch of violent turbulence and all came too, realising we had all been going to sleep! If further south we crossed the enemy coast, and started losing height to increase the ground speed to lose fighters, which would still be lurking. Down at 10,000 feet we took our oxygen masks off and some that smoked lit up a cigarette to go with the last of the coffee. Now we were in over the English coast but still keeping a wary eye out for intruders. About 10 miles from base we would call up to get a good place in the 'stack' and land in our turn. Then we taxied round to our hard standing, stopped engines, dropped the ladder and piled out to breathe in God's good English fresh air and to be greeted by the duty ground crew who were pleased to see us back again. The Flight Truck arrived to pick us up and we are soon in the Ops Room for debriefing with another cup of coffee, laced with rum this time. The CO came round and said, 'Good show chaps' and off we went for our bacon and eggs or some to be greeted by WAAF girlfriends who would have waited for them if it was a reasonable hour of return. If we were back early, we would maybe have a game of billiards before going to bed. If we were late back, then it was up in time for lunch and then we would start the cycle all over again, weather permitting. In a later spell, we were to do ten operations in sixteen days from 25 February until 12 March 1943, which entailed about 66 hours of operational flying.

Aircrews were the least class conscious of all branches of the three services and we found this was even more so on an operational squadron. From flight lieutenant downwards of the commissioned ranks and all those non-commissioned were generally on first name terms and it was very unusual to hear anyone called 'Sir'. When we arrived I was the lowliest sergeant but Cliff Giles introduced himself as Cliff so it was Cliff and 'Smithy' from then on. This sense of equality stemmed, I believe, from several things. First, we all trained together with a few being commissioned when training was complete with the majority going on to be sergeants and to become commissioned, as I was, when on operational service. Secondly, apart from the trial of navigator captains, the pilot was captain of the aircraft and although, as in our case, democracy reigned, he was the one with the final word. However, he was not necessarily the highest ranking in the crew and it was not unusual to have a NCO pilot with one or several commissioned officers in the crew. Another contributory factor was that we were all in it together and senior wing commanders got shot at just the same way as the most lowly of sergeants. There were no deeper dugouts for them and the risks were the same for all. In my experience, respect was more easily given to those with a lot of operational experience rather than those with badges of rank on their shoulders.

Our Lancaster *K-King* had at that time performed fifty-seven operational sorties, which was more than any other Lancaster in Bomber Command. We had flown in her forty-three times, of which twenty-five were operational sorties – 176.33 hours in all. Except for our first and third trips in Lancs and when she had the engine change, we flew her throughout the tour with great affection for a first class, extremely reliable aircraft. After the complete engine change in early March, immediately after the engine went on fire over Berlin, we had complete reliability on fifteen operations and, repeating myself, she really did go like a bomb so that we were always amongst the first back. Sadly, she was lost on her seventy-eighth operation to Mannheim on 10 August 1943.[10]

As a result of this tour, Gordon and I were awarded Distinguished Flying Crosses and Sammy and Woody, Distinguished Flying Medals, while Gordon, Sammy, Doc and I were all commissioned during or soon after, the tour. The awards for Gordon, Sammy and I were promulgated in August and Woody's slightly later. Whether or not Doc got any award, I do not know, as he was to finish his tour with another crew due to his absence through being wounded. Frank Emerson went back for a second tour on 61 Squadron with Flight Lieutenant Bill Reid and was with him when Bill got his VC and Frank got a DFM after that episode.

We obviously had a considerable sense of achievement and satisfaction in completing our tour without too much trouble, but there was a certain sadness at the break up of a highly efficient team, which had worked so well for over eight months.[11] Of course, lady luck played a big part in the survival of an operational tour, but it was a fact that the greatest danger of going missing was during the first five trips. Consequently, skill must have played a considerable part and, looking back, I have no doubt that we were a skilful, conscientious and efficient crew. A slap-happy crew with all the luck in the world would be unlikely to survive even half a tour, while a good, efficient, well organised crew would do a great deal to provide luck for themselves.

We were not particularly happy to be moving on from operational life, which so many aircrews enjoyed. That life was quite different from all other parts of RAF service, in that you were doing what you had been trained to do in company with others with whom the strongest of all bonds had been formed because our very survival had depended on each other.

Notes

1. 91 (OTU) Group put up 236 Wellingtons and twenty-one Whitleys; 92 (OTU) Group put up sixty-three Wellingtons and forty-six Hampdens.
2. Of the 956 aircraft dispatched, 545 were Wellingtons. Thirty-one bombers were lost, fifteen of them Wimpys.
3. On the Cologne raid the losses suffered by the OTU crews (3.3 per cent) were actually lower than the 4.1 per cent casualties of the regular bomber groups. Calculations also proved that those training aircraft with pupil pilots suffered lower casualties than those with instructor pilots! (*RAF Bomber Command War Diaries*, Martin Middlebrook and Chris Everitt)
4. Flying with 49 Squadron on 12.8.40 he was awarded Bomber Command's first VC of the war for a particularly determined attack in which his Hampden was hit.
5. Sergeant Stan Southgate was in Sergeant M. K. Matson RCAF's crew, whose Wellington III crashed in the vicinity of Dortmund with the loss of all five crew.
6. Of 479 aircraft dispatched, 242 were Wellingtons, thirty-three of which were lost, fifteen of them OTU aircraft. Pathfinders successfully marked the target using 'Pink Pansies' in converted 4,000 lb bomb casings for the first time.
7. Method of marking a target where sky markers were put down in such a place where, if bombed on the correct heading, the bombs would fall on the target.
8. Ground marking with coloured target indicators.
9. Mosquito night-fighters. On 8 November 1943, 100 Group (Special Duties, later Bomber Support) was created to consolidate the various squadrons and units using the secret ELINT and RCM in the war against the German night-fighter air and defence system. In tandem with this electronic wizardry, 100 Group also accepted 'spoofing' as a large part of its offensive armoury and it also controlled squadrons of Mosquitoes engaged purely on *Intruder* missions over Germany. See *Confounding The Reich* by Martin W. Bowman and Tom Cushing (Pen & Sword Publishing, 2004).
10. *K-King* (W4236) which had been accepted by 61 Squadron on 19.9.42, had flown a total of 639.55 hours without damage, or prolonged servicing, was shot down *en route* to Mannheim by *Leutnant* Norbert Pietrek of II./NJG4 on the night of 9/10 August 1943. Sergeant J. C. Whitley and three of his crew evaded. Three were killed.
11. Flying Officer Derek Smith flew a second tour (1.9.44–12.3.45) as a navigator on Mosquitoes in 692 Squadron, 8 (PFF) Group and was awarded a bar to his DFC. See *The Men Who Flew The Mosquito* by Martin W. Bowman (Pen & Sword Publishing, 2003).

CHAPTER 10

Memories of a 218 Squadron Bomb Aimer

Harry Barker DFC

When Sterling's spent on Stirling
We get our money's worth
In bombs by dozens hurling
Our wrath on brownshirt earth.

'The Aeroplane'

I joined up in 1941 as soon as I was 18 and began training as a pilot in July. The Arnold scheme had just started to train pilots in the USA and I was lucky enough to be sent to Albany, Georgia, to be taught to fly the Stearman PT-17. The first stage of primary training went well, but when I moved on to the next phase I failed to achieve the standard required in the Vultee B-13a and was sent to Canada to join an Observer course in Saskatchewan in March 1942. Although shattered by having to leave my friends on the pilot course, I made the best of the situation and the weather. The Canadian winter was a shock to my system after the hot climate of the Deep South. The Observer course was in fact the last one and all future aircrew would be trained as navigators or bomb aimers. I graduated as a sergeant bomb aimer and returned to England at the end of 1942 to complete the training, which consisted of day and night flying in Wellingtons, followed by conversion to the four-engined Stirling with familiarisation, practice bombing and navigation flights whenever weather and ground school schedules permitted. In May 1943 I joined Flying Officer John Overton's crew to fly Stirling Mk Is at Downham Market, the base for 218 (Gold Coast) Squadron.

The Stirling was enormous compared with all the training aircraft we had encountered and the pilot's task was daunting to say the least. There were a number of training accidents as the Stirling was not the easiest aeroplane to fly, with the pilot sitting twenty feet up from the ground and the well-known tendency to swing on take-off and landing. However, once airborne she was well behaved and very strong. There was plenty of room for the crew compared with most other bombers and I found that the bomb aimer was required to act as second pilot, so some of my earlier training could be put to good use. There were dual controls and take-off and landing required the assistance of the bomb aimer to ease the load on the pilot, holding throttles open, setting flap and calling out airspeed on the approach etc.

The crew of seven comprised the pilot, navigator, bomb aimer, flight engineer, wireless operator, mid-upper gunner and rear gunner. All our crew except John Overton were NCOs so we were not all together in our billets or mess but we formed close friendships and John was an excellent skipper.

We arrived at Downham Market on 20 May 1943 and our first flight was a short cross-country to practise with the *Gee* navigational aid and get to know the Stirling Mk I. On 25 May we were allocated a Mk III and flew with Wing Commander Saville[1] on an acceptance test, then our first operation was a mining trip to the Friesians. This was uneventful and lasted 4 hours but gave us a gentle introduction into action in enemy territory. Downham Market airfield was close to the tiny village of Bexwell and our billets were dispersed among the fields away from the airfield. The Officers' Mess was the rectory and all other ranks lived in Nissen huts with a large building for our mess hall. We all found the place quite pleasant, even if the new construction was obviously only partly completed. The fact that the weather was warm and everywhere seemed bright and green helped us to settle in. We soon borrowed old bikes and most evenings set off to explore the local villages for suitable pubs and places of interest.

On 29 May we were briefed for an attack on Wuppertal in the Ruhr. This has stayed in my memory because during the briefing the target was designated a dormitory town serving the factories of the Ruhr and it was clearly intended to destroy housing to disrupt the workers' production. We had a job to do and at that time bombing attacks on our own cities, London, Coventry, Birmingham and many others created a demand for retaliation. Sixty years later, the views of many people have tended to forget that we were all fighting for our lives and the very real fear that defeat was possible and probably very likely, has not been understood by the majority of people today. We were ordinary young men who had volunteered to undertake a special role in defending our country and our families. For my part I did not dwell on the damage and death resulting from our attacks. Instead, I pictured the scenes shown in the press of Coventry and London burning. We were expected to hit back and that was what we did.

The raid on Wuppertal was at times a bit scary; we saw flak and searchlights for the first time and our trip lasted 4 hours 25 minutes. I remember the rewarding breakfast we had on return of bacon and egg and then getting back to our billet for 6 or 7 hours' sleep. When I awoke and had my lunch in the Sergeants' Mess, I wandered off on my own and lay down on the warm turf outside our hut. It was beautiful day; there was a bright blue sky and birds were singing. I reflected on the incredible situation I was in. I was a very immature kid at 20 years old, stretched out on warm Norfolk turf having very recently flown as a crewmember of a huge bomber to drop bombs on a

German town. Then I had helped to fly back to my well-earned bacon and egg before getting ready to do the same thing again. It all seemed so unreal.

The other thoughts that I tried not to dwell on were the inescapable facts of losses by enemy action. They were just as determined to stop our attacks, as we were to carry them out. I cannot remember whether we lost any of our 218 aircraft on the Wuppertal raid but by 21 June our crew took part in four attacks on Ruhr towns: Krefeld on the 21st, Mülheim on the 22nd, Elberfeld on the 24th and Gelsenkirchen on the 25th. Now all the targets we attacked after Wuppertal were either factories or rail centres in the towns concerned. Target maps were given to all crews. Generally, coloured flares marked the aiming points and there was no question of simply dropping bombs just anywhere on the town concerned. In reality, after the first few minutes of the start of bombing, smoke obscured the target area and aiming depended on the markers so semi-blind bombing did result, but I clearly remember the objectives being industrial targets except in the case of Wuppertal.

My job as bomb aimer suited me fine. I had got over my disappointment at failing the pilot course and privately accepted some doubt about whether I would have been up to the huge responsibility carried by the skipper of a Stirling crew. John Overton was an excellent pilot. The secret of survival for a bomber crew was to avoid all straight and level flying whenever within reach of enemy fighter planes or flak. It was essential for the pilot to corkscrew continually; this made navigation far from easy as the track made good was an average heading achieved from the constant changes of course and height. It was a navigator's nightmare but John and our skilful navigator George Dennis were a very successful team and between them we survived for thirty operations. As I said before, part of my job was to act as second pilot assisting on take-off and landing from the right hand seat. In order to provide some relief for the skipper on the first part of a trip, I flew some of the easy legs, well out of reach of the dangerous stuff. Then I would take up my position in the front gun turret armed with two Browning .303 machine-guns. This was my position until we got within 50 miles or so of the target, when I got down from the turret to the bomb aimer's position and prepared to carry out the sole object of the trip.

The Stirling was fitted with the Mk 14 bombsight, which was very sophisticated for 1943. Most of the vital information was fed in automatically and the only input from the crew was to fly straight and level at a constant airspeed during the last few minutes and during the bombing run. The bombs were released by a rotating switch unit, which made electrical contact in a pre-arranged sequence to release one bomb at a time. The sequence was chosen to ensure that letting too much weight go suddenly from front or back during the release did not upset the balance of the aircraft. The first part of the bomb dropping operation was to check that the bombsight was switched on and prepare to identify the target area. Once established on the approach to the target, the pilot would open the bomb doors and the bomb aimer would 'arm the bombs'. This meant engaging a switch, which ensured that the safety pin through the bomb fuses would be withdrawn when the bombs were released.

Once in position, the bomb aimer guided the pilot on the intercom to fly so that the target was held on the red line reflected in the gyro-stabilised glass of the bombsight. A short line indicated the release point across the approach line and the release button was pressed when the cross was on the target. At this point it was essential to maintain straight and level flight until all the bombs had gone. This took several minutes and was a time of great stress for the crew who wanted to escape from this very vulnerable situation with all speed. When the bomb aimer reported 'bombs gone' the skipper would reply 'bomb doors closed' and we could get the hell out of it!

We completed our June operations with a raid on Cologne. This was a 4-hour trip and we were hit by flak, which broke the windscreen and slightly injured the skipper. Fortunately, he made very little of it when he found that all the liquid running down his face was from melted ice and not blood! I was also greatly relieved because I had visions of having to fly home and carry out my first night landing.

Cologne was the target again on 3 July and this time it was not too dangerous and we got good target photographs. These were taken automatically when the bombs were released by a camera running with an open shutter taking a number of shots recording a ground view illuminated by a photoflash flare. Our next trip on 24 July was to Hamburg and this was the occasion when the new defence against enemy radar called Window was used. This was in the form of narrow strips of aluminium foil dropped down the photoflash chute at short intervals. This screened us from radar and caused total confusion to night-fighters and flak guns. We had some losses, including our Wing Commander. The Hamburg raid was a horrendous event with vast areas set on fire. No doubt this was a clear signal that as a terror factor, the Germans did not have it all their own way in bombing. If we had known the result of our effort, I think we would have said that they started it . . .. But we did not know. Our bosses sent us again on 25 July to Essen and on the 27th back to Hamburg.

On 28 July we had a week's leave and all set off by train for our homes. In my case it was to London for Maidstone where we lived in a small village. It was hot and sunny so on my first day home, I set off for one of my old haunts in the Weald of Kent to a river where I used to spend happy times fishing and swimming. I swam and lay in the sun. It was here on 15 September 1940 that I had watched the Battle of Britain being fought out on just such a sunny day in a cloudless sky. As a 17-year-old I knew fairly certainly what was in store for me and here I was and it was for real. Now, three years later it did not seem so bad; I suppose I had grown up.

We returned to Downham on 5 August to find that our aircraft 'A' had been flown whilst we had been on leave and had not returned so we took on 'W'. As John was now 'A' Flight commander, he would arrange that our aircraft was 'A'. This was a privilege, which generally was granted to him throughout our tour, the exceptions were due to maintenance requirements.

The routine on the squadron continued much the same; we had to carry out air tests and ground maintenance on our guns and turrets, cleaning the Perspex and stripping down the guns, cleaning and oiling them. The Perspex

During the Battle of Hamburg over four nights 24/25 July to 3 August 1943, 3,000 bombers dropped 10,000 tons of HE and incendiary bombs to totally devastate half of the city and kill an estimated 42,000 of its inhabitants. After the fourth raid on the night of 2/3 August, 1 million inhabitants fled the city. (IWM)

used to get covered with squashed insects, which had to be removed to avoid visibility problems in the air, which of course are much worse at night. A clean turret could save your life.

We tended to relieve any boredom from the flying duties by some fairly heavy drinking sessions at the local pubs. I regret to say that the journeys home by bike were sometimes more hair raising than the ops. I frequently pranged and my bike, which cost me five guineas at Bennetts in Downham Market, suffered grievously. One handlebar broke off and I was forced to get used to riding a single-sided machine thereafter, which was even more difficult to control at the end of a heavy session of 'black and tans' – our favourite drink. John Overton encouraged us to socialise and test all the local pubs. This was the norm for crews and helped form the vital bond that was essential for men working together and knowing that each man could depend on the others totally. We usually went out as a party of four or five and soon found that the 'Carpenters Arms' in Denver was most welcoming and hospitable. We could settle down for pints and a singsong until closing time. It had a fairly large room with a bar at one end and a piano at the other but, best of all, there were a couple of pleasant young female members of the family who were accomplished pianists. The 'Chippies' soon became one of our favourite 'targets for tonight' when we were not flying. In fact, our ground crew had already sorted it out as the nearest home from home and we often found quite a large assembly from the squadron ordering pints at the bar. After a few weeks of regular attendance at the Chippies, the landlord George Tingey and his wife Grace invited two or three of us in turn to share their Sunday dinner with them. Bearing in mind that this was during stringent civilian rationing, sharing their excellent roast beef and Yorkshire pudding was extremely generous!

On Saturdays there was a dance in the Denver village hall and this was popular with those of us who had consumed sufficient beer. I had found that Molly, the youngest granddaughter at the pub, was friendly and very attractive. She played the piano and the accordion and was therefore very popular. I found her company more and more desirable, so visits to Denver were organised whenever possible, which provoked considerable ribbing from the rest of the crew.

August was a busy month for flying. On 10 August we had a 7-hour trip to Nuremberg. I noted that it was long and dull but we got some good photos. Two days later we were off to Turin, eight and a half hours with spectacular views of the Alps at 15,000 feet with Mont Blanc looking much the same height and glistening in the moonlight. There was very little opposition but Flight Sergeant Arthur Aaron's aircraft was shot up and he received severe injuries. His bomb aimer flew the crew on to North Africa and they landed at Bone. Aaron insisted on carrying out the landing and he later died of his wounds. His bravery earned him the VC.

On 16 August we returned to Turin but on the return trip we had to land at Ford on the Sussex coast due to fog at Downham. Just to complete the month's activities, we were briefed for Berlin on 23 August. This was of course heavily defended and we had our hands full. We dropped our bombs and then the rear gunner shouted that a fighter was attacking us. He fired back and we

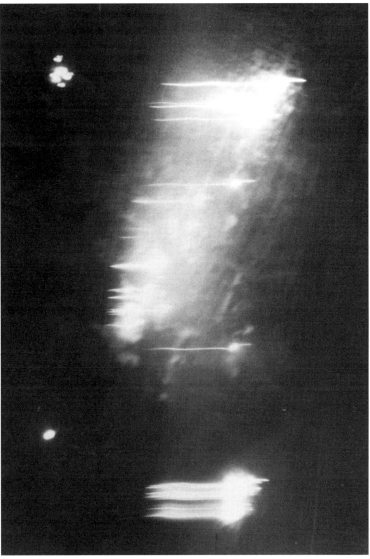

*Target photo of the raid on Turin on 16/17 August 1943 taken from 14,000 feet.
Flight Lieutenant John Overton's crew of a Stirling Mk. I of 218 (Gold Coast)
Squadron at Downham Market, went to the Italian city on 12/13 August which
Harry Barker noted was '8½ hours with spectacular views of the Alps at 15,000 feet
with Mont Blanc looking much the same height and glistening in the moonlight.'
Overton's crew were one of 103 Stirling crews who returned to Turin on 16/17 August
for the final Bomber Command raid on Italian cities but on the return trip they had to
land at Ford on the Sussex coast due to fog at Downham. In all, 154 bombers of 3 and
8 Groups were despatched and one Stirling was lost.*

were aware that we had been hit. The empty paper packets, which had
contained the Window anti radar strips, had been set on fire and Benny our
wireless operator seized a fire extinguisher and he and Alf, the flight engineer,
set about the flames. They managed to put out the fire and then Benny
admitted that he had been hit. Frank, the rear gunner, also called on the
intercom that he had been hit in the leg. In the meantime, I had moved from
the bombing position into the front turret to prepare for further attacks. John
flew brilliantly and got us away from the target area, which was a huge mass of
smoke and flames with searchlights by the dozen and anti-aircraft gunfire to
light up the sky. As soon as things quietened down I went back into the centre
of the aircraft to help with the injured crew. There were stretcher-like beds and
Benny lay on one with Frank on the other. Benny had received a bullet or shell
splinter in his back and was beginning to feel poorly. Frank had two bullets in
his leg and his flying boot was full of blood. We made them as comfortable as
possible and proceeded to get home without any more aggro. I must admit to
feeling decidedly dubious about the certainty of getting back to base on this
occasion. Whilst I had been in the bomb aimer's position, I had been aware of
unusual cracks and bangs around me and later I found a couple of bullets on
the deck, which had ricocheted off the interior of the cabin and ended up
harmlessly beside me.

*Stirlings of 90 Squadron taxiing at West Wickham for a raid on Berlin on the night
of 23/24 August 1943 when 727 aircraft took part including 124 Stirlings, one of
which was flown by Flight Lieutenant John Overton's crew of 218 Squadron from
Downham Market. (IWM)*

Our return route was north to the Baltic and then west to the Norfolk coast. We landed safely and the medics took care of Benny and Frank. Two days later, three of us went to Littleport hospital to see them and we were pleased to find them in reasonable shape. Benny's injuries were more serious because of the damage to his lung. Frank's leg healed fairly well but he spent two or three months off on sick leave and did not return to rejoin the crew until November.

In October we were only detailed for two operations; the first was to Kassel on the 3rd, which had to be abandoned because our compasses were u/s and then we attacked Bremen on the 8th. This was a good trip and took us 4 hours 35 minutes. On 27 October Tony Cattell (mid-upper gunner), George Dennis and I received our commissions. We got immediate leave for 48 hours to go to London to buy our officer uniforms. We were all amazed and proud. This would mean dramatic changes for us in some ways but our crew relationship would remain the same. When we returned to camp, we had to move into the Officers' Mess, which at that time was the Old Rectory. We had to get used to the apparently smoother way of life; we had a batman to clean our buttons and shoes, to make our beds and look after our clothes – it seemed as if we were living in another world! And on top of all this, all non-commissioned ranks had to salute us and call us 'Sir'. I have often heard chaps say they would never accept a commission, I always thought they must be mad and now knew this to be true.

We frequently had to carry out air test or practice gunnery exercises during the day. On one occasion, we did a formation flight with five other Stirlings of the squadron and this was a really great experience. We flew from west to east along the south coast at about 2,000 feet. John let me fly for part of the time and I found it easier to keep station than I had imagined. The Stirling was a delightful aircraft to fly.

Looking back, I find it surprising to see that my last entry in my diary for 1943 notes that 'it has been a most enjoyable and eventful year. Let's hope that by this time next year, the war will be won'. I have not made any reference to the losses we suffered. Very few crews ever completed their allocated number of thirty operations, which entitled them to be given a rest from the squadron and sent to training command. We were shocked when crews did not return, but the effect was tempered by the knowledge that on this occasion we had made it. Perhaps we would last a bit longer after all. However callous this may seem, I think it must have been our defence against the knowledge that, to have given the situation serious thought, would have seriously damaged our morale. We accepted that losses were a factor that bombing heavily defended enemy targets involved. We called it 'getting the chop'. All the men knew that the odds against getting away with it were slim, but we all believed that we could make it.

The chances of this were much better for experienced crews but how to gain this experience without becoming a casualty was the great question. We always hear our C-in-C referred to as Bomber Harris. We all called him 'Chopper Harris' without any disrespect or animosity. He was our boss and we would have done whatever he asked of us.

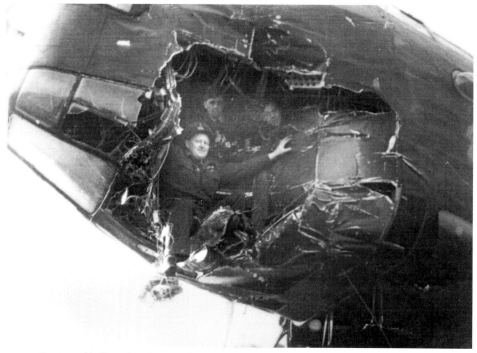

During a 'Bullseye' on 6 November 1943. Stirling R9192 of 1657 HCU at Stradishall (an ex-75 Squadron and 15 Squadron (fourteen sorties) aircraft) collided with Wellington III X3637 of 27 OTU in shadow of cu nim cloud at about 2000 hours. The Wellington, which took off from Lichfield at 1940 hours for an evening navigation detail crashed at Raden Stick Farm, Little Walden, 2 miles north of Saffron Walden, Suffolk. The all Australian crew including the pilot, Pilot Officer M. E. McKiggan RAAF were killed. R9192 was captained by Flying Officer D. W. Thomson RNZAF. Also on board were Flying Officer Vern L. Scantleton DFC RAAF, QMSI I. Colley and Flight Sergeant W. Mitson, army gunners for experience of AA. Stirling returned to Stradishall and landed safely at Stradishall. The Stirling was SOC on 12 June 1944. (CONAM)

We all knew that in 1943 the average 'life' of a crew was ten operations so you can imagine that everyone was a bit jumpy at their thirteenth! If you really begin to analyse it the options open to us were limited. We had to consider the following: (1) We had all volunteered to do the job. (2) We all wanted to hit back at the enemy, who were attacking London, Coventry, and Liverpool etc. (3) The camaraderie was so strong on the Squadron that no one would seriously consider letting his friends down. (4) There was a keen determination to achieve thirty ops and complete the tour. (5) The alternative was refusal – followed by a court martial and the awful consequences. (6) The reward on returning from an op was a breakfast of bacon and egos, a luxury only available to successful aircrews. When you take this lot into account, together with the youthful confidence that 'only other crews get shot down', you may understand how we felt about the incredible risks we were taking. It is similar to the attitude of cigarette smokers who are all convinced that it is only other people who get lung cancer!

In general the morale of aircrews was good. It was easier for the young unmarried and unattached men to cope than it was for those with wives, children or steady girlfriends. One could cope with the prospect of death if this did not result in the misery and hardships for others. This inevitably caused some differences in attitude to the war and the way we behaved under fighting conditions. I am not saying that the men with family commitments were any less dedicated to the job, but I believe they were under much greater strain than many of the rest of us. We did tend to 'let ourselves go' when off duty. We drank a great deal of beer and used any excuse for a party commonly described as a 'piss up' either in the mess or at a local pub. We got to know the locals who were always friendly and understanding. Some shared their Sunday dinners with us and of course there were the girls . . .. Life on the Squadron was a mixture of fun, laughter, friendships, excitement and hell, just around the corner. In the Officers' Mess we had a very good standard of living. The food was very good. The sleeping quarters were comfortable and we had either a batwoman or batman to look after us, cleaning shoes, brass buttons etc. and pressing uniforms and making beds. I usually had a cup of tea brought to me in bed every morning!

At the end of January 1944 John Overton was now a Squadron Leader and 'A' Flight was moved to Tempsford, which was the centre for supplying the Special Operations Executives in Europe with personnel and materials. This work was carried out mostly during full moon periods, to make map reading by night easier, when supplies were dropped to agents who marked a dropping zone with lights, and bombers were used to drop containers of weapons and materials to supply the resistance fighters. We were at Tempsford for one month and took part in three of these operations, not very successfully I have to admit, due to poor weather conditions and other problems. At the end of our stay, the squadron was moved from Downham Market to Woolfox Lodge near Stamford, which was our new home for the next seven months. I was very sorry to leave Downham and the friends we had all made there. But this what service life is like and it was pointless to moan.

Frank had now returned to the squadron but Benny needed a long recovery period and a new wireless operator, Ron Partridge, had taken his place in the crew. In April 1944 we attacked three targets in France and then began training to use a new type of *Gee* called GH. This would enable the navigator to direct the pilot to fly to within a few yards of a position on the ground to allow bombs to be dropped blind. We practised during May using Lincoln cathedral as our target and taking photographs to record the results. This work continued in the first week of June. Then on 5 June we took part in a special operation code-named *Glimmer* to simulate a naval attack on the Pas de Calais area in order to deceive the Germans into believing that the D-Day landings were there and not Normandy. This was achieved by flying a progressive square search pattern between Newhaven and Boulogne, dropping

Lincoln cathedral seen through the Mk. 14 bombsight, which was very sophisticated for 1943. In April 1944 Squadron Leader John Overton's Stirling Mk. I crew in 218 (Gold Coast) Squadron at Downham Market, began training to use a new type of Gee called GH. *This would enable the navigator to direct the pilot to fly to within a few yards of a position on the ground allowing bombs to be dropped blind. They practised during May using Lincoln cathedral as their target and taking photographs to record the results. Then on 5 June they took part in operation* Glimmer *to simulate a naval attack on the Pas de Calais area in order to deceive the Germans into believing that the D-Day landings were there and not Normandy. (Author)*

Window continuously. The plan was successful and we shared the task with 617 Squadron with additional crewmembers to ensure that a continual dropping of the packets of Window was maintained. I understood that no aircraft were lost during this risky operation. We returned to Woolfox Lodge after 5 hours 15 minutes' of demanding flying. After the usual breakfast we slept for a few hours and awoke to find out on the 1 pm news, that today, 6 June, was D-Day and the landings in Normandy had begun. In my diary I noted that it was cold and miserable at home.

The evening social activities were curtailed due to lack of transport. Woolfox Lodge was 7 miles from Stamford on the Great North Road so John and I decided to buy old cars. He bought an Austin Seven and I found a 1933 Morris Minor in Oakham for £40. Mine was towed to the camp for me to try on 20 May and I soon decided to keep it. After a few minor adjustments, it was deemed fit to venture to King's Lynn for a trial run. We succeeded in returning home safely and the car was passed as roadworthy. From now on this little box on wheels was in great demand for visits to Stamford and the local villages to find the best beer.

On 7 June I received news that my father had had a stroke and I got immediate leave to go home to Maidstone. I arrived at midnight after an interesting journey through London, this being the first time I had driven a car on my own! I learnt quite a lot on the 150 mile trip. Father was in a coma and I did what I could to comfort Mother but I had to return to camp after three days. He died twelve days later and I returned home in the Morris Minor, a much more experienced driver by now. I stayed for a week, during which time the first flying bombs arrived over Maidstone to add to my mother's distress. We only had one more night bombing in June. This was to Lens in France and took less than 3 hours.

In July we began to attack the new flying bomb sites in northern France using GH for bombing blind in daylight through cloud cover. This was very successful and we did two of these exercises then, on 28 July, we had completed our thirty operations (John Overton had done thirty-two) and we had finished our duties with 218 Squadron and we were all due for seven days' leave. We all gathered at the aircraft dispersal for an official crew photograph after we had each added graffiti in red paint to the side of our aeroplane. I had very mixed feelings – delight at having survived against all the odds, tempered with apprehension at the thought of having to fend for myself without the support and friendships of the crew. Then on 30 July, Squadron DROs (Daily Routine Orders) stated that Frank had been awarded the DFM and I the DFC. Some celebration was called for and duly took place. Then we all went off on leave.

I became engaged to the daughter of the owners of the Railway Hotel at nearby Essendine and we were married in November 1944. I was eventually posted to Little Rissington as an armament instructor. Alf Aubrey joined 35 Squadron in Burma on Dakotas and sadly he was killed in action in 1945. The rest moved on to training posts, except for John Overton who was posted to Waddington where he was responsible for converting the squadron from Lancasters to Lincolns.

I am one of the few who survived and it seems dreadful to admit that I enjoyed the life on the Squadron. The only way I can admit this is in the belief that my friends who were lost also shared the good side of this time of battle for survival. That is how we saw it. The tragedy was in fact that so many did not survive.

Note

1. Wing Commander D. T. Saville DSO DFC and six of his crew FTR from the fire raid on Hamburg on 24/25 July 1943 when his Stirling was shot down by *Feldwebel* Hans Meissner of 6./NJG3 8 km NNW of Neumünster.

CHAPTER 11

By Chance and Good Fortune

Frank Diamond DFC AE

. . . my guardian angel was there – by chance and good fortune – to save me

Frank Diamond

I was born in 1922 and was fortunate to live to see seventeen. Living in Kent in the summer of 1938 I rehoused a colony of honeybees from a travelling box to a hive. My rough handling through fear and lack of knowledge made the bees very angry indeed. The fifty or so stings to my neck, legs and hands could well have been fatal and I was in bed for three days to recover. I suppose I did demonstrate a determined approach to life and some tenacity in controlling difficulties when they arose, plus a degree of courage. I am sure that anyone who has had a close encounter with a wasp's nest will wonder at the desire to handle stinging insects and to do it as I did over a period of several hours. I had to close and reopen the travelling box and the hive several times as I plucked up courage to return to the task, which I did complete rather late that warm and pleasant summer's evening.

In the same year I had two cycle accidents. One morning as I was riding to school and looking to wave to a friend who was riding along a converging lane I rode into the back of a stationary vehicle and somersaulted into the middle of the A20. Luckily, there was no following traffic to run over me. A gradual upward slope on the same road was part of my homeward journey and the speed of heavily loaded lorries at this point was low enough for an energetic boy to ride up behind and have a free tow. I grabbed a hanging chain. However, the chain was long and the swaying of the vehicle caused it to curl round the centre part of my handlebar. A quick decision was to open my legs and let my bicycle go on so that I could step on to the road. I landed reasonably well and ran behind until I could disconnect the chain. Free tows were illegal so my parents would not have been told of this incident.

In June 1939 I joined the Territorial Army and the local battalion of the Royal West Kent Regiment. The 1914–18 War was still fresh in the memories of those whose close relatives had served and all too many had died. An uncle of mine had been a regular soldier of the Royal Horse Artillery in India prior to that time, and was in France and later in the Army of Occupation in

Flying Officer Frank Diamond in 1943 proudly wearing his 1939–43 Star. Altogether, he flew twenty-two ops on Stirlings, fifty more on Mosquitoes on his second tour and he was promoted to flight lieutenant and also awarded the DFC. (Frank Diamond)

Germany. He was my tangible link to the Empire, which covered a quarter of the Earth's surface and was something greater than anything seen before and we were proud to be a part of it. Our school atlas had large areas coloured red to show how broadly it was spread. With this background it seemed right for those of my age to accept that if the country needed to be served again, however terrible the previous conflict had been, we should be prepared for the eventuality. I had some foreboding when in late August 1939 the Territorial Army was mobilised in anticipation of the declaration of war, which did follow just one week later on 3 September. This early introduction to the dangers that life may have had a profound influence on me. I am quite sure that it fostered in me the will to live life to the full. In October an over enthusiastic fellow soldier who was demonstrating the use of a rifle with fixed bayonet struck me over the left eye. I still have the scar.

My days in the infantry and involvement with my regiment's part in France and the Dunkirk evacuation was averted by the introduction of an age limit of 19, below which servicemen were transferred to Home Defence units. However, two years' service with anti-aircraft units proved rather dull so I volunteered for something with more excitement. The burly CPO (Chief Petty Officer) at the RN recruiting office in Reading put a fatherly hand on my shoulder and said, 'We have plenty of recruits lad. You should speak to the RAF. They want chaps for aircrew duties'. I thought about that and wondered whether it might be a bit too exciting according to the stories I had heard, but I soon came to the decision to give it a go. In May 1941 I was interviewed by the RAF. After a written examination I was told that being good at figures, I would make a good navigator. I saw no reason to argue. I was just pleased to have been accepted. But my acceptance for aircrew duties was to be a far more extreme test of fate.

Initial training in the basics of flying, meteorology, air navigation and general airmanship, which I found so interesting following my dull two years or so in the army and at Torquay too, was like taking an enforced holiday. And, as an additional bonus I was destined to join those fortunate ones who were to be sent to Miami, Florida, for training at the Navigation School of Pan American Airways. The Atlantic crossing was in January 1942. Our ship was the SS *Volendam*, a Dutch cargo vessel of the Holland America Line. (In 1938 I had handled a *Volendam* cargo manifest when I was a junior clerk in the Caribbean Steamship Agency in London.) We were accompanied by the Canadian CPR (Canadian Pacific Railway) ship *Montcalm* and two small US destroyers, fifty of which had been passed to us by the Americans under a leasing deal. Those who know the Atlantic will confirm that January is a particularly bad month to choose. During the first of three severe storms we encountered we lost contact with the *Montcalm* and it was reported that the destroyers had returned to Milford Haven. The ship was put on a zigzag course and we proceeded on our journey to Halifax, Nova Scotia. I proved myself suitable for the Navy – that Reading CPO missed signing a very good man – as I was one of an exceedingly small group who were not seasick to the point of near death. On arrival at Halifax we were told that submarines had been very active along

Pilot Officer Hugh 'Wendell' Wilkie, a very competent 20 year-old New Zealander pilot. (Frank Diamond)

the eastern seaboard and there had been a particularly large number of sinkings. We had been assumed lost, as we had been at sea for much longer than expected. We had had ten very eventful days and I shall never travel on a ship again and view a wave from its trough to its peak as high as the side of a good sized house – or was it bigger?

The chance of a sudden demise now subsided. The train journey to and from Miami could hardly be called hazardous. It was an experience and the time there was something not to be missed. Take-off and landing in flying boats has its risks, but it was the return crossing of the Atlantic in June, when the ocean had barely a ripple, when we thought a submarine might just have the temerity to send us to a watery grave. However, we were home safely and further navigation training commenced at No. 3 AFU (Advanced Flying Unit) at Halfpenny Green (Bobbington), Shropshire. The fundamental change was the weather pattern and we were now required to fly with clouds in the sky! And usually the aircraft were past their best, so the accident rate was a threat to survival. It was only in later years that I knew that 8,000 of Bomber Command trainee aircrew perished in the training units through engine failures and trainee pilot errors. On 11 August we flew a navigational exercise in an Anson to Wales to find a crossroads north of Monmouth. We found the

Sergeant Hugh 'Wendell' Wilkie (far left) and his all sergeant crew who crewed up together in October 1942 at 11 OTU at Oakley before flying Wellington ICs. Next is 32-year old William 'Bill' Mudge, the 32 year old wireless operator; Frank Diamond; T. 'Curly' Palmer, New Zealander bomb aimer, and Jock Palmer, tail gunner (Frank Diamond)

crossroads but lost our way on the flight back. Finally, I said that castle below looks like Windsor Castle. It was! We ended our daylight exercise at night!

Next, in October 1942, it was to No. 11 OTU at Oakley, where we crewed up before flying elderly Wellington ICs. Sergeant Hugh 'Wendell' Wilkie, a very competent 20-year-old New Zealander was my pilot. He was a year younger than I was and all the others except our wireless operator who was considered old at 32. We were all sergeants. The bomb aimer was 'Curly' Palmer and the wireless operator was Bill Mudge. Jock Palmer was the tail gunner. We were to become operational on the Stirling and at 1657 Conversion Unit at Stradishall we acquired John Ledgerwood, the mid-upper

126

gunner, a nicely spoken Englishman with something of a wry smile, and a Welsh flight engineer. The crews were usually seven. The earlier practice of carrying a co-pilot had been discontinued purely on the grounds of waste of manpower. The bomb aimer stood in in that capacity to give the normal assistance with take-off and landing controls. Should a pilot be killed or injured, the crew would look to him to fly the machine if it were possible to do so, rather than the ultimate of abandoning it and relying on a parachute. We were all young and short on experience. I have no idea how many hours flying the others had but I had 180.

The flight engineer's main function was to monitor the engines and, as the Stirling had fourteen fuel tanks, he had to ensure that fuel was fed to them and taken in the correct order to maintain the optimum balance of the aircraft. Our wireless operator's most important function was to listen out to base in case there should be a recall signal. To miss it could not only mean flying on to the target when everyone else had gone home, but result in failure to be alerted to adverse weather conditions. It was rare indeed for him to transmit as a transmission could show our position.

Our tail gunner and our mid-upper gunner each sat in a power-operated turret, which could be turned to a limited degree in a sideways arc and their guns could be raised and lowered through about 60 degrees. They searched the sky continuously for the dark shape of hostile aircraft. It was the tail gunner's responsibility to give the pilot instructions as to the turns that should be made when a fighter attacked from the rear to ensure that the attacker could not bring his guns to bear on our aircraft.

With all the hazards of OTU flying we arrived at No. 15, our operational squadron at Bourn, Cambridgeshire, in March 1943. The squadron then moved to Mildenhall, Suffolk. From then on the Reaper stood beside us. A tour of operations was thirty and we soon found that it was difficult to find tour-expired people. The loss rate was especially high among Stirling crews. It was slow and with a load could reach about 16,000 feet, whilst with evasive action over occupied territory it was at around 12,000 feet over a Ruhr city. At that height it was also vulnerable from above if a Lancaster at 20,000 feet released bombs. Bombing times were set to prevent this but not every crew kept to its time slot. The first of the four-engined bombers, its wingspan was 9 feet less than the original design. This was by special request to Short Brothers, the makers, to allow it to pass through the doors of the standard RAF hangar! This was an important requirement if it were to be serviced away from the elements, but this fundamental change caused problems. It had to have a huge undercarriage, which meant that the cockpit window was 20 feet from the ground. The Stirling was slower and had a much lower ceiling than the Lancaster or the Halifax, both of which came later and replaced the Stirling towards the end of 1943.

The decision to operate under cover of darkness was a direct result of catastrophic and unsustainable losses in daylight attacks in the first years of the war. Our slow and lightly armed aircraft were outmanoeuvred by the German fighter aircraft and they had weapons of higher calibre and range. Our techniques were very different from those of the US daylight formations, which relied both for navigation, and the release of bombs on the leading aircraft in each formation. Their arrival over the correct target depended on the skill and the survival of the lead navigator and the lead bombardier gave the signal for bombs to be dropped. I believe it was only the pilot and these two key members of a crew who always flew together. The crew of each RAF aircraft operated separately and lost contact with the other aircraft in their squadron as they climbed away from their base into a dark sky. Each aircraft operated without navigation lights; the navigator's chart table was illuminated by a small orange lamp and he was surrounded by a curtain. The engine exhausts were masked as far as was practical. Care was taken in every way to avoid detection. Each member was responsible to the other crewmembers to give of his best in his particular function, as the lives of the others were dependent upon it. The bond within crews illustrated just how strong this was and to have another man fly with you as a replacement because of a regular crewman's sickness was regarded as a bad omen indeed. The fear of disaster on such operations was there right up to the point of a safe return.

It was usual for crews to keep to the same aircraft. Pilots preferred it that way and it was their responsibility to air test the machine in the afternoon prior to a night operation and liaise with our ground crew to ensure that every function was as good as it could be. The support we had from those who worked in all weathers to give us a safe and reliable aircraft was great and the erks, as we sometimes called them, were never given sufficient praise. (It was for them in particular that Bomber Harris fought for a Bomber Campaign medal to recognise their loyalty and he even refused a peerage because they were not given the honour he considered to be their due.)

Navigation was my function. Each operation started with the preparation of my chart: drawing the route, measuring the distances, and calculating the courses to fly by using the forecast winds the weather man had given us. It would be a continuing task in the air to fix the aircraft's position. Air navigation at that time was so very different from anything that came later. We did have maps with some surface detail and colouring for daylight flying, but not for high-level night flying. We used charts with a scale of 1:1,000,000 so this gave us the eastern side of England and much of Europe. It was plain black and white and the black was there just to show coastline, major rivers and inlets lakes and large cities. We had room for plenty of pencil work. It was fixed to the navigation table and was the focus of constant endeavour. As a Mercator projection, lines of longitude were shown as parallel and vertical lines on which a protractor could be placed in order to draw compass lines, a fundamental requirement if one was to determine a course to fly and transfer it to the pilot's compass. Further, the degrees of latitude shown on each side of the chart each divided into 60 minutes, with 1 minute equivalent to 1 nautical mile. (Distances were measured in nautical miles and speed was expressed in knots.) From 1942 when the Pathfinder Force was formed the less experienced crews were given guidance by the use of pyrotechnics particularly for target marking, and electronic aids for positioning became available to all crews. Nevertheless, the basic method still relied on the ingenuity of each navigator in splendid isolation to bring his aircraft to complete its task and return to base, this being written with all deference to the vital functions performed throughout by the pilot and others in the crew.

Prior to an operation there was a navigation briefing at which pilots, bomb aimers and navigators were shown the route, heavily defended areas and other problems, which might arise. We were briefed on the fuel and bomb loads, both of which would be influenced by the target and its distance from base, and, most important for Stirling crews, the time to be over the target. The Lancaster and Halifax crews flew up to 10,000 feet higher than we did, but if both their timing and ours were as planned all was well. However, I know of one instance when an incendiary dropped from above was caught in the wing of a Stirling and the pilot of that aircraft kept it for many years. He used it as a doorstop in his house.

Take-off was always an anxious time. We had confidence in Hugh Wilkie, but there was always the possibility of a failure outside his control. Engine failure with a full load had only one outcome.

It was lonely when the last dimmed lights of our base were left behind. Those of the crew who had a view, both the wireless operator and I being excluded, would be scanning the sky for other aircraft. Collisions were surprisingly rare but with several hundred aircraft flying the same route, we did feel the occasional disturbance as we crossed someone else's slipstream and were reminded that darkness had its dangers in other ways.

New navigation aids and a target marking device code-named *Oboe* was coming into use early in 1943, but the effective range for both was limited. With the new aids and the approach of shorter nights, as well as the requirement that we should attack the industrial cities, the bomber offensive was directed towards the Ruhr. Our tour started in March as this began.

My first training flight had been in a flying boat of Pan American Airways in Florida on 11 March 1942. It was on 11 March 1943 that we completed our first operation. Our task was to lay mines in the waters off the Dutch coast. We did three of these relatively easy trips and were fortunate not to meet any opposition, but there was still the grim reality of flying at night with no contact at all with our base and against an enemy out to destroy us.

The Ruhr was well defended. The twinkling display of shell bursts as we approached the target area was intimidating to say the least. German nightfighters had airborne radar to find us on the blackest of nights. And we were unaware of a new and deadly tactic by which, having found us, the fighter could with stealth come close and fly in the blind spot beneath us and deliver fire with upward-firing guns. They soon learnt to direct their fire at the wings instead of the fuselage. An exploding bomb load could bring the destruction of the fighter as well as its victim.

I did not keep a diary, a source of great regret, and with hindsight I suppose I was not mature enough to think of writing for posterity and for that matter we thought more of survival. The nights we did not fly were cheerful occasions when the odd glass of beer helped all of us to relax and get a good night's sleep.

It was quite early in our tour when on 20/21 April our squadron was included in an attack on the Baltic port of Rostock.[1] My record just gives a start time of an hour before midnight, that it was low level and took 8 hours – the longest we ever did. Our departure point on leaving home territory was Southwold on the coast of Suffolk. We were instructed to fly on a course from there to a point on the coast of Denmark. By flying at 2,000 feet we were told that we would escape radar detection and the presence of a full moon would not cause problems. It was unusual to fly close to the sea and I am sure that those who did not have the curtained area, which was mine, enjoyed the scenery. However, my pleasure came in a different way. I had always been interested in the way that Pan American Airways had put emphasis on astro navigation, which had been so very important to them in the pioneering days of the 1930s when they circled the globe with their passenger routes. This came through whilst I was at their school in Miami, Florida, during my time there in 1942. So, here was my opportunity.

To be successful with a bubble sextant it is vital to have a steady platform. The short explanation is that the instrument is held in both hands and with one eye at the eyepiece a small bubble in the liquid contained in a chamber at that point is illuminated to give a circle. When the star, or in this instance the moon, is brought into the centre of this by adjusting the sighting mechanism, its altitude can be read on the sextant's scale. An unsteady platform will cause the light circle to move and make an accurate and useful measurement impossible. At that point we were flying on automatic pilot, George as we called it, so the machine was more stable than if it were being flown manually.

The moon was at about 40 degrees above the horizon and on the nose of the aircraft – a near perfect position. I suppose we were over that part of the North Sea for about 2 hours.

During the last 40 minutes or so I took several shots of the moon and the calculations gave position lines at right angles to our track. These were most valuable as we converged on the coastline and ensured that we crossed it at the correct point. To cross too far south would have put us in danger. A Stirling of another squadron, which crossed to the south, was shot down over Esbjerg airfield. The flak gunners could hardly miss an aircraft at that height.

After the coast we were over the Kattegat and turned south and through the islands to the Baltic. It was here that we had our first experience of light tracer from flak ships. It was quite disturbing to watch. You see it leave its source and snake up towards the aircraft gradually twisting closer then seeming to accelerate to a point where we must be hit, only to see it move away and eventually be out of range. Others were having the same treatment, but the gunners seemed to have no successes. We continued to Rostock, where our industrial targets included an aircraft factory. As always, we carried out our instructions and were glad to return without any problems. Only four days before we had been hit by flak over Mannheim.

In May we went to three cities in the Ruhr. The defences there were quite fearful. The Mosquito marker aircraft using the very accurate *Oboe* system had to face their particular share of flak These Mosquito crews flew at 25,000 feet along a radio beam and released their pyrotechnic marker on the appropriate signal from the controller in England. And the marker fell within yards of the intended point. To do this the aircraft had to be flown with precision and the flak gunners soon found the release point so up went every available shell and those crews had to keep straight on into them. These target markers were to make our attacks more effective but ultimately it still depended upon the skill of the individual bomb aimers to placed the bombs on the industrial targets that we were sent to destroy. This was the only accessible part of Germany during the short nights. The press called the concentration on these cities 'The Battle of the Ruhr'. Anti-aircraft guns were moved there from other areas and I believe there were in the region of 40,000 there at that time. Fighters were still a menace on the fringes of the area. My logbook has a note that on 29 May our rear gunner fired at what he thought was an Me109.

However, our near demise came on the night of 11/12 June in Stirling III BF470 *G-George*. I have never been at all superstitious but it was our thirteenth and it could have been a Friday![2] We were over Düsseldorf and fortunately we no longer had our bomb load. We were turning away for home when the port outer motor was hit. The engine was very quickly an inextinguishable fire and the propeller turned ever faster. The engine noise was terrifying. I had a window in the fuselage to give me a full view of the engine as I sat at my table. John Ledgerwood, the mid-upper gunner, had the best view and his was the first voice over the intercom. He was very calm. We all were. Hugh said very little. He was working hard to handle a crippled aircraft, but he was quiet and efficient and, like the rest of us, he was never one to use bad language and curse if matters did not go as planned. John Ledgerwood's voice was calm and his comment to Hugh was that the propeller was likely to leave the engine and he suggested that a gradual dive and climb movement would ensure that when it did come off it would go over or under the aircraft. Little was said by anyone and Hugh proceeded as suggested.

Meanwhile, the noise from the runaway engine became louder and the propeller boss glowed red hot and then white hot. That noise and my clear view of the engine was scary but John's calm voice and Hugh's silence kept us all in a shaken but hopeful mood. The situation was under control to a degree, but the outcome was still in doubt until another comment from John, who was best able to monitor the situation, that the propeller had come off and had spun over his turret. He was greatly relieved that his turret had not been damaged and with hindsight we were pleased that the tail of the aircraft had not been hit.

Our height over the target area had been 12,000 feet. We were now at 8,000 feet. The weather was not entirely against us. Above, we had a clear sky, almost no moon and the blackness made the canopy of stars brilliant. Below us a sheet of cloud with the top a few thousand feet below. How lucky we were to have remained above the cloud whilst disposing of our propeller! Hugh's task would have been infinitely more difficult if he had been battling to cope with our problems in cloud. In fact, it could have been impossible.

We now had problems in my department. The violent movements of the aircraft had caused the gyro of our master compass to topple. This can be corrected but it takes time, during which there is no steady pointer to steer by. However, I could see the North Star – Polaris – very clearly. And, with Polaris on the right, to starboard, I knew we were flying a westerly course. The engine we no longer had was the one that operated the generator for our navigational equipment, so fixing the aircraft's position had to be by other means. The cloud prevented recognition of ground features, but we had no maps for that purpose and it is very difficult on a dark night to identify even large landmarks. Radio fixes were not available except near or over England and to transmit a signal for that purpose was to invite any enemy station to also take a fix. We were much slower now as well as low in the sky. We were an easy target for a fighter pilot who could increase his tally with very little effort. The only way to fix our position would be in the manner of the pioneers! To fly straight and level over enemy territory at 8,000 feet was not a popular suggestion at all, but essential as I have described previously. From the technical viewpoint it was a nigh perfect position as I stood under the Perspex blister we called the astrodome. There were brilliant stars all round so that I could choose three for each fix and have them positioned nicely through the circle. Apart from the time required to identify and select the stars to be used, the sextant had an averaging, wind-up mechanism, which whirred away and took sixty readings over a minute to produce an average. Directly after noting the read-out it was vital to note the time, and to the second. Our watches were always checked against Greenwich before departure. To the minimum 5 minutes needed to take these observations, it took more than another five before three lines could be drawn on the chart to mark our position, as it had been 10 minutes or more earlier! After correcting the sight readings for dome refraction, as the sighting was taken beneath a curved surface, and for the effect of the earth's rotation on the bubble, calculations were then made using the tabulations printed in the Air Almanac. We were a very worried crew, but in the light of this, and the fact that I fixed our position three times in this way, is some testimony to the way we handled our near calamity. It was important that we should know that we were not only tracking to the west and homeward, but that we were to break cloud near to Mildenhall, our base. The cloud sheet over the Ruhr extended far in to England. We had a base beacon, placed at a distance from the airfield and repositioned daily. It was indeed a relief when we saw it flashing. For 2 hours or more Hugh had flown the aircraft on three engines and, much to everyone's relief, he put it down safely at our home base. *G-George* was repaired and we flew it again eight days later to Le Creusot.

We operated over the Ruhr on seven more nights in June. Our rear gunner exchanged fire with a Junkers 88 on the 19th and on 28/29 June, our return from Cologne was on three engines. There were other life-threatening incidents and one was blissfully ignorant of the near misses, but when we began to lose hope of reaching the stand down figure of thirty for no one we knew had done so, there came sudden and totally unexpected relief. Our commanders did recognise our plight.

My last two operations were in the last week of July. We were on the first of the heavy series of raids against Hamburg, which caused such catastrophic damage that Albert Speer invited Hitler to see it for himself and reported that a few more such attacks would make it impossible to continue the war. It was beyond our capabilities at that time too. The raid on 24 July was also the first time a radar countermeasure, code named *Window*, was used. Basically, the defences were showered with narrow aluminium strips about 6 inches long, each backed with blackened paper. These reflected the radar beams and created a mush of false signals on the defender's receivers. It was so effective that out of a force of 791 only twelve aircraft were lost that night. The losses on well defended cities at that time were normally 6 per cent, so this could be compared with fifty aircraft. *Window* could be said to have saved the lives of 300 aircrew. Just 125 of the vulnerable Stirlings were there; perhaps it was another near miss for us?

On the following night, it was a 4-hour flight to Essen. This compared with 6 hours to Hamburg. There was nothing exceptional to record in the logbook, but I am sure we had a lively reception and it was probably the weather that brought about the change of target.

If we had known that Essen was our last op there would have been great jubilation, but it was Hugh's twenty-sixth so we were still fearful as to the outcome of his last four. We would not have quite thirty but we anticipated a stand down with him. I had just twenty-two so my aprehension was that I shoud be required to fly with another crew. However, my guardian angel was there – by chance and good fortune – to save me.

On our next op, early in August, we were taken right up to the wire, so to speak, by the normal daytime air-testing of our machine, attending briefing and having the usual meal in the Mess. It was then when we were thinking of boarding the aircrew bus for the aircraft with some unspoken foreboding, for we never talked about survival in any negative way, that the message came that our tour was finished and we were 'tour expired'. A person pardoned on the scaffold could not feel greater relief!

Two months later my squadron converted to Lancasters and the Stirlings ended their time as tugs for gliders and general transport aircraft.

The crew broke up and we each went to training units to pass on our experience to others. Sadly, and within months, in April 1944 our pilot Hugh Wilkie was killed whilst night flying in a Stirling at Stradishall. On his take-off run he hit three airmen on bicycles who were crossing the active runway as they took a short cut across the airfield after their evening out. They were killed and damage to the wing of the aircraft caused the sea rescue dinghy to be released from its storage and for it to wrap around the tail controls. Hugh gained sufficient height for the trainees to use thir parachutes but he could not land the aircraft and it dived into the ground a mile from the airfield. To this day I feel anger that his death was due to thoughtlessness and stupidity of those three who died with him.

The operational training units – the final stage before crews joined squadrons – used aircraft considered outdated and too old for operational use. Staff pilots flew with crews until they were allowed to go solo. Staff navigators had to fly as captains on their cross-country exercises. I was always fearful of a crash on taking off or landing and they did happen with terrible consequences. The twin-engined Wellingtons were fabric-covered and fire in these circumstances was horrible in the extreme.

Rumours of a forthcoming landing on the continent were reinforced in April 1944 when the armourers were required to exercise their skills in loading bombs on to our training aircraft. The thought of flying as captain of a pupil crew over a battlefront seemed to have little future to me so I volunteered immediately for another tour. In three weeks I was training to do this on the de Havilland Mosquito. At the time it was the fastest and highest flying machine on either side. Made of wood with two Rolls-Royce Merlin engines, it looked beautiful. It could be troublesome on take-off, but all pilots said it was a truly wonderful aeroplane to fly. Navigators had to get used to working faster. We still had to work with a pencil a chart and the other basics. At 1655 MTU at Warboys I crewed up with Flight Sergeant Ron Hemming and we were posted to 571 Squadron at Oakington. As my pilot was not commissioned we did not share the same Mess. This was unfortunate but it did not interfere with our operational efficiency. We were destined to fly with the Pathfinders and operated alongside a Lancaster squadron with the role of providing some cover for the heavy bombers by creating diversionary trails and raids. Having in mind our wooden airframes, our friends on the Lancs dubbed us 'the model aeroplane club'.

Our casualty rate was much lower than theirs was. This was acknowledged later in our tour when it was suggested that we could extend it from thirty to fifty, and this we agreed to do. However, predicted flak and radar-controlled searchlights were a threat up to 30,000 feet and flak once put our port engine out of action over Kiel. We took Mosquito MM156 to Berlin and on our approach a master searchlight caught us. Escape was made impossible as others immediately backed it up and we were held for 12 minutes into and away from the target area. At first we were fearful of being taken by a fighter circling above us. Just after releasing our 4,000 lb bomb and turning away there was a flak burst close to the tail. It had missed us. As we had now jettisoned our wing fuel tanks and no longer had the bomb, we could increase speed and dash for home. Speaking of the experience the following day, I said that as a true veteran of flak in a Stirling over the Ruhr, that it was a bit close but really nothing that bad. However, I agreed to go to the hangar and take a look at the damage. The holes in the tail unit were being repaired. The jagged holes in the skin were being trimmed with a fine-toothed saw and inserts cut to fit and be glued into place before taping with fabric and painting. I thought no more of it. We never flew that aircraft again but this was of little significance to my mind. The ground staff officer had taken a much closer look and found serious damage to the main structure in addition to the skin and he had ruled it unfit for further use. I now know that the Reaper was denied our scalps by a very narrow margin indeed. If that shell burst had occurred at a mere fraction of a second earlier it would have been a direct hit. And, at age twenty-two I would not have lived to enjoy a further sixty years or more.[3]

To mark my eightieth birthday my daughter's present was a trip in a hot air balloon. She said she could not be sure, but she thought that a list of the many things I had done did not include a flight in a balloon. Anyone who flew on operations over Europe or anywhere for that matter will understand that the thought of flying in an aircraft that was 'on fire' had not seemed particularly desirable until then.

Notes

1. Eighty-six Stirlings were dispatched to attack the Heinkel factory near Rostock, but a smoke screen concealed this target and bombing was scattered. Eight Stirlings were lost.
2. Some 783 aircraft including ninety-nine Stirlings took part in the raid. Thirty-eight aircraft, including two Stirlings, were lost.
3. Frank Diamond spent the last three years of his RAF career, 1945–47 on Dakotas in 271 Squadron. In 1945 they evacuated wounded from the battle zones and later PoWs and personnel from Europe, the Mediterranean and India.

CHAPTER 12

'If Yer Can't Take a Joke Yer Shouldn't Have Joined'

Ron Read DFC

> *Many airmen will not see tomorrow's dawn*
> *To their after-life they will have gone*
> *That is the price main airmen will pay*
> *They'll have no tomorrow and no today*
>
> *But every full moon when skies are clear*
> *This awesome sight will once again appear*
> *If each bomber's moon we always do send*
> *A thousand planes out, this war will end*

'*Bomber's Moon*', 7 October 1944, from *No Place To Hide*
by Sergeant George 'Ole' Olson RCAF, air gunner

As the winter term of 1934/35 drew to a close, my thoughts became occupied with the future. During schooldays the future consists of the next day, week, examination, football or cricket match. The rest lies in the lap of the Gods. I was unable to see any way I could start a career in aviation, which I so desired, with my limited qualifications gained at local south London elementary schools and Technical College in Southall. But radio was becoming increasingly associated with flying and perhaps employment with a radio company could provide an entry into the magic world of flying. My first job was with HMV or the Gramophone Company, where my father had been a long-term employee. By April 1939 I was working in the Road Surfacing Section of the Road Research Laboratory at Harmondsworth. Soon after the war started I decided I wanted to join the RAF as a fighter pilot. In February 1940 I went for my conscription interview but there was no recruiting for the RAF. In June 1940 this changed and anyone over the age of 18 was eligible to apply for aircrew. Finally, in October I was successful and was told to report to Uxbridge RAF depot where I was recommended for pilot training. In June 1941 I was on my way to Canada for flying training on the Tiger Moth and Harvard single-engined trainers. Then, for reasons that

Pilot Officer (later Flight Lieutenant DFC) Ron Read who flew a tour as a Halifax pilot on 78 Squadron in 4 Group at Middleton St George, County Durham and Linton on Ouse. (Read)

were never made clear, nine of us were selected to fly old twin-engined Avro Ansons. By early December 1941 I was commissioned as a pilot officer. In January 1942 it was back to England for six weeks at the reception centre in Bournemouth and then No. 3 Advanced Flying Unit at Leconfield in Yorkshire on 30 March. Ground school lectures were about fighter operations and tactics, but in the second week the need for fighter pilots was no longer urgent and the calls of Bomber Command for all available pilots and crews was overwhelming. We were to change our syllabus to bomber pilots. Disaster had struck. All through training I had a grim vision of me sitting in an old Wimpy bomber flogging my way in the night through the flak-filled skies of Germany. The previous week I had happily put aside that bad dream for a life in fighters but it was not to be now. To say we were disappointed was putting it mildly. However, there was nothing we could do about it. We just had to accept life as it turned out and get on with our training. As the flight sergeant said, 'If yer can't take a joke yer shouldn't have joined'.

On 1 April, an appropriate date as the laugh was on us, our training as bomber pilots started when we passed on to the flying wing to make our acquaintance with the Oxford. On 15 June 1942 our time at Leconfield came to an end when we were posted to 12 OTU, Benson in Oxfordshire. Meanwhile, I had been given a rating of 'Average' for my flying assessment. Six of us left for Benson on a sunny Tuesday 16 June. We arrived at about six to meet a very surprised adjutant. 'Are you here to fly these new aircraft we're just getting?' he asked. 'What new aircraft?' we asked. He invited us to accompany him after dinner. Intrigued, we followed him to a hangar. He unlocked the doors, opened them a slit and led us inside. There, resplendent in an eggshell blue finish stood the most beautiful aircraft I had ever seen. It was the first Mosquito issued to the RAF, ready for its introduction into service as a photo reconnaissance aircraft. We were enthralled but sceptical. 'I wish it was for us but I don't think they've sent us straight from AFU to fly that.' The next morning the adjutant had the bad news. 'Solved the problem lads, 12 OTU moved to a place called Chipping Warden. They're expecting you.' It was the end of another dream and goodbye to the lovely Mosquito before we'd hardly met. Yet another long rail journey took us to Banbury, where our

137

transport to Chipping Warden was waiting. Now we were back to real life. Stumpy, black Wellington bombers awaited us.

At Chipping Warden, or Chippy, we were introduced to another life style. On the wartime RAF stations, the Nissen hut reigned supreme. We shared a ten-bed Nissen hut, ate in a Nissen-hutted mess, took ground school in a Nissen hut and went into a Nissen hut at flights. At first sight, a Nissen looked anything but cosy. However, as wartime servicemen we could settle down anywhere and a Nissen wasn't too bad, although we certainly missed the comforts of the permanent buildings at Leconfield. It was summer time though so we escaped the condensation on the walls and the water on the floor that affected winter dwellers. Outside the aircraft were old Vickers Wellingtons, the Wimpy. I know they said, 'If yer can't take a joke, yer shouldn't have joined'. But this was beyond a joke. It was my nightmare scenario and it was here.

The first day we were there excitement pervaded the station. They were preparing for the next '1,000 bomber raid' that night. It was the third of the massive raids Air Marshal Sir Arthur Harris put on, to show the enemy and British alike, just what he meant to do with Bomber Command. 'Butch' Harris, as his crews were to call him was a rough, tough, vulgar egomaniac who was just what Bomber Command needed. He feared no foe, senior officers or politicians. He brooked no arguments from juniors and pooh-poohed any from those of equal or senior status who held a contra opinion. Harris knew what he was going to do and proceeded to move Heaven and earth to do it. Woe betide anyone who stood in his way. He was as firm believer in the Trenchard doctrine and with it he was going to win the war. The first 1,000 bomber raid involving 1,046 aircraft had been on Cologne on 30 May. It had been a success. The massive number of aircraft had overwhelmed the defences and created great damage by the standards of those days. Of forty aircraft, an acceptable 3.5 per cent were lost. The next night, 1 June, 965 aircraft attacked Essen and thirty-one aircraft were lost. Essen as usual was well hidden by broken low cloud, the industrial haze that always covered the Ruhr, plus the artificial smoke the Germans poured out when warnings sounded. Essen had escaped almost entirely. The bombing effort was so dispersed, the Germans didn't even know it was the target.

The next effort, was the one that all at Chippy were preparing for on 25 June. It was to be Bremen. The aircraft were manned by mixed complements of instructor pilots and navigators flying with trainee crews. It was to be another 1,000 bomber raid effort, although eventually only 904 aircraft set off. In order to reach the magic figure of 1,000, Harris had to order into the line training aircraft from OTUs and other units. But this was the last time he would do so; the subsequent disruption to training programmes was too costly.

We watched our aircraft take off with mixed feelings. It would have been nice to be taking part, but in a clapped out old training Wimpy, well perhaps it was as well we weren't. Again, it wasn't a good result; many aircraft failed to reach the target and losses, at forty-four aircraft, were high. We lost two aircraft from Chippy. One resident from our hut, a Canadian wireless operator, didn't return. We watched his effects being collected the following morning. It was a first indication that operations weren't going to be all fun.

Most of our instructors were New Zealanders and tended to be rather serious. All the instructors had recently completed operations and we were avid for their advice. However, when we asked the inevitable, 'What's it like, going on ops?' they found it difficult to explain. Answers varied from 'Bloody dangerous' to 'It's a bit like running out for an important football match playing for your school. Difficult at first but not bad once you get started'. On 30 June we started flying Wimpys. At the commencement of flying we found our crews. I found Vic Inman, the navigator, a modest fellow who didn't have much to say for himself. He then brought along a gunner and a wireless operator for my selection. On the radio was Taff Lewis, a thin, dark little Celt from Newport. A clarinet player in a local band before he joined up, we had something in common. He was also a bit of a wit. Coming from a small Monmouthshire village he was the youngest of a large family of ten and most unworldly. In 1941 he received his call-up papers. His elderly mother was sure the country could win the war without him and fully expected him to be returned to her as unacceptable. But he was accepted for wireless operator training and fully expected to become a ground operator.

Harry Laidlaw was the bomb aimer, allotted to us from the two unclaimed. Bomb aimers were a new breed, the result of Air Marshal Harris's desire to achieve better target identification and results. The first thousand or so were converted from navigators. Navigators had previously dropped the bombs, when near enough to the target to see it, but the poor results revealed by the Butt Report, made it necessary to specialise this post. At the same time as introducing bomb aimers, Bomber Command dropped the second pilot. The loss of two pilots with every aircraft was too much of a strain on the training resources to continue. The new bomb aimer would assist the pilot at take-off and landing when not in the front turret as gunner, or in his bombing position for the run up to the target. The changes were not altogether welcomed. One pilot in a large aircraft had plenty on his hands at critical moments and there were plenty of cases where the pilot had been injured and the aircraft flown home by the second pilot. While bomb aimers were to be given some training by their captain pilots in flying straight and level, they were not expected to land an aircraft. The idea was that the bomb aimer would fly the aircraft to friendly territory, where the crew would bale out. They had severe limitations if the aircraft was damaged or if a crewmember was wounded.

Laidlaw was older by about five years and married, two attributes that set him apart. Tall and sallow, he had a slight stoop and his slow Mancunian drawl was accompanied by a slow mind, at least as far as technical matters went. He didn't share our sense of humour either and remained on the outside of things. The more irreverent members of the crew soon christened him 'Septimus'. It seemed apt. To complete our crew we had a big, moon-faced gunner with flaming red hair, Sergeant A. F. Smith, known as Sunshine. He seemed sleepy most of the time and once honoured my night circuits and bumps by sleeping through three landings. The rest of the crew were amazed at such a feat. We were a mixed bunch and I felt that I had a lot of work to do to make a satisfactory operational crew.

I was assessed as 'Above Average' as a heavy bomber pilot and was very pleased to be up with Geoff Hobbs who I had met at elementary training in Calgary. The best pilot all the way through all our various courses, we'd been friends for over a year. I now hoped to fly Lancasters, but I expected to be posted to Stirlings. Chipping Warden was primarily turning out pilots for 3 Group Bomber Command and it was currently converting from Wellingtons to Stirlings. I was posted to 78 Squadron at Middleton St George, County Durham, a Halifax squadron in 4 Group. I had missed Stirlings, which was a relief but hadn't much hope of Lancasters now as 4 Group was all Halifaxes. Sergeant Tommy Thompson, Geoff Hobbs and E. G. 'Morty' Mortensen, my long-standing friend who I had met on the SS *Volendam* on 25 January 1942 when we returned from pilot training in Canada, reported to Middleton St George on 3 September. Morty was an educated Cockney. His father was a Dane who had come to London as a young man in the tailoring business. He had drifted to the East End of London to set up his own business. He must have done well as Morty went to Highgate public school. Dark, saturnine, with a long, serious face, which denied his satirical sense of humour, Morty was a mixed up person. Strongly anti-Semitic, a bit of a snob without any reason to be, I had never met anyone with his views before and found them hard to take at first. Much of his attitude was a pose, acquired from a conflict between his public schooling and his residence in a predominantly poor Jewish community. Apart from those idiosyncrasies, which we soon learned to laugh at or ignore, Morty was a wryly humorous person who became a lot more likeable on closer acquaintance. He joined up with Geoff Hobbs and myself and by the time we reached Gourock, we had become firm friends. Trained in Carbury, Manitoba near Winnipeg, he had been commissioned and shared the dubious distinction of wearing the white armband.

Middleton St George was a busy station. Apart from being at full blast on operations over Germany, it was preparing for a hand over to the Canadians as the first bomber station of their new 6 Group Bomber Command. Our squadron commander was 'Willie' Tait, later to become one of the legendary, elite bomber pilots who commanded 617, the famous Dam Busters squadron. There, he led the raid that finally sank the battleship *Tirpitz*. Already the possessor of a DSO and bar and a DFC and bar at Middleton, he was to become one of very few men to win four DSOs when he was awarded a further two bars later. Willie was a reserved man, dark and introvert and a tough CO. He had a strong motivation for being a bomber pilot. It was said his young WAAF officer wife had been killed in the Blitz on London. He was, in RAF parlance, a 'Press On' type and he expected his crews to be the same.

We spent the day checking in and making ourselves familiar with the station. In the mess at lunchtime the squadron crews were just getting up after their previous night's operations. We eavesdropped on their talk, not daring to say a word. This was the stuff of experienced veterans. Soon, we hoped, we would be able to share these conversations, talking from our own experience. We learned that two crews were missing, including one that had completed

*Halifax II W7676 TL-P of 35 Squadron, which was lost with Sergeant D. A. V. John and his crew (all KIA) on the night of 28/29 August 1942 when it was hit by flak and crashed into the Westerschelde off Koewacht in Zeeland, Holland on the operation to Nürnburg. Of the 159 aircraft despatched, 23 (including 2 Halifaxes and 14 Wellingtons) were lost. Bombing was very accurate, crews having been ordered to bomb from as low as possible as Pathfinder aircraft marked the target with target indicators (adapted from 250 lb bomb casings), for the first time. (*Flight*)*

twenty-five operations. We were a little shocked to realise that even at twenty-five you weren't immune from the 'Chop'. These matters had been thoughts harboured secretly, but never considered openly. Here was stark reality.

We were invited to attend one briefing as observers. Willie Tait, cold and stony-faced, gave a tough series of instructions to his crews. Now we felt the cold blast of the reality of life on operations blowing right down our necks. The smart uniforms, the carefree flying, the girls, the dancing and the good times all faded into the background. Now was the time we had to pay the piper. It was obvious from the chat around us that Willie Tait demanded payment in full.

We spent ten days waiting at Middleton without flying. Our Conversion flight was merged with that of 76 Squadron at Croft and moved to a new airfield at Riccall to become 1598 Heavy Conversion Unit. The squadron itself was moving to Linton on Ouse, which it would share with 76 Squadron.

We flew down to Riccall with our instructors one wet Sunday morning on 13 September 1942. We had time-expired aircraft for training. They were pretty clapped out. Some were still original Halifax Is with low-powered Merlin X engines. They all suffered from problems, not least glycol leaks. At Riccall Jimmy Goodwin, a 20–year-old fresh-faced 6 feet 2 inches quietly spoken Rhodesian, joined my crew as flight engineer. This was a new trade, to replace the old second pilot in the four-engined bombers. It was their duty to look after the management of engines and systems, constantly watching temperatures, pressures, outputs of hydraulics, electrics, pneumatics, fuel consumption and so on. They were intended to sit in the second pilot's seat and aid the pilot on take-off and landing, but were unable to do this on the Halifax. The aircraft was designed in 1936 to provide for the earlier, two-pilot concept with a separate engineer. As a result the instruments the flight engineer had to monitor were located in a large panel facing the wrong way behind the two pilots' seats. Old Harry still had to act as my assistant pilot.

My rear gunner, sleepy old Sunshine Smith, was loaned to Linton on Ouse and went missing with a 76 Squadron crew.[1] We would have to find a new gunner. Worse, my friend Geoff Hobbs had also gone missing on 2 October with an experienced pilot and crew on their twenty-eighth trip. Geoff was doing his obligatory 'second dickie' trip. Three Halifaxes were lost from the thirty-nine sent to Krefeld by 4 Group that night. I was shocked at the news of Geoff, the best pilot all the way through all our various courses, from elementary at Calgary, to heavy conversion at Riccall. We'd been best friends for over a year. Now he'd gone without even flying one operation as captain. What a waste! Now I knew ops were for real. A little chill ran down my spine. Morty Mortensen gave me the news when I called from Riccall. Morty had completed his 'second dickie' trip and was about to start operations. 'You'd better hurry up Readey,' said Morty, 'or we'll all be chopped before you get here.' I hurried through the rest of my course and travelled to Linton on Ouse by air on 18 November to rejoin the squadron and my companions. Willie Tait had been posted and we had a new wing commander. Gerry Warner, at 23, was cheerful and brisk. I was allocated to 'A' Flight, whose flight commander was Bertie Neal, a rough diamond of a New Zealander. A lumpy six-footer, round-faced with dark hair cut short in the approved RAF fashion, Bertie looked like a sheep farmer, although we never asked. In Bomber Command, living for the day ahead, we had no time for reflective conversations on the past. Bertie had a raucous laugh and a slight speech impediment that gave him a sort of 'slussching' lisp. The morning of our arrival Bertie told me I was 'on' that night as second pilot to Squadron Leader MacDonald, 'B' Flight commander. I didn't mind that. A squadron leader and a flight commander, I was sure he must be an experienced operational pilot. Reporting to him in the afternoon, I met a tall, fair-haired man, with a typical RAF pilot's moustache, who gave me a welcoming smile. Accompanying him to briefing, I noted his calm demeanour and the way he noted down points of importance. He's done this before I thought. I'll be safe enough with him and his experienced crew. His presence relieved some of the natural tension felt in going on my first op.

The butterflies were there all right but they fluttered less with Mac as my skipper.

Going on ops was the first real test of going into action under fire. The Blitz had soon become easy to handle, the bombs had been impersonal and random. It was soon obvious that survival was a matter of pure chance. Our life style accepted that and we enjoyed ourselves, even during the worst times. Flying in hostile skies for the first time, was a different proposition. Highly trained people on the ground and in the air were spending their lives trying to stop RAF bombers reaching their target. Tonight [18/19 November] we would be subjected to their attention. I felt added relief when we learned the target was Turin. There were seventy-seven aircraft going. Italian targets were supposed to be easy, the briefing certainly made it sound so. There had been two raids on Genoa previously [13/14 and 15/16 November] and the squadron was going back to continue the pressure on the Italian defences. The Italian targets came as a welcome relief to those crews who had been engaged in the nasty little battle of Flensburg, the week earlier. In the first attack five Halifaxes were lost out of twenty-eight. Two nights later, twenty-eight went again but they were recalled after 2 hours. One didn't get the recall and bombed the target all on his own, to return safely. A second, who presumably didn't get it either, failed to return.

I was glad I was starting on such an easy target as Turin, with such an experienced crew. Although nervous, it was more the sense of adventure of embarking on a new experience, rather than the fear of going into battle that I felt. I was fairly relaxed during the tense waiting period, between briefing and take-off, confident that the experience of my captain and the easy target would provide a smooth introduction to ops.

We took off about 5.30 pm, into the dark November night. I was surprised to note that Mac had a problem correcting the swing on take-off. We almost had our starboard wheel on the edge lights before we got off. I assumed that she behaved more awkwardly than ever, with a full load. We had a quiet ride all the way to the Alps. The one scare came when we heard the rattle of a machine-gun, very close indeed. It must be close, damn it! We could even smell the cordite. We frantically scanned the dark sky, until the bomb aimer in the front turret, called, 'Sorry Skipper, don't worry, it was me. I leant on the button'. We all laughed and relaxed. No wonder it had sounded so close. Privately, I thought it was an odd happening for an experienced crew.

We were over cloud as we passed Paris. There were a lot of searchlights underneath, which looked as though they were following us. Feeling a pygmy among operational giants, I tentatively mentioned this to the skipper. He nodded his acknowledgement but took no action. I kept quiet after that, confident that he knew what he was doing. We had a marvellous view as we crossed the Alps under the rising moon. We could also see the unaccustomed sight of the lighted towns and villages of Switzerland, just down our port side. At 18,000 feet, progress seemed slow but eventually the Alps slid under us and there, ahead of us, I had my first sight of a target. It wasn't all that impressive. There were a lot of searchlights waving about rather aimlessly, some light flak was popping up, but it didn't seem threatening at all. There were a few fires burning on the ground. Nonetheless, it was a target and there were guns shooting at aircraft. Soon, no doubt, they would be shooting at us. I felt the twinges of apprehension grow as we approached, although I was sure Mac would cope. It took a quarter of an hour to reach, then we let down to 8,000 feet to make our bombing run. As we closed in, the searchlight activity seemed even less than before and the guns had almost stopped. There was just the occasional flash at random. It was the reverse to all we had been led to expect.

The run up came just as it had in training. A 'left, left', a 'steady' and finally, 'bombs away', from the bomb aimer and we were done. There were lots more fires below as we closed the bomb doors and climbed for the trip home across the Alps. The flak and searchlights were now inactive. Hope it's always like this, I wished silently to myself.

It was a long, uneventful flight home and we made it to Linton on Ouse, after being airborne for 9 hours and 10 minutes. We landed and were on our way back to flights in the crew bus.

'OK chaps,' said the Squadron Leader, 'that's our third.'

'Pardon sir,' I asked. 'You mean that was your third trip?'

'Yes, what did you think it was?'

'Well, I – er, I thought – er, we did our second dickie trips with an experienced crew.' I said, somewhat tactlessly.

Mac laughed. 'Well, we're getting to be an experienced crew now. Any complaints about tonight?'

'No sir, not me, I'm quite happy thanks.'

That was it. My first op, my one and only second dickie trip completed. Now I knew how it felt to go on ops. Or did I? Thoughtfully, back in my own flight office, I crossed off the 'ops completed' square against my name, newly chalked on the crew board. There were twenty-nine adjacent squares awaiting the same treatment. If they were all like tonight it wouldn't be too bad. But I had no illusions; there would be tougher nights than this. I didn't think too much about those. Next time I'd be on my own, except of course, for the anxious fellows who awaited me at flights the next day.

'How did it go Skip? What's it like? Have any problems?'

'No. Piece of cake really. If they're all like that, we'll have nothing to worry about.' But I knew in my heart there wouldn't be many like that. Bomber Command didn't provide too many 'pieces of cake' for its crews. They knew that too. I also discovered that the 'What's it like?' question was impossible to answer. This was partly because we'd had such an easy trip, and partly because I couldn't put into words, the unique experience of knowing that other people are trying to kill you.

The weather was bad for the next ten days. On 28/29 November the squadron went to Turin again, I expected to be 'on' but there was only a non-operational aircraft available. To prevent us from getting rusty, we did a night cross-country. I was disappointed; it would have been nice to start our operations to a target I knew. In fact, the only one I knew and easy at that. We completed our cross-country and waited for our call to arms. It came on 6/7 December. The target was Mannheim and we were 'on'. I had not yet been given any gunners, so we carried two spares, whose crews were otherwise occupied. At briefing, we learned we were part of a force of 272 aircraft, Halifaxes, Lancasters, Stirlings and Wellingtons. Our route took us down England to Dungeness, south beyond Paris, into the heart of southern Germany itself, Mannheim.

I was busy before take-off, keeping the crew in good spirits, seeing that they were doing their 'things' and having a chat with our two strange gunners. They all seemed unruffled and we cracked a few feeble jokes as we waited for 'start up'. On board, the checks on the aircraft and the crew kept my mind busy and from thinking too much about what lay ahead. Taking off with a full load of bombs and fuel, she was slow. Mindful of Mac's swing, I took it easy and made sure that I had her under control all the way to the lift off. We took up a lot of runway that way, but at least we stayed on it. She climbed slowly and was sluggish under the load but I expected that. What I didn't expect was the effect of the turning of the turrets at altitude. It quite shocked me. Over 10,000 feet they acted like a rudder and pushed the aircraft in the opposite direction to their turn. Worse, they pushed the nose down and lost a hundred feet of precious height. I asked the gunners not to turn too quickly or too frequently unless it was for real.

The fun started while we were circling Dungeness, waiting for our correct departure time for France. We became involved in a German air raid on Dover. While I wasn't too impressed with English flak, I did think it would be too stupid for words to be shot down by our own guns before we'd left England .... The rest of the outward journey passed without incident. Our only sight of Paris was of gun flashes beneath the cloud and flak bursts in the sky. They were not too near us, just close enough to aid navigation. The cloud persisted to the target. The forecast of a clearance over the target remained that, just a met forecast. It was covered too.

We saw a few Pathfinder flares go down before we reached the target area. I flew towards them but they had vanished by the time we arrived and had not been replaced. I stooged around for 20 minutes waiting for more flares. They never arrived, but there were a few areas of fires showing through the cloud. I picked one, which I estimated had been closest to the Pathfinder flares we had seen and bombed through cloud on it. It was a flat and disappointing experience. We flogged back across Germany without incident. As we crossed the Channel, Jimmy Goodwin, the engineer, called: 'We're getting short of fuel Skip.'

I couldn't imagine how that could happen; we'd followed all the recommended engine handling procedures and hadn't been hit. 'How short Jim. Can we make Linton?'

'Don't think so Skip. I reckon we've got about half an hour's.'

Down below, the beacon of a coastal airfield blinked invitingly. It proved to be Bradwell Bay. A check confirmed the runway was long enough for a Halifax, so in we went. A day bomber station, they were used to helping night bomber crews in trouble and we were well looked after. I called Linton on Ouse to advise them of our safe landing. Our first operation was over but we slept in strange beds that night.

In the morning I had breakfast with Johnny McPherson, the quiet American I'd last seen sixteen months earlier in Red Deer, Canada. He was now at Bradwell, flying Bostons on daylight raids to France. He sounded reasonably happy with his lot. We flew back under very low cloud but we were a light-hearted crew, who'd completed our first op safely. The crew's general reaction was that it couldn't be bad if it always went like this. It paid to be optimistic in Bomber Command. The next day our rear gunner arrived. He appeared in the morning, almost as a manifestation. He stood in front of me as he was introduced, a slouching, gap-toothed, sloppily dressed, thin faced cockney, wearing a big grin, who called himself Jesse James. I wasn't too sure I really wanted him. I had a word with Shorty, our new Gunnery Leader. Shorty said he was good.

'But he looks so scruffy,' I protested.

'Depends on what you want a gunner for,' said Shorty. 'To look smart or shoot 'em down.'

Finally, I conceded to Shorty's arguments and took him on.

We were on ops again on 9/10 December. Once more the target was Turin. I was happy about that. It would be a good one to break in the full crew – a long run in operational conditions without, I hoped, too much opposition. There were 227 aircraft scheduled for the trip, of which forty-seven were Halifaxes. I didn't have to do much cheering up of the crew in the wait before take-off, Jesse James was irrepressible with his cockney humour. His outrageous, much exaggerated accent, greatly amused the crews, especially the Canadians. Young Mac McQueen was also keen to get into action and not at all worried about his first trip. The rest were veterans of one trip and Turin was easier than our last target, Mannheim.

All went well on the outward journey, except that soon into France, *Gee*, our wonder navigation aid was jammed and we had to rely on Vic's dead reckoning for the rest of the trip. The flak around Paris and later the Alps, sticking up ahead, helped point the way well enough. At the target the scene was much the same as my first trip. Searchlights were ragged, the gunfire, not hostile to start with, was hardly present as we flew over the target. We didn't see much; it was still smoky from a Lancaster raid the previous night. The crew were quite professional in their actions and I was pleased with our performance. I noted that after I operated the lever to close the bomb doors, they didn't close, so I pushed it down again and this time they did.

We were high above the overcast in France, when we got a scare. 'Midupper to pilot,' came Mac's urgent call, 'Fighter overhead going port to starboard. Turn to port, go.' I flung her into a descending left turn. The recommended response at that time was to turn into the attacking fighter. I could see nothing in the black sky as I headed down for cloud cover, the Spit's superiority that morning, strong in my mind.

'Anyone see anything?' I asked.

'It seems OK Skip,' came Mac's voice again. 'Perhaps he couldn't have seen us, he went straight on over us to starboard.'

I was now just on top of the cloud. We all looked for the fighter as we dropped into it. I sat tight about a hundred feet below the top for 15 minutes, changing course several times. When we popped up again nothing was in sight, the sky was pitch black anyway. *En route* again, Mac told us he was sure it was one of the new Me 210s, a formidable foe indeed. Upon reflection, Mac thought that he'd seen us and made a beam attack, heading straight for us. For some reason, he couldn't fire his guns.

We were highly alert for the rest of the trip. But I noted Vic was irritatingly slow to give me an estimated time for crossing the enemy coast. We were well across before he pinpointed us in mid-channel with a *Gee* fix. I put it down to the long trip, without any real help from any other aids. At the English coast Jimmy reported that we were again short of fuel. I really couldn't believe it but he insisted. I decided to go back to Bradwell Bay, where they had been so helpful.

It was very bumpy as we came lower and there was a strong wind below cloud. We passed over Bradwell's runway at 6,000 feet and obtained permission to land, number two. As I descended, unknown to me, Jimmy opened the hydraulic valve that isolated the flaps. This was always closed over enemy territory, to prevent damage to hydraulic pipes, causing the flaps to fall down inadvertently. At 2,000 feet I opened up the engines to slow our rate of descent, but the aircraft kept going down at a high rate. I couldn't understand why.

'Have we lost an engine?' I asked Jimmy, who replied in the negative. We continued down in a hurry. I opened more throttle while scanning the instruments for our problem. Finally, I had full power and we were just about flying level at 600 feet. I couldn't think why the aircraft was so heavy and sluggish. We now had a big problem, I couldn't climb and when I put the undercarriage down, I didn't see how we could stay in the air. What's more I would have to be very late putting flaps down, if I could put them down at all. Flaps! Something stirred in my memory. Hastily scanning the instruments, for the umpteenth time, I spotted the flap needle. It was showing 'Full Flap'. Thank God! That's it, we'd got full flaps down. I eased them up, gently at first, then a bit more, as we slowly regained circuit height.

It was a very rough night and I flew gingerly around the circuit, working hard to keep her in line with the runway. As we made our final approach, just before landing a strong gust pushed us hard to the right. I applied full left rudder and it went hard over to the stop. We were just above the ground and it only came back very sluggishly. We touched down on one wheel and bounced to an untidy landing along the edge of the runway. It was a nasty end to what had been a reasonable trip. I had found out the hard way two of the worst design aspects of the Halifax. First, was the proximity and similarity of the flap and bomb door levers. They were together, on the right hand side of the pilot's seat. The flap lever was a little longer, with a small round knob on its end. It operated in the normal sense: to put flaps down, push down, flaps up, pull up. The bomb door lever was the same shape but with a little spindle protruding a little through the centre of the knob. It operated in the opposite sense: bomb doors open, pull up, to close, push down. Leaving the target, intending to close the bomb doors, I must have pushed the flap lever down in error, the first time. Because the flaps were isolated from the hydraulic system, nothing happened. My second try, using the correct lever, closed the bomb doors. The flap lever remained fully down.

When the engineer opened the valve to feed fluid to flaps, they were already selected down and they came fully down without my knowledge, causing us to lose height so rapidly. I was looking for the reason for the height loss in the engines and it took time to eliminate those instruments. Fortunately, I thought about the flaps, just in time to retrieve our situation. The juxtaposition of two similar levers, functioning in opposite senses, was a design fault that could easily have killed us.

The other fault was in the rudders. They were so designed that at low speeds, using heavy foot force, it was possible to push the rudder fully to one side. Because of the design, it was not easy to force it back to a central position. Many Halifaxes were lost as a result of this fault, known as 'rudder stall'. I was fortunate that when it occurred, we were so low that the wheels touched the runway before we could come to any harm. From more than 50 feet up, it could have been an almighty prang. Later rudders were modified to correct it, not entirely successfully.

But the whole situation arose because of the dreadful design of the fuel system. Back at base, I had a long session with Jimmy as to why we were always running short of fuel. He told me that he was changing the tanks when the gauges, notoriously unreliable, showed empty. He did this to save me from the problem of engines cutting if he waited for the tanks to run dry. Standard practice for a tank change was for the engineer to watch the fuel contents and pressure gauges closely. When fuel pressure started fluctuating, he warned the pilot, left his position, and climbed over the main spar into the centre of the aircraft. There, he had to look under the rest beds and make his choice of moving two of the five levers, which he could only see at night with a torch. He had to turn the tank in use off, before turning the next on, to avoid air locks. Then probably, just as he returned to his position, he'd have rush back, to do the same for the tanks on the other side. All this time he was off intercom and couldn't hear the pilot. Jimmy wanted time to ensure he didn't, as so many engineers had, select the wrong lever and put engines onto empty tanks, thus cutting more than one engine.

The whole system was a mess that was never satisfactorily resolved. Even today, the Halifax fuel system instructions read like a Chinese puzzle. For crews with only a few hours on the aircraft, it was frighteningly dangerous under operational conditions. There has always been conflict about the relative merits of the Halifax and the Lancaster, which goes on today among the survivors. There is much to be said for both. It is pertinent to the arguments, that the Lancaster had its gauges and a mere two fuel cocks, next to the second pilot position. The engineer rode there in the Lanc. Whether seated there, or standing up behind in the astrodome on look out, he had no need to move to change tanks. Indeed, it was not difficult for the pilot to change the tanks himself, an impossible task in the Halifax.

As a result of losses and strong criticism, the Halifax rudders were modified in later marks but the awful fuel cock system and the adjacent flap and bomb door levers, stayed with them for the rest of the war. As a result of our

148

experience, Jimmy and I perfected a procedure to allow the tanks to drain till the pressure gauge fluctuated. He'd warn me of the engine concerned, hop back in double short time, quickly changing tanks to avoid a full engine cut. We had a couple of occasions when the engines lost power from loss of fuel flow but we never suffered from shortage again. From that night, too, he warned me whenever he was turning the flap isolating cock on. I checked the flap lever and we never encountered that problem again.

We reported our encounter with the Me 210 to the Intelligence officer at Bradwell, who was most interested. They were only just coming into service and had not been seen by any of their crews. At breakfast, I saw Johnny MacPherson again and told him about the Me 210. He was in a thoughtful mood. On their sweep over France the previous day they had lost two aircraft from Me 109s. He said things were getting tough and looked rather pensive. It was the last time I saw him and I never heard how he fared.

We were briefed for a trip to Duisburg on 20 December but our Halifax had developed a coolant leak and I said I was not taking her in that state. Our next scheduled trip was on Christmas Eve. 'Butch' Harris was not at all popular for this one. We were briefed for Essen, the toughest target of them all. It was not much of a Christmas present for anyone. The jokes, as we waited for our buses, were more forced than ever. Even Jesse was subdued. As we were glumly driving out in the bus, there were a lot of Irish labourers working on the taxi track.

'Good luck boyos' they called out. 'Give him one for us. Wisht we was goin' wid yer.'

'I wish you were going instead,' I called back.

We reluctantly climbed into our aircraft and set about our checks. All completed, we were looking at the tower for the green Very flare, the 'start up' signal. It was long delayed. Eventually, a red flare soared into the dull December sky; it was the 'Scrub' signal, cancelling the operation. Cheers went up all round, in and outside, the aircraft. We piled into the buses, laughing and joking with genuine humour this time. It was a great relief not to have to spend Christmas Eve over the Ruhr. There was a party in the mess that night that went on until early Christmas Day. The next day we were stood down, so the previous evening's celebrations continued. After the traditional serving of the airman's Christmas dinner by the officers, we returned for our own. By then the mess waitresses, especially Peggy the pretty blonde for whom we all made a play, had to do a lot of dodging of mistletoe-clasping, girl-grabbing hands. It was a dreary bunch of bomber crews who fell into their beds that Christmas night in 1942.

On 8 January 1943 we did a minelaying trip to the Baltic. We had icing problems and almost lost it. We went on leave for two weeks. When we came back we did a trip to Cologne on 2/3 February. We now had our own aircraft, *C-Charlie* in squadron terms, HR657 in official documents. It was not new but had only done three trips. We didn't worry about that. She was ours, to me as pilot, my very own 'kite'. We mightn't have been so sanguine had we known that the average life of a Halifax was ten trips but we didn't know and were never told those unpleasantries. We would have ignored them if we had known. There was nothing you could do about it.

Technically, Cologne was not in the Ruhr but for us it was our first trip to the Ruhr. Happy Valley, to all who'd been there and most that hadn't, was a trip that brought out all the butterflies. It was the real thing at last. It was here that we started our own little superstitious rituals. Mac had been given a stuffed penguin mascot by a girlfriend. He became our travelling companion on all our trips, fixed to the bulkhead behind the engineer's panel. Called Percy, we had his image painted on the side of the cockpit. He was riding a bomb and beneath him, the ground crew painted small bombs for each trip we completed. Taxiing out I started my own little ritual by singing 'We're Off On The Road To Morocco', from the movie I had seen on my last leave. It was meant to keep us all cheerful and show my confidence in our venture of the next few hours. I never asked what the crew thought but no one complained. They were probably too numbed by my singing to do so. Completing the ritual, I patted the Percy painted on the outside of the cockpit, on the rump. I don't know how useful these superstitious rituals were, but they helped. Many crews had one and I'm here to prove ours worked.

The Cologne trip was a good one. We were spot on with heights and turning points all the way round. Our first sight of the Ruhr was impressive. One of Bomber Command's folklore stories was of the pilot who asked what the flak was like over the Ruhr, and replied, 'Well, it was so thick over the target old boy that I put the undercart down and taxied across'. It wasn't quite as bad as that, but there was a lot of it about and plenty was coming our way, accompanied by hundreds of searchlights probing the sky to seek us out. We bombed at midnight and that day Jimmy was 21 so we all sang 'Happy Birthday' to him as soon as I turned off target. I was feeling a little happy, so I said a few rude words over the radio to the Germans. It was certainly a coincidence, but they replied with a big thump under our tail. I shut up and we ran for the coast. We were quite a happy crew when we landed that night. We had gone to the Ruhr for the first time and what's more, we'd come back.

We were destined to see a lot more of it during the next three months. While January had been a quiet time for operations, February was to be the reverse. The bad weather of the previous two months improved and we were to fly the hardest month of operations of our tour. On 3 February we were 'on' to Hamburg. I had a bad trip and reluctantly turned back. I felt a little better on landing, where I found several aircraft had turned back ahead of me. Many aircraft returned early because of heavy icing conditions over the North Sea. There were four missing out of eighty-four Halifaxes, among the 323 aircraft operating that night. Sixteen aircraft were lost all told, 6.5 per cent of the force. We had a break until 11 February, then we were off to Wilhelmshaven. We had a long wait between briefing and take-off, waiting for better weather. We found that the weather was still bad over the target, so we were to bomb on 'sky markers'. This was the first use of a new Pathfinder technique. The coloured markers floated high in the sky on parachutes. We had to pass over them on a given heading and bomb when they were in the bombsight. We had a few problems, as the clouds were so high that almost as soon as the markers

150

were dropped, they disappeared. We had to chase three markers, until we just managed to catch one before it disappeared. It was a frustrating experience, but it was later reported that the bombing caused much damage to the port below. There were only three aircraft lost from the 177 who operated. This was more like it.

Two nights later, on 13 February, fortunately a Saturday, we were on again, to Lorient. Lorient was an easy target and only seven aircraft were lost from the 466 despatched. We were on again the next night, 14 February, to Cologne once more. Over the target, we again used sky markers and this time we had more time to line up before they dropped below cloud. It was a good trip for us, although the results were unsatisfactory, as there were no photographs because of the cloud cover. We liked sky-marking nights though, most of the fighters were grounded and the searchlights couldn't get you. Only nine of 240 aircraft were lost, about sixty crew. We had a night off, to catch our breath and then we were 'on' once more to Lorient. We had a good trip and could see the target clearly. Unfortunately, we could only inflict accidental damage on the town, as the submarine pens were more than proof against our bombs. After three nights on operations out of four, I was very tired and could hardly keep my eyes open. As we flew up the length of England I found myself falling asleep a couple of times. Reaching Suffolk and Norfolk, we started to pass through the landing traffic of the many bomber aerodromes there. I put my second pilot to good use and told him to keep a good look out for other aircraft and make sure I didn't go to sleep. I sucked a caffeine tablet to keep me awake and finally with the aid of my drug, Linton on Ouse's beacon hove into sight. Out of 377 aircraft sent, only one, a Lancaster, was lost.

We had a whole night off on 17 February, but we were off again on 18/19 February to Wilhelmshaven. I had Flight Sergeant Ginsberg Morton back again as navigator. I was happy about that. A good New Yorker from the Bronx serving in the RCAF, Ginsberg was an old hand and a very cool head. I liked his style. He was positive about his work and seemed to have plenty of time to spare. He would come and stand between the second pilot and me for a lot of the time. (This was quite a novelty. I'd once asked Vic to come up and have a look at the flak and the target. Vic had popped his head over the cockpit coaming for about 10 seconds, whispered to himself 'Christ' and quickly disappeared back into his compartment below, never to be seen again.) This time the target was clear but the bombing didn't seem very effective. We had no problems but four Lancasters were lost out of the total of 195 aircraft sent.

As the results were doubtful, we were detailed to return to Wilhelmshaven the following night, 19/20 February. We never liked going to the same target two nights in a row. We always felt that the defences would be more alert and more practised, the second time around. It seemed a good effort, though the resultant fires were subdued. We noted that the defences now waited, until they were sure that the target was marked, before opening fire. This meant that the early Pathfinders ahead of us had a relatively quiet reception. Our task as the second wave, carrying mostly incendiaries, was to start fires to illuminate things for the Lancasters following up with their big 'Block-buster'

4,000 lb bombs. Once they were sure that the target was identified, the German defences gave us all they had. Their gunners at the start of a raid were always more accurate and quicker than later on. Seven aircraft were lost that night, but still no one from Linton on Ouse.

On the first raid, 195 aircraft were sent to Wilhelmshaven. Four Lancasters were lost. The bombing certainly was not 'very effective'. Although the Pathfinders claimed to have marked accurately in clear visibility, most of the bombs fell in open country west of the target. On the second raid, 338 aircraft were despatched. Twelve aircraft were lost. This raid also failed, with the Pathfinder marking causing the Main Force to bomb north of Wilhelmshaven.

The pace of things kept up until the end of the February. We went to Cologne on 26/27 February and to St Nazaire, for more pounding of impregnable submarine pens, on 28 February/1 March. Both were good trips for us. We had a problem returning home from Cologne. A lot of our incendiaries remained in the bomb bay, because they'd been iced up and failed to release. The ground crew were beneath the aircraft, pointing this out as we climbed out. Vic, getting his nav gear together, was last out, and last to look at the hang-ups. As he did so, the ice must have melted and one case of incendiaries fell out onto him. Fortunately, it just struck him a glancing blow on the shoulder. I was worried that they would light up and got ready to leap back into the aircraft to move it. However, they remained dormant and safe. As we turned away, another aircraft landing spread a host of incendiaries along the side of the runway. They caught and burned spectacularly for a short while. I resolved on future to open the bomb doors somewhere on the way home and give the aircraft a good shake to get rid of any hang-ups. The raid by 427 aircraft on Cologne cost ten aircraft and most of the bombs dropped fell to the south-west of Cologne.

Coming back from that St Nazaire trip, to avoid a repeat of hung up incendiaries, I opened the bomb doors and shook the aircraft quite violently. I'd completely forgotten we were flying over France, until Mac called out, 'Hey Skip, you've done something rotten there. I can see a good fire going down below. You must have set some farm or something alight.' I felt quite guilty about that and resolved to think more carefully about where I dropped any hang-ups in future. That was always assuming we had one. The operation to St Nazaire by 437 aircraft cost five aircraft.

February 1943 had been a month of hard operational flying for Bomber Command. I flew 72 hours, all but 3.30 hours on operations. We had been to eleven targets and my total of trips reached fifteen, including the abortive trip when we had failed to reach Hamburg. I had discovered that since we had crossed the enemy coast, it counted. That was half my tour. As we'd enjoyed a low casualty rate and I'd had some good trips, I began to feel that I knew a bit about operational flying. I wasn't over-confident and realised more than ever, that luck was going to play a major part in survival. I just hoped that with a sensible approach to any situations I might encounter, I could help luck along in my favour. We were getting along well as a crew, although our frequent change of navigator was unsettling and threw a lot of work onto me every time we had a new one. One result of our continuing good luck was the squadron now had a hard core of good experienced crews. This gave the new boys confidence and made them feel that there could be a future for them too.

Note

1. Sergeant A. F. 'Sunshine' Smith was killed on the night of 6/7 December 1942 when Pilot Officer W. C. Hillier MiD's crew in Hallifax II BB242 of 76 Squadron failed to return from the raid on Mannheim.

CHAPTER 13

There But for the Grace of God

Arthur R. 'Spud' Taylor DFC

*... Continuing to fly on the Ops that he was ordered to
While the fear he'd keep inside him continually grew
Fear that any member of an aircrew can understand
But apparently not understood by our Air Command
When orders came to fly missions, he'd have to obey
A refusal to fly was a lack of 'Moral Fiber' they'd say ...*

'*Fear*', 28 November 1944, from *No Place To Hide*
by Sergeant George 'Ole' Olson RCAF, air gunner

It soon dawned on me when I was being trained as an observer that once you were airborne in those days you were absolutely on your own. You could not drop anchor, ask anyone the way or, when on ops, break radio silence except to give a Mayday call. At night a blackout operated all over Europe, which made identification of objects on the ground very difficult. On moonlit nights you discovered that you could see best looking into the moon, and on cloudless nights without a moon, you could with practice distinguish coastlines, large rivers and lakes. You knew that from the amount of flak coming up that you were getting close to ships, towns or aerodromes and that gave you a clue. Navigation depended on a knowledge of wind speed and direction and these were given to you by the Met Officer at the briefing, but they were not always accurate. Another factor was that both wind speed and direction altered as you climbed and they would also change on your way to and from the target. Also, it was important that you arrived at the target at the correct height and time. Map reading was a major and constant part of my job and fortunately I had been well trained in this skill as an observer. I suspect that people who couldn't map read could quite easily run out of fuel and end up in the North Sea. There were other dangers, especially during training. One night in July 1942 when I was undergoing training at OTU at Bircotes, two kites, both without navigation lights owing to an air raid, collided and crashed with the total loss of their crews. Their charred bodies lay in the mortuary. At the time, I wrote in my diary that it was a fact that more lives were lost on training than on ops. In sharp contrast, 16 August 1942 was a wonderful

Arthur R. 'Spud' Taylor DFC

warm day. Everything seemed transformed by the light. The corn in the field across the road looked more gold and yellow than ever; the trees seemed to shimmer in the heat, their leaves like some green fountain and even our kites, which looked so black and ugly on the ground, seemed transformed and graceful.

It was at 25 OTU Bircotes, Nottinghamshire on 19 August 1942 that Sergeant Victor Page became pilot of our crew. On 14 February 1943 we arrived at Lakenheath to fly Stirlings in 149 'East India' Squadron. No. 149 Squadron's excellent motto was '*Fortis Nocte*' and their badge was a horseshoe with a streak of lightning running through it. It was at this camp that Middleton VC was at and they hadn't lost a kite since the previous December,[1] which was cheering. It was a highly dispersed drome and our billet (a tin Nissen hut) was in amongst some pine trees. The ground was very sandy and there were trees everywhere! We noted that the 'grub' was excellent and there was no 'bull'. What more could you ask?

While we waited to fly our first op there was a raid on practically every night. Only three crews were lost since our arrival, two riddled and a few prangs. One brought down a Ju 88 over Munich and returned with a wounded gunner. He died later. On 10 March Vic went off on his second dickie trip, a mining expedition to Bordeaux. I hoped he was coming back because he was wearing my Irvine. It was a pretty rough do apparently. There was some flak through his kite but they got back OK and he flew a second op, to Stuttgart, on 12 March, poor swine. We were still waiting for a navigator when Vic went to Essen on 13 March. Poor old Vic never returned.[2] We were quite stunned at the idea of never seeing the laddie again. I went for a long walk that night out along the Brandon road.

On 27 March we left Lakenheath for 1657 Conversion Unit, Stradishall, to acquire a replacement pilot. We got there long after others had already 'crewed up' and when we were shown into a large room there was only one pilot left. He looked rather thin and weedy but there was no one else. We introduced ourselves. He said his name was Bill. We asked him if he would be our pilot? He laughed and said, 'You'll regret it.'

155

Crew at Bircotes, the satellite of 25 OTU Finningley, in 1942. Sergeant Arthur 'Spud' Taylor; bomb aimer; Sergeant Jason Ives, WoP/AG; Sergeant W. 'Jock' Stewart, rear gunner, Sergeant Vic Page, pilot; Sergeant Laurie (?), observer. (Arthur Taylor)

We laughed back, putting it down to typical British understatement.

Stradishall was the usual monotony of circuits and bumps, which were brightened only by a remarkable series of lousy landings. Bill's weak point apparently was landing, while they had been Vic's strong point. Bill hadn't much grip and we came pretty near to a prang on one landing. After bashing down in an unusually hearty manner on the deck, he suddenly decided to take off again (we were then about halfway up the runway) and in a series of sickly swerves we closely missed the roof of the hangars. However, on 18 April we were posted to Downham Market and 218 'Gold Coast' Squadron, also flying Stirlings.

For seven days, 20 to 26 April, there was nothing much but DIs [daily inspections] and occasional short flights. Then they seemed to think it was time we did something and so we went *Gardening*. We stooged out to the island of Juiste in the Friesians. The cloud was pretty thick and Bill wouldn't go through the cloud to pinpoint (an essential thing on these efforts). He seemed to panic a bit when I said I saw some lights. I heard the short staccato directions in German over the R/T and knew a fighter was being vectored on to us but Jason Ives, the WOp, falsed him up with 'tinsel' [Window]. I saw these lights through a break in the cloud and I suppose this must have been

Juiste. However, Bill wouldn't let me drop the mines though Shorty and I were all for it. I took over for about half an hour on the way back and got to bed about 8.00 the next morning. I would sooner be bomb aimer than the navigator. I had the front turret, bombs, took photographs and map read for the navigator. The camera I used was a Kodak pocket camera with leather bellows, which had originally belonged to my elder brother Andrew who was in the Army and was killed in Belgium at the time of Dunkirk. The camera's viewfinder required you to look vertically downwards to get a forward view. This made it tricky to operate in the confined space of a bombing compartment, but I managed to take a few aerial shots, some of which came out quite well. As more equipment was invented (*Gee*, *Fishpond*, *H2S* etc.) space became more confined and we really had to be a pretty agile bunch of young men. Also, the bomb aimer lowered and raised the flaps and undercart, which is why he was sometimes called 'Second Pilot'. The old navigator on the other hand, sat in his little office with no view on the situation at all and on the big kites machines that seemed to do most of the work for him surrounded him. As far as I was concerned, as a bomb aimer/front gunner I was always positioned in a small compartment in the nose of the aircraft. Over my head were the turret doors and a metal bar. To get into the turret I opened the doors, grabbed the bar with both hands and lifted myself into the turret. I would shut the doors behind me in the very cramped space available and I was then able to fire my guns. As most actions involving the use of guns took place in a matter of seconds I generally found that by the time I was ready to fire it was all over. I did however manage to get a burst in when flying at low level over an aerodrome in France one night and helped to put out a searchlight. Down below the turret in my compartment there was a bombsight, parachute, maps, thermos flask and rations and piles of Window so that there was very little room to move about. In addition, I was plugged into the intercom and to the oxygen. Temperatures could get very low owing to air getting in via the turret and I could remember once pouring tea from a thermos, which then turned to ice in the cup.

My flying equipment included a leather helmet with earphones, which was strapped under the chin. Attached to one side of the helmet was an oxygen mask, which also incorporated a speaker that could be switched on and off as required. A parachute, Mae West and escape kit were issued before each flight. Other equipment included three pairs of gloves – silk, soft wool and leather – fur-lined flying boots and Irvine jacket and a large woollen polo-neck jumper. As they aged, these jumpers often stretched to the knees and I saw many an aircrew wearing one of these do an impromptu dance in the locker room before take-off. Sometimes two men would get into one jumper and do a tango! There was a whistle in case you ditched in the dark, an inner and outer suit (something like a boiler suit in shape) and finally, a similar-shaped suit, which could be plugged in like an electric blanket. I never use this as it considerably hampered my movements. On take-off in Stirlings I sat next to the pilot until the wheels were up and then I went down to my compartment, where I either lay down or crouched depending on what I was doing. On landing I sat next to the pilot and pulled the four throttles back when he

157

gave the order to 'cut'. In my compartment when the pilot corkscrewed (as happened a good deal on our first tour) I was pressed to the floor or sides and became almost weightless in a dive. Fortunately, I was not prone to airsickness, but it did make map reading rather difficult.

Our aircraft were not pressurised and you had to pinch your nose and blow to relieve the pressure on your eardrums. But to compensate for all this I had the best forward and downward view of anyone in the aircraft. With the bulkhead door open I could look back and see the pilot and flight engineer immediately behind and above me. They were moderately warm and needed fewer flying clothes than I did. Behind them came the navigator and wireless operator in the warmest positions of all, then the mid-upper gunner in about the same sort of temperature as myself. Finally, came the rear gunner, hidden by the metal back of his turret, in the coldest and loneliest position of all. Both he and the mid-upper gunner had to keep alert the whole time, staring out into the dark and identifying dark aircraft against a dark sky. As far as possible, they had to be careful not to lose their night vision by staring at lights and they had to constantly sweep the sky with their turrets and guns. The front and mid-upper turrets were mounted with two Browning machine-guns each while the rear gunner had four. The Browning fired .303 bullets (the same as we used in our Army rifles in 1939) interspersed with tracer and armour-piercing ammunition, while German fighters were always armed with cannon, which had a greater range and were more devastating.

The German night-fighters almost always had the advantage over our bombers. They had the edge over us in height, speed and firepower and could pick us out silhouetted against the bright lights below. This is why we were so vulnerable in the target area and it was only due to the skill of our two gunners that we managed to fight off the attacks that were made on us.

As well as all this the aircraft was equipped with a large inflatable dinghy capable of holding all seven of us. This in turn was fitted with a sea anchor, a kite, which provided an aerial when flown, and a waterproof transmitter. When a handle was turned on the transmitter it gave out the Mayday signal. We were also fitted with a Very pistol and were given cartridges with the colours of the day before take-off. In our case we never found this was of any help if we passed over a convoy escorted by the Royal Navy, as they invariably took a pot shot at us and occasionally brought one down. And finally the rations, with which we were issued before ops, included items that were in very short supply for civilians, such as a bar of Cadbury's milk chocolate, barley sugar and glucose tablets. 'Wakey Wakey' pills were also issued, but I found them quite useless and if I couldn't give them away I would flush them down the lavatory.

Briefings for raids took place in a large Nissen hut several hours before take-off. At one end of the hut was a low stage with a large map of Europe over which curtains were drawn. The crews had no idea where they were going and sat awaiting events with a distinct air of anticipation. The station commander unveiled the map on which tapes showed the route to and from the target. He explained the purpose of the raid, occasionally read out a message from our chief, 'Bomber Harris' and wished us 'good luck'. The various specialist senior officers then gave vital details, i.e. the colours of the day, times, exact route, TI colours, bomb load, wireless frequencies, the position of convoys, the weather, etc. Notes were taken and maps marked with routes. As a map reader and bomb aimer I found two maps particularly useful. The first was a map to cover the route and the second was a target map. Both were excellent. After briefing we had a supper of bacon and eggs and got all our gear ready. Debriefing occurred on our return to base when an Intelligence officer interviewed each individual crew. We were red-eyed from staring into the dark, and tired, with the marks of the oxygen masks still on our faces and the taste of oxygen still in our mouths and our hair flattened by our helmets when we were interviewed. While this went on we drank coffee laced with rum and smoked fags.

On 1 May our kites went out mining in Stettin harbour and we lost three. We flew another *Gardening* op on 5 May and on the 11th we were briefed for the Ruhr but it was cancelled at the last minute. On 12 May we set out for Duisburg. It was a big effort. We had to turn back though because Jock [Stewart] and Len [Durrant], the two gunners, couldn't get any oxygen through. They had forgotten to withdraw their bobbins. Shorty and I egged Bill on to complete the trip at 10,000 or 11,000 feet but he was too windy to try it.

On 13 May we were off to Bochum, pretty well in the centre of the Ruhr, in Stirling III BF480 *I-Ink*, carrying all incendiaries. We were determined to get there at all costs. We crossed the Dutch coast off track and wandered pretty close to Antwerp. The searchlights and flak were pretty strong. It was a beautiful moonlight night and we managed to pinpoint quite easily. The *Gee* went u/s sometime before reaching target area and we turned up, all unaware, over Düsseldorf. (On the way out I pinpointed our position exactly on the Dutch coast and gave a fix to Shorty, our navigator. Through a fault in his calculations, he then gave an incorrect course to our pilot. This meant that by the time we reached the Rhine we were some 20 miles north of the main force, and this in turn meant that we approached the target from completely the wrong direction. It was fortunate for us that we didn't collide with one of our own aircraft, who, by the time we reached it, were leaving the target in a northerly direction.) Being the only kite over the place, they gave us all they'd got. I did my best to pinpoint but was dazzled by all the lights.

Bill panicked and circled about in a frantic endeavour to get out, losing height all the while. Before we left Düsseldorf we were at 6,000 feet. Immense cones of 30/40 searchlights picked us up at a time and we were a sitting target for light, medium and heavy flak. There was plenty of it. I should think that something like 200 to 300 guns were firing at us at any one time. It was at this point that Bill gave the order to bale out. I replied that if we did no one would reach the ground in one piece. Bill then said, 'You bloody well fly it then!'

I went up the steps and grabbed the second pilot's controls and steered a straight course. In a few minutes we had left Düsseldorf behind. Ten minutes after that Bill had recovered sufficiently to take over again. We then passed over the southern outskirts of Essen and for several minutes we were coned by searchlights and fired at continuously. When flak hit the aircraft there was a clap like thunder and a strong smell of cordite. Finally, we arrived at the target. The place was ablaze. Immense fires covered the ground and reflected red on a great pall of smoke, which hung above the town. Meanwhile, Jock, our rear gunner, had obeyed the order to bale out, but he had pulled the ripcord too early and his parachute had partially opened, jamming him in the escape hatch. In this position, with his head, shoulders and arms out of the aircraft, he had received the full blast of the explosions. Having bombed, I tried to get Jock on the intercom and had no reply, so I went back to see how he was, to find him half in and half out of the hatch. He was in a dazed condition when I pulled him back in. I then sat next to Bill. *I-Ink* was shaking so badly that I had to hold the throttles in position from then on. At last we lost the searchlights and headed north into the seemingly quiet fighter belt that ran right the way from Northern Denmark down to below Paris. The *Gee* was still u/s, but I managed to pinpoint the Zuider Zee. There was only just enough petrol to get home.

We arrived back at base in the half-light of early morning. The TR.9 was u/s so we landed without permission. Just as I thought everything was OK, I looked at Bill to find that he had let go of the controls and had both hands over his eyes. The kite swerved suddenly to port and the next thing I knew we had cut a lorry in two, killing a couple of poor blokes just back from the raid.[3] We also knocked two cars for yards and partially demolished the briefing room where debriefing was taking place, before finally pranging into the operations room with our right wing. A few people in there were injured. *I-Ink* finally came to rest on the control tower. I headed for the hatch but Paddy, who was wielding an axe in a desperate attempt to hack his way out, blocked the way. I tapped him on the back and asked him if he had tried the door and with that we all ran out of the kite, fully expecting it to burst into flames. We all went to the MO [medical officer] who gave us two little yellow pills each, which all but knocked us out before we reached the billet! Next day, we looked over our kite. It had had it. We walked round counting flak holes and there were about 100 – several extraordinarily close to where we were sitting. Len's turret had five or six holes in it, one piece of shrapnel grazing his nose on its way through. The astrodome was whipped away while Paddy was looking through it and Jock had a deep cut in his head. I was lucky to escape injury myself as shrapnel broke off a 6-inch piece of metal from my compartment, which hit me on the head, but fortunately, my leather helmet saved my bacon.

After breakfast we were told to report to the CO. When got to his office we gave him our account to do with the raid on Bochum. I told him that we had no confidence in Bill and did not wish to fly with him again. The CO looked at some papers on his desk and told us that we were Bill's sixth crew and that he had crashed the lot! This was news to us but the main thing was that he granted our request. (We thought that Bill would have been grounded but later, at Stradishall, we found him with another crew. I will never know for sure what happened to Bill eventually. Some months later I was in a pub chatting with a bomb aimer from another squadron who told me that he thought he had seen Bill's Stirling heading into the Channel for no apparent

Stirling III BF480 'I-Ink' of 218 'Gold Coast' Squadron lies wrecked at Downham Market following the crew's disastrous operation to Bochum on 13/14 May 1943. 'I-Ink' ploughed into a truck killing two airmen who had disembarked from Stirling BF413/T and were about to enter the Operations Block for interrogation. BF480 was damaged beyond repair. (Arthur R. 'Spud' Taylor)

reason with all guns firing).[4] As for Jock, in the month that followed, he went missing a few times and was found wandering around the fields near the aerodrome, barefoot and in his pyjamas. We never saw him again.

We were posted to 90 Squadron at West Wickham [in August 1943 the airfield, in the parishes of West Wickham and Little Thurlow, 3 miles NW of Haverhill on the Cambridgeshire side of the boundary with Suffolk, was renamed Wratting Common] and our pilot was Pilot Officer Ted Mills. On 30 July 1943 we flew an op to Remscheid – a small town in Happy Valley, just east of Solingen. We passed over Dunkirk on the way out where we got a fair amount of flak. From then on it was fairly clear up to the target as our route took us south of Cologne. The target itself was an impressive sight. The whole town was ablaze with a red blanket of smoke belching from it. Every so often a great white flash in the middle of it all would show where a large bomb had exploded. There were few searchlights left working in the place and a few guns. The sky above the town was dotted by flak puffs, which showed like balloons in the light of the fires. My bombsight went u/s and I used the 5/2 finger method to lay the incendiaries smack across the centre of the blaze. Then we got out. We had to pass out of the main Ruhr defences (about 20 miles thick) where the searchlights were pretty thick. I saw a kite caught in a big cone and go down with sparks and flames shooting out from behind. The

Pilot Officer Ted Mills' crew in 90 Squadron. Mills is centre at the back with 'Spud' Taylor on his left. Len Durrant is far left in front row. (Arthur Taylor)

lights followed it right down. I also saw a German fighter belting along under us like a dainty silver toy – pretty but deadly. Thank God he didn't see us! We were last to land, which was a bad show.

On 10 August we went to Nuremberg. It was a 7-hour trip and quite tiring after the shorter efforts we had got used to. Mannheim had been attacked in force the night before and the wretched people there were kept awake the whole time by occasional kites off track and a few flares dropped on purpose to give them the wind up. Going there and coming back the guns and searchlights were busy! There was about 9/10ths cloud over the target, but we managed to prang a marker. The bombing generally was very scattered from what I could see, but there were quite a few hearty fires going. A Ju 88 passed quite close to us with both its navigation lights on, but it didn't see us. It was a quiet trip on the whole. We had engine trouble on reaching the south coast due to petrol shortage I think, so we lobbed down at West Malling, a Mosquito station, where we managed to get about 2 hours' kip in the mess before flying back to West Wickham. We arrived home in the afternoon feeling somewhat shagged.

On 23 August we went to Berlin in *M-Mother*. In all, over 700 kites went, mostly all four-engined.[5] There was not much trouble on the way there. The visibility was good so we were able to watch the attack as it developed. In six

Flight Lieutenant Robert Young Rodger's crew in 90 Squadron walking out to their Stirling at West Wickham prior to the raid on Berlin on the night of 23/24 August 1943. 727 aircraft took part including 124 Stirlings, one of which was flown by Pilot Officer Ted Mills' crew. Fifty-six aircraft including sixteen Stirlings were lost. Behind Sergeant Robert 'Tug' Wilson, air bomber are Warrant Officer Roy Child, mid-upper gunner, Sergeant Leslie Griffiths, navigator and Bob Rodger bringing up the rear with Howell Jones and their ground crew chief, Sergeant Arthur Stubbs, nearest camera. This photo appeared on the front page of the Daily Sketch *on 2 September 1943. On 9 November 1943 Rodger and Wilson were killed when their Stirling was involved in a collision with a Hurricane during a fighter affiliation exercise. Roy Child, who was absent from the crew that day, became a PoW when he was shot down on 19/20 February 1944 flying as part of Squadron Leader K. G. Davis' Lancaster III crew on 7 Squadron. (IWM)*

short minutes the place was glowing with fires and enormous flashes were lighting up the ground. Searchlights and flak were not very intense, but there were bags of fighters. Making our final run-up on to a marker we were suddenly attacked from very close range by a Dornier. She scored several hits on our kite but Len and John kept their heads and brought her down. Once in flames, the Dornier was picked up and finished off by searchlights and flak. We bombed dead central on a marker and got out like bats out of hell. I counted six of our kites going down in flames in the short time we were over the target. Over the target there was a plane circling around the whole time with one of the PFF laddies making a continual running commentary telling us where to bomb and cheering like mad whenever we scored a hit. This fellow was called the Master of Ceremonies and he was used on all the big raids.[6] His job was to cheer you on and then tell you which were the live and false TIs. The Germans were no fools and soon caught on to the ideas of dropping similar flares well away from the target. All this made the job of a bomb aimer much easier as we were told at briefing simply to bomb a particular colour, which was so bright that it could be seen from miles away. In the meantime the Pathfinders became a prime target for fighters and I think there is no doubt as all that they carried out the most dangerous tasks performed by Bomber Command. The crews I served with regarded the target area as the most dangerous and spent as little time there as possible. On the way back we got quite considerably off track crossing the Baltic and there were doubts about us even reaching England. Also, one engine packed up for a while. We threw out quite a lot of things though, including my guns and ammo, and we just made Coltishall with 80 gallons left. We had been flying for about 8 hours 40 minutes and we were damn tired.[7]

I always had the greatest admiration for the Pathfinders and it was noticeable that with their arrival we began to bomb accurately and cause real damage to the enemy. They operated by identifying the target at low level, flying in Mosquitoes that dropped a TI onto the objective. Meanwhile, their high-level Lancasters circled above and kept dropping further TIs onto the target until the raid was over. A remarkable example of their skill became apparent one night when the target was completely obscured by 10/10ths cloud. We were told to drop our bombs on the spot where the TIs entered the cloud, which meant that the Pathfinders had to allow for our speed, height and direction, as well as the trajectory of our bombs in their calculations. As photos proved the next day, they were spot on. Later, I volunteered to join them but was not accepted, presumably because I was not up to their high standard.

On 8 September we did a good op, to gun positions outside Boulogne, carrying six 1,000-pounders and eight 500s. We pranged the target fair and square and got a beautiful photo but we saw no big explosions. There was a fair amount of heavy and light flak, but we didn't see a fighter. We were only up for 3 hours. The next day we found out that our raid was merely a cover for a 'large scale amphibious exercise', whatever that meant. The air war had now taken a completely new turn. Before, a target was defended mainly from the ground by searchlights and flak – bags of it. Now, it was nearly all fighters. Sometimes searchlights and fighters co-operated. Searchlights lit you up and fighters pumped shot into you.

On 15 September we bombed a rubber factory near Montluçon in central France. We had to run in pretty low because of cloud. The target was pretty well ablaze by the time we got there and dense clouds of smoke (we could smell the rubber) were rising high above it. Our aircraft was shaken considerably by large explosions on our run in, which I thought was flak but turned out to be blast from the bombs. We were heading into an enormous great pillar of black smoke, when Shorty, who was in the second dickie's seat, noticed two other kites converging on us, so he pushed the stick right forward, and with the

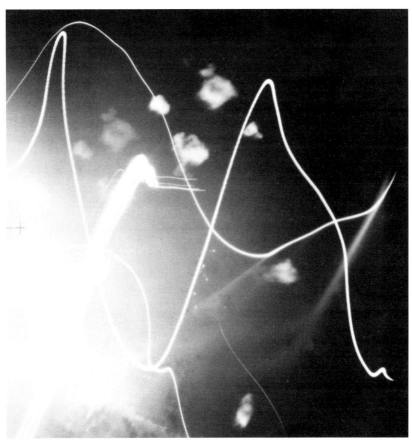

On 8/9 September 1943 'Spud' Taylor on Pilot Officer Ted Mills' crew flew an op to gun positions outside Boulogne, carrying 6×1,000 lb and 8×500 lb bombs. Taylor reported that they 'pranged the target fair and square and got a beautiful photo' but saw no big explosions. Altogether, 257 aircraft were despatched including 119 Wellingtons and 112 Stirlings and no aircraft were lost. However, the raid was not successful as the Oboe *marking and the bombing were not accurate and the battery appears to have escaped damage. (Taylor)*

steepness of the dive fell forward onto it and lost control. All four engines cut at the same time and we went screaming down this pillar of smoke until at about 3,000 feet Ted Mills pulled us out. Otherwise, the trip was uneventful, flying about 6 hours in bright moonlight. Coming home, I looked back and saw the smoke, black and enormous in the moonlight, reaching up to about 10,000 feet like a great mushroom. It was a good prang.

The next night we were on ops again, this time to a place called Modane, one of four vital railway tunnels between Germany, France and Italy. The target, in a valley with mountains rising steeply on either side to 10,000 or

165

11,000 feet, was about 10 miles east of the Italian border. About 60 miles north the same border joins Switzerland. It was a lovely night and a wizard moon lit up the ground like daylight. On the way out we passed Montluçon, which we could see quite clearly still glowing from our previous night's effort. After passing Lyons, we came to the high country, a sight I would not easily forget. There were great jagged peaks and ridges standing out hard and clear, with the valleys mostly thrown into shadow. We seemed to be flying extraordinarily close to the tops and I thought what an uncomfortable place it would be to land on!

The first few bombs were falling as we began our run on to the target, flying up a valley. I wondered what the echoes must have sounded like, as we were all carrying HEs. There was no opposition at all and we made our run straight and level just like practice bombing. After this I thought there shouldn't be much railway left around those parts. I saw Mont Blanc 50 miles away quite clearly on our starboard coming out. I also noticed a strange thing crossing the coast on way home. A round of incendiary flak shot up vertically into the sky till it reached about our own height, when it began to move parallel to the ground. Shortly afterwards there was a great flash and an aircraft (presumably one of our own) fell down in flames, hit by this strange missile. It looked strangely like Black Magic to me. At debriefing the Intelligence Officer said it was a new radar-directed shell that Jerry vectored onto aircraft. It was an 8-hour trip and I felt damn tired.

On the night of 21/22 September 1943 we set out for Hannover but we never got there because we developed engine trouble not far from the Dutch coast and had to come back early. The squadron lost one kite over the target and there was more trouble over our base. We got to about 8,000 feet over the drome and while waiting to land another of our kites, which was at the same height and not far from us, suddenly caught fire. She kept a pretty steady course for about a minute, then seemed to hover, and shot vertically downwards like a stone. Before she reached the ground the fire had spread to both wings, the engines had disintegrated and were blazing away in separate fires. Then the kite crashed with all its incendiaries and bombs. I never thought anyone could be alive after such an accident, but the mid-upper gunner survived and recovered in hospital. All the others were killed.

Two nights later, on 23/24 September, we went to Mannheim. The target was pretty hot, lit up for miles around by fighters, flares and fires. It was a good prang. I noticed for the first time lanes of yellow flares dropped by fighters to show our route in and out and, of course, the usual walls of searchlights with us and the fighters in between. We came off pretty lightly with one hole in Len's turret (that man led a charmed life!) and a few dents in the old bus. These long trips put a damn strain on the eyes. We lost one kite over the target and another was badly hit. One other came back on two engines and pranged just inside the east coast.

We went back to Hannover on 27/28 September. Just as we were about to taxi on to the runway for take-off, 'M' went u/s. It was her engines again! We dashed into 'Q' and set course as we took off. I saw a good many fighter's flares on the way and also a fair number shot down, but there was no trouble to ourselves until we were on the bombing run (as at Berlin). Just as I was about to press the tit, I heard John's voice say, 'Fighter!'

I heard the rattle of guns and saw a dirty stream of tracer shooting under the bomb window. We dropped the bombs (nineteen cans) onto an inferno of fire below and weaved away out of the target. We damaged the fighter and it shot away into the darkness. Hannover was one of the toughest targets I had been to. There were enormous cones of searchlights and plenty of fighters. Weaving away from the town I looked back and saw one enormous sheet of flame and smoke, the sky filled with flak puffs and searchlights and markers. It was the best prang I had ever seen.

Near Emden I saw one of our kites shot down in a combat. The rotten swine of a Jerry followed the blazing bomber practically down to earth, pumping lead into her. Ted and I saw it and we both swore.

Stirling III EF464 ZO-P of 196 Squadron took off from Witchford, Cambridgeshire on 4 October 1943 but evasive action en route *to Kassel caused the engines to over-rev and the port outer failed. Flight Sergeant G. H. Kogel, the pilot, turned back and made it across the North Sea but one mile from RAF Coltishall, a fighter station near Norwich, the port inner also failed and at 2143 hours the Stirling hit trees and crashed at Scottow, a small village near the airfield. Sergeant T. L. Dickie was killed and Sergeant C. D. Williams, who was severely injured, recovered and later flew with 514 Squadron. (via Mick Jennings)*

Flying Officer Bill Passlow's crew in 149 Squadron at Methwold. Back Row: L. W. J. 'Len' Durrant, gunner; Flying Officer Passlow, skipper; Jimmy Young, navigator; Warrant Officer Arthur 'Spud' Taylor; Eric, flight engineer. Front, kneeling: Burch, rear gunner, Poggy, WOp/AG. (Arthur Taylor))

Apart from the usual dangers over enemy territory, there was the added one of hitting one of our own kites in the dark. On average, at least once in a trip we had all but pranged another bomber. For this reason I spent a lot of my time sitting next to Ted. This night, coming back to base, the weather closed in until nothing could be seen but an occasional glimmer of light in the blackness. I happened to glance out of Ted's window and saw an enormous black shape sweeping towards us. Ted hadn't seen it and there was no time to warn him, so I heaved the stick back as hard as I could and we just made it. It was a near thing. One kite pranged near Haverhill. The mid-upper gunner and engineer were OK. Another came back with its rear gunner badly wounded and landed at Stradishall. Otherwise all were OK. We lost thirty-eight on this raid. I took a look at 'Q' next morning and found that one of the tailplanes was riddled and the starboard wing and one petrol tank were also holed.

Although the squadron only did about two mining trips in October, we managed to lose three kites. One crew [Warrant Officer Timlin] who were in our hut at West Wickham ditched on their first mining trip, on 7 October, shot down by one of their own ships. They were picked up after 6 hours but the wireless operator [Sergeant Miller] was missing.[8] This was a good start! Another crew[9] were landing in daylight on 12 October with three engines but judged wrongly and pranged about quarter of a mile short of the runway. There was an enormous explosion and the usual fire, with ammo and oxygen bottles exploding all over the place. The other crew were shooting up their old OTU, Benson, on 20 October, when they hit something and all were killed.[10]

On 13 October 1943 90 Squadron moved to Tuddenham in Suffolk. On 22/23 November we went to Berlin. There were plenty of high clouds and several small electrical storms. Our compasses did some queer things about 20 minutes before we were due at the target but, at zero-hour we could see some markers dropping and the clouds lit up some miles away. We went there and bombed. Through a gap in the cloud I saw a part of the town lit up by incendiaries and the continuous flashing of bombs. Before we left, the clouds had been turned to a dull red by the fires below. There was quite a lot of flak but not accurate. On our way back, while Shorty was taking a shot with the astro compass, we were picked up by some very accurate flak batteries that chased us out of their area.

On 1 December we set out for the Baltic just east of North Denmark. We flew low across the North Sea while it was still light, and could see the three other kites from the station, on each side and in front of us. Then it became dark and we climbed to get above some cloud and the compasses again went haywire. By this time we were over Denmark, parts of which I could see

Arthur 'Spud' Taylor and Marguerite's wedding on 18 November 1944. Best Man is L. W. J. 'Len' Durrant. (Arthur Taylor)

through the cloud. Jason dropped some pamphlets to encourage the inhabitants. Ted decided it would be foolish to add 200 miles to our route with the compasses as they were; I dropped the bombs this side of Denmark. We then went home. Our trip did not count. Of the other kites – one was shot down, another was shot up and the last, diverted.[11]

Notes

1. Flight Sergeant Rawdon Hume Middleton RAAF of 149 Squadron received a posthumous VC for his actions on 28/29 November 1942 when mortally wounded, he flew Stirling BF372 back to England after a raid on the Fiat Works at Turin, Italy. Five of his crew baled out to safety but when BF372 ran out of fuel it crashed into the English Channel and Middleton and his flight engineer and front gunner who had remained aboard to help their captain, drowned. 149 Squadron flew 2,628 Stirling sorties on 244 bombing and 160 minelaying raids, losing 87 aircraft, before converting to the Lancaster in August 1944.

2. Sergeant Page was flying as 2nd dickey to Flight Sergeant A. Pearson in Stirling I EF330 OJ-P. All 8 crew were killed when they were shot down by *Hauptmann* Wilhelm Dormann, a pre-war *Lufthansa* pilot, of II./NJG1, over Holland at just after 2200 hours. Page was flying as 2nd dickey to F/Sgt. A Pearson in Stirling I EF330 OJ-P. On 17/18 August 1943 Dormann, flying Bf110 Wrk Nr 6228 of 9./NJGI, was shot down by Flying Officers H. E. 'Harry' White and Mike Seamer Allen of 141 Squadron, their second victory of the war, flying a Beaufighter. Dormann's radar operator, *Obfw* Friedrich Schmalscheidt was killed when his parachute did not fully open. Dormann, who had fourteen victories, also baled out and suffered severe head injuries and burns. He never flew operationally again.

3. WOp/AG, Sergeant A. R. Denzey, and the flight engineer, Sergeant H. Lancaster, both of whom suffered a fractured skull, were from Stirling BF413/T flown by Sergeant J. B. Smith. They had disembarked from their aircraft and were about to enter the Operations Block for interrogation. BF480 was damaged beyond repair.

4. The increasing tempo of operations in 1943 increased the incidence of LMF cases, but they still remained a very low percentage of total numbers of Bomber Command. Throughout the war, 4059 cases were considered – 746 officers and 3313 NCOs. The 'charges' against most were dismissed and only 2726 (389 officers, 2337 NCOs) were actually classified as LMF, less than 0.4 per cent of all the aircrews of Bomber Command. The NCO total was higher, because there were more of them then officers.

5. 710 Lancasters, Halifaxes and Stirlings and seventeen Mosquitoes.

6. Master Bomber, Wing Commander J. E. 'Johnny' Fauquier, CO, 405 'Vancouver' Squadron RCAF.

7. This was Bomber Command's greatest loss of aircraft in one night so far in the war with a total of sixty-two aircraft twenty-five Halifaxes, twenty Lancasters and seventeen Stirlings, or 8.7 per cent of the force despatched. Thirty-one bombers fell victim to fighters in the target area with another seven crashing on the way home as a result of fighter attacks over Berlin. *M-Mother* was left at RAF Coltishall, its tailplane and rudder full of holes.

8. Timlin's Stirling EF147 WP-V was hit by flak from an Allied convoy returning from a *Gardening* sortie to the Friesian Islands. EF147 ditched in the sea 10 miles east of Cromer. Timlin was killed on 12.11.43 during an air test when his Stirling crashed at Hundon, Stradishall, after the control lever jammed. His air gunner, Sergeant Briscoe, was also killed.

9. EF426 WP-W, flown by Pilot Officer Hilton, overshot on an air test with the starboard outer feathered. He turned into the dead engine, the wing dropped and they hit the ground, killing six crew.
10. Sergeant Edwards and his six crew were killed while on an air test, EF497 WP-L crashing at Woodhouse Farm, Benson.
11 During 1944 Flying Officer Arthur Taylor flew on operations in support of the *Maquis* in France from Tempsford. He completed a second tour as a Warrant Officer observer on Lancasters in Pilot Officer Bill Passlow's crew in 149 Squadron at Methwold, February to May 1945, and he received the DFC on 20.7.45.

CHAPTER 14

'The Condemned Men Ate a Hearty Breakfast'

Ron Read DFC

Men who had thought their last flight over,
All hoping gone, came limping back,
Marvelling, looked on bomb-scarred Dover,
Buttercup fields and white Down track.
Cottage and ploughland, green lanes weaving,
Working-folk stopping to stare overhead –
Lovely, most lovely, past all believing
To eyes of men new-raised from the dead.

'*The Bomber*', Anon

March 1943 came in with a roar, when on the 1st we were briefed for Berlin – 'The Big City' as we knew it. It was a feared target and there was no doubt it would be defended fiercely. Cheshire [the CO of 76 Squadron] was going and Jock Hill, his wireless operator, was going to Berlin for the fourteenth time. Jock, a good friend of mine, was determined to make a full tour of thirty trips to Berlin if he could. He was the Signals Leader of 76 Squadron and could choose his trips. They were always the difficult ones. He had made several to Berlin with Cheshire on their first tour.

I had, for my last few trips, given up trying to get our aircraft *C-Charlie* up to our briefed bombing height. She was dreadfully slow on the climb and wallowed like a waterlogged boat at maximum altitude. I always became impatient and levelled off a couple of thousand feet below the stipulated height. This gave me more time on the run-in and a steadier platform over the target. It also made me look rather daring, always bombing at a lower height than most, although I didn't realise that at the time. These tactics were not at all popular with my crew, who believed, probably correctly, that every inch of height should be taken. They insisted that going to 'The Big City' I should climb all the way up to our bombing height of 20,000 feet. I felt perhaps this time they had something and promised to do so.

Setting off before dusk, it was dark when we got to the North German coast. The plan was to fly north along the coast across Schleswig Holstein and turn south somewhere east of Hamburg. It was intended to indicate that we might be going for one of several targets, Kiel, Hamburg, or Rostock. We would pass them closely, before making a last minute turn south to Berlin. Over Germany, the winds were all over the place and we were soon well off track. We flew over Kiel by mistake and got a very hot reception. It even woke Taff up from his job of monitoring and jamming German R/T transmissions by using tinsel. All aircraft carried a microphone in an engine nacelle. When he heard any German broadcast, the wireless operator pressed his key and the noise of the engine was transmitted on the German fighter frequency, to distort any instructions.

As we bounced about the sky, Taff, while listening out, had been reading his musical magazine, *The Melody Maker*. Seeing the title of a popular melody of the day, he came up on intercom: 'Hey Skip, it says here that, "Anywhere On Earth Is Heaven".'

'You're bloody right Taff,' I replied through my teeth, hanging on to the shaking control column. 'And I wish like Hell we were anywhere on earth now.'

We ploughed on to Berlin, me hauling and coaxing old *C-Charlie,* higher than she'd ever been before. Finally, I told them we were at last at 20,000 feet. There were muted cheers all round. When we reached Berlin the Pathfinders, affected by the fickle winds, were late, so we had to stooge around. After a while, some fires and flares appeared ahead and Harry led us to them. We were quite close to them when Mac said that there were other flares going down behind us. I looked around over my shoulder. No doubt about these, they were the real ones and the ones we were chasing were dummies, well east of the target. Now I had to go back against the stream of incoming aircraft. There were over 300 that night. As I turned I saw a few more aircraft doing the same. Making my turn fairly sharp, *C-Charlie* lost a bit of height. By now there were aircraft all around us, going in all directions. It was bloody dicey. Wanting to get over the target, drop the bombs and get out as soon as possible, I pushed the nose down to speed things up.

We soon had a good view of the correct marker flares but I now had to go the full distance back across the target, among the heavy flak and against the oncoming stream, before turning once more onto the correct heading. By the time we'd done that I was down to 17,500 feet for the bombing run. Once more I hadn't managed to bomb from the full height. However, the crew weren't complaining now, they wanted to get it all over with and get out just as quickly as I did.

It was hot over Berlin all right. We saw several Halifaxes coned in search-lights. Having dropped our bombs in the approved fashion and spent ten long seconds waiting for our photoflash to go off, I turned for home at just about the correct position. At least we thought it was. Harry claimed another pinpoint, a junction of river and railway, just where they should have been. If we really knew where we were then, it was to be the last time for three more hours.

As we headed back over Germany, we saw flak coming up at aircraft in almost every direction. Normally, the location of flak and searchlights was a good aid to navigation, but this time they seemed to be everywhere. I was pretty sure that the flak ahead was the Ruhr. I noted two aircraft at least go down in flames. It was coming up in such quantity; there must have been a lot of aircraft ahead of us in the same predicament. I took some small consolation from that and pressed on. Fortunately, I had held height after we left Berlin and we were still at 15,000 feet. I wasn't crossing the Ruhr lower. We ploughed our way through the flak, getting bounced about in the process and eventually, 30 minutes later, came out the other side. Ahead lay the coastline, but we were heading for yet another concentration of flak. I flew north of most of it, but we were hit just as we passed out to sea. It wasn't bad but noisy, as a lot of shrapnel rattled our tail.

Back at Linton, waiting our turn to land, a Halifax came flying along over the runway shooting off red Very flares. We made way for him immediately. It was Roger Coverley, literally coming back from a spin to avoid the searchlights. He managed to pull out at around 2,000 feet. All his radios and electrics were out and he had to make a landing without any communications. He made it OK, the final happening of an eventful night. Counting the cost next day, we found that of the force of 302 aircraft setting out, seventeen were lost: a nasty 5.5 per cent. Six of them were Halifaxes. No. 76 Squadron lost two crews. Pilot Officer [N. S.] Black [RNZAF] and Sergeant [J. L.] Fletcher [DFM MID], both of whom had been with us since December. In 78 Squadron our luck still held but it was a frail thread, as we were to find out.

Later that month I was promoted to flight lieutenant and appointed deputy flight commander. One day I had a long and controversial conversation with a couple of Intelligence Officers about 'Chop Rates'. They were averaging 4 per cent per sortie. I mused, that with thirty sorties to complete, the average crew had a minus 20 per cent chance of surviving. Their reply was instant and consoling but spoken from theory, not experience.

'Oh no,' they said. 'It doesn't work like that. The statisticians say it starts from zero, for every trip. So it's only ever 4 per cent.'

'Nonsense' I said. 'If you only had to go once, it would be 4 per cent, as long as you don't go again. If you go again your percentage chance of the chop must go up. I've got to find a way to get on to some one else's percentage.' They laughed and tried to convince me by insisting the statisticians had proved it was only 4 per cent. I said if they'd find me a statistician who'd completed thirty operations, I might believe it. Otherwise, I believed myself. By this time into a tour, one became quite cynical. The illusions of youth had fallen away. Gone were the images of single-engined knights of the air jousting in the blue skies, fostered by the Battle of Britain. We saw the raw, ugly face of death and destruction all around us, when nightly flying those hostile skies across the North Sea.

Giving the matter some thought, I developed what I called my 'percentage' approach. I decided that we should go in a little behind our own wave, to be able to assess what had gone before. This would take us round the course, over and through the target when, hopefully, the guns and fighters were still busy with the keen young pilots pressing on in front. There were always some. Whilst they were being attacked, we would follow in the relative calm and slip through. Each battery of guns and each enemy fighter was dealt with by a

174

ground radar controller, handling a box some 30 miles deep. He picked an aircraft as it entered his box at its western edge and if it wasn't lost or shot down, handed it over to the controller of the next box 30 miles east. I felt I could take advantage of this system. I decided that we should be up to 2 minutes late at each turning point. My theory was that when we entered a box the controller would be busy with the people in front.

When I saw anyone being fired on by flak or fighters or coned in search-lights I would edge up to him, not too close but enough to feel shielded by the interest of the enemy forces in him. Once he escaped or was shot down I hoped to be too close to the controller's far boundary for him to bother with me. I reasoned that he would turn his attention back to his western boundary to pick up some one just entering it, thus missing me. In this way I thought I might get a little of the percentage of survival chance of those aircraft shot down near me, hence my 'percentage' system. It was crude and cynical perhaps, but flying a bomber over Germany in the spring of 1943 was a crude and cynical business.

Our aircraft changed in recognition of new German tactics. Some time in January 1943 the front turrets were removed and a new nose section fitted. There wasn't much point in carrying a front gun. Nothing was slower than we were and unless an enemy aircraft was foolish enough to fly in front of us and throttle back we weren't going to be able to shoot it down. In early February, our mid-upper turrets were also taken out and faired over. This was a Cheshire modification. Again, there was little use for them. Almost all fighter attacks were now being made from below. It was decided that the reduction of weight would give more speed and height. To help the illusion along, aircraft so modified were recoded from a Halifax II, to a Halifax Mk II Series 1 Special. Whatever they called it, it remained a lumbering, under-powered sitting target for enemy night-fighters.

Now we had only the rear turret to fight back with. With four puny .303 in Browning machine-guns of limited range, we were at a great disadvantage to the Ju 88 night-fighters, who now carried three 20 mm cannon and three 7.9 mm machine-guns in the nose, as well as a 13 mm machine-gun facing the rear. We asked for .5 in machine-guns, to give us a chance of reaching them, since sitting behind us out of range, they could pump cannon shells and heavy calibre bullets at us with impunity. We never got them, although later, a few 5 Group Lancasters were fitted with them.

We were slowly becoming aware that most of the attacks were now being made from the blind area beneath us. With the withdrawal of the mid-upper turret we had a spare gunner. To help to improve the total blind spot that existed below, a small blister window was fitted in the floor of the fuselage. Here, the poor mid-upper gunner had to lie on his belly, with his head poked into the blister, to try to spot a climbing fighter. Someone could do this for a short period, but lying on his stomach, head lowered through the floor into the blister, it was absurd to expect anyone to stay alert for the long hours over enemy territory.

Another change was the removal of the shrouds covering the glowing exhaust pipes either side of each engine. Their effect on the airflow over the wings reduced performance. With their removal we gained a hundred feet or two in height but were left with eight red-hot glowing exhausts, displayed to the world above and behind. On one occasion a British Beaufighter flying in bad visibility thought that the exhausts he saw from a Halifax was a flare path and tried to land along it. We were always vulnerable and the improving fighter radar was making life even more difficult.

One reassuring story we were given by our intelligence staff, was that of 'scarecrow' shells. These were said to be anti-morale shells, fired in the path of a bomber stream to dishearten the crews. They represented aircraft being blown up. As they burst nearby, they showered flaming oil and petrol, together with the pathfinder flares and colour signals carried by RAF aircraft. In fact, all the symptoms of an exploding aircraft. Briefings referred to the probability of 'scarecrows'. Having been briefed, we would report that 'scarecrows' were active tonight. We saw them often and used to say how realistic they were. We wondered how the Germans could portray an exploding aircraft so accurately. At the end of the war, when German anti-aircraft personnel were interrogated, it was discovered that they had no such thing in their armoury. The 'scarecrows' that we dismissed so casually were real RAF aircraft blowing up. In a way, it was just as well that we didn't know. It was a comforting illusion that saved us some concern. Not that it would have made much difference if we'd known the truth. We were of the generation that would do what we were told, in the name of duty and honour. This was to be well proven in the winter's Battle of Berlin. Most of us were far more afraid of being thought afraid, than we were of flying over Germany. The period ahead of us in March 1943 was to test that loyalty to orders to the limits. We were entering the Battle of the Ruhr.

Flogging night after night over enemy territory in our Halifaxes, with ever increasing numbers of Lancasters flying above us, slow Stirlings below and the dwindling Wellingtons around us, we were known, as a whole, as 'Main Force' squadrons – the work-horses of Bomber Command, making up the main body of any attack. We ploughed our way almost nightly, across Germany, to targets personally selected by our Commander-in-Chief. Our private hopes lay in doing as good a job as our aircraft and equipment would allow and to survive the night, get back home, ready to fight again.

By March 1943, excluding the light daylight bombers of No. 2 Group, there were fifty-one Main Force squadrons operating, increasingly equipped with four-engined aircraft. At an average of twenty-four aircraft per squadron there were, theoretically, 1,224 aircraft available, although it was probable that only about 50 per cent were ever available at any one time. The rest were in use for training, under repair from damage, under routine maintenance, or meeting other calls upon them, such as minelaying, or working for Coastal Command. Allowing for the ten squadrons still flying Wellingtons with five-man crews, we numbered about 8,000 trained aircrew, the tip of an iceberg, reaching down all stages of training, from HCUs to recruitment depots. With the five new squadrons of Pathfinders to lead us, we were a formidable force.

Down the bottom of the ladder at squadron level we were totally unaware of the momentous decisions taken in Bomber Command. Almost all were taken personally by our chief, 'Butch' to us all. At that time there was little of the mutual affection that was to blossom between him and his crews post-war. Then, he was a remote, steely-eyed figure, who made announcements to the press about our activities. We basked in the glowing tributes the press paid to our efforts and believed the glossy interpretation of our results portrayed by Harris. We were unaware that much of his optimism was self-deception, brought on by his obsession, shared by many senior air chiefs, British and American, that the bomber on its own would be the war-winning instrument. To us, he was a man that sent us back to targets several times in succession, increasing the risk each time. He was responsible for sending us in bad weather to undertake almost impossible tasks, which our aircraft and equipment was incapable of fulfilling.

It would have been impossible to please aircrew in the choice of targets. The one place that was unlikely to be top on anybody's list was the Ruhr. But it was top of Harris's list in March 1943. On 5 March we were briefed for Essen again. It was the most heavily defended of the Ruhr towns, the big bogey one that had escaped serious damage to date. I sang 'Off on the Road to Morocco' quite cheerfully as we taxied out.

We were one of ninety-four Halifaxes from the total of 442 aircraft going. If we didn't know before, we found out what was meant by the Ruhr defences being tough, on the way in. It looked quite frightening from afar. There was solid flak ahead and already plenty of fighter activity. However, our own passage wasn't too bad and I managed to pick our way safely through the worst areas. We were in the first wave, with a mixed batch of 4 lb and 30 lb incendiaries and a couple of 1,000-pounders. Our task was to start the fires that the following Lancasters and Stirlings could use as a target guide. We got there on time and Pathfinder flares were going down as we made the target area. We had a good run up, although it was through the heaviest flak we'd yet encountered. We dropped our bombs accurately on the flares below. We couldn't see anything of the target itself, as the usual haze covered Essen. But it looked, as we turned for home, as though there were heavy fires breaking out. Leaving the target, we saw two aircraft shot down by fighters close by. [Fourteen bombers were lost.] I made a sneaky detour towards the scene, on the basis that the attacking aircraft would be on their way elsewhere to seek some other unfortunate victim. It seemed to work out; we had no problems finding our way to quieter skies. Upon return two Linton, aircraft were missing. A few days later we learnt that, for the very first time, the Krupps works was severely damaged by our efforts. We felt quite proud of ourselves.

Although his main objective during spring 1943 was the Ruhr, to stretch the German defences Harris varied the attacks with some long-range trips to southern Germany. On 9 March we went to Munich and on the 11th to Stuttgart. On the whole they were a softer option than the Ruhr, not quite such a frantic and frightening scene. Mind you, you could be killed going there just as easily as anywhere else. On the Stuttgart trip we saw a couple of night-fighters flying over the target. One of them attacked us unexpectedly on the way out. I was surprised and thought he had us cold. I flung the aircraft around, expecting a long battle but we evaded him easily. We decided he must have been a 'Sprog'. On the Munich trip, out of 264 aircraft, eight were missing – none of them ours. On Stuttgart eleven out of 314 aircraft were missing. Once again at Linton, we had a charmed night, although six of the missing were Halifaxes.

On 12 March at breakfast our talk was of the night before to Stuttgart. It had been a longish trip of 7½ hours. We compared it with the trip two days earlier to Munich, of 9 hours. Both by the standards of the day were interesting but not too 'dicey'. Coming out of Stuttgart we had been attacked by a fighter. I'd prepared for the worst but he had given up rather easily after we returned fire, as I weaved violently out of his range. We thought he must have been a 'Sprog'.

The next mystery in our shortish lives was learning what our activity was for the coming day. Would we be given a day off, after being 'on' every other night since 3 March? By the previous pattern of operations we were due for one and looking forward to tasting the joys of Betty's Bar in York. But we'd learned the hard way that it didn't do to make assumptions in Butch Harris's Bomber Command.

Breakfast over, we wandered down to flights to report to our Flight Commander, his to dispose of as Bomber Command wished. Squadron Leader 'Bertie' Neal was a lumpy, dark haired, round-faced New Zealander, about 6 feet in height. He looked and talked like a sheep farmer, although he could have been a bank manager for all we knew, or cared. In Bomber Command, living for the day ahead, we seldom had time for deep conversations on the pre-war past. In fact, such was our life style, the conversation seldom reverted to anything more recent than our activities of the preceding operation or last night out in York.

Bertie laughed a lot and spoke with a sort of 'Slussching' lisp, particularly prominent when he was excited. Having counted the heads of his available pilots and learned that their crews were accounted for and available, he took himself off to the office of Wing Commander Gerry Warner, to learn our fate for the next 24 hours.

'You never know,' said Bertie hopefully, 'We might even get a schtand down. Ha ha ha!'

We spent the next hour checking with our crews and ground crews, obtaining the serviceability of our own aircraft after the night before.

'Shorry blokes,' said Bertie, when we returned to flights an hour later, 'We're on again tonight. Maxshimum effort.' That meant all available crews and aircraft.

Most crews departed to their various tasks. 'Morty' Mortensen and I, as deputy flight commanders, stayed behind to receive any further instructions. There wasn't much Bertie could say, no one could learn the target before briefing.

'By the fuel loads, it's going to be "Happy Valley",' was all he could add.

'Happy Valley' was the RAF's euphemism for the Ruhr. The most feared and heavily defended targets in all Germany lay within its sprawling maw. The little peanut-sized knot that always lay in the pit of my stomach on ops days swelled a little more. I just hoped it wasn't going to be Essen, the hardest of them all, again. We had been there the week before on 5 March. It wasn't an experience I was anxious to repeat.

The rest of the morning passed with the testing of equipment in the aircraft, culminating in an air test, where everything we could test we did. We couldn't test the guns without going out to sea, which needed special clearance. We would test those after we crossed the English coast, clear of shipping but well before the enemy coast. Everything else we could test, we did: navigation systems, radio, autopilot, bomb doors, turrets and, hopefully, landing gear upon our return. Everything worked and after a short discussion with the ground crew we retired to our respective messes for lunch. Briefing was scheduled for 1600 hours.

The briefing room was on top of Station Headquarters at Linton, reached by an outside wooden staircase. Extinguishing our cigarettes below, we clattered noisily aloft to take our seats inside. The big wall map at the end of the room was covered with a canvas curtain. The two wing commanders entered, followed by the station commander, Group Captain John Whitley. The chattering ceased and we clattered noisily to our feet, until told to be seated.

Briefing tonight was to be by Wing Commander Leonard Cheshire, the CO of 76 Squadron, our sister squadron at Linton. The two squadron commanders took it in turns to take the briefing. Gerry Warner was the CO of our squadron, 78, but we all preferred Chesh's briefing. They came from much more experience.

Wing Commander Leonard Cheshire DSO DFC and bar had been recently promoted from squadron leader to take over 76 Squadron. Already, at 24, he was something of a legend in Bomber Command, because of his book *Bomber Pilot*, published earlier in the year. For the first time, it put down on paper the experiences and feelings of a bomber crew at war. Reading it while in training, we had our doubts about the author. It flew in the face of the RAF's tradition of never 'Shooting a Line'. Who was this chap, openly talking of his operational experiences, not just in the mess but to the world at large? He must be a real 'Line Shooter' putting it all down in a book. Many were the reservations we held about him.

We looked at him as he first came into the mess. He looked harmless enough. Could he really be the chap that wrote that book? In fact, he was, and as soon as we had spoken and listened to him, our doubts dissolved. He was a quiet, modest enough individual in any company. But he was also dedicated to the business of winning the war and wanted to share his experiences with other crews, to help them and the world at large, to promote the war effort – especially that of the RAF. Before his 76 Squadron appointment he had been a member of a British mission to the USA on a tour to bring home to the American public the facts of being at war with Germany and to raise help for the RAF and Britain's cause. We soon found him an entirely open and helpful commander, who would give assistance and advice to any member of aircrew who needed it, irrespective of his squadron. He was already developing new tactics to assist in countering the German defences. We had received the minimum instruction on this during our training. There had been no formal lessons, just casual tips from those of our instructors who had completed a tour and the 'no line shoot' tradition muted those to mere references. Chesh was providing a lot of light in our darkness. So we were all agog for his message that night. He stepped up onto the platform, we sat down and he pulled back the curtain across the map with a flourish, saying,

'Gentlemen, our target for tonight is Essen.'

Glug! Our hearts dropped. There it lay, at the end the red ribbon delineating our route, passing through the massed, red hatched areas indicating the heavy anti-aircraft defences and fighters of the Kammhuber Line, which protected the interior of Germany from Denmark to south east of Paris. The section passing around the Ruhr, the most heavily defended of all.[1] Not that the Kammhuber Line itself made a lot of difference, we had to fly through it to get to almost any North German target. It was just that going to Essen, the intensity of the defences increased when you passed the line, rather than decreased, as they did when you got through anywhere else. The little knot in my stomach grew to a pigeon's egg.

Chesh told us that there were 457 aircraft going, one of the highest numbers for some time – 158 twin-engined Wellingtons and 156 Lancasters, but only ninety-one of our Halifaxes. 'Hallies' had taken a beating on the previous two raids. There were also forty-two Stirlings and ten Mosquitoes, the latter acting as Pathfinder markers.

Our role was that of fire raisers, following in immediately after the first Pathfinders had dropped their marker flares. We were dropping incendiaries and two 1,000-pound bombs, to stir things up and light the fires for the following Lancasters to plaster them with their 4,000 lb 'Blockbusters'. We were beginning to find our fire-raising role a little onerous. The German defences had the habit of waiting until they were certain that the target was properly identified. They held their fire until the initial markers went down and then gave the following aircraft – us – all they had.

Having given us our route and general advice, Chesh stepped down and we listened half-heartedly to the intelligence briefing on the defences, which, as always, was optimistic. We knew what they were really like and didn't need to be told by an ancient, non-flying officer, what he imagined was in store for us.

The weather was good and the Pathfinders were using the new *Oboe* technique of marking the target with special flares dropped by Mosquitoes, directly controlled by radio beams from England. At least we ought not to be hanging around waiting for the markers, as had been the case sometimes in the past. Take-off was to be at 1900 and, briefing over, we left for our messes once more, to partake of our operational meal, always of real eggs and real bacon, unavailable to almost anyone else in war-time UK, except through the black market. They were fattening us up for the kill.

'Morty' Mortensen had a macabre sense of humour. As this culinary treat was being served he made the statement 'The condemned men ate a hearty breakfast'. This was a statement that, in those days, accompanied the notice of the hanging of a murderer. We ignored him and chewed doggedly on. By now, the knot in my stomach was reaching the size of a hen's egg and the bacon tasted like leather.

180

Leaving the mess, we returned to flights to prepare for take-off time. This waiting time was always the worst period and the hen's egg in my stomach grew steadily into an orange.

The crews all met in the locker room, to dress up for the cold night skies. Depending on the anticipated weather, we could don long johns and string vests, or retain our normal underwear. We could wear our battle dress tops and cover them with the fur-lined Irvine suit, usually just the jacket. In between these, was the long, heavy, white sub-mariner's jersey, which some quirk of supply branch humour labelled 'Air-crew, Frocks, White'.

In summer the battle dress alone was sufficient. There was some heating in our Halifaxes, although it was not wholly reliable or effective. March though, was still a time for Irvine jackets over battle dress and jersey. Dressed, we stood around talking and joking with the other crews. By now the jokes were pretty forced and we'd heard them all before. But they were part of the ritual and we laughed as best we could.

Finally, the time came for us to step into the waiting crew buses, three crews to a bus, or the back of a three-tonner, if you weren't quick. I had my favourite little WAAF driver, known as 'Blondie' to the squadron. She had short, curly blond hair, sparkling blue eyes and a broad Glaswegian accent. The rest of her was enveloped in battle dress. Her sharp Glaswegian humour made her stand out from the other drivers. I managed, as usual, to grab a seat in the cab beside her and her Glaswegian chatter kept me occupied until we reached the aircraft.

My orange-sized lump had reached Jaffa proportions by this time but as I got to work it subsided. Outside checks in the company of Jimmy, my Rhodesian flight engineer, were completed. I joined the rest of the crew aboard, already stowing their gear and busy checking what equipment they could before the engines started. I checked the fuselage interior on the way up to my seat. Once ensconced in the cockpit, I got to work in earnest, preparing for start-up. The lump that had been in my stomach all day had disappeared. I was too preoccupied now to think about it. And so it would remain, at least unless some serious danger threatened later.

Five minutes later the green Very signal for 'Start up' rose from the control tower and thirty Halifax captains gave the thumbs up to the crew chief, standing below his cockpit. The fitter under the fuselage pressed the button on his battery cart and the skipper pressed his starter buttons. The noise reverberated around the airfield as 120 Rolls-Royce Merlin engines roared into life. Now that all power sources were operating, each crewmember tested the rest of his systems. I checked with Jimmy that all the engines were running OK and he told me when they were ready for run up. Starting with the port inner we tested all four through each operating cycle. Run ups completed, each crewmember called in to say their equipment was OK; now we were ready to taxi. Two or three aircraft were already moving, as we moved out of dispersal onto the taxiway.

Our dispersal was quite a way from the runway, so I usually finished up about seventh or eighth in the line of aircraft waiting to take-off. This gave me time to study their take-offs and the possible effect of a cross-wind, as well as to gauge the length of take-off likely to be needed. These were useful little snippets of information that could help in an emergency.

Finally, on the end of the runway, the green lamp from the runway control van cleared us for take–off. Giving a quick wave to those lucky people assembled at the control van to see us off, I opened the throttles and we were away. Sluggishly and slowly the Halifax came to life. Watching the increasing airspeed and feeling the beginnings of life flowing into the controls, I held her down until the speed was 10 knots above the recommended take-off speed, every cautious pilot liked to have an extra 10 knots for Mother. Then, wheels up and off on the long, slow, bomb laden climb, that would not stop until we were somewhere over Holland.

We circled Linton for 20 minutes before setting course at the specified time. Joined by another fifty or more Halifaxes from adjacent airfields, we climbed individually into the fading light, towards our destiny. In an hour we would be the playthings of fate.

We were all aware that some of us wouldn't return. The self-protective aspects of human nature made us believe that it couldn't be us. Although sometimes, a little secret, traitorous voice, kept asking 'Why not?'

If I cared to think about it, I knew quite well why not, the current chop rate was 4 per cent per sortie. Since you had to complete thirty sorties before being taken off operations for a rest, there was a strong mathematical probability that you wouldn't. So I didn't think about it. Take each day and especially each flying night, as it came, was the common Bomber Command crew's attitude.

Thirty minutes later we lumbered across Flamborough Head, to head for Egmond on the Dutch coast. This was our usual route and the Germans were aware of it. They had a fighter station adjacent to Egmond that could catch us on the way in and out. This seemed to make little difference to the plans of Bomber Command. We went that route with monotonous regularity when going to the Ruhr or north Germany. Going to South Germany, we departed via Southwold, the regular crossing point for the Lancasters based around Lincoln of 5 Group and the 3 Group Stirlings and Wellingtons, operating from Norfolk and Suffolk. Going further south, we always left via Dungeness. And they said the Germans were inflexible.

It wasn't long before we could see the flashes on the horizon that indicated the arrival over Holland of the first wave of Pathfinder aircraft. But it wasn't at the coast that the action began, the German flak ships stationed a few miles off-shore, were always ready to pop off a hostile reception for the unwary. One of the benefits of being behind the front runners was that I could pinpoint them and fly a course to avoid them.

We tested our guns as soon as we saw the flashes and I warned the crew to tighten up their look out for fighters. We saw nothing of anything in the black sky, but every now and then we humped across the slipstream of an aircraft in front. Although that meant he was probably dangerously close, I took comfort from it. It showed we weren't entirely on our own. Crossing the coast, weaving through the growing bursts of flak, we set an easterly course for our final turning point, before the run to the target.

Now above 16,000 feet, the aircraft was sluggish and slow to respond to controls. I tried to avoid sharp movements, as that led to a loss of precious height. But out of self-preservation I always gave a hank to the left and right every 5 minutes or so, just to give the lookouts a chance to note any crafty fighter climbing up from below.

There were one or two bursts of air-to-air firing close to us, indicating fighters in action. We redoubled our look out. Now, well into the heavily defended areas of the Kammhuber Line, the intensity of the flak was increasing. Just ahead of us was the Ruhr and there it was already an inferno of brilliant explosions, which appeared to fill the sky.

'Christ it's worse than last time.' I called on the intercom. 'Come up and have a quick look at this Vic,' I invited the navigator.

'No thanks Skip, I'm too busy, anyway I saw it the last time. Your course for the target is 156 in 2 minutes.'

I knew he wouldn't come up. He'd only ever looked out once, after a glance of less than a minute at the angry sky, he returned to his little enclosed world of the nav cabin, never to appear again until we were ready for landing. He was lucky, some of us had to look out: the two gunners, Jimmy the engineer in the observation dome, Harry Laidlaw the bomb aimer, who was now going down on his pad to peer at it all through his bombsight, and me. I banked steeply onto the last course, having a good look around below as I did so, from here we had to keep straight and level if possible.

The flak was heavier than ever on the run up. We were bounced around by the bursting shells below and the stink of cordite from those bursting in front, filled the cockpit. I clung onto the controls, to try to keep things level for old Harry, peering down through his sight. Taff our wireless operator groped his way past me going back to the flare chute at the rear.

His job was to make sure the large magnesium photoflash slid down the chute when we released the bombs.

Shrapnel rattled against the fuselage. Our only consolation was that the flak wasn't predicted and aimed just at us, just the usual blanket stuff pooped up at random now they knew our approach path. Not that that was much of a consolation, flak was all a matter of luck. But looking out into the face of that inferno I needed all the consolation I could find, as well as all the luck. I could see the marker flares ahead quite clearly. So could Harry. I opened the bomb doors and told him we were all his.

'OK Skip, I've got the markers in sight. Steady, hold it at that.'

Just as he said it, we got a roaring bang under the tail that pushed the nose down and way off to the left.

'Right, come right, you're a long way off, come around about ten degrees right, quick,' called Harry. I stomped on the rudders and swung us around. We were still a bit off to the left.

'More right,' Harry called urgently, I pushed her round against the flak bounces. 'A bit more – more, that's it, steady, steady. Hold her.'

The marker flares had disappeared under the nose but there was plenty to see. Some aircraft had already dropped their loads and fires were lighting up the ground. Among them I could see the flashes of HE bombs exploding.

'How far now Harry? We don't want to overshoot.'

'OK Skip, it's coming up now, steady – steady – steady.' I thought he'd never stop saying, 'steady'.

Essen was at its worst; we were still bouncing around from the flak and I was sure Harry was overshooting.

'Come on Harry for Christ's sake. How much further?' Harry was not to be hurried and I shouldn't have been impatient; but.

'Just a little more left left, a little – steady.'

Just as I reached bursting point, 'Bombs gone' he called.

Now came the most testing time of all. As the bombs were released, a little red light came up on the panel before me. It was the photoflash light. As the bombs fell, they were followed by the photoflash, which, exploding above the site where our bombs would strike, would enable our camera in the fuselage to take a picture of that point.

According to the height from which it had been dropped, that photoflash took between six and ten seconds to go off. I had to keep the aircraft flying straight and level across the target until the light went out, when every instinct screamed for me to fling the aircraft away from it and head for home. I closed the bomb doors and settled down for the longest ten seconds in the history of world. The flak was getting worse, as more and more aircraft entered the target area. I hung on until, thank God, the light went out.

I started a full right turn away; just as I did I saw sparks going forward over my turning starboard wing. Now, there were always sparks flying back from the engine exhausts when they were at full power, but these sparks were going forwards. Christ, they weren't sparks, they were tracer bullets. We had a fighter, which none of us had seen.

Halfway round my turn away from the target, I could only go one way, down and back into it. I pushed the aircraft down into the flak-filled sky below and hoped for the best. Fortunately, the fighter either lost me, or decided on discretion and not to risk being shot down by his own flak.

Now down at 11,000 feet and still descending, my full turn had carried us right back over the target again and I had to get us out into the clear. I didn't want to go lower, into the light flak at around 10,000 feet. It looked un-healthily close already; a loud bang under the port wing pushed us into an even steeper turn. I wrenched the controls back into a steep lumbering turning climb, up and away from the target area. That's when the engineer Jimmy took a hand.

'Port outer heating up Skip, it's going off the clock. You'll have to feather it.'

Jesus, that bloody port outer. We'd had lots of trouble with it on previous trips. This was the fourth time it had let us down. That was, if it hadn't been hit. That flak burst was certainly close enough. Anyway, I couldn't leave it to run and not feather it, that could lead to a fire. There had been several engine fires in the air in Halifaxes recently. Not only would a fire probably force us to abandon the aircraft, but if it really flamed, we'd be a clear target for every gun and fighter around.

184

I feathered and our not very rapid climb dwindled to a slight upward stagger. That was when Taff our wireless operator, back in his cabin, re-entered the fray. 'Hey Skip, I think there's a fire down here. There's a lot of smoke coming up from somewhere. What shall I do?'

I couldn't think of any other answer than, 'Well put the bloody thing out of course'.

While I pondered on our state, if you can call a quick mental debate of baling out now or trying to drag it away from an undoubtedly hostile Essen below, 'pondering', we somehow staggered to 12,000 feet, gradually clearing the target area into the quieter skies to the west. Taff called back quite soon,

'It's OK Skip, it's out. Don't know what it was but it's all clear now.'

Thank goodness for small mercies, if you could call not having an engine on fire a small one. Now we could start the long haul home. It would be a long haul too, on three engines. Once in the clear, I checked to find all the crew still in one piece, excited and glad to be clear of the target area. But we were low and slow, lower even than the poor old Stirlings, who usually caught the flak. It was not a good place to be, but I didn't want to descend in case we lost another engine and we couldn't climb at all.

'All right chaps but we're not home yet. Don't relax, keep the look out going. And Vic, what about our course, any change after all that weaving?'

'I don't think so Skip, I think it's all right. Just keep her on 283, we should go out north of Antwerp.' Vic was never quite sure where we were, until after we'd left it behind.

We ploughed on at a snail's pace of 130 knots so that I could climb a little more, to give us room for manoeuvre as we crossed the coast. I noted sporadic fighter action around us and kept giving a tilt to right and left for the gunners to view the sky below. But there was little venom left in that night for us. We made our departure from Continental Europe quietly. Although a flak ship or two were still having a last word, it was not with us.

After the long flog across the North Sea, we saw the welcoming flashes of the red airfield beacons in England from 20 miles out and flew in over Filey Bay to land at Linton 5 hours 30 minutes after take-off, glad to be once more on terra firma. The more firma the less terror, we always said. Once on the ground, we discussed our night with the ground crew, while waiting for the bus to take us back to our next chore, debriefing.

We were in mixed mood of relief, exhilaration and fatigue – pretty standard feelings after a hard flight. The one thing we wanted was to get back to the mess and have a drink, eat our second bacon and egg meal, which I would enjoy much more than the first, simmer down and get to bed. But we had to be debriefed first. That meant a joust in the briefing room with the intelligence staff, never a welcome task. Quite apart from the RAF tradition of under-statement and never 'Shooting a Line', most aircrew were not ready to give long, detailed descriptions of the night's events so soon after.

On the other hand, the intelligence staff was anxious to obtain the imme-diate impressions, so that they could report to the Group headquarters. Group themselves were required to report to Bomber Command. Thus there was a little conflict between the crews and the debriefing staff. We tended to minimise events, whereas the intelligence staff tried to press us into revealing every detail. Our reports were normally laconic and terse, while they tried to coax us into expanding them into detailed sagas.

I was fortunate in that one of the WAAF Intelligence Officers, Pam Finch, had a sympathetic understanding of the way aircrew felt and was a good friend. As we walked into the briefing room, to find several other crews waiting, she rounded off the debriefing she was engaged in, just in time to call us to her desk. She almost always managed to do that. Aware of our feelings, she usually accepted our brief statements without probing too much for detailed expansion. Consequently, we said that it was a good 'prang' on the target, we had seen a fighter that had shot at us unsuccessfully, though we couldn't see the type, the defences were heavier than last time, otherwise it was pretty well a normal Ruhr trip.

The next day we found that things were getting tougher over the Ruhr. Out of 457 aircraft, twenty-three, 5 per cent, were missing. Seven were Halibags and two were from Linton – one from each squadron – so new that I didn't know either of the pilots or crews. We older crews tended to hang together and though we helped the new crews when they asked for it, we were by now too pre-occupied with our own problems to go out of our way to do so. We had to do thirty trips for a tour of operations. Then it was six months' rest, before starting another tour of twenty trips. You didn't have to be a mathematician to wonder how it could be done. Still, that was just another mystery in the day to day the life of a Bomber Command crew, vintage 1943. Sometimes I pondered on that other, greater, mystery. Just what was I doing here and how did I get roped into this bloody dangerous pastime? Not that I really had anyone else but myself to blame. Anyway, in the words of every RAF flight sergeant listening to complaints from recruits, 'If yer can't take a joke, yer shouldn't have joined'.

Morty went on leave after the second Essen trip. We had a good break for twelve nights, as the weather was too bad to operate.

On 26 March we went back to the Ruhr, this time to Duisburg. I was again on special reconnaissance. Special recce on Hamburg was one thing but the Ruhr was another. Wherever you hung around in the Ruhr, you were over another town and the defences embraced both. They were fierce everywhere and growing more so. Once again the first wave after Pathfinders, we could expect the same warm reception we got at Essen. As special recce I had to hang around to report what happened. Giving the matter some thought, I extended my 'percentage' approach. I decided that we should go in even a little more behind our own wave, to be able to assess what had gone before. This would take us round the course, over and through the target, when hopefully, the guns and fighters were still busy with the keen pilots pressing on in front. We would follow in the relative calm behind, slip through quietly if possible and observe. It worked on Duisburg like a charm. Four minutes late, we sailed in and out having a good look at the action below as we went round. I worked my way in following two aircraft, one engaged by flak and the other by a fighter. Over the target we could see little on the ground and I couldn't say much in my recce report. Again, I wasn't very enthusiastic about what I saw. Again I was right. The Pathfinders had gone awry – the raid was scattered.

We were briefed for Berlin on 27 March. There were 396 aircraft going. As it was beyond the range of our fuel capacity, we were to carry 240 extra gallons in a bomb bay tank. It reduced our bomb load but as we were now fixed in our role as fire raisers, the loss of the two 1,000-pounders made little difference to our effect. It was a fine Saturday evening as we taxied out. Well loaded with our extra fuel, I knew we were going to use all the runway for take-off. When our turn came, I was careful to give her full power as soon as I could and to hold her down for as much of the runway as I could get. She came off well. But almost as soon as I got the wheels up, Mac's voice came on the intercom: 'Hey, is it raining outside Skip? There's all water coming into my turret.'

It was fine and clear outside and I wondered what was happening in Mac's turret. I was still thinking of a funny answer, when Jimmy called urgently 'Christ it's fuel, the bloody over-load tanks leaking'. I felt him leap back into the fuselage. Looking back around my seat, I could see a fountain of fuel spurting out of the bomb bay inspection cover in the floor. A light spray was flying back to the rear, into Mac's turret. I was really glad that I had insisted on a strict no smoking regime at all times. Looking out of my cockpit window, I saw all the sparks of red-hot soot flying back from the exhaust pipes. They always accompanied a take-off at full power and didn't bother us. But tonight they were flying back into a stream of raw petrol. I hastily throttled back, until the flow of sparks became a trickle. They weren't a pretty sight. There were still some, indicating that we were still literally sitting on a time bomb. If a spark reached the fuel, a flash back could see us finish up as a spectacular firework display.

The smell of petrol was overpowering. Telling everyone to put on their oxygen masks, I turned it on to full flow and opened the cockpit windows, creating a flow of air through the aircraft. I glanced back at Jimmy and saw him face down on the floor, his arm down the bomb bay hatch, immersed in a diminishing flow of petrol. Somehow he got the flow stopped. By this time I was at 1,000 feet, heading for Filey Bay on the Yorkshire coast. I knew we couldn't make it to Berlin and back without at least 150 gallons of the over-load fuel. We flew on to Filey Bay out to sea and dropped our bombs 'safe' in the approved area. Flying back, we could see the other aircraft climbing outbound. With everything now normal, I felt guilty again, perhaps we should have gone on. But to finish up baling out over Germany, or floating in a dinghy in the North Sea, wasn't a future I sought. Normal Bomber Command activities exposed us to it often enough, without us making our own contribution. We made a quiet return and told our tale to an unbelieving Timber Woods, our engineering officer. Inside, the aircraft all looked normal now. The next day, our overload tank drained out at about 120 gallons. If I'd flown very slowly, we might have landed in the North Sea, just within reach of our rescue services.

Post-war analysis showed that the raid on Berlin that night was a failure. The Pathfinders marked two areas but they were short of their aiming points by 5 miles. Consequently, none of the bombs came within 5 miles of the target area in the centre of the city. So they didn't miss me much. Out of 396 aircraft despatched nine were missing.

Two days after our last 'shaky do' on our Berlin take-off, Jock Hill told me he was on that night. I knew it was 'The Big City' again. Trying to make thirty Berlin trips, Jock only went there. I hoped we'd have better luck than the last time. The briefing was a nail biter. The weather forecast was awful – thick cloud most of the way, with a high icing index, just the formula I hated. Miraculously, the cloud was supposed to clear over the target. At briefing we were told that Churchill particularly wanted an RAF presence over Berlin that night. There was a Nazi Party rally and Göring was to be present.

We carefully checked the overload tank cap. At take-off time there were low clouds on the deck and pouring rain. We were all pleased when the red Very light for a 'scrub', went up from the control tower. We weren't so pleased when we learned that it was only a postponement, we were to take off 2 hours later at 2000 hours. At 2000 we went out, only to be told to position our aircraft on the taxiway for a 2200 hours take-off. Our nerves by now were pretty taut. At nine thirty we went out again to our pre-positioned aircraft. It was a terribly rough night. The wind was howling, rocking the aircraft as we sat in it. The rain was hammering on the wings and fuselage. We wished Churchill would go and get Göring himself.

Engines started, *The Road to Morocco* was definitely not on the pro-gramme, we still expected a scrub in such awful conditions, when incredu-lously, at ten sharp the first aircraft got a green light and lumbered off down the runway. I was number four for take-off and still hoping for the 'scrub', I pointed *C-Charlie* into the black night and got the dreaded green light. I crossed my fingers and gingerly poured on the throttles; the strong wind lifted us off in no time. It was a struggle to keep the aircraft on an even keel. She was being bounced all over the sky. We entered cloud at 600 feet and the bouncing got worse, until at 6,000 feet she settled down to a slightly smoother ride. We left the English coast at 6,000 feet and she wasn't climbing very well. I knew what was happening, we were picking up ice. I felt sick, I really had to go on tonight, after the last debacle.

We struggled up to about 9,000 feet and had been flying for just over an hour. Suddenly, there was a big bang from the port inner engine and a great black mass sailed over the cockpit, striking the roof with a resounding clunk as it went. I thought we might have hit another aircraft. The port inner made a lot more noise and I was ready to feather it, but scanning all the instruments, I could see no malfunction and it still seemed to be turning. A check with the crew revealed no other problems.

Peering out in the pitch-black night I couldn't exactly see what had happened but it looked as though there was a big hole in the inner engine cowling. I still thought we might have clipped someone's tail wheel somehow. The port inner still sounded funny, noisy and rattling, and still below 10,000 feet we weren't climbing much either. My thoughts ran riot. 'Christ! What would they think? Two Berlin trips and we turned back on both. OK, we could do little else on the previous one. But problems with the aircraft again, who will believe it?' I gave it another 10 minutes. We weren't climbing at all now and the engine still sounded very different, somehow it was all wrong. Sick at heart, I was forced to concede defeat and turn back for Linton. (The whole engine cowling had flown off. Passing over the aircraft, it hit the top of the fuselage and carried away all our aerials. It appeared that it had not been properly fastened.) When we called on the only communications we had left – the trailing aerial – we were No. 7 to land. Out of twenty-two Linton aircraft setting out, only five claimed to have reached Berlin. This made me feel a lot better.

We went to Essen again two nights later, 2 April. This time I had a second pilot of some standing. We had four visitors from the Central Flying School, Hullavington. They were all Canadian and all squadron leaders, new appointees to the School, visiting Linton as an introduction to an operational station. While they were there, learning that we were operating that night, one made the usual visitor's remark, he wished he were going with us. Whether they meant it or not, the others echoed this sentiment. Almost every visitor did and we were a bit sick of hearing it. But someone took them at their word and obtained permission from Group for all of them to go. I'm not sure that any of them were really happy at such a premature and unexpected exposure to the realities of war, but having expressed the wish, they couldn't really refuse when permission had been obtained. I noted that between briefing and take-off, all our visitors were writing furiously, presumably to their loved ones. This was a sure sign that they had not expected to be going with us.

On the trip all went well but the flak was heavier than ever over Essen. Back at Linton, we found three of our aircraft were missing – two from 78 and one from 76 Squadron. Out of 348 Lancasters and Halifaxes going, twenty-one were lost, twelve of them Halifaxes. The 'Chop Rate' was still 6 per cent. I hoped my 'percentage' theory was working. If it was, there were enough RAF aircraft shot down near me that night, to keep me going for a while. The next night, 3 April, we went to Kiel. It was the largest number of aircraft we had operated with so far, 577. There were 116 Halifaxes. It was a cloudy night, with sky marking to bomb on, not much flak and no sign of fighters. After Essen it was a 'piece of cake', everybody said so. Only twelve aircraft were lost, just 2 per cent. If only they were all like that!

By this time, as a deputy flight commander I was no longer going on every trip. The first time I didn't was a novel experience when, on 8 April, they went to Duisburg without me. I felt great relief at not going, but considerable guilt as I watched them take-off. They were going and I was staying safely on the ground. It didn't seem quite right. Before start-up I had driven around with the Wing Commander and Timber Woods, wishing them luck. I forbore to tell anyone that I wished I was going with them, it would have been an outright lie.

The next operation was on 10 March, to Frankfurt. I was not going again and just beginning to get used to it. The Group Captain was going though, having managed to get Group's permission. Normally station commanders were not allowed to go on ops. It was considered that they were privy to too many secrets. 'Groupy' Whitley was different. He'd been an operational pilot with the squadron in 1940–41 and wanted to get an up-dated view of the problems of his crews. He was that sort of man. He was going with Flight Lieutenant Hull of 76 Squadron, an experienced pilot who'd started at the same time as me. Accompanying Gerry Warner, we drove out to Hull's aircraft, saying good luck to Groupy and the crew. Groupies didn't go on ops very often. I was OC flying for 78 Squadron that night. I remember the long weary wait, as it became apparent that Hull wasn't coming back. The Group Captain was missing. A little shiver ran through us in the control tower. If they could get old Groupy we felt they could get anybody.[2]

I went on leave a week after Groupy went missing. I returned to London from leave in Torquay in not a very happy frame of mind. On the way, I read about the latest RAF raid the night before [16/17 April 1943] on Pilsen. They had lost thirty-six aircraft, the highest loss to date. Phew! 'That's a bit hot' I thought. When I arrived home on Saturday evening, 17 April, there was a telegram that had arrived that afternoon from Pam. It said: 'MORTY MISSING LAST NIGHT 16TH, ON PILSEN.'

Oh Hell! Morty gone! It was a shock and yet not more than I had feared. I was somehow expecting it. I felt that he was going to go the minute he came back and told me he was married. It was just the way things were on the squadron at the time. He may have gone anyway, but I had felt he was tempting fate, marrying in mid-tour. I know in his heart, he thought so too. I had a couple of days' leave left but I went back to Linton the next day. I wanted to find out what I could and to screen Morty's effects. It was customary for a close friend to do this, just in case there were any articles that might have been embarrassing to the family. The return journey on Sunday seemed slow and dragging. I had a lot of time to think. As ever, one felt there was always the chance that he and the crew would have baled out and would turn up eventually as prisoners-of-war. That was a standard palliative for friends and family. It saved the immediacy of the alternative. It had worked out that way for Geoff Hobbs.

When I arrived, I received a few tentative looks and words of sympathy. We had been very close, the sometime Terrible Twins. Close friends were worried about how I would take it. I got what details were available. Pilsen should have been a 'piece of cake'; it was a long flight into Southern Europe, well away from the heavy defences. The Wing Commander had chosen to go himself. Unfortunately, it was a night of bright moonlight and the fighters got into the bomber stream early. From then on it was a fight for survival, with mainly luck deciding who was caught. There were 197 Lancs and 130 Halifaxes on the trip. Eighteen of each were lost – 11 per cent of the force. This was the highest loss since the early days of the daylight raids and certainly since I'd been operating. It was soon learned that the target – the Skoda armament factory – was not affected by the raid. The major damage was to a lunatic asylum, 7 miles away. It was a terrible waste of crews, at least 252, and of poor old Morty, my closest RAF friend.[3]

I cleared up Morty's things the next day, with a sympathetic padre. I didn't tell him that Morty went because he'd forsaken our pact with the Devil. He wouldn't have appreciated it, though Morty would. There were no skeletons

Halifax II HR657 C-Charlie *of 78 Squadron, which Ron Read (3rd from right, front row) flew his final op of his tour to Dortmund on the night of 23/24 May 1943. (The other flight crew are L–R: 'Taff' Lewis; 'Mac' McQueen; Vic Freeman; Jimmy Goodwin and Harry Laidlaw). Although the troublesome port outer had been changed for the fourth time no sound reason was ever found why this engine always failed. Read and his crew made it home with the port outer feathered but 38 bombers from the 829 aircraft despatched failed to return. After this trip* C-Charlie *was 'ripped apart' in an effort to find the cause of the failure, a loose piece of rag was found blocking the oil pipe. The troublesome Halifax was finally lost on 24 June 1943 when over the target a Lancaster dropped its bombs on* C-Charlie, *flying directly below. The 4,000 lb bomb went diagonally through the upper fuselage leaving two gaping holes. A number of incendiaries fell directly into the cockpit, one knocking off the earpiece from the engineer's helmet. The engineer threw these out of the cockpit windows. A few lodged in the wings. The port outer propeller was shattered and the engine revolutions ran off the clock before Flight Sergeant Wilson flying only his second operation, could stop it. The port inner propeller had two blades severely damaged and it ran very roughly all the way home but just kept turning. 'Charlie's wounds were mortal' [sic] says Ron Read. 'Having done her one good deed she obviously felt life wasn't worth going on without me to plague her with her temperamental unserviceabilities'.* C-Charlie *passed to 1667 HCU and finally 1662 HCU and was finally lost on 7 March 1944 when it was involved in a collision with another aircraft during a cross-country and crashed near Haxby, Yorkshire. (Read)*

191

'Hello-Goodbye'. Group Captain Wilson (2nd from right) at his first and last party for two years, at Linton-on-Ouse in May 1943. Flight Lieutenant Ron Read (far left) recalls that 'Group Captain [D. E. L.] Wilson was a dry humourless Australian, who had been mainly engaged in training and had no experience whatever in operations. What made him very unpopular was his attitude in his first couple of briefings, telling us, most all veterans of many ops, how we should press on more than we do and not be slow to attack the heavy Ruhr targets, which we were doing two or three times a week in some cases. At the party we got Wing Commander Gerry Warner (centre) and the new 76 Squadron Commander, Wing Commander Smith, to suggest Wilson should be coaxed into trying one. Perhaps he would not so critical and, we slyly thought; he might go for the chop himself. He did go for the trip and the chop [on 22/23 June 1943 on the raid on Mülheim when he flew with Pilot Officer J. Carrie's crew, one of whom was killed, the rest being taken prisoner]. He was sent to Stalag Luft III *where he became the Senior British Officer [replacing Group Captain Herbert Massey DSO MC after he was repatriated to Switzerland on 11 April 1944) and continued to try to treat the other PoWs in the same high-handed ways.' (Read)*

in Morty's effects and they were sent off to his new wife. I sat down and wrote her a sympathetic letter, with as much cheer as I could find in it. Then set out to get on with life. I had seen quite a few of my friends go and it was an accepted aircrew tenet, that we put our lost friends behind us and forgot them as quickly as possible. Although he had been my closest friend for a year and a half, I was determined to adhere to this philosophy. I reasoned that Morty was a good pilot and if any one could have made it he could. If he hadn't, well he was as aware as we all were, of what could happen. He'd often philosophised on the, 'If yer can't take a joke' joke. Unfortunately, it was now on him. No doubt we should learn in due course what had happened.

Meanwhile, life had to go on and it was just as well to embrace that old secret aircrew belief, 'Whoever it happens to, it won't be me' though in deep thinking moments, a little voice still murmured, 'Why not?' The answer was, don't think too often, or too deeply, about these things. Play the role of a light-hearted bomber aircrew. Remember, 'The Devil looks after his own'. Eat, drink and be merry and to hell with tomorrow.

The Pilsen trip cut a swathe through the Linton aircrews, probably because they were in the second wave once more. Apart from Morty there were four others missing: Flight Lieutenant Paddy Dowse, a pleasant Irishman of 78 Squadron on his second tour and three sergeants and crews from 76 Squadron.[4] It was our worst night to date – a total of five crews or thirty-five bods. I knew few of them personally, as many were replacements for recent casualties. There were lots of new faces in the mess now. Final news of Morty came a few weeks later with a letter from a PoW camp from his wireless operator [Sergeant C. A.] 'Steve' Stevens. Hit by a fighter, the crew had baled out. Meanwhile, the aircraft was getting lower and by the time they were all out it was too low for Morty to jump. He was killed in the ensuing crash. Typically Morty and typically a pilot's end. It had happened many times and would happen many more. Now to forget it. There was plenty to get on with.[5]

Notes

1. Named after *Generalleutnant* Kammhuber, *General der Nachtjagd* (General of Night Fighters) who introduced a continuous belt of combined searchlight and radar positions stretching from the Schleswig area over Kiel, Hamburg, Bremen, Ruhrgebiet, Arnhem, Venlo to the Liege area and further to the south. A second belt protected Berlin covering the Gustrow-Stendal area and extending in the direction of Gardelegen.
2. Flight Lieutenant A. H. Hull was found dead in the wrecked cockpit of Halifax II JB871 MP-V. Group Captain J. R. Whitley and three others evaded. Three were injured.
3. The Pathfinders mistook a large lunatic asylum near Dobrany for the Skoda Works. The result was that though 249 crews claimed to have attacked the target, only six had got their bombs within 3 miles of it.
4. Flight Lieutenant A. P. Dowse DFC and crew in Halifax II DT773, who were shot down by a Bf 110, survived and were PoWs.
5. Flight Lieutenant E. G. 'Morty' Mortenson's Halifax II (HR659 EY-A) was brought down by the combined fire of a Bf 109 and a Bf 110 (possibly *Feldwebel* Paul Faden of 11./NJG4) and crashed near Trier. (Faden claimed a Halifax S of Bitburg at 0307 hours.) Five of the seven crew were PoWs. Sergeant D. A. Pitman was KIA along with Morty. Ron Read finished his tour in May 1943 and he was posted as an instructor to 1664 Heavy Conversion Unit, 6 RCAF Group. In a 4½-month period he converted eleven pilots and crews to Halifaxes. What we left behind didn't occupy our thoughts very much. We certainly didn't dwell in the past and in view of our circumstances didn't devote much time to the future either. The next day's activities or at longest the next leave was about the limit of our aspirations. Those Ruhr battles of 1943 provided the blueprint for the bomber offensive for the rest of the war. I was both sad and glad to leave 78 Squadron. In effect it was where I grew up. In my time with them I had seen 19 squadron crews go missing, approximately 150 aircrew members. In addition, 27 crews of our sister squadron 76, were lost – 195 aircrew. More friends were to go after I left. Just average Bomber Command figures for any station. I was relieved to be free of the constant knowledge that the next night I might have to stick my neck out once again. I should now be able to sleep easy in my bed. It was like a reprieve from the condemned cell of poor old Morty's corny, pre-ops statement: 'The condemned men ate a hearty breakfast'.

CHAPTER 15

Low Level to Stettin

Tom Wingham and Louis Patrick Wooldridge

Rain is falling, silver-lead'n in the dark and tortured night,
Flick'ring streaks of incandescence from the phantom shrouded light,
Glim'ring dim upon the runway – mist enclosur'd tarmac strip,
Guarded still by sombre sentries, haven for the broken ship.
Watching for the twin lights burning o'er the darkened Yorkshire plain,
Winging home to blacked out England – pilots of the German main.

'*Grey Dawn*', Robert S. Nielsen

Sergeant S. T. 'Tom' Wingham was a Halifax II bomb aimer in Sergeant Dave Hewlett's crew on 102 Squadron in 4 Group based at Pocklington, Yorkshire. Pilsen had been their fifteenth op since being posted to the squadron in February 1943 and it had been in a full moon. With the moon still full it was with some trepidation that Wingham realised from the petrol and bomb loads that they were in for another long trip on 20/21 April 1943. All told, 339 aircraft (194 Lancasters, 134 Halifaxes and eleven Stirlings) were to visit Stettin, an 8½-hour round trip, while eighty-five Stirlings were despatched to bomb the Heinkel factory near Rostock. Wingham recalled that, 'With briefing came enlightenment. Bomber Command had come up with a new plan to beat the German GCI – a low-level trip.'

At another 4 Group airfield, at Snaith, Flight Sergeant Louis Patrick Wooldridge,[1] a mid-upper gunner in Claude Wilson's Halifax crew on 51 Squadron was also 'on' this night. Wooldridge explains the reason for the raid on Stettin.

> Information obtained from Russian intelligence sources revealed that a large quantity of German fighter and bomber aircraft had been concentrated at Stettin for use on the Eastern Front and the Soviets had requested that the RAF eliminate this menace to their forces on the Leningrad-Moscow fronts. Our Halifax II, HR750 MH-W, was fitted with an auxiliary petrol tank in the bomb bay for the 600-mile trip to Stettin and another pilot, on his first operation, accompanied us as a crewmember to gain operational experience. Judging by the number of bomb symbols painted in yellow beneath the pilot's window HR750 was a bit of a veteran. In addition, the aircraft bore the words, '*WANCHORS*

CASTLE' and carried an emblem of a small castle and a knight with a coat of arms on a shield.[2]

We took off at about 2100 hours and on leaving Snaith the weather was clear and almost cloudless with brilliant moonlight. As a result of the forecasted weather conditions the operational flight to the target was carried out at fifty feet, climbing to 12,000 feet at Stettin to release the bomb load, thereafter dropping down to 50 feet for the flight to base. Approaching the Danish coastline, I observed a U-boat on the surface of the sea. Wilson passed the details to Peter Finnett, navigator, who recorded it in his log and informed Don Hall, WOP, who in turn sent a coded wireless signal to base. Receipt of this information after decoding, would then have been forwarded to the Admiralty in London for appropriate action by naval units in the North Sea. Meanwhile, the U-boat crew had obviously seen us. There was feverish activity in the conning tower and the sea foamed about both sides of the U-boat as it blew its ballast tanks and crash-dived beneath the silvery surface of the sea. Neither Les Sharp in the rear turret nor me could aim and fire our machine-guns. The rear turret was unable to traverse to a suitable bearing and the mid-upper's safety gear interrupter solenoid, which prevented a gunner causing accidental damage in the heat of combat, would have prevented my guns from firing. All the same, I do not think that any of the U-boat crew required any medical laxatives for quite a while.

Tom Wingham's Halifax, meanwhile, had climbed on take-off and crossed the North Sea at 10,000 feet, reaching the Danish coast near Esbjerg, where they descended to 700 feet.

Now began one of the most exhilarating trips I took part in as 350 heavy bombers streamed across Denmark between 400 and 700 feet. Lying in the nose map-reading did feel a bit hairy as we were constantly being hit by the slipstream from other unseen aircraft. In the brilliant moonlight all the ground detail was clear and Danes came out of their houses flashing torches and waving. Occasionally, a little light flak came up to port or starboard as aircraft strayed off course or the sky was lit up as an aircraft hit the deck.

Flight Sergeant Louis Wooldridge continues.

Flying at low level had its compensations in the exhilarating feeling of power and speed as the Danish countryside and gleaming rail tracks illuminated by the light of the brilliant full moon flashed beneath the wings of the speeding aircraft. We flew over an L-shaped farm with an orchard and the door to the farmhouse was suddenly flung open and a shaft of light appeared in the doorway. Four figures emerged and they ran out each frantically waving a large white cloth like a bath towel. I turned the mid-upper turret slightly towards their direction and rapidly raised and lowered the four .303 in Browning machine-guns in acknowledgement of their greeting and the grave risk this family was taking. Shortly afterwards I saw two motor vehicles speeding along a road

195

towards the German border. According to intelligence reports only German military forces, *Gestapo* personnel and their collaborators operated on roads after night curfew. I turned the mid-upper turret to port and lowered the guns and waited until we overtook the speeding vehicles, but they entered a large wooded area to stop until we had left the area.

As the flight would be of 8½ hours duration I decided I would use only two of my four guns so as to conserve ammunition. In between my legs was a mechanism called the feed assister (in Lancaster, Stirling and late models of Wellington aircraft a mechanism of similar type was known as a Servo feed), which operated the rate of fire, approximately 1,200 rounds a minute. In view of later events my decision was correct.

Tom Wingham continues.

We continued low level across the Baltic doing a cruise among the islands until on our last leg with the North German coast on our starboard we climbed to a bombing height of 14,000 feet. As we approached the target, Stettin was well alight and in the glare from the fires below and the brilliant moonlight. It was like carrying out an aircraft recognition test. It was the first time I had seen Fw190s and Me109s as well as 110s and Ju88s, all clearly visible flitting about among the silhouettes of Lancs and Halifaxes. Somehow we were not singled out for attention as we went in and bombed. Immediately after completing the bomb run we dived for the deck and went out the same way we had come.

Flight Sergeant Louis Wooldridge, approaching the Baltic, continues.

Off the starboard bow at about 11,000 feet I could see 'white' flashing harbour lights in the vicinity of Lübeck and Rostock, as we awaited the 'yellowish' marker flares of the PFF Force about a mile ahead of the bomber stream indicating a course turning point. A mile west of Lübeck three Lancasters of the PFF Force released clusters of flares spaced across the night sky and burning brightly to indicate the way to Stettin. The flares, which floated slowly down on parachutes, could be compared in purpose with the 'Stave Leys' of times when knights of old found their way across Britain by staves or staffs interspersed across the country. Observing the marker flares Claude Wilson informed Peter Finnett who remarked, 'They're dead on time'. Suddenly, two of the three Lancasters in the starboard beam about 3,000 feet below were enveloped in black smoke and red flames and the bombers fell rapidly towards the moonlit sea 6,000 feet below. No parachutes emerged from any of the stricken aircraft and Peter's casual remark on the Pathfinders' punctuality took on an entirely new meaning. A lack of flak puffs that always hung about the sky for some considerable time after the explosive burst seemed to indicate that enemy fighter activity was the cause but we failed to see any enemy aircraft in the area.[3]

We left Lübeck and Rostock behind and had reached the bombing height of 12,000 feet as our Halifax altered course onto the final approach leg to Stettin. We were part of the first wave of Main Force bombers to arrive in the area, which was bathed in brilliant moonlight. The view from my turret gave the impression that the area below was peaceful but this was just an illusion. The air raid warning sirens would already have sounded to enable the inhabitants to take shelter and to alert the flak gunners. Suddenly, red and green TIs were released into the night sky by the Pathfinder aircraft directly ahead of us. (This type of target marking was known as '*Musical Parramatta*', which was devised for visual ground marking. In the event of the target area being obscured by 10/10ths cloud conditions, a sky marking technique consisting of similar coloured flares attached to parachutes for a slow descent and known as '*Wanganui*' was used. Both were reputed to have originated from the choice of the Commanding Officer of 8 Group, Group Captain Don Bennett. As Parramatta is a place name in Australia and Wanganui a place name in New Zealand it would appear that there is an element of truth in the matter.) As the TIs cascaded through the air, burning brilliantly, all Hell was let loose. Numerous heavy flak bursts dotted the night sky and probing mauve (master) and white (coning) searchlight beams sought various individual aircraft of the bomber stream. Instructions broadcast from the Master Bomber of the Pathfinder Force informing the oncoming Main Force bomber crews to bomb the marker flares concerned were received over the bomber intercom system, as they commenced their run into the target area. As the flak bursts decreased, tracer streams criss-crossed the moonlit sky indicating the presence of night-fighters over Stettin and aerial combats between the British bombers and German fighter aircraft. Miraculously, although troubled slightly by predicted flak, we managed to evade any engagement with any German night-fighters and after the release of our bomb load our aircraft swiftly descended to 50 feet for the return flight to base.

Suddenly the ditching hatch immediately forward of my turret swung downwards, leaving a gaping hole about 2 feet by 1½ feet and 'Ginger' Anger the flight engineer waved towards me. I then remembered that he had a load of propaganda leaflets to dispose of. As 'Ginger' threw the leaflets out the air current of about 200 mph whipped them up into the air high over the turret to stream rearwards above the rear turret where Les Sharp observed them fluttering gradually to earth to give the impression of a gigantic paper chase over Germany. The military authorities always collected the British leaflets as soon as possible after they had been dropped, but on this occasion their task would have been difficult as many settled on the roofs of numerous tall buildings that the Halifax bomber flew over. We flew over a large town with a tall white building in the main street, which I presumed was the town hall. A clock illuminated by the brilliant moonlight indicated that the time was 0130. To test the guns for sighting accuracy and to disrupt the German war workers dependent on the clock to rouse them from sleep, I fired at the building

197

and observed two of the clock faces disintegrate. At the same time I felt a tug on my left leg and looking down I saw 'Ginger' Anger looking anxiously up at me through the open hatch. Apparently he had thought that I was engaged in combat with a German night-fighter aircraft, but after assuring him otherwise he carried on with the disposal of the leaflets.

Shortly afterwards we emerged over a German aerodrome. Turning our turrets to starboard Les and I fired tracer bullets into the glass panels in the hangar roofs and then we directed our fire against aircraft parked outside. The door of a long wooden hut suddenly opened emitting a shaft of light and numerous figures ran to a wood nearby or towards the parked aircraft. I presumed that the figures running towards the wood were to man anti-aircraft guns so my gunfire was directed at them first and then again at the parked aircraft and the figures running towards them. Finally, the wooden hut was strafed with gunfire. By now the Halifax was flying over the wood leaving the German aerodrome with its casualties and damage in the distance.

Briefly relaxing for a few minutes the crew was suddenly brought into instant reaction by what seemed to be coloured lights floating through the night sky towards us. The German aerodrome had obviously telephoned information of our approach to flak defences ahead of us. Our arrival over what appeared to be peaceful meadow bounded by a small wood was suddenly marred by the criss-crossing above and below of numerous red and green and white light anti-aircraft shells. They rose ever so slowly from ground level, giving the false impression that we could reach out and take hold of them as they sped towards the aircraft but a true indication of their speed was obtained when the shells whistled past the aircraft. Explosions carried away the external wireless aerial about 2 feet above my turret. Another shell exploded behind the Direction Finding (DF) loop immediately aft of the pilot's escape hatch in the upper fuselage. Allowing deflection to the right and behind I fired two of my guns at the fringe of the wooded area, my tracer fire speeding its way in a straight line before gradually curving slightly to the right of the source of the flak shells about half a mile distant. The gunfire suddenly ceased and was not renewed for a few minutes, by which time our aircraft was leaving the area.

About a quarter of an hour later I observed some light flak off the port bow about 3 miles ahead. As we neared the coastline I discovered that the gunfire originated from a source in the sea. We were approaching Kiel and observations revealed the silhouette of a surfaced U-boat. Allowing deflection, I fired the two Brownings and observed the tracer fire snaking its way toward the vessel and then veer in all directions as it struck the U-boat. Apparently, Claude Wilson had hoped to pass the U-boat without attracting fire but I had cancelled that idea. By keeping an intense vigil on the source of the light flak I failed to notice about half a mile away a large U-boat depot ship with about half a dozen other surfaced U-boats positioned about the centre of her starboard side. Suddenly, I glimpsed the large dark shape of the depot ship emerging into view against the background of the moon. Figures could be seen running all over the ship and I turned the turret slightly more to port and concentrated my gunfire on to the vessel and its cluster of U-boats. Gunfire was returned as the Halifax continued its flight homewards over the Baltic towards the NW German coastline and Denmark. When I suddenly observed the dark shape of a Lancaster ahead of us off the port bow I realised that this was the reason for the solitary U-boat's gunfire.

Our aircraft went off course and we suddenly emerged over the Danish port of Esbjerg, which was heavily fortified by the German forces. Our lone arrival resulted in the entire defences being directed against us. Turning the turret to starboard I found that the guns could not be depressed far enough to return fire so I called Claude on intercom to bank to starboard. Obligingly, Claude banked the aircraft steeply to starboard so that the Halifax appeared to be standing on its wingtip, allowing me to return fire and eliminate the source. I had to return the favour for Claude as the searchlights were forming a cone on the aircraft and were blinding him as he endeavoured to fly the Halifax towards the North Sea. Firing at the searchlights, Les Sharpe and I managed to extinguish some of them as Claude weaved the aircraft over the rooftops and through the red, green and white tracer shells of the light flak defences to eventually emerge unscathed over the North Sea. Settling down to a straight and level course Peter Finnett made some quick calculations and gave a corrective course alteration for the Yorkshire coast. The North Sea was covered with clouds at this time. Claude requested the second pilot to take over for a brief spell so that he could visit the Elsan toilet. While he was gone he was unaware that Peter Finnett gave the second pilot a course alteration for the flight to base. After a period of time on this course Peter said on intercom that base should be appearing at any second but minutes went by with no sign of base. Sqeaker noises on the IFF set were heard and everyone was mystified, as there were no barrage balloons for miles in the vicinity of base. Anti-aircraft shell bursts were then heard and I briefly glimpsed a Heinkel 111 among the clouds, crossing ahead and slightly above the Halifax. As suddenly as it appeared, it just disappeared from view. A quick check revealed that we were over the London area! Claude resumed control, obtained a reciprocal course and set off for base. We landed at Snaith at about 6 am amid the code words, 'Bandits in the area'. We were about the last aircraft of the squadron to return. Next day inspection revealed that there were only about forty rounds of ammunition left from the 2,400 rounds in my mid-upper turret boxes!

Tom Wingham concludes.

For such a long-range target, over 600 miles from England and well outside the range of *Oboe* it was probably the most successful raid during the Battle of the Ruhr. There were a lot of very tired pilots when we got home. We still lost between 6 and 7 per cent[4], which was the going rate for the job, so presumably Harris felt there was nothing to be gained by repeating the exercise. As far as I know this was a one-off and the tactic was never used again on such a large scale.

199

Notes

1. Louis Patrick Wooldridge was born in Stalybridge on 4 June 1921, about 400 yards from the theatre on Corporation Street, where in January 1912, the song 'It's a long way to Tipperary' was first sung. On attaining 18 years of age he left civilian employment as an apprentice engineer with Henry Simeon & Sons Ltd at Stockport to enter regular RAF service as a ground staff flight rigger and part time aerial gunner. In 1940 during the Battle of Britain he served on a Maintenance Unit, repairing and modifying all types of aircraft. In 1941, after experiencing the Blitz in Manchester, he went overseas to Singapore where he became an LAC Flight Rigger on 243 Squadron, which was operating single-seat Brewster Buffalo fighter aircraft from RAF Kallang at Singapore airport. He left Singapore for Africa at the end of 1941 and by May 1942 had completed an air gunner's course. Arriving in Britain on June 1942 and after a short period flying on Bothas with Polish pilots, he became a rear gunner of a 20 OTU Wellington crew at RAF Lossiemouth. On completion of Halifax conversion training at RAF Riccall he finally became a member of 51 Squadron at RAF Snaith, Yorkshire, on 1 January 1943.
2. This aircraft and Warrant Officer A. H. Beeston's crew FTR from Essen on 28.5.43 when they were shot down by a night-fighter.
3. Five Lancasters (and three Halifaxes) were claimed shot down by *Nachtjager* crews who also claimed five of the eight Stirlings lost from the eighty-six sent to bomb the Heinkel factory at Rostock.
4. Twenty-one aircraft (thirteen Lancasters and seven Halifaxes) FTR from Stettin and eight Stirlings FTR from Rostock. NJG3 was credited with twelve and NJG5 with another six confirmed victories.

CHAPTER 16

The Tour

John 'Jimmy' Anderson Hurst

I profess not talking only this
Let each man do his best
And here draw I a sword whose temper
I Intend to stain, with the best blood that I can meet
With all In the adventure of this perilous day.
Now esperance Pathfinders and set off
Sound all the lofty instruments of war
And by this music let us all embrace
For heaven and earth Some of us never shall a second time
Do such a courtesy.

Henry IV, Sir Henry (Hotspur) Percy before
the Battle of Shrewsbury

We were all keen to go on ops. I was a tail gunner. Little did we know that in November 1942, when several of us from the Halifax HBC at RAF Topcliffe joined 102 Squadron, that of the ten crews who arrived at Pocklington in Yorkshire ours would be the only one to complete a tour. All the others were killed, seriously injured, or became PoWs. The majority of my ops from 6 November 1942 to 13 May 1943 were over the Ruhr. We hit most of the main cities – Essen, Munich, Cologne, Frankfurt, Mannheim and Stuttgart, etc. Then of course there was Berlin and three to Italy – Turin and Genoa – a 9-hour trip, as well as minelaying around the Friesian islands, so I had an exciting an eventful war and lived to tell the tale. We were a happy confident crew – no bickering or arguing. We just gelled. (We almost won the *Croix de Guerre* in 1943. The French government sent our squadron seven of them. They must have been impressed with our efforts. The names of the crews involved were put into a hat and those drawn were given the medals. What a way to win, or not to win, the *Croix de Guerre*!)

Our first operation was minelaying off Ameland in the Friesian Islands on 6 November 1942. Mines were dropped from 200 feet and at such a low height we received a lot of attention from ground fire. Tracer was hosed around us but we were not hit. That was our 'baptism of fire' but we had yet to encounter night-fighters. They were always a problem. The worst encounter that we had was with an Fw 190 that attacked us from astern. He was very determined, but

I had seen him before he was within range and warned the skipper. At the critical moment, as he came in, I told the skipper to corkscrew, this entailed the aircraft diving a few hundred feet to port or starboard and then climbing again on the opposite tack in a corkscrewing motion. This could be quite a violent manoeuvre, but was effective in shaking off a fighter. A few minutes later the fighter found us again and came in from port and I told the skipper to turn hard to port and as the Fw 190 broke away the mid-upper and I gave it a short burst. He came at us again, this time from starboard, and we repeated our evasive action. As he broke away he gave us a burst but did no damage and we did not see him again.

Most of our ops entailed flying through areas heavily protected by anti-aircraft guns. It sounded like hail as it hit the aircraft after the shell had burst above us; this was not too lethal as it was in free-fall on its way to the ground. The most dangerous was from shells that burst close to the aircraft as the hundreds of hot jagged fragments had the momentum to penetrate the plane and kill or injure crewmembers and cause mechanical damage, often resulting in the aircraft crashing. On one occasion we were on our way to Essen in very heavy flak, when there was a loud explosion in the aircraft and a rush of cold air and the plane bounced around. The skipper checked on the intercom that we were all OK and the flight engineer went to see what the damage was.

What had happened was that a piece of shrapnel had detonated the photo-flash, which exploded and destroyed its launching tube and blew a jagged hole in the starboard side of the fuselage just behind my turret. We measured it back at base and it was about 5 feet long by 3 feet high. This resulted in a gale blowing through the aircraft and made it very difficult for George, the pilot, to handle. Nevertheless, we flew to the target – Krupps – and bombed it, but with no photo of course and set course for base. About halfway home, still over enemy territory, we lost an engine due to mechanical trouble. This reduced our airspeed even more and we lumbered home an hour later than the rest of the squadron. Being behind the main stream and flying low as we approached the English coast, we attracted the attention of the Navy, who fired at us with pom poms. Despite us firing off the colours of the day, I recall sitting in my turret and hearing the pom, pom, pom of the guns above the sound of our three engines. When counting the hits on our plane – as we always did – we wondered how many were from enemy fire and how many from the Navy. It was surprising how much damage the Halibags could sustain and remain flyable. I certainly owe my life to this factor. As well as flak holes, there were sometimes unexploded incendiary bombs embedded in our wings – and this was where our fuel tanks were! This was the result of flying through an incendiary shower dropped by Lancs flying above us at about 20,000 feet. These would be removed by our gallant ground crew, of whom I cannot speak too highly. They did a great job keeping our aircraft in first class condition whatever the previous night's battle damage had been. They waved us off and they were there waiting for us to bring 'their' aircraft home.

Our CO, Gus Walker (later Sir Gus Walker) would also wave us off from beside the runway. He would stand there with cookhouse staff (who always waved us off), with the crew list in his hand. As each plane started its run down the runway, he would run beside it, waving to the crew and would be waiting in the briefing room when we returned and chat to each crew. He was popular with the crews, whom he called 'my boys'. He had flown quite a few ops but had to stop flying when he severely damaged a hand in a ground incident involving exploding bombs.

The cold could also cause problems for crews; it was not unusual for the air temperature to be $-20\,^{\circ}$C and ice would build up on the wings of the aircraft, often adding weight and making the plane difficult to fly and sometimes causing it to crash. The crews had little protection against the cold and on one occasion when we were returning through the Alps from Turin, my oxygen tube froze solid, cutting off my supply of oxygen. The crew became aware of this, because I had switched on my intercom and was singing into my mike. (This was due to me being starved of oxygen, which has a similar affect to drinking too much alcohol.) The skipper sent the flight engineer to my turret to see what the problem was. On finding my oxygen tube solid with ice, he went back into the fuselage and returned with a flask of hot coffee. He removed my mask and poured coffee into it and this quickly thawed the ice in the tube, enabling me to breathe the oxygen vital to survival at 18,000 feet. I was so starved of oxygen that I was hardly aware of what was happening. The quick thinking of the engineer surely saved my life – another of my nine lives gone!

I have not mentioned my skipper, George Barker – yet. I was always 'happiest' when flying with him. He was 21 years old and seldom flew straight and level. I was never airsick but invariably when a new member joined the crew they were sick on their first trips with George. To be aboard when he corkscrewed – descending 2,000 feet, weaving as we went, then up again – with a bomb load on, was something to experience, but it worked and on several occasions enabled us to escape when coned by a group of searchlights.

Searchlights, of course, caused problems on many ops. One would light our plane as it swept the sky but on 9 March 1943, when on our way to Munich, we were locked onto by a blue beam. These were radar-controlled from the ground and referred to as master searchlights. Immediately it illuminated us several other searchlights locked onto us and the skipper took violent evasive action. How he could see his instruments, I do not know, as so intense was the light from the beams that I was completely blinded. We seemed to be held for ages, but it was maybe a couple of minutes before we were out of the beam. So violent had our evasive action been that the gyro in the compass toppled and we had to abort our op and return to base. The engineer thought that at one stage the skipper had rolled the Halifax onto its back. We still had our full bomb load aboard during these manoeuvres and back at base we landed with them aboard. I can't recall just why we did not jettison them. We were lucky that night, as usually when a plane is caught by a master beam, fighters come in and shoot it down, whilst the crew is disorientated.

To fly with another crew as an 'odd bod' was something that I was not keen on doing. So many of my colleagues had failed to return from such ops. But on about three occasions, for various reasons, I flew as an odd bod. The one that comes to mind was when a 'Wingco' was flying an op and did not have a crew of his own as he seldom flew on ops! When he did he selected experienced men from other crews for the trip and I was detailed to fly as his tail gunner. It was to Essen, on 3 April 1943. I had been before [on 5 March] and I knew it was a heavily defended target. The flight to the target was normal, with the usual attention from flak, searchlights and fighters, but when we reached Essen, he seemed reluctant to leave!

We started a normal bombing run through heavy flak with the bomb doors open. This was always a vulnerable situation – the bomb aimer doing his usual drill directing the pilot to our aiming point, the rest of us waiting to hear him say 'bombs gone' and feel the pilot put the nose down and head away from the target. But in the midst of our bombing run, the pilot told the bomb aimer that he was not happy with our run and we would go round again and make another run. So the bomb doors were closed and we flew a circuit around Essen, which was well alight, and we came in for a second time. Again, the bomb doors were opened and the bomb run began. To our 'dismay' the skipper aborted again and we were taken over the blazing city. The AA gunners were very active. So for a third time we made a bombing run. By now, we all felt very vulnerable and that we were pushing our luck. This time the skipper was satisfied and our bombs were released into the inferno below. I had, on occasions, made two runs across a target, but never three, and it had then been the bomb aimer's decision to go round again, as he and not the pilot was in the best position to see if our aiming point could be hit.

We finished our tour with a trip on 13 May 1943 to the steel works at Bochum, a routine one as ops went, but we were all very much aware that it was not unusual for a crew to be lost on their last op. We were an experienced crew, but many an experienced crew went for a Burton. But we made it and the following day, we left 102 Squadron and went on leave.

CHAPTER 17

The Shining 10th

Jim Sprackling DFC

We sleep safely in our beds because rough men stand ready in the night to visit violence on those who would harm us.

George Orwell

On 5 June 1943 my Halifax bomber crew arrived on No. 10 Squadron (The Shining 10th) near Melbourne, 15 miles south-east of York. I was the flight engineer. Pilot Officer G. W. 'Bill' Lucas, the pilot, had blond hair and very blue eyes. He was older than the rest, possibly nearly 30 and had been a sergeant in the Royal Artillery and had volunteered for aircrew after Dunkirk, so he was battle hardened. Jock Ellis, a young Glaswegian, was navigator. Pilot Officer Len 'Butch' Butcher was bomb aimer. Paddy Seay, another older chap from Belfast, was the wireless operator. The only other country lad was Digger, who was half Aboriginal, and he had been brought up on a cattle station in Queensland. Digger Davis was mid-upper gunner. Ronnie Pentlin, a cockney, was rear gunner. So began fourteen months of very close association with six chaps from very different walks of life.

Flying started almost immediately. We had a local familiarisation flight, more fighter affiliation, a formation flying practice and then three more night cross-country flights. On the third flight, the navigator got lost and we finished up landing at East Wretham, a Lancaster base in Norfolk. This did not seem to matter because we were allocated Halifax ZA-V *V-Victor* and cleared for operations. On 11 June – just six weeks after my first flight in a Halifax – we were detailed for our first operation. Crews were alerted during the morning that there was a 'Call' and the flight commander detailed which crews were to fly and which aircraft. Group HQ nominated how many aircraft were required. Most bombing missions to German targets were maximum efforts, i.e. every available aircraft. During the afternoon the ground crew would prepare the aircraft, loading bombs and ammunition into gun turrets. The fuel load would be put on and everything checked over. The aircrew would go out to the aircraft and check that everything was to their satisfaction, each member checking his specialist equipment. The flight engineer would thoroughly inspect the whole aircraft, looking for any signs of trouble like small oil leaks and physically check the fuel tanks to see none had been missed – not too difficult with ten tanks on a Halifax. Then it was off to the mess for a meal before briefing.

About 3 hours before the scheduled time for take-off all the crews detailed to fly assembled in the briefing room. The airfield gates were shut and no one was allowed off camp. The briefing room at Melbourne was a standard Nissen hut. At one end there was a large map of France, Germany and the Low Countries, which at the time was covered by a curtain and a black board and easel holding a smaller map. There was a low platform with two or three armchairs in front of the maps and the rest of the room was filled with forms on which the crews sat. At that time the navigators had been doing pre-paratory work on their charts but no one, other than the briefing officer, knew the details.

On commencement of briefing, the station commander, a group captain, took one of the chairs, the squadron commander, a wing commander, stood by the covered map and the station intelligence and meteorology officer stood by. Also, the most senior member of each non-pilot aircrew trade, known as 'leaders', hovered. With everyone inside, the doors were shut and the roll was called, each captain answering for his crew. Then the curtain was raised and the target exposed. A large pin in the map indicated the city to be attacked and coloured string showed the route to be taken in and out of the target. The squadron commander gave a brief description of the target, the time the squadron was to attack and the height from which the attack was to be made. There was a murmur from the experienced crews. *V-Victor*'s crew remained very quiet. Then the intelligence officer took the stage. He gave a more detailed assessment of the target and what was expected to result from the attack. He pointed out all known German anti-aircraft batteries along the route, the known defences of the target and also known night-fighter bases likely to be activated. The target was Düsseldorf, an industrial city south of the Ruhr Valley in northern Germany. The Ruhr cities were known as 'Happy Valley'.

The last briefing, from the met man, was very important for many reasons. The navigators needed to know the wind strength and direction accurately because the aircraft flew at about 150–170 mph and wind speeds of 40–50 mph at altitude had a great effect on navigation. Also important was cloud cover. There were few navigational aids, so crews needed to be able to see vital land marks like the coast and the Rhine, but not too clear as some cloud cover made it difficult for the German night-fighters. Cloud also broke up the search-light patterns. What was ideal was low-level broken cloud over the night-fighter bases, with clear weather conditions above and a hole in the cloud over the target. It seldom happened. Tonight it was to be clear above broken cloud and the moon set early. These were reasonable conditions. The engineer leader confirmed fuel, ammunition and bomb load and stick pattern. The station commander wished everyone luck and we all trooped out to the parachute and locker room where everyone put on flying gear and collected their parachute from the specially aired and heated store. And so, out to the crew buses. These were the standard pre-war Bedford thirty-seat buses, except that the seats were down the side of the bus to allow room for the flying gear and equipment, such as navigators' bags, sextants, engineers' tool kits etc. Each bus carried two or three crews for aircraft in adjacent dispersals. And so to the aircraft. Usually, there was time to spare, so those who smoked would move away from the aircraft and have a last puff. Superstitious members had a pee on the tail wheel. Don't ask why, it was tradition. Then we all waited and chatted to the ground crew until it was time to go aboard.

A bomber airfield at night is an eerie place. There is silence once the crew buses have gone. There are just normal country sounds: owls, a cow mooing in the distance and, if it was really quiet, a night train chugging along a nearby railway line and the added rustle of small animals in the grass around the concrete pad. Then, suddenly, the unmistakable crackle of a Merlin engine coming to life as the first aircraft due off started up. Then it was all aboard and time to get to work. Aircraft took off in alphabetical order, so *V-Victor* (JD207) was one of the last.

Bill and I worked to get the engines running from the external starter trolley, checking that all the gauges came to life as each motor started. We always started the two inner engines first, as they carried the essential auxiliaries. When all four were running, we changed the ground flight switch to 'flight'. This put all the electrics on the aircraft's own batteries and the ground crew removed the external connection and towed the trolley/AC away. We then went through all our pre-flight checks and the engines were given a quick run up. The captain set the first course on the compass and the correct barometric pressure on the altimeter and we were nearly ready for off. Chocks were waved away and the aircraft gently taxied out onto the perimeter track and, in its turn, onto the runway. Twenty or so black monsters were trundling through the dark with only the faintest lights on the edge of the track to guide them. Except for the noise of the engines, all was silence. There was no radio or anything like that to warn Jerry that they we were coming.

A green light flashed from the caravan at *A-Able*, or whichever aircraft was first lined up on the runway. Momentarily stopped, another green light and then the roar of the four Merlin engines opened to full power and the aircraft started thundering down the runway. After what seemed an age, it slowly lifted off and started to climb away. The next aircraft was already lined up and off it went. At last it was *V-Victor*'s turn. The green light flashed. Bill eased her onto the runway and held her straight on the brakes. He opened up the throttles to full power. I had a quick look at all the dials. They were OK. The brakes were released and *V-Victor* started down the runway. There were two points of apprehension at this time. This was the first take-off with a fully loaded aircraft and *V-Victor* was a bit of an old lady – a Mk I Halifax, with the nose turret removed and replaced by a hand-beaten fairing. So, she didn't really leap down the runway, but eventually the magic speed was on the Air Speed Indicator. Bill eased the control column back and she slowly lifted off, out into the darkness over the Yorkshire countryside. There were no lights anywhere – just blackness. Gradually, we were gaining height and Bill turned on to course almost due south. I kept my eye on my engine gauges as the first five or 10 minutes were the only time they would be on maximum power. Bill straightened up when on heading and at 2,000 feet reduced the power and the long flog down the east of England began. Eventually, we went over the Essex coast and to the Scheldt Estuary of Holland. At 10,000 feet oxygen masks had to be worn and the superchargers' gears changed to 'S Gear' (i.e. fully super supercharged), to pump more of the rarefied air into the engines. And so up to cruising height, which should have been 22,000 feet, but we had been warned that poor *V-Victor* wouldn't go much above 19,000 feet until some of the fuel was used up. So at 19,000 feet the throttles were eased back a bit as fuel consumption was critical if we were to get back safely. The object of the exercise was to carry the maximum bomb load, so the minimum fuel safety margins were carried.

As we approached the Dutch coast we could see that the early aircraft had alerted the defences. Searchlights were throwing their beams in the air and, occasionally, they would form a tripod and an aircraft would be illuminated for a few minutes. Tiny stars – anti-aircraft shells bursting – would appear round it, but they didn't seem to be doing any damage. Except for this display, nothing exciting was happening. Although there were another 400 aircraft with us, we seldom saw another one. A black shape showing up against the skyline would stay for a while and then drift out of sight.

We crossed the Dutch coast and entered into enemy territory. Fortunately, searchlights did not bother us, so we pressed on. The great rivers of the Rhine estuary were quite clear underneath and the Dutch islands were easy to identify. The navigator confirmed that we were on course and on time. The time was essential as every squadron had its precise time over the target to avoid hitting each other. The whole raid was scheduled to last under 30 minutes, the object being to swamp the defences. Besides watching my engine dials and recording all their readings, I had to help with the lookout for enemy fighters. The astrodome was over my station and by standing up I probably had the best all-round view of any of the crew. And so we crossed Holland. The numerous glints of water below concentrated into one wide river, the Rhine, as wide as the Thames after it had passed London or the Severn opposite Avonmouth. They carried on south just west of the river. Then, some way ahead, what looked like a bright star appeared, which rapidly grew to look like a bonfire in the sky. Then it started twisting and dropping towards the ground. Bill remarked, 'Some poor sod has bought it, hope they baled out'. He warned every one of us to keep our eyes peeled for fighters.

Then down below in front of the port wing tip a fireworks display began on the ground. The attack had started. It was easy to see the explosion of the HE bombs and then, what looked like streetlights, coming on as the incendiaries lit up. Then the whole area was a blaze of light as more and more bomb loads were dropped. The navigator called up a new course and Bill turned the aircraft toward the target. We were starting our bombing run. There was a screen of searchlights ahead to pass and numerous little pinpricks of light showed that anti-aircraft shells were bursting ahead. Other aircraft were appearing as the force was concentrating into the run in to the target.

As the conflagration started to slide under the nose of the aircraft, Butch's voice came over the intercom, 'Bomb doors open', 'bombs fused', then called 'left' or 'right', then 'steady'. Bill kept the aircraft dead steady, ignoring the white puffs of smoke flying past, which were caused by exploding shells and fighting the slipstreams of other aircraft. Then, suddenly, the aircraft seemed to give a little jump and over the intercom we heard 'Bombs gone, bomb-doors closed'. Poor old *V-Victor* seemed very relieved. We spent another minute straight and level for the camera to record what we had bombed. The photoflash went off and then we turned north for home.

But we had obviously stirred up a hornets' nest. We were just clear of the target area, when a searchlight caught us and then two more joined in. Bill immediately started a corkscrew manoeuvre, but the white puffs of smoke started to appear again and we could hear the shells exploding (we had been told not to worry about flak unless we could hear it). Then there was a loud explosion and I suddenly felt my left foot knocked from under me. This caused me to lose my balance and I fell into the gangway, sitting painfully on the edge of an armour-plated step just behind the instrument panel. I switched on my mike and announced that I had been hit.

Bill said, 'There isn't much wrong with you or you wouldn't be making so much noise' and believe it or not there wasn't. A piece of 88 mm flak, about half the size of the filler cap, had come through the starboard side of the cockpit and hit the heel of my flying boot and then rattled down among the oxygen bottles.

Once I was back on my feet we had lost the searchlights and it was time to check for any other damage. Everything appeared OK. There was no vibration from the engines. All the gauges were normal and none of the ten fuel tanks appeared to be holed. I had a good look outside to see if there were any holes and a walk down the fuselage. There was no damage and nothing to report from the gunner. Next, the bomb bay inspection hatch was checked to ensure that all the bombs had gone and the doors were fully closed.

Soon the Dutch islands were beginning to appear and then they disappeared under cloud. After about another half-hour, Jock, the navigator, announced he didn't know where we were as he wasn't sure where we had started from after taking evasive action from the searchlights and we had not been able to pick up a landmark over the Dutch coast because of cloud. Bill said he would hold his northerly course while we sorted ourselves out. Paddy was told to get his radio going and try and pick up a one of the J Beams, which were beamed out from the east coast of England across the North Sea, to help aircraft in trouble. After about half an hour Paddy called that he had found one, and an interpretation by the navigator showed we were due east of Yarmouth. So at least we were clear of enemy territory. We knew we were somewhere over the North Sea, but how far from the English coast? It was decided to turn due west and make sure of making the coast, then if the fuel ran out we should be able to find an East Anglian airfield. After another half an hour we identified the coast and set a new course for base. It was now a question of whether or not the fuel would last. I set to work to make sure it did.

I set the engines at their most economic power setting and the aircraft was allowed to slowly descend. Then I drained all the six smaller tanks completely dry to concentrate all the remaining fuel in the four larger tanks, one connected to each engine, and kept a continuous watch on the fuel gauges. Eventually, we spotted a chance light beacon flashing the letters MB –

MELBOURNE. We did a quick half-circuit and then landed. We had only 15 minutes of fuel left. We had taken 6 hours to do a 5-hour mission. The crew bus was waiting for us. While the navigators were packing up their gear, Bill and I had a good look round the aircraft to see if there were any more holes. Surprisingly, none were obvious. Then we had our debriefing, which for a new crew was fairly informal. I showed off my souvenir piece of flak, which I had recovered from down among the oxygen bottles. The navigator's log would be thoroughly checked next day. We had a pat on the back from the CO and the station commander, then it was off to breakfast, bacon, eggs and baked beans. There was no rationing where aircrews were concerned. Then we went off to bed. Our first op was over.

The next week was quiet for our crew. We air-tested *S-Sugar* after some major repair and *V-Victor* was found to be due for major overhaul so we flew her to Pocklington, headquarters airfield for our clutch of airfields. A crew bus brought us back to Melbourne. We did another air-test on *S-Sugar* to check a faulty supercharger gear change. Then we did some more practice formation flying in *X-X-Ray* and then more formation flying in *V-Victor*. We had a surprise – it wasn't our old JD207 but a brand new Mk II aircraft with a plastic nose cone, a little Vickers machine-gun for the bomb aimer to use and huge 'barn door' fins and rudders instead of the half diamond fins of the old one.

Then on 19 June we had another call for ops. Something was different this time; we had more fuel and were equipped with all 500 lb HE bombs – no incendiaries. Also, besides a new aeroplane we had a new navigator. Young Jock had to go back to school for more training and we got old Jock, a Scottish schoolmaster, at least as old as Bill, probably 25, so we now had two old men in the crew. Old Jock was a flying officer so we now had two officers but Bill was still the captain and his word was law in the air. Briefing was a bit earlier and the target, the steelworks at Le Creusot, on the eastern side of the Massif Central, 200 miles south east of Paris, was a surprise. It was impressed on the crews that this was to be a pinpoint target. If we could not clearly identify the target, we were to bring our bombs home. It was hinted that the French Resistance would warn the French workers to take the night off. We were also told that we had very little fuel reserves so we would land at a south coast airfield and refuel. The operation went as planned.[1] Butch could clearly see the target and the photos showed that very few bombs missed the target. There was little enemy opposition. (We learnt the next day that the Lancaster groups had attacked a German target so the night-fighters went after them.) But we were getting pretty low on fuel by the time we reached the south coast and were very pleased to land at Tangmere. We refuelled, had a meal and a few hours' rest in the Sergeants' Mess, a magnificent pre-war building, and then it was back to base. Two ops finished and twenty-eight to go.

We were kept busy that week, only one day of rest then two nights in succession to the Ruhr area, Krefeld to the west of the Rhine on 21/22 June and Mülheim, which is near Düsseldorf, on 22/23 June. Next, one of the perks of Bomber Command aircrew was to have six days off with a rail warrant home every six weeks. On the way I dropped off in London for a couple of nights with Ethel [a girlfriend] at the dance halls and then went home for a couple of nights, with a chance to take a gun and knock over a few rabbits. On the way back Mum came as far as London and we went to a show, one of the Ivor Novello musicals that were on at the time. It was a treat as 9 July was my twenty-first birthday. Then we were busy again, *V-Victor* was serviceable, so we had a quick local flight. However, we were not happy with her, so it had another day being serviced and then we did an air-test to be sure. On 13 July we bombed Aachen and on 15 July had another long flog to the Peugeot motor factory at Montbéliard, a suburb of Sochaux in southern France close to the Swiss border. There was some excitement before one of these French targets. The bomb load was all HE – fifteen 500-pounders. On German targets all the bombs were released at once, as they were mostly incendiaries or barrel-type HE that had no fins, so they tended to broadcast themselves over the target. But with the precision targets in France the bombs were released in a stick. A timing device released each bomb individually. Well, on this occasion, while I was standing on the wing checking the fuel tanks Butch was checking the bomb gear. Somehow, the electrics, which should have been isolated, were live and when he checked the timer, all fifteen bombs crashed to the tarmac. Fortunately, none of the fuses were live, so none went off, but there was a problem. Some of the bombs had damaged action fuses, which might have activated, so they could not be returned to the bomb dump. I organised a team to hoist all the bombs back on board and they were delivered to the target a few hours later.

Then we had a week with nothing but another practice formation flying exercise. We wondered if we were being trained to emulate the Americans and operate in daylight but no, on 26 July we were detailed to attack Hamburg. This was the most effective Bomber Command attack yet. Hamburg was completely destroyed by a firestorm and our losses were possibly the lowest of the war. Not only was Hamburg almost a coastal target but it was also the first time Window was used to counter the German radar defences. Paddy had to push the bundles of metal strips down the flare chute, a bundle a minute. This was the first op that I had a seat, as they stored the packages on my platform. It was reassuring that from now onwards two feet of tightly packed aluminium foil protected my backside.

That finished July. On 2 August we went to Hamburg again, but we could not get near the target because of the enormous thunderclouds caused by the heat of the inferno underneath. Bill tried to fly through the cloud but was caught by a vicious down current and we dropped from 22,000 feet to 12,000 feet. By the time we recovered, the navigator said that Kiel was dead ahead, so we dropped our bomb load on Kiel and turned for home. Then it was back to formation flying again until 12 August. During the week I was commissioned as a pilot officer. Off came the sergeant's stripes and on went a thin blue bar on each shoulder strap. It meant goodbye to the Sergeants' Mess and over to the luxury of the Officers' Mess and a new way of life. I had a room all to myself, with a nice WAAF batwoman to clean my room and shoes etc. and a cup of tea when I was called in the morning. No money was allowed in the bar. All drinks were booked and paid for at the end of the month. There were no more pay parades, and I had a bank account and a nice lump sum every month from Cox and King, the RAF pay agents. Also, I was given a lump sum to buy a tailored uniform and greatcoat etc.

We had also completed ten operations without turning back once, so were considered an experienced crew. This experience affected our next operation, which was a long one to Milan, Italy, on 12/13 August.[2] All the fuel tanks were full and most of the bomb racks loaded with incendiaries, which, being made of magnesium, didn't weigh very much. But again, we were tight on fuel, with the expectation of landing on the south coast to refuel. In fact, some crews were to fly straight on to Malta and then to North Africa. Half of 10 Squadron had done this a few months before, expecting to bomb up and take another target on the way home. They didn't. Montgomery held on to them and they stayed out there for a year or more. At this time some bored Army officers from the artillery regiments volunteered to see what a bombing raid was like. *V-Victor*'s crew acquired one of these chaps. It was doubtful if he had flown before but he was put in the rumble seat next to the pilot and told not to touch anything.

The route out involved crossing the French coast before dark. We were conned that the coast would be cloud covered and with Window to upset the Jerry radar there would be no bother. There was cloud, about 5 miles inland. Also, we were going through at a relatively low level of 10,000 feet to save some fuel by climbing very slowly. The ack-ack fire made a good firework display, seeming to come up in front of the aircraft and curve away astern. No one appeared to be hit and we were soon clear and in cloud cover. We climbed clear of the cloud and carried on south. The Alps was a beautiful sight in the moonlight above all the cloud. Mont Blanc was a pinpoint *en route* and Butch, the bomb aimer, called when we were clear overhead. Jock then called up that we were 2 minutes late and could he have another couple of mph? The Army chap commented that we were lucky to be there the same day let alone to be within 2 minutes.

All went well. Milan was clear so a lot of Italians lost their sleep and then we went off home. On the way back Paddy, the wireless operator, announced that he was going to the Elsan (a W/C bucket in the rear of the plane). When he got there called up that the so-and-so ground crew had been using it and not emptied it. Bill said, 'Well open the rear door and empty it but be careful not to fall out!' We felt the rush of air as the door was opened. Then there was another call from Paddy, 'Navigator, where are we?'

'Just about over Geneva.'

'Well I've dropped the bucket!'

On reaching the UK we landed at Ford in West Sussex. They made us welcome, fed and watered us, refuelled the aircraft and, after a few hours' rest, we flew back to base. The next week was spent in local flying and flying crews down to Ford to pick up aircraft that had been damaged and needed repair after the Milan operation.[3]

On 22/23 August it was Leverkusen, the home of I. G. Farben Industry, the German chemical company. It was not a very satisfactory op, as the target was cloud-covered so we bombed 'blind'. Flares were dropped by the Pathfinders of 5 Group, which was now operational with all very experienced crews, one of whom was the Master Bomber, who gave instructions where to bomb if the flares were not on target. Then on 23 August we flew an op to Berlin, 'The Big City' in RAF jargon. This was another long flog with a mostly incendiary bomb load and only three HE bombs, although the total load was only 4,500 lb all the bomb stations were full with either cases of 4 lb magnesium fire bombs or 25 lb phosphorus bombs. The route to the target was mostly uneventful, across the North Sea to cross the coast between Bremen and what was left of Hamburg. Then we went to the target, which was brilliantly illuminated by the Pathfinders and a great area of the city seemed to be burning. Over 700 aircraft were on the raid and 4 Group were the last wave. All aircraft had to cross the target before turning for home. The powers-that-be had discovered that if the turn was made over the target then the bombing pattern gradually crept back, as crews tended to release their bombs as soon as the edge of the fire area was reached, resulting in the later waves bombing before they reached the target. Also, now the Master Bomber[4] would direct the attack at a specific area of the target required.

Soon after leaving the target I spotted a small aircraft astern and slightly above. At first sight it looked like a Mosquito but as it started overtaking us both Digger and I were sure it was an Me 110. It obviously hadn't seen us. We were probably in a blind spot under his nose cone, or else he was creeping up on another aircraft. We debated if we should lie doggo in case shooting at him attracted attention. If our gunners missed, then the Me 110 would make short work of a Halifax. However, he presented such a tempting target, well within the range of the gunners' .303 Brownings, that both gunners opened up together and immediately their tracer bullets flew in all directions off the target, which promptly dived away and was lost to sight. No further sign was seen of it or any other enemy action, other than the odd searchlight and we soon cleared the coast between Kiel and Hamburg and set course home across the North Sea. We of course reported the fighter engagement at debriefing and were told that other crews had reported seeing an Me 110 going down. The next day we were credited 'a kill' by Bomber Command. This finished our ops for August and it was also the last time that Halifaxes went to Berlin. After that, they were detailed to secondary targets to decoy the German defences while the Lancasters, with their bigger bomb loads, went to Berlin.[5]

We had now completed thirteen operations and were among the most experienced crews on the Squadron. At this time Bomber Command were suffering losses of 5 per cent on each operation, i.e. the whole force in twenty operations. However, the worst losses were in crews during their first five ops and as a crew became more experienced so the chance of survival increased.

At about this time the squadron started to carry 2,000 lb bombs. These were fitted to a special bomb rack carried on three centre 500 lb attachment points in the centre of the bomb bay. After leaving the target with the first one Butch reported that it had not released. It was a hang up. It was now my job to get rid of it. A check through the inspection hatch showed that it was partly released and hanging nose-down through the bomb-doors, which were not fully closed. This meant that the fuse link was pulled and the bomb was live. However, asking Bill to rock the aircraft, the manual release worked and away it went, unfortunately not on the target. Several other crews had the same problem, so something was wrong. The very next op the same thing happened again and this time nothing would move in the release mechanism so there was nothing for it but to get the tools out and dismantle the bomb rack. This involved driving out the pin on which the bomb retaining cable hinged. It was a long job, but eventually the bomb went near the Dutch border. This effort also solved the problem, as it was the first time a faulty rack had come home. It was found that the bolts in the bomb-release mechanism had been put in backwards and the nuts were jamming the release end of the cable.

We were back at work by the middle of September – another long flog to Montluçon in southern France, then Hannover and Mannheim. These three trips were in other crews' aircraft. Then on 27 September we collected *V-Victor* from overhaul and that night we set out again for Hannover, but this time we didn't make it. Just as we were approaching the enemy coast, one of the engines started exhausting white smoke. I had seen this before. (It was an internal glycol (coolant) leak.) The engine temperatures started to climb to the upper limit and the oil pressure began to drop. There was nothing for it but to feather the engine. It was rapidly decided that we could not reach the target with three engines, so we just crossed the coastline and jettisoned the bomb load, hoping that it might hit something, and turned for home. It was just as well, because as we neared base, another engine started playing up. This time something was broken and it had to be stopped. We restarted the first failure in the hope that if we were gentle with it we would get some power to go in and land, but Bill knew it had to be first time, as it would not take full power for an overshoot. We made it – 4½ hours mainly over hostile waters for nothing. An operation didn't count if you didn't reach the target. *V-Victor* was unserviceable for most of October 1943, which was spent training the navigator and bomb aimer using *Gee*.

19 November was another ordinary autumn morning on the plain of York. I was having a 'lie in'. The previous night we had been to Mannheim. It had been a long flog, but as we had taken off early, we had finished debriefing and got to bed soon after midnight. Normally, we would be left in peace until midday after an op and would wander up to the mess in time for lunch and then spend the afternoon up at the flights checking over the previous night's work. As flight engineer leader I would have to check through all the flight engineer's logs and discuss any irregularities with the squadron engineer officer whose job it was too oversee all aircraft servicing, repair damage and rectify faults. I would also check over my own aircraft – normally *V-Victor* – and have a chat with the ground crew. Finally, I had to check the sick, lame and lazy list to see who was able to fly. I was expecting just a quiet afternoon's work. But today was different. Soon after 9 o'clock my batwoman, a nice girl of about 20, gave me a shake. She put a cup of tea on the bedside locker and said there was a 'CALL' (the code word that we were wanted for another raid that night). All crews were to report for duty by 10 am. I never had any trouble sleeping no matter what the previous night's excitement, so I was soon up, washed and shaved and down to the squadron offices, where it was confirmed that there was to be another 'Maximum Effort'. Lunch was to be taken at 12

o'clock and briefing at 1 pm. This meant another early take-off and that all serviceable aircraft would take part if they could get crewed. Again, we would be crossing the enemy coast in daylight and it was probably a German city. Other targets were usually restricted to experienced crews only.

So I had a quick word with Bill, my skipper, to be told that we were on and that our own aircraft, *V-Victor*, was still unserviceable and that we would be taking *X-X-Ray* again. We climbed into my old Morris and drove out to the dispersal where our own ground crew was getting it ready. There was no time for an air-test but it had gone well the previous night so a quick look round would have to do. The fuel was already on – some 200 gallons short of a full load – so it wasn't going to be a long trip, probably the Ruhr, North Germany. A full bomb load was waiting to go on – nine 1,000 lb HE for the main bomb bay and six canisters of incendiaries for the wing bays. The incendiaries were a mix of 25 lb phosphorous bombs, twelve to a canister and 4 lb magnesium bombs: about sixty to a canister – enough to start a private war. Some of the HE had delayed action fuses to keep the show going as long as possible. We ran the engines up to make sure that everything worked and that the ground crew had missed nothing. The gunners checked their turrets and ammo loads, which were still on from yesterday, as they had not been used. The navigator and bomb aimer checked their magic boxes, which, if the weather was to be the same as last night, they would need.

Then we went to lunch. The mess was quiet, the bar closed and there was none of the usual banter and horseplay. To the old hands (those crews with more than ten ops – and there were not many of these), it was just another job of work. The newer crews were either very quiet, or noisy, depending on their temperament. Then we went up to the briefing room. I joined the other leaders and flight commanders on the platform while the crews were lined up on benches in the main body of the room. On the platform was a weather map of Northern Europe and at the back a large map concealed by a roller blind. Dead on time, 'Groupy', the station commander and 'Wingco', the squadron commander, the only old men (over 25) in the room, came onto the platform.

The flight commanders called a roll of the captains of their flight who confirmed that all their crews were present and the doors were closed. The met man was called to give the weather. The important news was that, like last night, fog and low cloud covered the whole of northern Europe. This meant that the German night-fighters would be grounded and the attack would be blind using target-markers dropped by the Pathfinder aircraft of 5 Group. The met man left and the screen was raised showing the target and the route to be flown in and out. The target was Leverkusen on the Rhine, about halfway between Cologne and Düsseldorf. It was a real military target, as it was the home of the I. G. Farben works, a vast chemical plant. We had had a go at it only a few weeks before, so we already knew it was heavily defended. It was confirmed that we would not see the target but that it would be marked by *Oboe*-controlled Mosquitoes backed up by *H2S* equipped heavy bombers. The markers would be green, corrected if necessary, by reds. A Master Bomber, who would advise which marker to aim at, would control the raid.

Then followed details of the bomb and fuel loads. The take-off time would be 1500 hours. We were given the height to be reached at each turning point *en route*, time and height and time on target. We were to attack the target from west to east and then circle south to miss Cologne, then across southern Belgium and north-east France and home. Known anti-aircraft sites marked were to be avoided! Signal codes were given. These included the colours of the day. Very pistols to warn off trigger-happy Navy ships or friendly (?) A/A gunners. Any questions were answered and the CO gave a final good hunting message and we went away to the locker room to get into flying gear.

The standard flying suit was a kapok-lined overall with loose-fitting Morland's sheepskin boots. Bill and I had acquired a full Irvin suit of sheepskin jacket and trousers and properly fitting fur-lined boots, much more comfortable and a status symbol. Pilots carried a seat-type parachute while the rest of the crew wore a harness with a detachable chute. Fully kitted and with a .38 Webley revolver pushed into my flying boot, I joined the rest of the crew on the crew bus and we were taken out to the aircraft. In November they didn't waste much time hanging around. The nicotine addicts had a quick smoke and the superstitious had a pee on the tail wheel, then we climbed aboard and closed the hatch. Other aircraft were already being started and soon the peace was shattered with the roar of eighty Merlin engines. A green Aldis lamp was signalled from the control tower and the aircraft started rolling. We took off in alphabetical order so again 'X' was one of the last to go.

After a green light from the runway caravan we rolled on to the runway. We took a few yards to get straight then the brakes were put on for as much power as the brakes would hold, then brakes off. As soon as the aircraft was running straight then full power was fed on. Acceleration was fairly rapid and at just over 120 mph the plane lifted off and a long slow climb began. As soon as a safe height was reached we turned SSE. We were already being joined by 6 Group Halifaxes from North Yorkshire (all Canadians) and were soon joining Lancasters from 1 and 3 Groups. There were even a few Stirlings but most of these had been relegated to glider towing for the Army. The total force would be about 600 aircraft and they would be so concentrated that the raid would be over in about 20 minutes. Although it was still daylight as we reached the enemy coast, below was a solid bank of cloud that the met man had promised. This didn't stop Jerry flak gunners from opening up, but with no searchlights and their radar jammed by Window, they were not very effective but the light ack-ack tracer shells gave a good firework display.

Once over Belgium and Holland, things quietened down. We were now at our full operating height of 22,000 feet, and although occasionally a searchlight illuminated the cloud, we could not break through so we were soon over the Rhineland and turning east for the target ahead. The first target marker appeared. It looked like a great green Christmas tree sitting just above the clouds. The Master Bomber's voice came over the radio. The first marker was good, clear for backup markers and to commence bombing. So in we went. Now the natives really became hostile. Leverkusen itself was heavily defended and also we were in the range of the heavy guns defending Düsseldorf and

Cologne. Bill, the skipper, was an ex-artillery sergeant and knew a bit about guns. He would never weave about as that only increased the time we were in range. If we had spare height he would put the nose down a bit and increase speed. But now Butch was beginning his bombing run patter so it was 'press on regardless'. Fortunately, we were now using Window, so most of the flak was at random as the German radar would be overwhelmed. In fact, the flak never looked lethal, just pretty white puffs of cloud, but if you could hear the shells exploding that was different matter.

We ran in to the target. 'Bomb doors open, left, left, steady, steady, bombs gone, bomb doors closed.' We could feel the aircraft lift as five tons of deadweight dropped off. Bill and I adjusted the power settings of the engines a little, but allowed the aircraft to climb to get away from the flak guns. There was no sharp about turn for home. Experience had shown the planners that if this was allowed then the bombing pattern crept away from the target as crews dropped their bombs early, also there was a danger of meeting late arrivals head on as they approached the target.

Tonight we were to fly straight ahead for about 10 miles to clear the defended area then south for 20 miles to clear Cologne on the westerly run home across the Rhineland and the Ardennes south of Belgium. Once clear of the target my job was to check all my dials and what I could see of the aircraft for damage, or if any of the bombs had 'hung up'. It was my job to get them released, preferably over enemy territory. Everything seemed OK so we settled down for the run home, when suddenly, things went wrong. We were bracketed by flak, in salvoes. We must have drifted out of the mainstream with its Window cover and presented the gunners with a clear single target. Bill opened up the engines to full power and Paddy, the wireless operator, started pushing bundles of Window down the chute as fast as he could go. This worked because the flak bursts drifted behind and then ceased.

But this time our luck had run out. There was no visible damage and all four engines were running smoothly, but the fuel tank supplying No. 2 engine, the port inner, was losing fuel at an alarming rate. Switching tanks soon made it obvious that fuel pipes to the engine were damaged, so there was nothing for it but to shut down the engine and isolate it from the rest of the fuel. This in itself was no problem as the Halifax, with no bombs and only half its fuel load, flew quite well on three engines and could maintain height and speed. The problem was that the damage had almost drained No. 1 tank on the port side, which held 300 gallons and which had been held back for the return journey. Bill liked to use the outboard fuel first as this kept the weight of the fuel inboard and improved the aircraft's manoeuvrability. I got my pencil out and calculated how long we could fly on the remaining fuel. On checking with the navigator it was obvious that we could not reach Yorkshire. So we decided to stay with the main bomber stream until over the Channel (we had enough personal attention for one night) and then head for the Sussex coast where there were several airfields just inland. We had recently called on the Navy at Ford on the way home from Milan so we chose that one.

All went well across the Channel and we arrived over Ford with enough fuel to do a circuit and land. We called for priority and were given No. 2 behind a

Stirling, which was also in trouble. Everything was going smoothly. We could see the Stirling reach the runway, so wheels and flaps down. They all still worked. Paddy, the wireless operator, could see the port wheel, which was in the port inner engine bay and it appeared to be OK. Bill called, 'Positions for landing' and started his landing run. Then just before reaching the airfield, a red Very light was fired from the caravan and we were told to go around again. The Stirling had crashed on the runway.

Bill opened up the engines and retracted the wheels and we seemed to be climbing away but suddenly Bill called, 'Can't hold her – we're going down. Everybody brace'. I was sitting on two bundles of unused Window, between my instrument panel and the pilot's seat and I stuck my head between my knees and waited for the inevitable crash. Then it happened. There was an enormous jolt and the noise of grinding metal as we crashed through a hedge of small trees. Bill had got the wings level so the aircraft did not stick a wing tip in and cartwheel, which was always fatal, but it slid along on its belly through a herd of cows until the nose dropped in a rife (water meadow ditch) and it tore itself apart. I had the impression of being inside a barrel being tossed in all directions, with a noise as though half a dozen blacksmiths were beating the outside with sledgehammers. Then everything came to a stop – there was no movement, no noise. There was absolute silence except for the gentle hiss of escaping oxygen from the bottles over which I had been sitting. This quickly brought me to my senses. I appeared to be in one piece and I realised that a mixture of oxygen and spilt petrol was something to get away from. There was some moonlight and fortunately no fire and I soon found a hole to scramble through. I unclipped my parachute harness and scrambled through. Once out I could see what was left of the plane. The whole nose section had been ripped away from the centre section. Most of the starboard side of the cockpit was missing and there was a wheel in its place. Jock, Paddy and Digger appeared out of the centre section, so that was four of the crew accounted for. Then help started to arrive from the nearby railway station but, panic, they were carrying a hurricane lamp! I yelled at them to put it out. There was spilt petrol about.

Now to find the rest of the crew. I crawled back in the hole I had left by and scrambling around, found Bill conscious but trapped in the remains of his seat. I got his harness and parachute undone but could not move him. He was moaning that his arse was cold – he was sitting in the bottom of the rife in six inches of pretty cold water! Paddy came and between us, by hauling his sheepskin jacket, we were able to pull him clear. Bill was also complaining that his shoulder hurt and that we were making it worse but we had got him out alive. Jock and Digger had found Ronny, the rear gunner, half out of his turret with a chunk of his knee missing. Six out of seven were accounted for but where was Butch? There was nothing left of the aircraft where his seat had been so where to look? Then he appeared, climbing out of the rife, wet and muddy but in one piece. He must have been thrown clear through the side window. Seven out of seven.

The Navy soon arrived with stretchers. Bill and Ronny were loaded on two of them and we all trudged out of the field to an ambulance waiting on a nearby road. We were all given a standard Navy noggin to cheer us up and carted off to St Richard's hospital in Chichester, where we were cleaned up and put to bed for the rest of the night. Next day we were more thoroughly checked by an orthopaedic surgeon who pronounced that except for Bill, dislocated shoulder, and Ronny, badly damaged knee, we were all in one piece. Butch was very badly shaken up and was being checked for internal injuries but we were told that we were all being kept in for another day in case any other injuries became apparent.

My answer to this was that if they didn't have to go back to base, I might just as well go home, which was only 12 miles away. The doctor thought this was a good idea and I was allowed to use the phone to call my parents. Half an hour later Paddy and I were on our way to the farm. No one made a fuss at home. Pop was a WWI survivor and Mum had been a VAD nurse, so they were not excitable parents. We were given a good lunch (rationing didn't apply on a farm) and I pinched Pop's chair by the fire and dozed off. When I awoke it was a different story. I ached in every limb and muscle and I didn't move from the chair all afternoon. To make matters worse, Paddy was OK, had been given a gun and was taken out rabbit shooting – my favourite pastime. He didn't hit anything – the report was that he couldn't hit a stationary barn door!

After another night's sleep the bruises began to wear off and in the afternoon we were taken back to St Richard's, where after another check over we were pronounced fit to return to base the next day. That evening, we all gathered around Bill and Ronny's beds and it was agreed that we all would wait until Bill was fit and we'd finish our tour of ops together. We had a chuckle over a report in the local paper. A bomber had crashed into a herd of cows and killed eleven of them. I remarked that the owner was one of the wealthiest farmers in West Sussex and he could afford it!

Next day five of us caught the morning train from Chichester and that evening we were back at base, the end of op nineteen. But it wasn't quite the end. A few days later, a package of personal belongings arrived that had been salvaged from the wreck. In it was my tool bag and in it our mascot, the Scarlet Woman, a rag doll given to me by a girlfriend, Ethel. The doll had lost a leg – the only permanent casualty

It was important, and still is, to get in the air again quickly; so on 2 December we did a cross-country trip with Johnny Hullah. The navigation equipment failed and we came back early. Johnny was just back from a month at Brighton[6] for being caught low flying. The local bobby came in with Johnny's tail wheel in a wheelbarrow. Johnny had left it on the chimney of a girlfriend's house he was beating up and got a bit too low! I was strapped up at the time as my ribs still hurt. The doctor concluded that I had broken a couple of ribs. The strapping was more painful than the ribs so I had a hot bath and stripped it off. Eventually, the ribs healed. I was given the rest of the month off and went home for Christmas. Then another disaster. I had a letter from Ethel. She had caught TB, very common among young people in London at the time. (There was no penicillin or streptomycin in those days). Three weeks later she was dead.

After Christmas Bill returned and we started flying again. I was packed off to St Athan to learn about Bristol Hercules engines, which as I had built them for six months was easy. We were scheduled to get the new Halifax III aircraft fitted with Hercules engines. I was back on the squadron and flew down to Gravely with a second tour pilot to collect our first Mark III from 35 Squadron, a Pathfinder squadron, who were converting to Lancasters. I also had to set up a training course for flight engineers and pilots, on what the effect of the new engines would have and how to handle them. Also, another piece of radar equipment, H2S, was arriving and this was fitted to the rear of the bomb bay. It contained a transmitter and receiver and the receiver measured the returned transmitted signal to paint a picture of the earth's surface below the aircraft. It picked up major geographical features, the coast and the rivers and built-up areas etc. Bomber Command was becoming an all-weather force.

Something was even done to combat fog at the base airfields and Melbourne was one fitted with FIDO.[7] This consisted of a series of large scale Bunsen burners set along the side of the main runway. The object was to create enough heat to lift the fog to form a tunnel down which the aircraft could land. It worked, one night over fifty aircraft successfully landed at Melbourne in foggy conditions.

Earlier in February I was appointed as engineer leader of 10 Squadron, which meant promotion to flight lieutenant and another substantial pay rise. Bill, who was now fit again, was also promoted as senior pilot of C Flight. It made no difference to the crew. We were a team and all mates, each a professional whose sole object was to carry out the duty given them and get home in one piece. That is not to say to say we didn't get up to mischief. One night Bill and I went to a 'do' at Market Weighton. We missed the bus home so we had started walking. On the way we saw a horse in a field and being country lads and a bit 'the worse for wear' we decided to catch the horse and ride it home. The horse thought differently and after half an hour of drunken attempts to catch it we gave up and walked home.

On another occasion we were invited to the Sergeants' Mess of a nearby artillery unit, Bill's old outfit. Here they played a game where the victim was laid face down on a table and it was pretended to paralyse the victim's leg, foot upwards. The unit's commanding officer volunteered, after a demonstration by the crew. He should have known better, when his foot was up in the air half a pint of beer was poured down his trouser leg. We weren't invited again.

At the end of February we were back on operations again and a new experience called *Gardening*. This was laying anti-shipping mines in enemy waters. We were detailed to do this first of all in the Kattegat, the narrow sea channel round the north of Denmark. The following night we went right into the home of the German Navy in Kiel Bay. Both ops were uneventful. We dropped four mines each time, each about 7 feet long and 18 inches in diameter, with a parachute fitted to one end. They had to be dropped from low level for accuracy. Fortunately there were no mountains in Denmark. In the first week in March it was back to French railway yards, but now much closer to home, Moulems, Le Mercier and Trappes, just outside Paris. This was obviously the early work towards D-Day, three months later.

Another squadron celebration took place at this time. Jack Trobe, a popular Aussie squadron leader, CO of 'A' Flight, had gone missing around Christmas. Then one day he walked into the mess, having walked home via Spain and Gibraltar, with most of his crew. He had been brought out by the French Resistance. He got himself trained on Mk III Halifaxes and stayed on the squadron as a conversion instructor. I flew with him a number of times instructing new crews and testing the operational capacity of the new aircraft. One U/T pilot swung off the runway on take-off and snapped the port undercarriage off, fortunately quite gently and the aircraft was not badly damaged.

Flight Lieutenant Jenkins, a Welsh pilot, also fairly experienced, caused another piece of excitement. He came back one night after an argument with a German night-fighter, with most of his elevators shot away either side of the rear turret. He got the aircraft down superbly, but ran off the runway and broke the undercarriage. On his very next trip he repeated the performance, but this time he had much of his bomb load still on board. So he was ordered to bale his crew out then head out to sea and abandon it. He was nicknamed 'Bring 'Em Back Alive Jenkins'.

Then we had another surprise. Bill and I were awarded the DFC. This was uncommon before completing a tour and unusual for a flight engineer anyway. The rest of March and early April 1944 were spent converting the Squadron to Mk III aircraft. On 18 March operations began again with *V-Victor*. We had two easy ones to start with – Tergniers on the Belgian border on 18 March and Ottignies south of Brussels on 20 March, both pre D-Day interdiction targets. And then the real stuff, Düsseldorf again on the 22nd. This time it took only 4½ hours, which shows the improvement in the Halifax Mk III. We had a *Gardening* op in Kiel Bay again on the 23rd, a long flog to Karlsruhe on the 24th and then went to Essen on 26/27 March. We had completed our thirty operations, although I had only completed twenty-nine. The crew had all gone to Leipzig one night without me, when I was doing the Mk III training. We had flown six operations in eight nights – the previous twenty-three had taken nearly a year!

On the 28th op, to Karlsruhe on 24/25 April, Jerry had one more go at us. On the way home I saw a dim shape of what looked like a hostile aircraft astern and below on the port side, which was rapidly overtaking us. It disappeared under the tail plane so I asked Bill to bank the plane so that we could look underneath. As he did so, fortunately quite violently, a stream of tracer shells came up between the wing and the tail plane, followed by a fighter aircraft. Digger, in the mid-upper turret, got a full burst at point-blank range. We could see his tracer hitting and bouncing off the target, which quickly fell away and disappeared from view. Our luck was still holding. For Essen Bill managed to coax the aircraft up to 24,000 feet, the highest we had ever attacked a target. All the crew put on parachutes over the target, the first time we had done that. The markers were clear and we were attacking from the south. We had plenty of fuel so we left the power on and put the aircraft into a shallow dive to get maximum speed. We were back over the Rhine estuary north of Antwerp in 14 minutes; then we eased up and made for home.

At the debriefing we were targeted by the press representatives who had been allowed in. I made the mistake of talking. It was nearly a year since we had attacked Düsseldorf for our first operation. I said that the defences were now so weak that they must be short of ammunition. This made the centre page of the *Daily Mirror* next day and drinks were demanded in the bar – very expensive! Then began 48 hours of one enormous 'booze up'. None of us would have to go operations again unless we volunteered, except for me. After a thrash in the mess bar, where amends were made for the remarks to the press the previous night, we agreed that we would all go to London, so we all drew warrants home via King's Cross.

The plan was to have a short afternoon sleep and then catch a night train to London, which we duly did. We parked our baggage in the Left Luggage and set out for town. Ronny, being a Londoner, knew where to start. Covent Garden Market pubs opened at 3 am for the porters, so that is where we started. As soon as the locals found out what we were celebrating, that was the end for the need for money and we were feted until he market closed at about 9 o'clock. Then we went back to the Strand for some breakfast and by that time the Irish pubs were opening, which kept us going until early afternoon when Bill said he knew an Afternoon Club that was open from 1 pm to 6 pm. So, off we went. By the time that closed we were hungry again so we had a meal somewhere around Piccadilly Circus. Then we thought we would give the booze a rest and all go to the Windmill where we cheered the girls and booed the comedians but were not thrown out. After the show we decided to finish the job properly and set off for Shepherds Market. Somehow we got back to King's Cross station in the early morning and collected our kit and went our various ways.

I never saw three of them again. Bill was killed instructing on Whitley bombers. Someone flew into him at night. Butch (Len), who was sure we would never complete a tour, volunteered for a second tour on Mosquitoes and was killed in a training accident. Digger presumably went back to Australia.

Notes

1. Some 290 aircraft of 3, 4, 6, and 8 Groups, 181 Halifaxes, 107 Stirlings and two Lancasters, were sent to bomb the Schnieder armaments factory and the Breuil steelworks. Two Halifaxes were lost. All crews bombed within 3 miles of the centre of the target but only about a fifth managed to hit the factories.
2. Some 504 aircraft – 321 Lancasters and 183 Halifaxes – were to bomb Milan and 152 aircraft of 3 and 8 Groups – 112 Stirlings, thirty-four Halifaxes and six Lancasters – were to bomb Turin.
3. Two Halifaxes and one Lancaster FTR from Milan. Six Lancasters and two Stirlings were lost on the Turin raid.
4. Wing Commander J. E. 'Johnny' Fauquier, CO of 405 Squadron RCAF.
5. This was Bomber Command's greatest loss of aircraft in one night so far in the war with a total of sixty-two aircraft – twenty-five Halifaxes, twenty Lancasters and seventeen Stirlings, or 8.7 per cent of the force despatched. Thirty-one bombers fell victim to fighters in the target area with another seven crashing on the way home as a result of fighter attacks over Berlin.
6. A disciplinary or 'Refresher Course', as it was officially called.
7. Fog Investigation and Dispersal Operation.

CHAPTER 18

Lady Luck

Tom Wingham DFC

A Guardian Angel today was watching
Protecting me from the fate that I dread
When a bullet passed through the turret
About an inch or so behind my head.

'*Guardian Angel*', 26 August 1944, from *No Place To Hide*
by Sergeant George 'Ole' Olson RCAF, air gunner

There is no doubt that whatever the skill or experience of a bomber crew, at the end of the day, Lady Luck inevitably had the last say. A random shell or fighter in the right place would negate all the craftsmanship of the group of aircrew who had joined together to become as one. To some extent aircrew had the opportunity to decide their own destiny in that they themselves, in most cases, chose with whom they would crew up. Even so, one can often trace a string of circumstances, which led to a single event.

In May 1943 Squadron Leader Stan Somerscales DFC completed his first operational tour with 10 Squadron at Melbourne and he and his crew split up to act as instructors at various training units. He and Flying Officer Jim Lewis DFM, his navigator, were posted to 1663 Heavy Conversion Unit at Rufforth while the wireless operator, Flying Officer Jack Reavill DFM, and engineer, Pilot Officer Sid Stephen, ended up at 1652 HCU at Marston Moor, of which Rufforth was a satellite. The rest of the crew went to other stations. It was at Rufforth that Stan flew as an instructor under Squadron Leader Hank Iveson who was one of the flight commanders at the HCU, having previously flown operationally with 76 Squadron.

Meanwhile, I had been flying as bomb aimer with Pilot Officer David Hewlett on 102 Squadron. We had three more operations to complete our tour in June 1943 when we were sent on a five-week secondment to the Intensive Flying Development Flight at RAF Boscombe Down to carry out 150 hours' flying on the Halifax III prototype. The five weeks became five months, at the end of which, upon returning to Pocklington early in November, our crew were screened and split up. Offered the choice of posting, I elected to go as a bombing instructor to 1663 HCU Rufforth. Navigators and bomb aimers were of the same genesis and at Rufforth had adjacent offices in a shared hut. This made for a chummy atmosphere and as I already knew several of them from 102 Squadron days, there were many combined drinking operations at the 'Half Moon' and the 'Hole in the Wall' in nearby York. Invariably, Jim Lewis and Nell, his wife, could be found at these gatherings with the odd pilot now and again throwing in his lot with us.

The countdown to the events of 22/23 April 1944 began a week or so before Christmas 1943 when Squadron Leader Hank Iveson was promoted to Wing Commander and posted to lead 76 Squadron based at RAF Holme-on-Spalding Moor. When vacancies occurred for flight commanders, where else to look but to Rufforth, to those officers whom he had had the opportunity to assess; first he requested Kenny Clack and then, the last week in March, Stan Somerscales. Ideally, Stan would have wished to reassemble all his original crew, but neither his gunners nor bomb aimer, a cousin of Jack Reavill, were available, Ralph Reavill having returned to operations with 158 Squadron a little earlier. He was to be killed over Aachen at the end of May. The gunners were replaced by Warrant Officer John Rowe, rear gunner, and Flight Sergeant Harry Poole, mid-upper, who came from Driffield where they had been instructors at the Survival School that was located there. John had carried out his first tour with 76 Squadron during the time it was commanded by Cheshire and Harry's first tour had been with another bomber group on Lancasters. The question of a bomb aimer was left almost to the end, but when Stan found the original member of his crew was otherwise engaged he and Jim came with all sweetness to the Bombing Section looking for a volunteer. Being somewhat bored with instruction and with a view to once again enjoying squadron life, I did not need much persuasion and so the die was cast.

RAF Holme-on-Spalding Moor, to give its full title, the home of 76 Squadron since June 1943, was a bleak wartime airfield with very few comforts, just south of Market Weighton on the York–Hull road. It was here that Stan and his crew started to settle in after their posting on 28 March. A few days followed in getting acquainted with the station and squadron routine as well as the Halifax III, before pushing off for some leave prior to commencing operations. This gave a respite to get over the shock of the loss of Kenny Clack, one of the flight commanders we had known at Rufforth, together with two other crews on the Nuremberg raid of 30 March. Experience did not appear to count quite so much.

The Wingco's aircraft had gone for a Burton with Kenny and it was arranged that the squadron commander would share an aircraft with Stan Somerscales, who was 'A' Flight commander, when a replacement arrived. Upon return from leave we carried out two raids on railway marshalling yards at Ottignies and Tergnier as part of the preparations for what was to be the Normandy invasion. Then a new Halifax came on the strength, which the ATA pilot considered the best Halifax she had ever flown. Nominated *I-Ink* (or Iveson!) the Wingco decided to take it on its baptism at the first available opportunity. So on 22 April his name went in the battle order and we were stood down; but this state of affairs was to change as the telephone began to buzz between Heslington Hall (4 Group HQ) and Holme-on-Spalding. The CO had 'forgotten' that he had completed his quota for the month and was being reminded of this oversight by the staff at Group. For an hour or so calls went backward and forward between Hank Iveson and Group with our crew hovering around waiting for the decision as to whether we were 'off' or 'on'. Eventually, as Stan and I stood in Hank's office the telephone rang for the last time. It was the AOC, 'Tiny' Carr, and we understood from Hank that the conversation was very brief and on the lines of, 'Hank, you will not fly tonight. That is an order'. At which point, the phone was hung up. So for us ops were on.

The target was Düsseldorf in the Ruhr, or in Bomber Command parlance, 'Happy Valley'. It was well-known to all of us in the crew and certainly I had been to the target twice before during the period that became known as the 'Battle of the Ruhr' during April to July of the previous year. Briefing followed the usual pattern that had become all too familiar to those who had operated before. The Ruhr always produced apprehension even in the most experienced veteran and tonight was no exception. I had been over the Ruhr ten times in 1943 and losses sustained during that period were always heavy and in terms of average aircraft numbers put up each night it would hardly be an exaggeration to say that the Command had been wiped out nearly twice in that time. The route was always a matter of great interest and tonight the coloured string on the wall map took us down to the south coast and then east across northern France, before swinging north east at the last moment over Belgium and south-east Holland to reach Düsseldorf. Two other major operations to Brunswick and Laon were also being mounted that night to keep the German defences guessing and at full stretch; in all, around 1,100 heavy aircraft would be attacking. The station intelligence officer had his usual say on the target, giving an update on any known alterations to the defences on the way in before the met officer was able to promise good clear weather *en route* and over the target. He was followed by navigation, bombing and W/T briefings, before Hank Iveson, as CO, finally rounded off the briefing with a few well-chosen words.

We drifted out of the briefing room and went about our various tasks in preparing for the night before spending the last hour or so stretched out on a bed. As usual, this night, at the appointed hour we made our way to the mess for an operational supper of bacon and eggs, afterwards filling our flasks with hot coffee before making our way to the crew room. The time-honoured routine followed. We turned out our pockets, removing all forms of identification, put on flying boots, for gunners heated flying suits as well, Mae West and harness. We collected rations and parachutes, codes, signal cartridges of colours of the day and any other paraphernalia required, before moving out to the waiting bus or truck, which was to transport us to our waiting aircraft a mile or more away around the perimeter track at Dispersal. We were somewhat quieter than we had been some 24 hours earlier in the 'Half Moon' at York. Jim Lewis had a Morris 8 open four-seater, but somehow it always managed to carry six. The previous night, on our return from a raid on the marshalling yards of Ottignies, photographers and reporters from a press agency had been visiting 76 Squadron and as the most experienced crew on the squadron we had been interviewed and photographed leaving our aircraft. So had been celebrating in good style and we had a rumbustious ride back to Holme. Pride, literally, doth go before a fall!

At dispersal we climbed into the Halifax (MZ578), which had that smell of all things new, stowed our parachutes and carried out last-minute checks. A last smoke in the cold night air and then we were all in again to take up position as the time came for start-up. Each of the four engines roared into life and, after warming up, we checked for magneto drop to minimise the risk of engine cut out during take-off. One of the ground crew brought the Form 700 to Stan for his signature (this was to indicate that the aircraft was accepted by the pilot as being in a satisfactory condition, a ritual before any RAF aircraft left the ground). Following his departure the hatch was closed and we were on our own. Slowly, we moved out of dispersal in the inky darkness on to the perimeter track in order to wend our way round to the end of the runway, there to take our turn for take-off with the rest of the 76 Squadron, some twenty-two aircraft in all.

We lifted off at 2236 hours in clear conditions with no moon and settled down to the slow climb with full bomb load to the operational height of 19,000 feet. Having assisted Stan with the take-off, I folded down the second pilot's seat to allow Jim and Jack Reavill to come forward, as I also moved down to the nose. Very little conversation took place on the intercom other than routine chat on course and height between Jim Lewis and the skipper and comments by the gunners on other nearby aircraft. The usual thoughts passed through our minds as we crossed the English coastline. Open seas were always viewed as a potential grave. God knows how many Bomber Boys were swallowed up by them. However, tonight was a short sea crossing and it was not long before I was reporting 'enemy coast ahead'.

We roared ahead with everything around us completely obscured by the blackness of the night with only the stars glowing above us. It could be said that, apart from the odd bit of AA fire to be seen as some poor aircraft strayed, life was rather quiet – if one ignored the thumping drone of the four Hercules engines. Occasionally, we were assured that we were not alone by a bump as we hit the slipstream of another bomber. There was little sign of enemy activity as the aircraft reached the end of our easterly run and the navigator gave Stan the new course for the last leg of our approach to Düsseldorf, tracking north across the east of Belgium and Holland.

As the Halifax crossed Belgium and began to move up Holland between Maastricht and Aachen all was still, with no sign of the enemy. Suddenly, there was a soft muffled thud and at least three voices including Stan and Sid Stephen's cried out, 'What was that?'

For probably no more than two or three seconds there was complete silence. Then, 'The wing's on fire!' This was from Harry Poole, the mid-upper.

Again, there followed a silence, which was quickly shattered by Stan's order, 'Bale out!'

It was an order on which he did not have to agonise. A fire in an engine or in the fuselage could be dealt with by fire extinguishers, but a wing – that was a different matter. With hundreds of gallons of high-octane petrol in each wing it does not need much imagination to visualise the inevitable end. In order to give Stan a lighter aircraft I jettisoned the bomb load, hoping to make the aircraft easier to handle while everyone got out. That done, I threw off my oxygen mask and helmet, clipped on my parachute and turned to help Jim Lewis remove the escape hatch just behind me under the seat where he had recently been sitting. Being new, the hatch was proving troublesome, but the combined effort of the two of us quickly overcame the problem and we dropped the hatch out into the night.

John Rowe in the rear turret had already run into trouble and his situation soon became desperate. His seat was in the recumbent position in order to give him as much downward vision over the guns as possible, but now the guns and the seat refused to return to the normal position due, no doubt, to the fire, which may have affected the hydraulics. This meant that his legs were jammed under the guns, making it almost impossible for him to leave the turret. He rotated it manually to the 'fore and aft' position then slid open the turret doors before reaching behind to get the bulkhead doors open.

Everything in the dark had to be done by touch and with his hands behind his back. In John's own words:

> I found my chute in the rack, unclipped it and pulled it over my head into the turret. I was dead scared I was going to catch the rip handle in something and spill it open in the aircraft. I clipped it on and manually turned the turret on the beam. The seat was still stuck so it made it almost impossible to get out through the turret doors and, with the aircraft belting down in a port spin, I was being thrown all over the place. Eventually, throwing myself backward I was left in the position of hanging outside by my knees over the turret ring with my feet trapped under the guns because of the seat and being swung round as the aircraft, by now with only one wing, fell out of the sky. I got one leg out and then, with much effort, wriggled my other leg out of the boot leaving it in the turret. Falling clear, I pulled the cord and all was well when all the noise, smoke and flame suddenly ceased.

Jack had just pulled his parachute in time as he had but a few hundred feet left. For the rest of his life he suffered from one broken knee and the other one badly damaged.

Jim Lewis was first out of the stricken aircraft. A tall thick-set Herefordshire farmer, Jim squeezed through the dark hole and needed a little push as I wished him, 'Good luck', before he dropped away into the darkness, only to find that the slipstream had whipped away one of his boots as he emerged from the aircraft. The parachute having opened, he drifted downwards, watching the blazing aircraft dropping out of the sky and then exploding before crashing into the ground, where it continued to burn. In a short time Jim, too, had landed but in the black of the night had been unable to avoid crashing into the trees on the edge of some woods and with his parachute caught up in the trees was still a number of feet from terra firma.

Having seen Jim on his way, I crouched by the hatch reluctant to follow him. This sort of thing didn't happen to us – only to other people. There was almost a dreamlike quality to the whole thing. It occurred so quickly. There had been no anti-aircraft fire and no apparent night-fighter attack; there had been nothing against which we could have taken action to produce a fighting chance. Less than a year ago I had been in a bale-out situation just after bombing Dortmund when our aircraft was falling out of the sky without power. At that time, although my skipper had given the order, 'Prepare to bale out' we had done little other than clip on our chutes. In the event, our engines picked up and we got away. Having also heard of crews who had been baled out, only for the pilot to regain control or the fire to go out, I was a rather reluctant candidate for a drop in the dark. Was there a chance of the fire going out? Various other thoughts crossed my mind as lying there in the dark I debated the matter with myself. I stretched out and looked back up into the cockpit. Jack Reavill was standing in there with his parachute on and had another one in his hand, which he was trying to clip onto the Stan's harness. Behind him was a dull red glow and smoke was drifting in from the fuselage. It was time to go! How much time had passed since I had discarded my helmet and oxygen mask I didn't know – maybe a minute or so – but as I dropped through the hatch I felt a bit muzzy and so almost immediately I pulled the ripcord. The last thing I remember was the black bulk of the port wing above and then, nothing, until I awoke on the ground.

Pilot Officer Sid Stephen was in his normal position as flight engineer directly behind the pilot when the Halifax was hit by a Bf110G-4 night-fighter with *Schrage Musik* cannon, piloted by *Oberfeldwebel* Rudolf Frank of 3./NJG3. The Halifax was the *Oberfeldwebel*'s forty-third 'kill' but he, too, was nearing the end of his career. On the night of 26/27 April, after having shot down two further RAF bombers, he also was shot down, near Eindhoven and killed with his crew,[1] whether by a Lancaster or *Serrate* Mosquito night-fighter is not certain. He was posthumously promoted to *Leutnant* at the end of April on Hitler's birthday. Of this Sid was not to know for another forty-eight years. But then *Schrage Musik* seems to have been a secret kept just as well by the Air Ministry in late 1943 and early 1944 as it was by the Germans. Certainly, very few operational aircrews were made aware of this type of attack at the time.

When Stan gave the order to bale out Sid put on his parachute and then checked to see whether it was possible to halt the fire. Seeing the wing was on fire in the wing bomb bays he realised the fire was beyond control and came back to the cockpit with the intention of going out of the forward escape hatch, which he could see being opened by Jim and me. However, as Jack Reavill, who was getting the pilot's parachute, stood blocking his way forward, Stan ordered him to go out through the rear entrance hatch. Sid turned back into the smoked-filled fuselage only to meet Harry Poole, the mid-upper gunner, who was coming forward. Both being without intercom, Sid grabbed Harry by the arm, turned him round and then they made their way back to the rear hatch. It is probable that Harry had already tried to open the hatch and failed. Sid tried to release the catches but found it very difficult, probably because the aircraft was so new and it took the combined effort of both of them, Harry pulling at the catches while Sid used his feet to push against the hatch. It took an age, or seemed like it as they crouched in the dark working desperately to escape.

They felt trapped. And then in Sid's words: 'We eventually opened the door and that's the last I remember before wakening on the edge of a wood, which had been set on fire by our aircraft'. Probably, the wing dropped off at the time when Sid was levering at the hatch with his feet, thus throwing him through into space and trapping Harry Poole in the fuselage as the aircraft went into the spin, which was throwing John Rowe all over the place in the rear turret. When John got free it meant that four had reached the ground and there was only to be one more survivor, Jack Reavill.

Upon receiving the order to bale out Jack keyed a distress call back to base on his radio and then clipped on his parachute as he made his way up to the cockpit. Locating the pilot's chute, he unstowed it and then reached across trying to assist Stan to clip it on his harness. While struggling to do this there was an explosion as one of the wings broke away and the aircraft went into a spin, leaving John in the grip of 'G' forces that rendered him helpless. There was then another explosion, of which Jack knew nothing. It threw him clear of the cockpit for he woke up to find himself in space falling with no parachute on his chest. As he came to and sized up his predicament, he realised that his parachute was still with him, floating above his head but attached to only one of the straps. Reaching over his shoulder and grabbing the strap, he drew it back and pulled the ripcord to release the canopy. Barely had it opened when he hit the trees in the Wachelder woods. It is probable that Stan Somerscales had also been blown clear by the same explosion, for he was found dead not far from the aircraft with his parachute streamed out above him in the trees. Harry Poole was never able to leave the aircraft.

Tom Wingham and Jim Lewis were able to evade capture and after four and a half months returned home to RAF service. The official German communiqué stated that Squadron Leader Stan Somerscales, Flight Sergeant Harry Poole and one unidentified airman were killed and Pilot Officer Sid Stephen, Flying Officer Jack Reavill and Acting Warrant Officer John Rowe were PoWs. This information was at a later date passed to the International Red Cross at Geneva. No satisfactory explanation has ever been discovered for the 'unidentified body' given out by the Germans. One can only speculate that perhaps the local German commander was seeking to discourage the local Resistance from helping two evaders or was covering his own back against charges of allowing two aircrew to escape rather than one. There seems to be little likelihood of a satisfactory answer.[2]

Notes

1. *Oberfeldwebel* Schierholz and *Oberfeldwebel* Schneider in Bf 110G-4 720074 D5+CL.
2. After compulsory two months' leave and being given an open invitation to decide his own posting, Wingham volunteered for Mosquitoes and, after a navigation refresher course at OTU ended up in 8 Group (PFF) on 105 (Oboe) Squadron at RAF Bourn at the end of March 1945, with whom he completed four ops before the war finished. In April 1946 on recommendation of AOC-in-C Bomber Command he was awarded the DFC, American, for his successful evasion, the list for British awards having been closed in June 1945.

CHAPTER 19

Surrounds of Glory

Louis Patrick Wooldridge DFC

Amidst the night sky, studded with stars bright to fair,
Sometimes graced by a brilliant silvery moon – at other times bare,
Borne upon outstretched wings of speed,
The RAF 'Knights of the Air',
Upon their wood, fabric and metallic steeds,
Like their counterparts, the bold Knights of Old,
Rode out to give battle,
Not with Shield and Lance,
But to the accompaniment of cannon and machine gunfire rattle,
The fortunate few returning, albeit covered in surrounds of glory,
Whilst alas, the unfortunate many, by fate's decree – their frames so bloody gory.

Knights of the Air, Louis Patrick Wooldridge DFC

By January 1944 Halifax gunner Louis Patrick Wooldridge was a second tour member in Sergeant Jim Allen's newly picked crew at 15 OTU RAF Harwell, Berkshire. They were training on Wellingtons prior to transferring to the Halifax Conversion Unit and then on to 578 Squadron at Burn, Yorkshire, for their first operational tour. Allen himself was a Yorkshireman born in Hornsea, but whose family had moved to Essex. He was an apprentice instrument maker at Plesseys in Ilford before joining the RAF. He maintained that the main requirements for survival were 'crew confidence, crew discipline and a very good guardian angel'. The crew were all NCOs except for Warrant Officer Cohen, the wireless operator (who entering his second tour, later opted to join an experienced crew and was replaced by Sergeant Ron Adams). All except Wooldridge, who was 23, were under 21 years of age. Norman Phillips was bomb aimer and second pilot, Ron 'Geordie' Stobbs, flight engineer, and Eric G. Dunton, gunner. Colin 'Joe' Dudley, the navigator, recalls:

> Jim Allen was not only a brilliant pilot and a lucky one but he was very 'highly strung' and lived perpetually on a high level of adrenaline. He also felt very keenly his responsibility for the lives of his crew. The whole crew had absolute confidence in his skill and his courage and intelligence, but some of them found his intensity hard to live with at times. But they

couldn't ever fly with anyone else, although on one occasion they came to me to try to persuade Jim to ease up and relax a bit, which he very sensibly did.

At 1800 hours on the night of 21 January 1944 Jim Allen's crew were detailed for a cross-country flight, including the North Sea area, in a new Wellington III LN487 KK-U. 'Wooly' Wooldridge recalls:

The aircraft was laden with a full load of 10 lb practice bombs for the bombing exercise. As I was due to occupy the rear gun turret that night, I left Joan, a WAAF M/T driver I knew, standing at the tail of the aircraft whilst I entered at the nose and walked along the interior catwalk to the rear turret. Entering the turret, I manually turned it to face to port and opened the two sliding doors of the turret in order to speak with her until it was time to leave Harwell on the cross-country flight. After a few minutes conversation, Jim Allen informed the crew over the intercom that it was time for us to leave the dispersal point. I informed Joan that I would have to close the turret doors prior to leaving the dispersal point for the take-off runway. At that moment, whether by second sight, instinct, or other means, Joan suddenly reached up before I could close the turret doors to kiss me fully on the lips. Afterwards, she repeated several times the words, 'Take care' before I had closed the turret doors. As the aircraft taxied away from the dispersal point, along the perimeter track to the runway concerned, I saw her waving towards the aircraft, from her position beside the stationary aircrew transport vehicle at the dispersal point. She was still standing at the same position as the Wellington roared down the runway during the take-off flight.

At about 1900 hours over the Doncaster area, the aircraft suddenly dived earthwards from our altitude of 15,000 feet, although the two Bristol Hercules radial engines were still functioning and the propellers rotating. I heard over the intercom system the hurried, desperate measures taken by Jim Allen and the rest of the crew, as they endeavoured to pull the Wellington out of its final destructive dive to earth. The extra assistance on the control column included placing both feet against fixed objects and with the feet thus braced to obtain extra leverage. As a result, the aircraft temporarily gained flying speed and levelled out for a few seconds before dropping to stalling speed and diving earthwards again. During these manoeuvres the landing lights in the wing of the aircraft emerged and swung down and forward ninety degrees. The lights illuminated the area ahead and crew in the front part of the aircraft could see that the nose of the Wellington was almost perpendicular to the earth and we were very low. As I listened to the crew's conversation on this latest predicament they gave, in desperation, a final heave on the control column, which had sufficient effect to pull the aircraft out of its final dive.

During the rapid descent, about 5,000 feet a minute, emergency Mayday wireless call signals were broadcast over the radio telephone system and several RAF stations in the area, including Rufforth, East Moor and Marston Moor, responded. These three stations were heard repeatedly answering our emergency distress call signals and we assumed that the aircraft's position was in the vicinity of these stations. Suddenly, as the aircraft levelled out from its final dive, I felt a severe jolt to the starboard side. Before I could ascertain the cause, I suddenly observed the roofs of numerous wooden huts flashing past about ten feet at the most beneath the rear gun turret. I heard Jim Allen shout over the inter-com system, 'Brace yourselves lads. This is it. We are going to hit the deck any second now'. And almost immediately I felt the aircraft violently strike the ground, shudder violently and slew round to starboard by the pull of the port engine.

During these violent, uncontrollable aircraft manoeuvres, at which the Wellington was the complete master of the crew, I was thrown violently about the rear turret. I had turned the turret to starboard by using the servo feed mechanism at its base and raised my legs to avoid entrapment therein in case fire broke out. The aircraft was fabric-covered with highly inflammable dope paint. I was thrown against the gunsight and the turret guns, which caused injury to my head and face. I was dazed and apparently temporarily blacked out as a result. The centrifugal force action of the violent swing to starboard flung open the sliding doors of the turret and I parted company with the aircraft. I was deposited on the grass field as the aircraft, continuing its swing, passed over me and came to a halt with its fuselage framework broken in three places and at three angles, facing the direction we had been flying. The rest of the crew hurriedly vacated the aircraft and finding the rear turret vacant, searched the field to find me lying on the ground about thirty feet away with blood oozing from my nose and mouth. About this moment I regained consciousness.

Colin Dudley takes up the story.

My emergency position was against the main spar bulkhead facing rear-wards. Here I re-plugged my intercom. We then heard the pilot report that he had lost sight of the aerodrome but had got the aircraft level. I asked at what height we were at and he replied that it was 4,000 feet and he was about to switch on the landing lights. Then we heard loud exclamations from the gunners and the pilot, felt a couple of bumps, smelt flying mud and petrol, a sense of being spun around then silence and stillness. Phil and I scrambled out of the astrodome escape hatch onto the port wing and then onto the ground. There was little left of the port wing and the port engine had rolled away in front of the aircraft and was burning away merrily. The landing lights were still shining bright and lighting up the scene. We were in a muddy field with petrol pouring from the port wing onto the squelchy grass. Jim Allen, standing on the wing, began calling the roll. Everyone answered except Wooldridge. We all ran to the rear of the plane where we found Wooly spread-eagled on the grass under the rear turret, which stood about eight feet above us. At last Jim Allen's calm professional efficiency gave way. 'I've killed old Wooly' he cried out in great anguish. Geordie rose to the occasion and with great presence of mind and not a little courage, climbed back into the aircraft to retrieve the Very pistol and fire off a red flare to attract rescuers. His enterprise proved a little too enthusiastic, however, for instead of climbing out of the plane with the pistol he inserted it into its special socket and fired it out of the top of the fuselage. We took one horrified look as the brilliant flare soared into the air, paused and began to fall back towards the aircraft.

There was not a breath of wind. Each of us grabbed one of Wooly's limbs and we ran like hell to get as far from the plane as possible, until the flare, still burning, landed and fizzled out on the grass only a foot or two from the canvas-covered fuselage. Silence reigned except for the gush of petrol from the broken wing. We laid Wooldridge on the grass about 50 yards from the aircraft as Geordie clambered from his escape hatch. Wooly then sat up and said, 'What's happened?' to which Eric Dunton replied, 'You can see what's bloody well happened!' Wooly looked back at his turret and immediately exclaimed. 'What about my rations?' (The tin of chocolate and raisins that was issued to crewmembers on long flights.) 'You can go and get your own bloody rations' was Eric's vehement reply.

'Wooly' Wooldridge again.

Minutes later numerous male and female members of an Army search-light unit based on the hill nearby arrived on the scene. I noticed that about eight feet of our starboard wing was missing, revealing broken twisted metal spars and framework. In addition, the starboard engine complete with bearers and other components was also missing, revealing the red-coloured sponge rubber self sealing petrol tanks. In the distance I could see by the light of leaping flames a solitary line of trees. The starboard wing had chopped down one of them and the starboard engine was now burning fiercely at that location.

The arrival of the Army personnel at the scene included a Medical Officer captain who informed us that our crash location was at Askham Bryan about 3 miles and 1 minute's flying time from the centre of York. A few thousand feet higher over Doncaster at the commencement of the aircraft's loss of power would most probably have resulted in the aircraft crashing in the centre of York. His examination revealed that the bleed-ing from my mouth was slight and that the bleeding from my nose was due to damaged and burst blood vessels at the bridge of the nose. After his initial medical examination on the field the Army Medical Officer made arrangements with the searchlight unit personnel to convey me to York Military Hospital, but a group of RAF motor vehicles arrived from RAF Rufforth, near York. A car contained the group captain commanding Rufforth and the Station's Ambulance and Medical Officer and an Aircraft Crash and Fire Tender conveyed RAF aircraft crash guard personnel. A further examination by the RAF Medical Officer confirmed the diagnosis of the Army Medical Officer. Arrangements for my removal to York Military Hospital were cancelled and I was to be

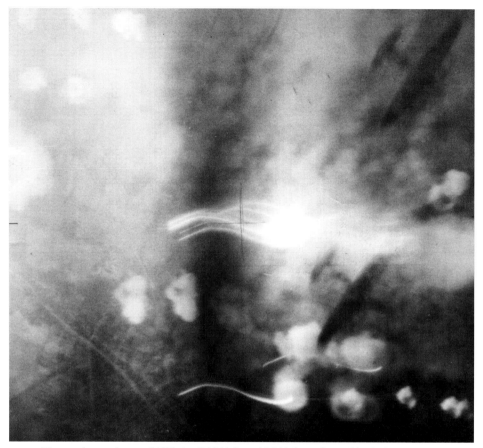

Target photo taken on 10/11 April 1944 from 11,000 feet of a raid by 148 Lancasters and 15 Mosquitoes of 3, 6 and 8 Groups on the rail yards at Laon, France. One Lancaster was lost and the marking was not completely accurate with only a corner of the rail yards being hit. Note the silhouettes of two Lancasters crossing the target below. (Taylor Coll)

conveyed to Rufforth and the Station Sick Quarters instead. On arrival at Rufforth I underwent further intensive medical examination, whilst the rest of the crew had a general examination. Afterwards, all the crew were conveyed to the Sergeants' Mess where a hot meal and drinks awaited us after our ordeal.[1]

Fully recovered within a few days, we transferred to a Halifax Conversion Unit and then joined 578 Squadron at Burn, Yorkshire, where we flew daylight and night ops before and after D-Day. On Tuesday 4 July we were detailed for the daylight operation on the V-weapon site at St Martin Le Hortier. It was the crew's second operation to this site, the previous operation in June being a night operation. We left Burn at about noon in Halifax LW473 LK-B and, joining the usual bomber stream, we flew towards France at about 18,000 feet. Approaching the target area I could see V-1 flying bombs several thousand feet below us in flight. Their distinctive white-hot jet exhaust flames trailed behind them as the bombs flew in the direction of the English Channel and the London area. At night, the flying bombs were more distinguishable by their jet exhausts, which appeared as white-hot incandescent spurts of light moving at a very fast speed through the dark night sky.

Arriving over the target area, the presence of the flying bomb sites could be ascertained by clearings within a wooded area. Tracks of vehicles entered the wood from one side only and to a depth of half to three quarters of the depth of the wooded area, whereas a roadway would have completely traversed the area. During the straight and level bomb run in and over the target area, which is the bomber aircraft's most vulnerable time, heavy predicted flak burst all round our aircraft. Consequently, the starboard outer radial engine was hit, causing the engine to cough and splutter violently. Due to the violent vibrations from the damaged engine being felt throughout the aircraft's frame, the engine was stopped and the three-bladed propeller feathered. Feathering caused the blades to be fully turned so that the thin edge faced the onrushing air and thus prevented 'windmilling'; that is, rotation of the propeller by the force of the slip-stream air due to the speed of the aircraft. If this manoeuvre had not been carried out, windmilling would have eventually caused the propeller increasingly to rotate. This in turn would have resulted in uncontrollable vibration being transmitted to the engine, bearers and mountings to the aircraft, causing additional control difficulties and the possibility of the propeller, engine and bearers etc. being torn from the mountings. In addition, damage had also been caused to the flight instruments. If this had been a night operation the aircraft would have been abandoned because without instruments the pilot could not have kept the aircraft in level flight or carry out banking and turning manoeuvres.

The aircraft had now become a 'Lame Duck'. We were part of the last wave to attack the V weapon sites and our aircraft began to lag behind the rest, which was quite an unenviable position from our point of view, but quite an enviable position for German fighter aircraft in the area. As the rest of the bomber stream aircraft gradually began to widen the distance between us, I rotated the mid-upper turret, keeping observations for vapour trails and small specks of approaching enemy aircraft. Whilst rotating the turret on the starboard beam, I suddenly observed a small speck about 2 miles distant and approximately at 1,000 feet or so above our aircraft, rapidly approach in our direction. I informed Eric Dunton in the rear turret of the approach of the aircraft and thought to myself, 'This is it. Here comes the first of them'. As the aircraft drew rapidly nearer, however, I identified it as a Spitfire. Apparently on observing our plight, the pilot had decided to take up a protective position about a thousand yards or so, level with our aircraft and almost directly opposite my turret. However, even though the Spitfire appeared to be a friendly aircraft, it

235

was known that KG200 operated captured British and Allied aircraft. KG200 would fly alongside an unsuspecting aircraft until sufficient vigilance had been relaxed and they had been accepted as 'friendly' aircraft, when the German crew would suddenly open fire on the British or American aircraft. I half inclined the mid-upper turret towards the Spitfire on the starboard beam of the Halifax in order to keep it under observation.

As we, the 'Lame Duck' Halifax bomber LK-B and the escorting Spitfire fighter aircraft, approached the French coastline, I observed in the distance, about 20 miles or so, two other Spitfires circling about a 1,000 feet over the English Channel. Our Halifax was flying on three engines and gradually losing height so I hoped that our altitude did not go below 10,000 feet before reaching the sea area. Captured anti-aircraft batteries known as 'Z' gun batteries could open fire on any aircraft, irrespective of identification, if it flew below this height.

Arriving safely over the coastline, I observed the two Spitfires concerned slowly circling in a forward movement above and around a Lancaster in its last moments of flight before it entered the choppy waters of the English Channel far below. At this moment, the pilot of our escorting Spitfire, his escort job completed, looked toward our aircraft and raised his hand in a friendly wave in my direction. I replied with rapid elevation and lowering of the four mid-upper turret Browning machine-guns. In acknowledgement, the Spitfire pilot gave a final wave, banking steeply to starboard, and dived towards the other two Spitfire aircraft circling the Lancaster as it ditched. Flying above and past the area, our Halifax continued its lone flight towards the English coastline at the tail end of the bomber stream, as the three Spitfires circled the area now far to our rear where the Lancaster entered the cold, choppy waters.

Shortly after crossing the English coastline, our Halifax aircraft arrived in the vicinity of RAF Farnborough, Hampshire. Due to the considerable damage caused by the German flak batteries, emergency landing facilities under the 'Darkie' emergency radio telephone procedure was requested. Almost immediately we received a request asking us what type of aircraft we were flying. Apparently, on another occasion, the pilot of a four-engined aircraft with an engine failure had requested emergency landing facilities and had been forestalled by the pilot of a Wellington, who, frustrated at having to remain in the air until the other aircraft had safely landed, had reported that he had only two engines! He was consequently given the preferential landing permission, causing much consternation to the Flying Control personnel concerned, when the Wellington aircraft suddenly appeared and landed on the runway. The pilot was apparently reprimanded for the incident.

Receiving landing permission from Farnborough Flying Control, Jim Allen brought the Halifax in for its landing approach, banking to port to keep the starboard wing with its dead engine in a raised position. As we approached the runway, I observed the RAF Station fire tender and ambulance move off and when we touched down and commenced our roll along the runway, the emergency vehicles followed until we came to a halt adjacent to Flying Control. A motor vehicle took us to debriefing. We observed an unusual-looking aircraft approach the airfield. As the aircraft drew nearer, we observed that there were no blurred discs of rotating propellers and it emitted an unusual whining sound instead of the usual pulsating rhythmic throb of an internal combustion engine. The aircraft landed and as it slowly approached we saw that it did not have propellers, but circular apertures where the whining noise was being emitted. The aircraft, which was also fitted with a tricycle undercarriage, was the Gloster Meteor jet and as RAF Farnborough was an aircraft experimental station, it bore a large 'P' within a circle.

On Monday 24 July we were notified that we were on ops that night but our Halifax (LK-B) was unserviceable, so we were detailed to air-test LL458/LK-C, whose regular crew was on leave, from the adjoining dispersal. LK-C was a comparatively new Halifax Mk III, having only completed two operations with 578 Squadron and it sailed through its air-test with flying colours. Everything – engines, navigational equipment (including the distant reading (DR) compass), wireless, gun turrets and the oxygen supply system – were in perfect order and functioning faultlessly.[2] Briefing revealed the target to be Stuttgart in southern Germany, about 600 miles south east of RAF Burn in a straight line and about 100 miles south-west of Nuremberg, the scene of the destruction of RAF bomber aircraft in March that year. It was the first of three heavy raids on the German city in five nights.[3]

Shortly after take off LK-C melted into the converging bomber streams heading to the *rendezvous* point high over East Anglia. All navigation lights were extinguished as the aircraft merged into one long, wide, bomber stream to cross the North Sea and English Channel to their targets. In each aircraft were seven men against the might of Nazi Germany. Approaching 10,000 feet, Sergeant Jim Allen informed the crew so we could clip on our oxygen masks and remove the 'bobbin' from our oxygen supply regulators. Each member of the crew informed Jim that they had done so and that the oxygen supply was working effectively or reported to the contrary. I removed the 'bobbin' from my respective oxygen supply regulator fitted in the mid-upper turret and attached my oxygen mask in position on my flying helmet. (The regulator kept the oxygen supply constant and avoided too much oxygen supply, which could cause the recipient to become 'oxygen drunk' and he could become overconfident and reckless.) Normally, I felt a slight puff of oxygen on my face when I did this, but this time there was no puff of oxygen on my face. I removed my oxygen mask's corrugated tube from the bayonet connection of the oxygen supply tube and placed the open end of the latter opposite my left eye to await the puffs of oxygen. None came. Meanwhile, the rest of the crew reported that their oxygen equipment was functioning correctly.

My failure to report prompted Jim Allen to call me on intercom. He asked if my oxygen supply was functioning. After my negative reply Ron

Stobbs came to the turret to offer assistance. Ron and I tried to find the reason for the failure of the oxygen supply to the mid-upper turret. As the aircraft ploughed onwards and upwards into enemy air space, Eric Dunton in the rear gun turret and Ron Phillips in the astrodome kept extra vigilance for any enemy aircraft in the area. We failed to find a loose lock nut or pipe becoming disconnected and decided that the cause must be in an inaccessible part of the supply system, behind the ammunition boxes and other equipment of the turret, which could not be removed at that particular time. We reported this to Jim Allen, who now had to decide whether to carry on to Stuttgart or abandon the operation. Failure of operational equipment, especially gun turret equipment, was a valid reason for a pilot of a bomber to abandon an operation and return to base. I suggested that a makeshift temporary oxygen supply line could be maintained by utilising the long corrugated flexible rubber hose situated in the 'Rest' position of the aircraft. This was normally used by the flight engineer for oxygen supply whilst changing petrol supply cocks and other work in the vicinity of my turret.

Ron Stobbs unhooked the flexible tube in the 'Rest' position, approached the mid-upper turret and stretching the tube connected it to my oxygen mask. Immediately, my oxygen supply was in efficient working order, but my defensive role was limited to two half-circles of 180 degrees, after which the flexible oxygen supply tubes reached the limit of their flexibility. Turning the turret half a circle and then reversing the turret to cover the other half, thus gave me complete operational coverage from port to starboard side, covering the rear, forward and beams of the aircraft. I had to remember that in the heat of any encounter with an enemy aircraft during the operation, I must not traverse the turret in a complete 360 circle. If I did, I would rip out the oxygen supply tube in the 'Rest' position of the aircraft and automatically deprive myself of oxygen. Jim Allen decided to carry on with the operation to Stuttgart, which was still a long way off, albeit with reduced operational defence efficiency.

Joe Dudley, as a result of his *Gee* fixes, now queried our course and asked Jim for the bearing reading of his master compass on his instrument panel. Jim supplied the information and Joe stated that the reading was different to the reading indicated by the DR compass repeater at his navigator position. Joe was of the opinion that the DR compass was faulty and that he would carry out further navigational checks to establish his findings. A few minutes later, Joe informed Sergeant Jim Allen and the crew, that the DR compass, which is switched on at base prior to the aircraft moving from its dispersal point to monitor bearings, was, in fact, faulty and that we were off course. A few minutes later, Joe provided a correct course for Stuttgart. To emphasise the fact that we were off course, several terrific bangs were heard and felt. As predicted, heavy flak followed the flight course of our aircraft. Evasive action by Jim Allen, however, resulted in avoiding a long line of bursting flak shells a short distance ahead and at the height of our aircraft. It was estimated that we were over the Koblenz area, situated on the River Rhine.

Although I could not see the river because of the dark and the German blackout conditions below, I pictured the area scene beneath the Halifax from memories of my previous visit to Stuttgart in March 1943. On that occasion the bright moonlight conditions revealed the Rhine stretching and glistening for miles like a silvery serpent, with its horseshoe bend at Koblenz shining like a silver horseshoe.

Later, as our Halifax continued through the dark night sky above Germany, a large circle of white coloured lights (similar to the 'Drem' system of the aerodrome landing circuit in Britain) came into view in the vicinity of Mannheim and Karlsruhe. Suddenly, against the outline of these lights, I observed the large black shape of a twin-engined aircraft as it crossed from starboard to port at about our height and 600–800 yards ahead of us. I identified the aircraft from its silhouette as a Heinkel 111 and I informed the crew of its position and course. I assumed it was on a circuit of some airfield, possibly in the vicinity of Karlsruhe, as the aircraft disappeared from view in that direction and no further sightings were made. Less than a minute earlier, our Halifax would have collided with the Heinkel.

Shortly after this incident, Jim Allen banked the Halifax slightly to starboard to head for the 'Stuttgart Gap', a small clearing in the other-wise extensive flak defence system surrounding the area. As we approached the city target area, Eric Dunton suddenly reported that the rear turret had now become unserviceable. The Boulton Paul turret hydraulics system had a free balanced floating piston, which equalised the oil pressure on either side to allow the turret to be moved quickly from side to side. Also, it enabled the tail gunner to fire one of the four .303 Browning machine-guns manually. We were fortunate to be flying a Halifax. If it had been a Wellington, Whitley, Stirling, or a Lancaster, which were fitted with the Frazer Nash hydraulic system, the situation would have required rapid winding of the turret's manual operating handle. This very slowly overcame the hydraulic oil back pressure in the extensive pipeline system and slowly rotated the turret.

We now found themselves approaching Stuttgart, one of the most heavily defended target areas in Germany, with the mid-upper turret power operating in two separate half-circles and the rear gun turret manually operated, with one machine-gun capable of being operated at any one time. And the DR compass was unserviceable. We needed it for accurate navigational bearings to reach the target and to return to Yorkshire. Our predicament was unenviable in any terms. We were over 600 miles from base, irrespective of the dog-leg tactics to avoid heavily defended areas *en route* and in the target area where there were numerous 88 mm anti-aircraft gun batteries, 20 and 40 mm light flak gun batteries and enemy night-fighter aircraft and airfields. However, as we levelled out and commenced a straight and level bombing approach to the target, luck was with us. We observed several combat duels above Stuttgart from criss-cross tracer fire and in the light reflected from the fire glow below, we crossed the target area. We experienced the usual sudden upsurge of the aircraft on release of its heavy bomb load and banked steeply to starboard to resume course for base.

At this moment, whilst my turret was facing to the rear, I noticed an aircraft rapidly approaching the direction of our own aircraft but at about 200–300 feet above and about 800 yards or so away from us. As I turned my turret in the direction of this aircraft, informing the rear gunner as I did so, I recognised the aircraft as being an Fw 190 fighter. I thought that if he commenced his attack now, in the circumstances, there wasn't much either of us gunners could do, although the mid-upper turret was in the more favourable position of the two. However, as the German fighter rapidly approached our aircraft across the fire illuminated target area below, he did not commence firing at our aircraft as he closed with us. Perhaps he had his eyes on another possible victim (although a quick search of the dark sky around our aircraft failed to observe any other British aircraft in our vicinity). Or, he was out of ammunition, which I doubt. Anyway, the Fw 190 disappeared from view to port of the Halifax and was never seen again, much to our relief.

Apart from numerous bursts of heavy flak (some box barrage, mostly predicted), nothing else occurred in consequence during the return flight, although the crew wondered which part of the aircraft's equipment would malfunction next before we reached base. The malfunctioning equipment and our consequential flight errors *en route* delayed our reaching the Allied lines area in France and the dark night sky had now assumed the early daylight hours of the morning. As a result, numerous bomber aircraft could be observed well ahead of us, above, below and abeam of our position. Our aircraft was in the unenviable position of being a 'Lame Duck' or 'Lone Ranger', only on this occasion the Halifax had four sound engines. Over the Allied lines, in the distance, on the starboard side of the Halifax, I observed a group of aircraft approaching at about our height of approximately 15,000 feet. As they drew nearer I recognised them to be US Flying Fortresses. There were eighteen in number, grouped in 'Vics' of threes and each stepped lower than its preceding group. Just as our Halifax was about to pass them, Jim Allen adjusted his position in the pilot's seat and momentarily caused the Halifax to 'waggle' its wings. In response, the central aircraft of the leading 'Vic' of three Fortresses did the same, apparently acknowledging the 'friendly' gesture. Each of us gave a friendly wave to the eighteen US crews as we passed by, with the jocular remark, 'There's the dayshift going on as we come off'. To quote the American expression that aeroplanes are referred to as 'ships', the ships passed in the night; one destined for RAF Burn, Yorkshire, the other eighteen for some destination in Germany and return, or a German cemetery and scrap yard.

As the Flying Fortresses disappeared and became specks in the distance, our Halifax crossed the English Channel. We dispensed with our oxygen masks below 10,000 feet and continued to base. During the debriefing session with the Station Intelligence Officers, our equipment defects were reported and, as a result, a detailed examination was held the next day.[4] On reporting for squadron flying duties, we were informed that investigation of the defective equipment had revealed acts of deliberate sabotage. The oxygen supply pipe to the mid-upper turret had been severed deliberately with something like an electrician's wire-cutters. Iron filings had been found in the magnetic DR compass and in the hydraulic oil sump unit of the Boulton Paul rear turret, causing a sump blockage and consequential power failure. As all the equipment was found to be in working order when LL458 had been air-tested, it was concluded that LK-C had been subjected to acts of sabotage prior to the night operation. Enquiries made to trace the person or persons responsible failed. However, the dispersal point for LK-C was adjacent to a public road, where the hedge had several gaps in it. After this incident, ground staff members obtained their evening meal in relays, so that the squadron's aircraft were never left unattended after an operational air-test, until the arrival of the respective aircrew concerned.[5]

After the Stuttgart operations 578 Squadron reverted to tactical targets, assisting the Army against the German Wehrmacht and operations against the V-weapon sites. In consequence, operations, both by day and by night, were carried out against such place names as Thiverny, Bois de Cassan, near Paris, Forêt de Nieppe, Forêt de Mormal and Hazebrouck. About the first week of August the Squadron was informed that a decision had been made to commence a 'Round the Clock' bombing campaign against Berlin. Instead of returning to our bases in Britain after bombing Berlin, we were to continue our operational flight eastwards, to land at pre-arranged bases in Russia, where the Lancaster and Halifax bombers would be refuelled, bombed up and re-armed for the return flight. Meanwhile, during the day period, the US 8th Air Force would commence their operational day flights to Berlin and Russia, to land at the Russian bases vacated by the RAF aircrews on their return flight to Berlin and Britain. Arrangements were made by RAF Bomber Command, the US 8th Force and the Russians, but after a few false starts, the operation was scrubbed. Annoyed, we questioned the reason for this. Apparently, Stalin himself had cancelled the operation because of supposed difficulties of aircraft recognition between unfamiliar British and American bomber aircraft by Russian aircraft. It is possible that if Stalin had agreed to the original operation code-named *Thunderclap*, upon Berlin in August 1944, Dresden might possibly have escaped destruction later in the war, 13/14 February 1945.[6]

Notes

1. Jim Allen was able to telephone the CO at Harwell, whose reaction was not to ask if anyone had survived, but only to curse the pilot for losing his best aircraft! They never discovered why both the Wellington's engines should suddenly fail completely and without warning, but the problem was manifest and often was related to the fuel tank change-over system. What made Allen's effort almost unique was that no one had ever heard of any other aircraft falling 3 miles at night with no engine power whatsoever and landing safely on its own accord in a dark and muddy field with all the crew walking away

    unharmed. At the end of the official Inquiry, which found no fault in anyone's actions, nor any reason for the loss of the aircraft, each member of the crew was asked if he wished to change to another crew. All except Cohen had no hesitation in saying that they wished to continue flying together with Jim Allen as their skipper.

2. The crew had landed from a raid on Kiel at 0405 hours and were very tired. Take-off that night was 2140 hours. Jim Allen recalls: 'We were a bit concerned during the afternoon when we saw belly *and* wing overload tanks being fitted; this indicated an 8-hour trip (say Berlin?) Our bomb load was half-normal because the extra tank took up so much of the bomb bay.'

3. 461 Lancasters and 153 Halifaxes were dispatched.

4. Seventeen Lancasters and four Halifaxes were lost on the Stuttgart raid.

5. Colin 'Joe' Dudley adds: 'There was no doubt whatever that *C-Charlie* had been deliberately and very skilfully sabotaged. Whoever it was needed a highly professional technical knowledge of the Halifax. The sabotage was designed to be undiscovered until late in the flight while in the event of a cancellation the evidence could easily be removed or repaired. The saboteur also needed solitary access to the interior of the aircraft so that his presence would not be challenged. There is no doubt in the minds of the pilot and the navigator who the clever murderer with the sharp cutting tool was. But if he sabotaged one aircraft he must have done the same to other aircraft on the squadron, sending them off track to be easily picked up by enemy radar, anti-aircraft batteries and night-fighters, but with both gun turrets out of action, unable to defend themselves. On 9 May *D-Donald*'s bombs failed to release due to an 'electrical fault' as happened to *C-Charlie* on 22 May. On 24 June *B-Baker*'s air position indicator was u/s due to an 'electrical fault'. On 20/21 July twenty-six aircraft of the Squadron had set off to attack Bottrop. Six failed to return to Burn. Two collided in the air near Hull with the loss of all crewmembers but the other four were lost over Europe, with the loss of twenty-two crew, the most disastrous episode in the history of the Squadron, while the total losses that night in Bomber command were very light. On 10 September *B-Baker*'s bombsight was u/s due to an 'electrical fault'. One has to consider seriously the possibility that the high losses on 578 that night were due to sabotage. What other reason could there be? And what about the two 51 Squadron aircraft reported by Louis Wooldridge as having exploded virtually simultaneously at Snaith because the bomb bay electrics had been wrongly wired up?' [During the middle of April 1943 Halifax MH-M caught fire and exploded as the fuel supply and bomb load blew up. Whilst fighting the fire, the airfield fire tender crew had to leave the now smouldering remains of the aircraft to race to the other side of the airfield where MH-H had similarly gone up in flames followed by explosion. The night's operation to the Ruhr Valley was 'scrubbed' and the aircrews returned to the aircrew room. Those of a superstitious nature stated it was an omen for the squadron due to the individual aircraft concerned being 'M' and 'H' and the target that night being Mannheim. The destruction of these aircraft caused all Halifax aircraft to be grounded until the reason for the fires was discovered. (Later, it was found that an electrical fault in the bomb bay caused circuit wiring to overheat and catch fire, igniting the incendiary bomb load.)]

6. Jim Allen's crew flew thirty-nine operations over Europe. At the end of the tour 'all nervous wrecks' as Colin Dudley recalls, the whole crew felt the need for a long rest from each other's company. On the other hand, they did not want to fly with any other crews, so they voted to apply for an immediate second tour on Special Duties. However, by September 1944 the Second Front was well under way and they were all sent in different directions and never met all together again.

CHAPTER 20

The Mystery of H-Harry Two

Martin Bowman

Where are the Aussies, the sports and the cobbers,
Talking of cricket and sheilas and grog,
Flying their Lancs over Hamburg and Stettin
And back to the Lincolnshire winter-time bog?

'*Lancasters*', Audrey Grealy

Australian airmen served in RAF and RAAF squadrons of Bomber Command during 1939–45, losing over 4,020 RAAF aircrew killed on operations and in non-operational crashes. In October 1944, 460 Squadron was the first of three Australian Lancaster squadrons,[1] having begun operations with Wellingtons in 1 Group in March 1942, and flying 307 raids from Breighton and from May 1943, Binbrook in Lincolnshire. Flying the most sorties of any other squadron, 460 suffered the highest Lancaster losses in 1 Group, losing 140 Lancasters and thirty-one more in accidents. On the night of 23/24 October 1944 when Bomber Command despatched 1,055 aircraft – 561 Lancasters, 463 Halifaxes and thirty-one Mosquitoes – to Essen to bomb the Krupps works, 460 Squadron provided twenty-six Lancaster crews. This was the heaviest raid on the already devastated German city so far in the war and the number of aircraft was also the greatest to any target since the war began. Altogether, the force carried 4,538 tons of bombs, including 509 4,000-pounders. More than 90 per cent of the tonnage carried was high explosive because intelligence estimated that most of Essen's housing and buildings had been destroyed in fire raids in 1943.

At Binbrook the seven crew of Lancaster III PB351 *H-Harry Two* in 460 Squadron had been an exclusively NCO crew up until September 1944, when the pilot, 22-year-old Dennis R. G. Richins RAAF, was commissioned. Of Pilot Officer Richins' crew, all were Australians except the flight engineer, 20-year-old Yorkshireman Sergeant Eric A. Sutherland. At 20 years old, Flight Sergeant Ken T. Frankish from Western Australia was the navigator. Warrant Officer John R. Treloar, the 21-year-old wireless operator came from the same town as Richins. Treloar's father had fought with the Anzacs at Gallipoli. The 19-year-old Flight Sergeant J. G. 'Jack' Cannon RAAF, the baby of the crew, occupied the mid-upper turret. Cannon had been a cub reporter on the Melbourne *Argus* before joining up. The tail gunner was 20-year-old Flight Sergeant Richard W. Bergelin. Flight Sergeant Wren Stobo (named after Sir Christopher), the air bomber, was at 28 the eldest, and was married with a small daughter. Stobo was a likeable eccentric, with a fund of superstitions. One of them was that he must always kiss one of the WAAFs before take-off. They always lined up to see the crews off, treating them like heroes. Sometimes, as this evening, they boarded the aircrew trucks in a flurry of banter and accompanied them out to dispersal. This didn't inhibit Stobo from performing his second superstitious rite of wetting the Lancaster's tail wheel. Everyone watched for it and cheered as he did it. The night of 23/24 October was no exception.[2]

Ralph Barker, writing in *The Sunday Express* on 11 December 1983, gives an account of what happened:

It was a blustery autumn evening, scattering the leaves and bringing a thin, driving rain. *H-Harry Two* took off at 1615 hours in daylight. Darkness would overtake them as they crossed the North Sea, providing cover when they reached enemy territory. Once clear of the English coast, Cannon and Bergelin tested their guns. *H-Harry Two* climbed to its bombing height of 18,000 feet and Cannon switched on his electrically heated clothing, but the temperature in his turret was well below freezing and he couldn't get warm. It was easy enough, in these conditions, to lose concentration, but he forced himself to keep on the alert. Over the French coast they ran into a cold front, giving thick cloud up to 18,000 feet and beyond. They continued in cloud to the bomb-line. The route had been well chosen to avoid the enemy defences and not until they were approaching Essen after 2 hours' flying did they meet intense flak.

The Pathfinders were less punctual than usual, but they saw the first marker, a single red flare, at 1935. This was followed by a single green flare, but no other markers appeared for seven anxious minutes. Then a red target indicator cascaded down but was soon lost in cloud. Groups of red and green flares followed, but the greens were too scattered to be of much help. The Pathfinders were having a bad night. Fixing their position as best he could, Frankish gave Richins a change of course and they left the main force and steered for their target. Even now the flak was no more than moderate, and there was no sign of enemy fighters. Searchlights, too, were absent. They were carrying one 4,000 lb bomb, five 1,000-pounders and six 500-pounders, plus about a thousand 4-1b incendiaries. Entrusted with a special task they were determined to fulfil it.

Getting what guidance they could from the markers, they began their bombing run. Cannon, from his station on top of the fuselage, peered down and watched the black and red puffs come eddying up towards them in deceptive slow motion. He could smell the sulphurous stench of the flak bursts, but there was nothing he could do about it.

They had just dropped their bombs when he saw something that looked like a red hot coal climbing into the sky towards them, lazily but inexorably. This one was going to be close. They said that when you could smell the flak you were for it. He knew now that this one had their name on it. He could still see the fiery, incandescent orb soaring towards him when oblivion came.

* * * *

The rain falling through the trees dripped incessantly on the body of a man dressed in flying kit who was either unconscious or dead. The question was not resolved for many hours. Then at last the rhythmic tapping of the raindrops finally penetrated sufficiently for the body to stir into involuntary movement. It was still some minutes before the first glimmer of consciousness. Then, reaching out into the impenetrable darkness, fingers scrabbled for the watch that was normally kept by the bedside. But there was no watch, only the dankness of rain-soaked undergrowth. Cannon had no idea where he was, but at least he knew he wasn't in bed. He was lying in a patch of damp bracken under a canopy of trees. He was not really sure whether he was dead or alive. It was still too much for his bemused brain, and he slipped back into unconsciousness. Then the raindrops, accumulating in the foliage above him before being released in larger globules, became so persistent that he stirred again. Where was he? Where did he go last night? Was he suffering from a massive hangover? Lingering in his nostrils was the same sulphurous stench he had sniffed in his last moments of consciousness. That was the key. Memory, still blank round the edges, was coming to life at the centre.

They had been sent to bomb Essen. That was it. A section of the Krupps works. Vaguely he recalled their bombing run, and that lambent ascending flame. It must have destroyed them. But where was the wreck of the Lancaster? What had happened to the rest of his crew? How had he escaped? At first he thought he must have baled out, but he had no recollection of doing so. He couldn't even remember collecting his parachute pack from its stowage. He felt for his parachute harness and was puzzled to find that he didn't seem to be wearing it. Yet he had had it on in the turret. He was quite sure of that. Without it he certainly couldn't have baled out. But why had he taken it off? Every thought that came to him only intensified his bewilderment. But one thing seemed certain. They had been shot down over the target, and he was lying in a forest somewhere on the edge of the Ruhr. They had been due over Essen at 1930. They must have crashed soon after that. His watch, which was still on his wrist, disclosed that it was now after midnight.

Dimly, he remembered from his subconscious that during his hours of oblivion he had heard shots. German guards would have seen the Lancaster come down and would be out searching for survivors. Very probably they had captured some of the crew already. Or shot them. He had to get moving. Richens had always made his crew take the escape and evasion lectures seriously, but it was an effort now to remember what they'd been told. A single phrase drummed on the membrane of his mind. *Travel by night, hide by day*. Before dawn he had to put some distance between himself and the crashed Lancaster. He had no doubt that their plane must have crashed. That was just about the only thing that made sense. But which way should he head? He remembered the scarf in his escape kit, stuffed into a capacious pocket in his flying suit. Printed on the scarf was a map.

The forest was now silent and there was no traffic noise in the distance. He would try to get started. He removed his collar stud and unscrewed it; the base was a miniature compass. Then he risked striking a match. Supposing he was still somewhere near Essen. He had two choices: to go west for Holland or south-west for Belgium. Eventually, he decided to head west-south-west to try to reach the British front line. It was an optimistic plan rendered still more so by his instant collapse when he tried to stand up. His left leg crumpled beneath him, and a head wound, which had stopped bleeding earlier, reopened, oozing blood down his face. He still had to get away from his pursuers, and he began, slowly and painfully to crawl like a crab through the forest. He had no clear idea whether he was scrambling away from the shots or towards them. He just had to keep moving.

The autumn was not yet sufficiently advanced to have denuded the trees, and the branches above him shut out the sky. It was like dragging about in a dungeon, with orientation constantly in peril. When he lit a match and checked with his compass he found he'd been going round in circles. But for hours he kept on. Suddenly ahead of him the tree-trunks acquired definition. Beyond them, he was sure, was an open space where some degree of reflected light seeped through. He would he careful to keep within the sanctuary of the forest, but he might get a chance to reconnoitre the route ahead. Once or twice he still fancied he could hear the occasional rapid burst of shot as though someone was firing a machine-gun. But he thought it was getting farther away.

Reaching the edge of the forest, he was disappointed to find that dawn was being presaged by a seasonal ground-mist. There was certainly open ground ahead, but otherwise he could discern nothing. Then, rising like wraiths above the mist, the dome-like turrets of a castle stood strangely suspended in mid-air. Nothing could have looked more menacingly Teutonic, and he floundered back into the forest. A place like that would be heavily guarded, and he half-expected to hear the barking of guard-dogs. Exhausted by his efforts and sick with nausea, he sank back to rest. Only one thing, he felt, could restore him, a cigarette. He inhaled the smoke avidly, hiding the glow of the cigarette under his jacket. Then he ate a malted milk tablet from his emergency food pack and felt better.

The morning fog might be a blessing. Instead of waiting for nightfall, he might get safely clear of the wood in daylight, putting a useful distance between him and the crashed plane. As first light seeped under the horizon the mists expanded, rolling around him as in some fanciful film. He almost wondered if he was in another world already. But a light drizzle, reassuringly earthy, was still falling. Now was the time to work his way into the open. Somehow, he had to evolve a more practical method of propulsion. Choosing a stout piece of wood from the forest floor as a staff, he found that with its support he could just about hobble along. Keeping a hedge at his shoulder for safety, he advanced laboriously across the field. He was halfway across when, not 20 yards distant, he saw something move. He dived at once for cover into the base of the hedge. It could be some species of cattle. But he knew in his heart it was not. It was a man, mercifully facing away from him, hoeing the ground. If he waited for the man to move on, he might crouch here all day. But his cover was flimsy. When the sun came up and the mist cleared, his hiding-place would be easily revealed.

He recalled another phrase from the escapers' guide. 'A man alone in a field is the best person to help you.'

Could it be true? So far as he could see the man wasn't armed. It might be worth a try. He had nothing to lose.

He pulled out the card in his escape gear, which listed simple foreign expressions. He looked for 'Where am I?' and found it in German, Dutch, Flemish and French. He would try it first in German.

Peering through the fog, he could still make out the ghostly outline of the farmer, as he supposed him to be. The man, intent on his hoeing, was still presenting his back to the hedge. There could be no half measures now. If things went wrong he would try to escape through the fog. But what would he do if the man proved aggressive? Tucked into his suede leather flying boots was another item of escape equipment – a long-bladed sheath knife. He drew it, then crept like a predator close to the ground. Dropping his staff and seizing the man from behind he stubbed the tip of the knife gently but firmly into his neck. '*Wo bin Ich?*' he demanded.

He judged that the man was in his middle forties, about his own height. His colouring was Aryan enough, but he also had the ruddy complexion of the countryman. The man looked round in utter amazement. In doing so, he caught a sidelong glimpse of an apparition. His attacker was a mixture of the madman and the macabre. His face was badly contused, and blood was dripping from a wound in his head. Momentarily shocked, the man was weighing up his assailant, wondering how easily he might be overcome. But feeling cold steel on his neck, he bided his time. Meanwhile, he made no attempt to answer.

Cannon tried him French. '*Comment s'appelle ce place ici?*'

When this too brought no response, Cannon increased the pressure of his knife on the man's neck. Desperately, his voice rising in a crescendo, he reverted to native Australian. 'Where am I, you silly old bastard?'

Slowly the man began to smile. His dialect was strange to Cannon, but the words uttered were the most incredible he had ever heard.

'Ye be in Norfolk, lad. Over there be King's Lynn.'

For a moment Cannon stood dumbfounded. Then he reeled with stupefaction and fatigue. The man grabbed his arm and helped him across what he now saw was a lawn. The man was the estate gardener; he had been hoeing an onion bed.

Cannon was taken into the turreted castle, which he now learned was Houghton Hall, home of the Cholmondeley family. The gardener – his name was Fred Dye – sat him down before a log fire and went off to call an ambulance and fetch his wife. Soon Daisy Dye was cleaning the blood off his face and examining the wound, making him tea, and cooking him a breakfast of bacon and eggs. They did not tell him they had been up half the night, trying to rescue his comrades.

He was taken to hospital at the nearby RAF station at Bircham Newton. There he was given sedatives, which silenced him for the next two days. Then came the questions. All he was able to learn was that after he was knocked unconscious his crew had somehow managed to fly the crippled Lancaster back across Holland and the North Sea. Staggering under a weight of ice they were unable to avoid because they could not climb above it, they had sent an SOS and tried to reach the airfield at Bircham Newton, crashing within sight of their goal. Of the seven men on board, Jack Cannon, already unconscious, was the one whose chances seemed slimmest. In fact, he was the only one to survive. It was assumed that he had baled out, but he had no recollection of doing so and could scarcely believe it but he did not ask any more questions. The shock of losing his mates shut all else from his mind. It was a mystery that one day he might try to solve.

Twenty years later, when working as London representative of an Australian newspaper, he went back to Houghton Hall and renewed his brief wartime friendship with Fred and Daisy Dye. His visit was intended to clear up the mystery. Instead, what he was told only complicated the riddle. The Lancaster, ploughing into the wood, had hit a huge beech tree head-on. Fred Dye showed him the tree. Savaged in its upper branches by violent amputation, it still had a lopsided look that the multi-coloured autumn foliage could not hide. After the plane hit the tree there was a terrific explosion followed by a sheet of flame, which spread over a large area. 'The flames were so brilliant that they lit up the whole picture gallery,' remembered Daisy Dye. She had gone there to adjust the blackout curtains, thinking there was an air raid. 'Then came a series of smaller explosions. My husband and young Lord John Cholmondeley, who was on leave from the Navy, raced towards the burning bomber but they were driven back by the heat. Within minutes dozens of men were on the scene, but we all knew that nobody could have survived that first explosion. For hours ammunition was bursting and zinging out in all directions.' These were the 'shots' Cannon had heard. 'By 3 am the last of the men had gone. We went to bed worrying about the men who had died and thinking about their families.'

Again, the only conclusion Cannon could come to was that he must have baled out. But when Fred Dye took him further into the wood, he changed his mind about this once and for all. First Dye pointed to where his parachute harness had been found – high in a tree 400 yards from the wreck. Next he took him to another tree, 500 yards in a different direction, where his para-chute pack, still unopened, had turned up some days later. Neither the harness nor the pack were anywhere near the spot where Dye estimated Cannon had found himself when he came to. Cannon had to agree. ... He can only conclude that he was either blown high through the air by the first explosion, which he believes might have been caused by a bomb – presumably one of the smaller ones – that hung up, or catapulted through the cupola of the mid-upper turret on impact with the beech tree. This would account for his head injuries ....

Severely iced-up and unable to climb above cloud, an SOS message had been received from the aircraft and PB351 was diverted to Bircham Newton,

Norfolk, on return. It is believed that while the Lancaster was making a very low circuit over Bircham Newton prior to landing, it struck a tree near Houghton Hall and blew up on impact at 2156 hours. Eric Sutherland was later buried at Shipley (Nab Wood) Cemetery, Yorkshire. The five Australians were buried at Cambridge City Cemetery. Ken Frankish's headstone records, 'Farewell Ken. A good innings. Well Played'. Stobo's says, 'Loved Husband of Flo and Daddy of Frances'. Treloar's has the Latin inscription, *Tradidit Lampada Vitai.*

In May 2004 in a million to one chance the Jack Cannon story surfaced again. It was during the prelude to the celebrations for the 60th Anniversary of D-Day. Martin Bowman was invited to accompany a Channel 9 Australian TV crew and two D-Day veterans to France to film a segment for the *60 Minutes* programme.[3] One of the D-Day veterans was 84-year-old Bluey Arthurs from Claremont, West Australia. He had been a Sub Lieutenant Watchkeeping officer/gunnery officer on LST 420 off Sword Beach on 6 June 1944. In all, Bluey took part in five landings – *Husky* (Sicily), Salerno, Anzio, Normandy and Tarakan, Borneo in May 1945. In the hotel in Bayeux one night Bluey was telling some war stories and when they dried up Bowman began to relate the story of the RAAF Lancaster crew that crashed on the estate of an old Norfolk mansion. When he got to the bit about Jack Cannon being blown out of the aircraft in his turret, Bluey, startled, asked, 'Who was the pilot?'

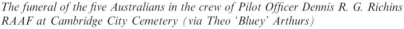

The funeral of the five Australians in the crew of Pilot Officer Dennis R. G. Richins RAAF at Cambridge City Cemetery (via Theo 'Bluey' Arthurs)

22 year old Pilot Officer Dennis R. G. Richins RAAF says, 'Ever in our hearts'.
Flight Sergeant Wren Stobo's says 'Loved Husband of Flo and Daddy of Frances'.
Flight Sergeant Ken T. Frankish's headstone records, 'Farewell Ken. A good innings.
Well played'. Warrant Officer John R. Treloar, the 21-year-old wireless operator has
the Latin inscription, 'Tradidit Lampada Vitai'. Tail gunner, 20 year old Flight
Sergeant Richard W. Bergelin's headstone says, 'His duty fearlessly and nobly done.
Ever remembered'. (Author)

From memory Bowman said, 'Ken [sic] something'.

Bluey leaped out of his seat and, completely astonished, said, 'Ken
Frankish?'

Bowman said, 'Yes I think it was, why?'

Bluey said that when his tour in Europe was up and he was waiting to return
home to Australia he had gone to Kodak House (RAAF HQ) in London,
where he was given a warrant to visit an Australian squadron at RAF
Binbrook. He was there on the night of 23/24 October where on the ops board
the Lancaster Ken Frankish was on was rubbed out. Bluey lived at 18 Walcott
Street Mount Lawley, Perth. Ken Frankish lived at No. 22!

Bluey, who attended the funeral of the crew at Cambridge City Cemetery,
explained that Frankish was a talented cricketer who would certainly have
played for Western Australia if he had survived the war; hence the inscription
on the 20-year-old navigator's headstone.

There was another incredible coincidence in September 2004. Martin
Bowman took a telephone call out of the blue from Rex Barker, who was
ringing after being put in touch by the Mosquito Aircrew Association. Barker
wanted information about a pilot called Richins who had been killed on

250

Mosquitoes.[4] The animated conversation between two aviation authors led to a scratching of heads and it turned out that the Richins killed on Mosquitoes was Dennis Richins' brother! Bowman then related the story of Bluey Arthurs and the gravestones in Cambridge. Barker, who had never seen the graves of the crew, said that he had Stobo's watch, which has inscribed on the reverse 'from Flo and Frances'. Sadly, Barker tearfully related that Stobo never saw his daughter before he died.

Notes

1. The other two were 463 Squadron and 467 Squadron while 466 Squadron operated Halifax bombers.
2. In all, five Lancasters and three Halifaxes were lost on the Essen raid on 23/24 October 1944.
3. *Remembering D-Day: Stories of Everyday Heroes* by Martin Bowman (Harper Collins, 2004).
4. *The Men Who Flew The Mosquito*; *Moskitopanik!* and *de Havilland Mosquito* are among several books on the aircraft and its crews by Martin Bowman.

CHAPTER 21

Dresden

John Aldridge

*How lonely sits the city
that once was full of people! ...
She weeps bitterly in the night
with tears on her cheeks; ...
she has no one to comfort her ...
they have all become her enemies ...
All her gates are desolate ...
and her lot is bitter ...*

> Jeremiah (when Jerusalem was destroyed by
> Nebuchadnezzar)

There was a lad in the year ahead of me at school who joined the RAF early in the war and told us how wonderful it was – flying seemed heroic to schoolboys like me and it was what we all wanted to do. The following year he was dead. But when I volunteered for aircrew in 1941, all I felt was excitement. As far as I was concerned, it was a big adventure. Training took six months and during that time the axe fell – they decided there were too many pilots and we were offered training as navigators or bomb aimers. I was 19 and desperate to get into action, so I chose the bomb aimer course because it was the shortest. Looking back, I didn't think about what being a bomber really meant.

As a flight sergeant bomb aimer I was part of a 49 Squadron Lancaster seven-man crew at Fulbeck, Lincolnshire. It was my job to aim the bomb and drop it at the right time – and get home as quickly as possible because we were constantly at risk from flak and enemy planes. Once in the air, we were a self-contained unit with no outside communication and, as a result, the crew became extremely close. At the back of our minds, we knew each operation might be our last. People from other crews always went missing. One night you'd be out drinking with them and the next they weren't there. Their beds would be empty and someone would come the next day and collect their kit.

Nine of the thirty-three operations I flew from September 1944 to April 1945 were on built-up areas. On 28/29 October we went to Bergen: most of 5 Group had not operated for several days, awaiting clear weather in which to attack the U-boat pens at Bergen. During the Saturday evening of 28 October over 240 Lancasters took off from Lincolnshire airfields (including eighteen from Fulbeck). Although clear conditions in the target area had been forecast, when the Group arrived over the pens they found 10/10ths cloud cover; forty-five Lancasters did manage to bomb, helped by two more from 49 Squadron. But eventually the Master Bomber conceded defeat and sent the remainder home. Three Lancasters and their crews failed to make that return leg. All 49 Squadron's aircraft arrived back over England to find they had been diverted. One put down at East Kirkby, one at Burn, nine at Rufforth and the remaining seven landed at Marston Moor.

My pilot, Flying Officer Ken Lee (PB519) diverted to Marston Moor. The op to Bergen was aborted and on our return flight we dropped 'part' of the bomb load in the North Sea. On the last leg, I was in the bomb aimer's compartment getting my gear together and unloading the guns in the front turret. I continued to sit on the step in my compartment when we joined the circuit and prepared to land. I could see that the skipper was going to land well up the runway and expected him to go round again – but he decided against it. With part of the bomb load aboard and a high all-up weight *Q-Queenie* ran out of runway and carried on through the overshoot area, hit a ditch, smashing off the undercart, and eventually coming to a halt across a main road. I can still visualise earth appearing at my feet as I sat on the step. As we ground to a halt, there was just a moment when we all held our breath (thinking of the bombs resting on the ground in the smashed bomb bay), then someone shouted 'Let's get out of this bloody aircraft!' We in the front, pilot Flying Officer Ken Lee, navigator Tom Gatfield and Lou Crabbe, the flight engineer, went out through the top hatch like scalded cats and down the wing into a ditch to be joined by Flight Sergeant Pye, wireless operator, and Flight Sergeant Powell, mid-upper gunner. Poor old Roy Wilkins the rear gunner came staggering along with the cocking toggle in his hand (with which he had been unloading the guns). His turret had swung as we bumped along the ground and he had fallen out of the doors. Needless to say, the Lanc's bomb load did not go up!

On 7/8 January 1945 we took part in the final major raid on Munich when an area attack was carried out by 645 Lancasters led by nine Mosquitoes. We were supporting the Pathfinder Flare Force (83 and 97 Squadrons), which meant we arrived at the target at the same time but we flew at 2,000 feet below them. This attracted the flak to enable them to carry out a straight and level run.[1] Tom Gatfield and I had been working *Loran* and obtained some decent fixes and we managed to keep to time, however predicted winds were all to cock that night and we arrived over Munich on time . . . but on our own! I went forward into the bomb aimer's compartment to prepare for the bomb run in our supporting role. The sky was one mass of flak bursts and we seemed to be the only aircraft around and we were leaving a contrail at that. We were well and truly hammered. One piece of flak came through the front Perspex and ripped the sleeve on my battle dress blouse. Searchlights also dazzled us and the skipper nearly stalled the aircraft taking evasive action. Tom called out that the airspeed was 110 knots and falling and there was a shout of 'Get the bloody nose down Skip!' Thankfully, he did.

We were then hit in one engine, which had to be feathered; this was the only occasion on which I removed my parachute from its stowage and laid it on the floor beside me. I remember looking down at the snow-covered landscape and thinking 'It's damned cold down there if I have to jump'.

We had to keep an altitude of about 14,000 feet as our route home was above the Alps skirting Switzerland. We saw the lights of that neutral country. Everything went well till halfway across France (by now mostly occupied by our own troops since D-Day) when another engine started vibrating badly and shaking the whole aircraft. The skipper and Lou Crabbe our flight engineer decided to feather that engine, so now we were on two! We decided that rather than land at an airfield in France we would go for a landing at the emergency runway at Manston in Kent, entailing a short sea passage on two engines. This was managed successfully, although the skipper risked unfeathering the last engine to give us trouble, to get a little more power if required.

We hoped another crew would be sent to pick us up from Manston but this was a bad winter with heavy snow and we were instructed to return to Grantham by train, where transport would collect us from the station. We travelled to London in flying boots and battle dress carrying our parachutes. In one pub where we went for a drink, Lou was actually offered £20 from a chap. We also went to the Odeon in Leicester Square where the manager, seeing us attired in flying gear, admitted us free of charge!

I took part in the 13 February bombing of Dresden. Afterwards, when I read criticism of the bombing, I did wonder what I'd been a part of. But at the time it was just a job we had to do. We bombed Dresden at 10.30 pm and joked that we'd catch the Germans just as they were coming out of the pubs. In hindsight I don't feel good about that. But for the most part, we didn't think in terms of people being killed but of areas we had to hit.

As far as Bomber Command was concerned the plan of attack on Dresden was as follows: 5 Group was to attack at 2215 hours on 13 February, using its own pathfinder technique to mark the target. This was a combination of two Lancaster Squadrons – 83 and 97 – to illuminate the target and one Mosquito Squadron (627) to visually mark the aiming point with target indicators from low level. The aiming point was to be a sports stadium in the centre of the city situated near the lines of railway and river, which would serve as a pointer to the stadium for the Marker Force, especially since it was anticipated that visibility might not be too good. The bombing technique to be carried out by the main 5 Group Lancaster Force was known as the Sector type, which had been developed by 5 Group in area attacks. This meant that each aircraft headed up to the aiming point on a different heading – in the case of the Dresden attack from about due south to about due east, each with differing delays for bomb release after picking up the aiming point on the bombsight. This meant that the bombing covered a wedge-shaped sector, resulting in a great number of fires being started over the whole sector, since a great proportion of the bomb load consisted of incendiaries.

When the illuminator force of the Pathfinders arrived over Dresden the cloud cover was 9 to 10/10ths up to about 9,500 feet. The Marker Force of Mosquitoes found the cloud base was at about 2,500 feet. The cloud was not too thick and the flares illuminated the city for the markers who placed their red target indicators very accurately on the aiming point. At 2213 hours 244 Lancasters, controlled throughout by the Master Bomber, commenced the attack and it was completed by 2231 hours. A second attack was timed for 0130 hours on 14 February by another 500 aircraft of Bomber Command. Calculations were that a delay of three hours would allow the fires to get a grip on the sector (provided the first attack was successful) and fire brigades from other cities would concentrate fighting the fires. In this second attack target marking was to be carried out by 8 Pathfinder Group. By the time of this attack, cloud cover had cleared to 3 to 7/10ths, but despite this the Master Bomber could not identify the aiming point due to the huge conflagrations and smoke and a decision was made to concentrate bombing on areas not affected. An area was marked by the Pathfinders both to the left and to the right to assist in concentrating the bombing and good concentration was achieved. So great were the conflagrations caused by the firestorms created in the great heat generated in the first attack that crews in the second attack reported the glow was visible 200 miles from the target.

In addition to these attacks the 1st Air Division of the US 8th Air Force despatched 450 B-17s of which 316 attacked Dresden shortly after 12 noon on 14 February. To assist the night operations of Bomber Command various 'spoof' attacks were made by Mosquitoes on Dortmund, Magdeburg and Hannover and 344 Halifaxes attacked an oil plant at Böhlen near Leipzig at the same time as the first attack. In addition to the above the routeing and feints carried out by the Main Forces involved caused night-fighter reaction to be minimal. In the case of the 5 Group attack our outward route consisted of no fewer than eight legs with feints towards the Ruhr, Kassel, Magdeburg and Berlin, using Window at the same time. An indication of the effectiveness of these operations was that out of over 1,000 aircraft taking part, only six were lost.

Much has been written about the tragedy of Dresden. Probably the primary factor (and here I may be prejudiced!) was the highly successful first attack by 5 Group, which resulted in an almost perfect 'sector' attack. Also, the great strength of the wind helped create the firestorm conditions and spread the conflagrations. At my own bombing height of 13,000 feet the wind speed was 70–75 knots.

An interesting point here is that on the very next night Chemnitz was to be the target of a similar attack, 330 aircraft to make the first and 390 the second attack 3 hours later. In this case Harris at Bomber Command (probably under pressure from Bennett of the Pathfinder Group) decided that 8 Group's Pathfinders would carry out the marking for both attacks and we in 5 Group would carry out a separate attack on an oil plant at Rositz near Leipzig. However, with cloud cover and with 5 Group low-level marking, 8 Group had to rely on sky marking and no concentration of bombing was achieved. I saw personal evidence of this as our (5 Group) withdrawal route linked up with the force returning from Chemnitz and I well remember the fires were scattered over 20 miles. Would Chemnitz have been a second Dresden had the same procedure as in that attack been carried out?

Personal recollections of the Dresden raid are few since, at that time, we were operating at considerable pressure, with deep penetration operations – in fact, three in six days of 9 hours 40 minutes, 9 hours 5 minutes and 9 hours 20 minutes' duration. Points that do stand out are: (1) The long duration of the operation (9 hours 5 minutes). (2) The use we were able to make of Loran, one of our navigation aids, despite jamming. (3) The wind speed set on the bombsight computer box was the highest I recall (about 75 knots). (4) The clarity of the red target indicators despite almost 10/10ths cloud. (5) As the target was relatively close to the advancing Russian lines, we were issued with Union Jacks to put across our chests – in case we were shot down behind their lines – with the words 'I am an Englishman' (in Russian, of course) printed on them. We thought they were not much of an asset – rather they would present a better target!

After the war we weren't treated as heroes like the boys from Fighter Command – in fact, Harris was vilified. People said that bombing German cities had been wrong. But that was unfair – we simply carried out our instructions to the best of our ability. Nothing was said about all our friends that lost their lives.[2]

Bill Gough was a PoW in Dresden in February 1945. He recalls:

> My three years as a PoW started in June 1942 at a place called 'Knightsbridge' in the Western Desert where we were surrounded by the *Afrika Korps*. After my time in two camps in Tripoli and Italy I was sent to Stalag IVB near Dresden. It was a small working camp of about forty men in an area, which we thought safe and peaceful. Our work on the *Eisenbahn* (railway) took us to many places in the Dresden area. The rail network in the centre was very busy so we rarely went into the main station. I remember being taken to the dentist in Dresden by a guard old enough to be my grandfather. That visit impressed me very much. There were streets of beautiful buildings of old architectural design. Later, after the RAF and US Air Force had done their duty, I felt sad that such a grand place had been reduced to rubble.
>
> The two days 13 and 14 February 1945 gave us all in the camp an experience that is almost impossible to describe. On the night of 13 February we were all in our bunks after lights out. (Our day started at 5 am so early to bed was the order.) The sound of planes approaching and flying over became so loud it was as if the planes were just above the rooftops. There had been no warning but these planes were not moving onto another target. They were too close. The noise of the aircraft and the thump of the bombs were frightening and I am sure we all expected our camp to be struck at any moment. How long it was before the noise faded away I have no idea but the relief was immense when all was quiet again.
>
> The following morning, 14 February, instead of small gangs being sent under guard to various work locations, we, the whole camp were marched into Dresden. The situation was chaotic. Civilians who had survived were fleeing the city and every street we could see was just a smouldering ruin. The intention was that we would assist the SS and civilian railway

Front page of the Daily Mail *with details of the Dresden raid.*

men to repair damage sustained to the tracks outside the main station. We refused and stood around doing nothing, whilst the Germans were trying to do the impossible. The whole situation was unbelievable. Germans were frantically removing rails with sleepers still attached pointing vertically from gaping holes. The total area was cratered and littered with burnt out rolling stock, including steam engines in the skeleton of workshops. We stood in the centre of this carnage and confusion like bewildered schoolboys doing nothing. I suppose we were fortunate that no one reacted against us or attempted to force us to take part in the clear up operation.

Just before the alarm sounded the USAAF arrived in formation. It was a clear blue sky and those enormous Flying Fortresses looked very menacing. We did not wait to welcome them. We just ran for shelter, which we found in the bolt holes built into the walls of a brick railway cutting. This saved us. A bomb dropped on our side of the cutting about twenty yards away. The blast ripped past and two of our lads were cut with shrapnel. Following this we were moved to an army barracks about 10 miles from Dresden where we suffered more machine-gun assaults from the USAAF and two of our party were killed. 'Enough is enough' I thought. The Russians were getting ever closer from the east, so I took off with a friend who could converse in German. We eventually met the Americans, who flew us from Leipzig to Reims and the greatest honour for me was flying home in the rear gunner's seat of a Lancaster bomber.

Notes

1. 'Supporters' first flew over the target area to draw flak while the markers dropped their flares and then re-crossed the target to drop their bombs.

2. On Sunday 8 April John Aldridge and the rest of the crew were among those briefed just after lunch for a raid on Lützkendorf. The oil refinery would be the target of 231 Lancasters and 11 Mosquitoes of 5 Group while 440 aircraft of 4, 6 and 8 Groups bombed the shipyards at Hamburg. Aldridge recalls. '1 Group Lancasters had attacked the Lützkendorf refinery [on April 4/5] achieving 'moderate' success and 5 Group was to finish the job. At the conclusion of the briefing W/C Botting, with a piece of paper in his hand, told us that we were tour expired since the signal he had received during briefing had reduced the number of operations required from thirty-six to thirty-three. We were scrubbed from the operation and the reserve crew (F/O Roger Cluer's) would take our place. Our rear gunner, Roy Wilkins had completed about three trips less than the rest of the crew (because of illness) and since Sergeant Pollington the rear gunner in the reserve crew had contracted ear trouble Roy volunteered to take his place. We all went out to the runway to see the lads take off and Pollington came with us. Sitting on the grass on this pleasant early spring evening awaiting Cluer to swing *N-Nuts* onto the main runway we idly picked clover. Pollington actually picked three four-leafed clovers in succession! Laughingly, we all remarked, 'You lucky bastard … it looks like your crew will get the chop tonight'. Many a true word spoken in jest! Roy gave us thumbs up from his rear turret as *N-Nuts* roared down the runway at just after 1800 hrs. Later we all went to the *Hare and Hounds* in Fulbeck village for a drink before rolling back into our hut. Although we never had the pleasure of knowingly flying our last op, the feeling of having finished was never the less fantastic. Next morning Roy's bed was still empty and we thought he might have landed elsewhere but nothing more was ever heard of him or the crew with which he was flying. Roy's loss was a very tragic experience coming right at the end of a long and distinguished tour. The raid itself was a total success with the refinery being rendered inactive. The cost had been six Lancasters and their crews.

CHAPTER 22

The Grim Reaper

Johnny Wynne DFC

Death rides my wingtips
As out bombing we go
It lays there in waiting
To claim friend or foe

The grim reaper will harvest
A very large crop tonight
Many souls he will garner
He will grant no respite

'*Death Rides My Wingtips*', 9 August 1944, from
No Place To Hide by Sergeant George 'Ole' Olson
RCAF, air gunner

On the night of 14/15 March 1945 when 244 Lancasters and eleven Mosquitoes of 5 Group attacked the Wintershall synthetic oil refinery at Lutzkendorf near Leipzig, two Fortresses of 214 Squadron at Oulton, Norfolk, in 100 Group[1] carried out *Jostle* radio countermeasure duties in support of the Main Force. One of these American-built/RAF-operated aircraft (HB802) piloted by Flight Lieutenant Norman Rix was shot down.[2] The other Fortress was HB799/K, a Lockheed-built III (B-17G) flown by Flight Lieutenant Johnny Wynne who until recently had been a flight commander of one of the Advanced Training Flights at 29 OTU Brunting-thorpe. Wynne had felt that it was time he returned to operations and he secured a posting to a PFF Mosquito squadron. Having completed his decompression tests he was awaiting marching orders when a request came through from Bomber Command for him to go to 100 Group. Wynne reluctantly agreed on the understanding that he could take his own crew from Brunting-thorpe. The crew, which was composed of second and third tour operators, included Flying Officer Dudley Heal DFM, the station navigation leader; Flying Officer James Vinall DFM the engineer leader and Flying Officer Sidney Matthews DFC the gunnery leader. All three along with the other six members volunteered to go with Wynne, who recalls:

Heal had completed his first tour in 617 Squadron and flew on the Dams Raid, successfully attacking the Sorpe Dam.[3] In the course of his training

Flight Lieutenant Johnny Wynne, who brought Fortress III HB799/K back alone from Lützkendorf near Leipzig on the night of 14/15 March 1945, in the cockpit of another Fortress, Take It Easy. (CONAM)

for that raid he had navigated at very low level at night for scores of hours. He was by far the most qualified night low-level navigator at Oulton. Matthews had flown seventy-odd missions with Bomber Command and aimed to reach his hundred. I would take him to that goal. Every member of this ten-man crew had been decorated during or after their previous tour except the two radio operators, Flying Officers Tom Tate and Gordon Hall. The 2nd Navigator was Flight Lieutenant 'Tubby' Pow DFC and the other gunners were Flying Officer Harold Frost DFM (top turret) and Flight Sergeants Norman Bradley DFM and Edward Percival DFM, the two waist gunners. More than one of the gunners had an enemy fighter to his credit.

The duties of the crew broke down into four basic groups. The navigator and pilot were responsible for the navigation and tactical operation of the aircraft. They were the 'Management'. The top and rear gunners were responsible for the air defence of the aircraft and for advising the pilot of tactical matters behind his field of view. The waist gunners augmented the top and rear gunners some of the time and outside enemy airspace, but for most of the time over enemy territory they fed Window into the chutes at a prescribed rate. This was a soul-destroying job: very cold, uncomfortable and muscle binding, sustained by high-pressure oxygen. The two wireless operators occupied the radio compartment in isolation from the goings-on of the rest of the crew. Hall was a straight W/Op keeping the aircraft in touch with higher headquarters. Tate was the Special Operator who had several functions including the operation of the *Jostle*. His role was so secret that he had a separate briefing from the rest of the crew and we were not allowed to ask him about his work. Geographically the crew was divided by the bomb bay into a front and an aft group. Collectively we shared more than 450 missions and knew that an operation was not over until the engines were shut down and the crew stood on the dispersal pan. It flew in silence except for instructions and maintained the same level of concentration from engine start-up to engine shut down. It landed with its guns loaded and cocked, contrary to local orders. I had flown half of my first tour out of Malta within range of German radars on Sicily and only 15 minutes Ju 88 flying time from an intruder base. We knew about intruders in the circuit and on the approach to touch down.

The two Fortresses flew at around 24,000 feet while the Lancs flew towards the target at 20,000 feet. For the homeward trip the Lancs and the Forts were to fly at 3,000 feet above sea level to make it difficult for the German night-fighters to locate and attack them. However, this of course made the heavies more susceptible to flak and small arms fire. Wynne comments:

I had to obey orders ... I had trusted that the planners had routed the force away from towns, airfields and other places that would be defended by guns. We now know that this was not the case. Of the sixteen bombers shot down on this attack on the Lutzkendorf oil installations almost all were brought down by light flak between Nuremberg and the Rhine.

Wynne's Fortress was within half an hour's flying time of the Rhine when his aircraft was hit, though he did not see a flash from the gun.

> This is why I thought that we were being attacked by a night-fighter from below. The fact that I did not see the flash means the gun was more or less vertically below us or slightly behind us. It would not have made much difference if I had seen the flash. We would still have been hit, perhaps in a fuel tank instead of the front wheel bay, which would have been bad news for us.

Wynne soon found that the oil pressure on the No. 2 engine was falling rapidly. The propeller refused to feather and about 6 minutes later the engine burst into flames. Wynne and his co-pilot, Flying Officer James Vinall, knew that they had only 20 minutes to fight the fire before it reached the firewall behind the engine. The fuel tank, which by now was half full, could explode at any time. Wynne flew on as the Fortress gradually lost height. By now they had flown 80 miles with the No. 2 engine on fire and they were 60 miles from the Rhine, where the land south-west of the river was occupied by the Allied armies. Unfortunately, strong winds had caused the Main Force to fly further south and east of the planned track and the Fortress had been hit 25 miles east of the position recorded in the navigator's log. The No. 2 engine gradually disintegrated but Wynne was sure that they had by now reached the safety of French territory though his navigator, when asked, was unable to confirm their position. Wynne decided to give the order for his crew to bale out. They put on their parachutes and all eight men vacated the aircraft in less than 5 minutes. Vinall first made sure that nobody was left behind and told Wynne this before his captain told him to bale out too.

Wynne now tried to reach Rheims and repeatedly he tried to make contact with the emergency field there but to no avail. The No. 2 engine was still burning fiercely and by now the autopilot was no longer functioning. The propeller was trying to turn a jammed engine and this created a completely asymmetrical load, which the trim system could not cope with. If Wynne left his seat and his control wheel, the Fortress would immediately turn to the left, drop its nose and plummet to the ground. A quick escape was his only hope. Wynne trimmed the ailing Fort as best he could, quickly took off his helmet, vacated his seat and rushed into the nose and the escape hatch. He knew he had but seconds before the bomber would begin its dive to the ground and total destruction. However, Wynne did not get very far for his oxygen tube got caught up with his parachute harness and he realised that he couldn't free himself unless he took off his parachute pack, took off his helmet and mask and put the chute on again. There was no time for all of this so he had no option but to return to his seat and try to balance the aircraft. Gradually, he got the aircraft back on level flight and he was now able to undo his parachute pack and place his helmet and oxygen mask on the co-pilot's seat. He refastened his parachute pack and put his helmet on again with the tube outside the pack this time. By now baling out was no longer an option, he was far too low and the aircraft refused to climb. Standing with his left foot by his own seat and the right one by the co-pilot's seat, he had to lean across to take hold of the wheel. Incredibly, the flames died down and finally the engine fire went out. He now had to work out his position and the only way would be to leave the cockpit and retrieve the maps from the navigator's compartment in the nose. Wynne trimmed the Fortress and went quickly down into the navigator's compartment, where he picked up the charts lying on the table where the navigator had left them.

Back in the seat Wynne levelled the aircraft off and sorted through the maps to work out where he was. To his utter dismay he found that the maps were incomplete! Wynne had to dash down into the nose once more and return to the cockpit with the missing papers. When he discovered that the log was missing he had to make a third dash into the nose compartment! By now he was talking himself and to God for guidance and this time remained in the navigator's compartment longer, gathering up every available piece of paper. He was determined not to have to return again! He clutched everything to his chest with his left hand and crawled back past the open escape hatch on his knees, holding on grimly with his right hand to stop himself being sucked out. Nearly back to his seat the D-ring release handle on his parachute pack snagged on something and the canopy spilled out. Wynne released the harness and threw it onto the flight deck, and still clutching his maps and papers, followed as quickly as he could. He found the log and began to sing. However, 30 minutes later the engine started to burn once more but after another 10 miles the fire again died down and finally went out. He knew he had to find an airfield and make an emergency landing. He crossed the English Channel at 0240 hours and, amazingly, reached England and sighted an airfield beacon just after reaching Beachy Head. Despite circling and firing off the colours of the day, no light came on and he was forced to fly on. After a nervous 15 minutes he saw a searchlight and he fired a red flare before circling and flashing his landings light. The searchlight gave him a heading straight over London to Bassingbourn in Cambridgeshire, ironically, an 8th AF B-17 base. Wynne made two circuits and received a green from the control tower to land. The landing was going to be hazardous because the No. 2 propeller had separated from the engine and was only held on by the pressure of the slipstream. Wynne skilfully went along the runway for 1,000 yards and then went down on the rim. The No. 2 propeller flew off and made a hole in the nose of the aircraft. The B-17 ground to a halt. Johnny Wynne was home safe!

Sergeant T. H. Dawson of the 91st Bomb Group recalls:

> The control tower told me a plane was about to land and they had no radio contact with it. I jumped into a jeep and got out to the runway the minute he landed. I could tell something was wrong because the escape doors were missing. An airman jumped to the ground. I was surprised to see an Englishman get out of a B-17. The first thing he said was, 'I'm sorry if I skinned your runway up a bit'. When I asked him where his crew was he told me they had baled out. ... I think we had our lights on for some reason. Anyway, he saw our field and made a safe landing. They had sent a truck from the tower to pick up the crew – so we sent it back empty. I took him to the tower in my jeep. He wanted to make a phone

call. I could only hear one side of it. His commander must have asked him about his crew, I heard him say, 'Oh, I left them over there!'

Wynne was taken to the mess where he was given 'pancakes with maple syrup, two eggs, bacon, delicious little buns with currants in them, unlimited butter, unlimited sugar for my coffee, pineapple, orange or apple juice and other things which were unheard of in Europe where we were all rationed'.

Wynne was sent on leave to await the return of his crew from France. He wrote to all the relatives to assure them that their sons or husbands were uninjured when they left the aircraft and that they would soon be returned. However, when the logs were examined it looked as if the crew had baled out while the Fortress was over the east side of the Rhine. The strong winds at low level had completely altered the situation. Most likely they had all become PoWs so Wynne wrote again to all the relatives telling them that it was most likely that they had been captured. (This is what happened to Rix and five of his crew, who baled out after their Fortress was hit by ground fire south of Stuttgart, some 30 miles south of the planned track and exploded. The four other crew landed safely in a suburb of Stüttgart and drove westwards in a fire engine they found. Whenever they were confronted they simply rang the fire bell and were waved on!)

Sadly, there was no such happy outcome for five of the nine men who baled out of HB799. Tom Tate, the wireless operator, and Flight Sergeant Norman Bradley landed close together and were soon captured. Their captors separated the two and Tom Tate was taken on a horse and cart to Bühl near Baden Baden. On one occasion Flying Officer Dudley Heal, the second navigator, was brought into the same room as Tate but he did not recognise him, probably because he was still in a state of shock. Flight Lieutenant 'Tubby' Pow, the other navigator, who was severely burned on the face and neck, landed in telegraph wires. He had also broken his ankle and he was hospitalised. Tate was put into a cell where he was reunited with six of the crew. Vinall and Bradley were there. So, too, were Flying Officer Harold Frost DFM, Flying Officer Gordon Hall, Flight Lieutenant Sidney Matthews and Flight Sergeant Edward Percival, whose wife Maud was expecting a baby on this very day. Tom Tate recalls the events of the next day

Next day was Saturday 17th March, a terrible day!

Five armed guards called for us in the morning, put us on a lorry and that lorry drove to the city of Pforzheim in southern Germany, about 20 miles further south. Near the Black Forest. And Pforzheim was a city of 80,000 people. In a valley. And you could stand on a hill at one side and more or less see the hills on the other side. And when I looked down I received one of the greatest shocks of my life. The city had been bombed three weeks before by our RAF on 23rd February and it was in ruins.[4] And these five guards – they ushered us down the hill to the town, down to the centre. The roads had been cleared. There was no traffic. The debris had been cleared aside. There was not a building standing. There were just mounds of bricks everywhere. Thousands of buildings – absolutely nothing!

And there were lots of people about and they recognised us for what we were. They started throwing debris at us and there were some anxious moments. The guards spread out with rifles ready and we got to the other side of the town. We climbed those hills and within a couple of miles we came to the village of Huchenfeld, and walked down the main village street. There was a school. It was occupied by German forces. Armed forces. And we were put in the basement; we were put in the boiler room. I shared a bucket of water and took my flying boots and my socks off. I washed my socks and hung them up hopefully to dry. Lay down on the coke. Went to sleep.

After a short time I remember being hauled up off that coke, hauled up that iron staircase. Out into the street, held by two or three people – there were lots of people around. I was taken down the road. I was thinking to myself, what on earth is all this about? I was in a daze. Suddenly someone hit me across the head. I knew that it was a lynching. I got further down the road; there was a turning on the right. I now know it goes to the church and the churchyard – 200 yards. But on the left there were big double doors of a barn and they were closed but the small door in that barn was open and there was an electric light on and I saw a very substantial beam with a rope or several ropes hanging from it. My imagination told me we were going to be hanged. This triggered the impulse, which fired me into action. I burst away from the people around me and I ran. I was in bare feet. I was dodging people – there were lots of people about. I was dodging them and I was running up the road, back to where we had come from. Then I started thinking: now I have done it! I thought to myself, was it better to go back? There was gunfire. I was impelled. I continued running up the road. Then I saw a pathway between houses. I turned right along this pathway. I was obstructed by hedges, fences, barbed wire. Came to a field. Crossed that field. Came to a pine forest. When I got into that pine forest it was too dark for me to see where I was going. Perhaps I was fortunate in entering, in arriving in that pine forest. There was a small plantation of oaks, oak trees. It was fortunate because there were leaves on the ground and I lay on the ground and I covered myself with leaves as far as I could because I think I was trying to hide myself. While I was doing that I heard a lot of gunfire where I had come from . . ..

Tom Tate was later apprehended by a group of about twenty *Wehrmacht* soldiers. He was later taken into custody by two *Luftwaffe* soldiers who escorted him to a PoW camp in Ludwigsburg. While waiting under guard for the train to Ludwigsburg he was saved from a lynching by the mob that was still roaming free by the intervention of one of his two escorts, Franz Woll, a *Luftwaffe* ground staff. Meanwhile, Tate's breakaway had caused such confusion that two other prisoners, Norman Bradley and James Vinall, managed to get away from their captors. Sidney Matthews, Harold Frost, Edward Percival and Gordon Hall were pushed towards the churchyard and murdered in cold blood. Vinall was free for a day and then he gave himself up to some *Wehrmacht* soldiers. He was handed over to the police, who had to give him up, and later murdered by a civilian mob and Hitler Youth. Norman Bradley evaded re-capture and reached the village of Grunbach, south-west of Pforzheim.

The five men of HB799 are buried in the Dürnbach RAF Cemetery. Knab, the Nazi *Kreisleiter* (District Leader) of Pforzheim was hanged in 1946 following the War Crimes Proceedings in Essen–Steele. He had instructed the commander of the local Hitler Youth, *Sturmabteilung* or SA and the *Volkssturm* to assemble with their men in Huchenfeld in civilian clothes and had incited the crowd to murder the RAF airmen. Johnny Wynne adds:

> HB799 probably returned to Oulton in April. Although she never flew properly after 15 March because of airframe distortion she took part in the last raid of the war with Flight Lieutenant Carter on the pole. I took over another Lockheed built B-17G, KJ117. While on 214 squadron she was lettered BU-E. Over several days when the weather was fine, sitting or standing on a servicing ladder out on *Easy*'s dispersal pan I painted a tableau of St Peter using the basic colours available in the Flight dope store. It represented a war operation 'Dicing with Death'. Historically it is interesting because it shows St Peter, who theologically is the keeper of the Gates of Heaven, with his Golden Chopper with which he harvested the Good Boys for Heaven. This was current Bomber Command myth- ology. Hence the expression to 'Get the Chop'. There was of course a third player in this game of Crap. That was *Easy* herself who took care of us. Hence the exhortation '*Take it Easy*'.

Wynne concludes:

> The losses on the Wintershall raid were unusually high for the period of the war. It appears that most of the losses occurred in the low-level withdrawal from Nurnberg to the Rhine. The bombers were routed at approximately 1,000–1,500 feet above the ground, without navigational aids, using a pre-briefed met, wind and without route markers to keep them on track. This sort of activity is fine for a single aircraft because it arrives and disappears before ground fire is alerted. But to pass 224 bombers over a 30-minute period (i.e. seven per minute) along the same general corridor was by any standard stupid.

... You for long alone, carried the war ever deeper and even more furiously into the heart of the Third Reich. There the whole might of the German enemy in undivided strength and – scarcely less a foe – the very elements, arrayed against you. You overcome them both. Through those desperate years, undismayed by any odds, undeterred by any casualties, night succeeding night, you fought ... isolated in your crew stations by the darkness and the murk and from all other aircraft in company. Not for you the hot emulation of high endeavour in the glare and panoply of martial array. Each crew, each one in each crew, fought alone through black nights rent only, mile after continuing mile, by the fiercest barrages ever raised and the instant sally of the searchlights. In each dark minute

Vol. VI. No. 136 · MAY 17, 1945

THE AEROPLANE SPOTTER

Incorporating the Bulletin of
The National Association of Spotters' Clubs

Proprietors:
TEMPLE PRESS LTD.
Managing Director:
ROLAND E. DANGERFIELD
Head Office:
BOWLING GREEN LANE,
LONDON, E.C.1
Telephone: TERminus 3636

FOR THE ALERT

ALTERNATE
THURSDAYS

3D

VICTORY · IN · EUROPE

of those long miles lurked menace. Fog, ice, snow and tempest found you undeterred. In that loneliness in action lay the final test, the ultimate stretch of human staunchness and determination.

'Your losses mounted through those years, years in which your chance of survival through one spell of operational duty was negligible; through two periods, mathematically nil. Nevertheless survivors pressed forward as volunteers to pit their desperately acquired skill in even a third period of operations, on special tasks.

'In those five years and eight months of continuous battle over enemy soil, your casualties over long periods were grievous. In the whole history of our National forces, never have so small a band of men been called upon to support so long such odds. You indeed bore the brunt. . . . To all of you I would say how proud I am to have served in Bomber Command for four and a half years and to have been your Commander-in-Chief through more than three years of your saga.

'Your task in the German war is now completed. Famously you have fought. Well you have deserved of your country and her Allies.

ACM Sir Arthur T. Harris KCB OBE AFC
'Special Order of the Day', 12 May 1945

Notes

1. In January 1944 214 Squadron, then at Downham Market and equipped with Stirlings, had transferred from 3 Group to 100 Group and, equipped with B-17G and G Flying Fortresses and *Jostle* jamming equipment and Window, flew patrols for the ten months preceding the end of the war, flying over 1,000 sorties on 116 nights. On 20/21 April 1944 when the Main Force went to Cologne, five B-17s of 214 Squadron, including one captained by the CO, Wing Commander McGlinn, flew their first jamming operation. No. 214 Squadron's role was to jam enemy R/T communication between the *Freya* radar and the German night-fighters. Among other countermeasures, they also jammed the FuG 216 *Neptun* tail-warning system. No. 214 Squadron moved to Oulton on 16.5.44. By the end of August, 214 Squadron, which shared the 24-hour watch on the V-2 rocket launchings with 192 and 223 Squadrons, had completed 305 successful operational sorties as a counter-measures squadron with the loss of only three crews. It had achieved a record of no flying accidents for six months. See *Confounding the Reich* by Martin W. Bowman and Tom Cushing, Pen & Sword, 2004.

2. 5 km SE of Baiersbronn, W of Eutingen at 2337 hours by a Bf 110 flown by *Hauptmann* 'Tino' Becker of *Stab* IV./NJG6 and his *Funker* (air gunner) *Unteroffizier* Karl-Ludwig Johanssen. The funker's burst of gun fire hit the Fort's No. 2 engine and the bomber was claimed as a kill. In all, Becker and Johanssen claimed nine bombers (eight of them Lancasters) this night, three of the victims falling to the air gunner's twin rear-facing machine-guns. This was the highest score by a German night-fighter crew in any single night and Johanssen's three victims counted towards the grand total of his 'driver', 'Tino' Becker. The B-17 'kill' therefore was Becker's 57th official victory. Johanssen was awarded the *Ritterkreuz* two days later. Becker's score at the end of the war was fifty-eight confirmed night victories.

3. On 16/17 May 1943 when nineteen Lancasters of 617 Squadron took off from Scampton to breach the Ruhr dams with 'bouncing bombs' invented by Dr Barnes Wallis, Heal flew in Lancaster ED918 *F-Freddy* piloted by Flight Sergeant Ken W. Brown RCAF.

4. On the night of 23/24 February 1945 over 360 Lancasters and thirteen Mosquitoes of 1, 6 and 8 Groups carried out the first and only area-bombing raid on the city from only 8,000 feet and 1,825 tons of bombs were dropped in just over 20 minutes, which killed more than 17,000 people. A total of 83 per cent of the town's built up area was destroyed in 'a hurricane of fire and explosions'. Ten Lancasters were lost.

CHAPTER 23

Reflections

J. B. Hughes

I was disappointed with my tour. Although it looked reasonable on paper I felt that I had not accomplished much more than the survival of the crew and myself. I had served my operational tour through the whole of the Battle of the Ruhr, unaware then, that it would come to be known by that name. To us it was a series of operations, mostly unpleasant, to the most heavily defended area of Germany. It was the build up to Air Chief Marshal Harris's plan for the systematic destruction of the German's capability to wage war by destroying its industrial capacity. It was also expected to break the morale of the civilian population to a point where they would abandon their towns and factories and, perhaps, rise up in arms against the Hitler regime. In spite of the failure of the London blitz to break British civilian morale, the Air Marshals, as well as some of the politicians, not least Churchill, were convinced that the German civilian morale was lower than British. They felt that it would collapse under the much heavier bombardment the new, 1943, Bomber Command could deliver.

Flight Lieutenant Ron Read DFC

Over the years, with monotonous and nauseating regularity, writers have delved into the musty labyrinths of wartime files and amongst the archives and dark recesses of this august institution have resurrected from its limbo the dossiers containing the battle orders, plans and counter-plans of RAF Bomber Command. The publication of these so-called histories and narratives has brought in its wake numerous letters and correspondence to the National Press and much of it has degenerated into a criticism of Bomber Command. How short memories are! What were great exploits and victories of yesteryear are today relegated into the realms of fifth-rate skirmishes and wasted efforts, directed by misguided warlords.

I have no desire to take to task these erudite and competent chroniclers but only to voice my resentment that after so many years these learned scribes with their impotent pens should try to prove that, in essence, the bombing raids on Germany and occupied Europe were a failure. This I take as an affront to the many who did not return.

What do these conclusions and charges do so long after the battles? Nothing, except raise and fester in the minds of those who lost their own, a bitter resentment and heartbreak at the supposed folly and stupidity that cost them their loved ones.

Of course, there were bound to be errors of judgement. What great undertakings ever went according to plan? Could one forecast the weather to a nicety and when the action was committed, should it change hundreds of miles away over the target area, could the High Command, at their behest and with the wave of a providential wand, command the elements to behave, to suit our death-dealing nocturnal marauders? Some forty years on, when the battles are over, it is easy to be wiser.

Can we take these learned scribes and quasi historians' opinions and narrations as gospel, or can they be sure themselves, that in another twenty years they won't be dug up once again, challenged, embellished, rehashed and taken out of context to give a completely different picture? I think not. Many are the diversities of tongues in history.

Who knows what damaging effect Bomber Command had on the enemy morale and war effort? Göring, in one of his bombastic moments, said 'The sky over Berlin would never be violated by enemy bombers'. But violated it was, not by two, three or four but literally by thousands. That in itself was a victory of great magnitude and when this empty utterance was thrown back into his face, did the German people not have doubts about their would-be saviours and masters?

I am not primarily interested in writing as to whether the tactics used were right or wrong, or whether Bomber Command could have been used more effectively, but on behalf of the many who made the 'flight of no return'. Those thousands of men who with undaunting valour and youthful exuberance took to the air, night after night, in the undying belief that they were in their own very small way helping to smash the fiendish ring that engulfed and enslaved Europe. It is possible that the belief in Bomber Command to force the Germans to a quick surrender may have been illogical. But make no mistake, they certainly gave the courage to others to hang on when everything seemed lost, by the very assurance with which they disdainfully saturated and pierced his defences.

Who is there to say how many were the silent and whispered prayers ushered up from those below in the throes of slavery, as they heard the drone of the bombers, night after night, carrying their death-dealing hope into the heart of the enemy bastions? It was the sound of the bombers, when everything seemed lost, that helped to bolster up the hope of the hard pressed peoples below and fan the embers of a dying Europe, which were fast going out. It gave its peoples the will to rise once again, like a Phoenix from the ashes, with deadly and telling effect, as witnessed in later years. These are the victories, which cannot be tabulated and measured in terms of cold figures and clinical narratives.

After the fall of France, what was it that gave us here in these small islands some vestige of hope and glimmer that we would stay impregnable and be victorious from the might and arrogance of a ruthless enemy that was already virtually knocking at the door, but the roar of the bombers, night after night, as they set course for the enemy coast? Without this comforting noise and the catch phrase 'they're ours', the morale of Britain would have been at a low ebb, particularly as we were having our baptism of fire from the *Luftwaffe*.

When our armies made a magnificent and providential withdrawal from Dunkirk, who was left at that time to challenge the mighty fortress of the enemy but Bomber Command. Whilst our armies regrouped, re-equipped and consolidated, the men of Bomber Command with their infectious abandon took off into the stygian darkness and flew hundreds of miles into enemy territory, to become the awful gnawing wound in the side of the German High Command. From an embryo it grew, matured and emerged in size, gathering momentum all the time, penetrating his defences when and where they liked and finally helping to grind his potential war effort to a standstill.

Who was to know what effect the bombers had on the morale of the German armies, engaged in mortal and devastating combat on the Eastern Front and on the West by a populace seething with hatred and resentment and poised ready to strike when the opportune moment arose? Surely the cumulative effect of their battle reverses, plus the stories from men returning to the front from the homeland about the air attacks, may have stiffened their will to resist, but at the same time lowered their morale. How many times during the raids on London did one hear vivid and erroneous accounts of the attacks? By the time it reached the ears of our troops overseas it had been embellished out of all proportion to give a very depressing picture, which was certainly not conducive to a high standard of morale. Wasn't it natural when their own were in the front line?

It's all right now to sit back in smug complacency, judging and moralising, but let's not be so bloody self-righteous about it. If tomorrow we were attacked by nuclear weapons, would we not retaliate? In times of stress and danger, self-preservation is uppermost in all minds and men act not irrationally but naturally to fight back with what power they can command.

If the attack had not been mounted on Peenemünde in 1943, who is there to say that from this infernal melting pot of demonical weapons of V-1s and V-2s, might they not have produced an atom bomb that would have blasted all our self-righteousness, smugness and histories to smithereens? The losses were heavy in this attack but nothing comparable to what the losses might have been on a London defenceless against this type of missile, had not Bomber Command annihilated the laboratories of death and delayed the perfection of these missiles. Or again, when they searched the woods and byways of the Continent seeking out and blasting the death-dealing launching pads and rockets right out of their camouflaged pastoral setting. Or was this a wasted effort?

When Bomber Command mined the waters in Danzig Bay and traversed the length and breadth of the fjords of Europe, up the Skaggerak and Kattegat, they had their losses. But who was to know what German troopships and U-boats it impeded and destroyed, apart from the battleship *Tirpitz*, which could have played havoc with our lifelines, had Bomber Command not cornered and reduced it to an impotent rubble of steel in the Norwegian fjord where it lay skulking. Or again, when the Ardennes offensive broke right

271

through, it was halted when Bomber Command cut off the fuel supplies to the German tanks, which in due course brought about resultant defeat.

If these quasi historians must commit themselves to opinionating on facts and figures, they must weigh very, very carefully what might have been, taking into the account this unknown factor. This is an appraisal that is impossible. Surely, history is a narrative of events and times compiled from documents or eyewitnesses, the least of its objects is dwelling into the realms of suppositions and forming conclusions.

Albert Speer, Hitler's highly efficient and intelligent Reichsminister for Armaments, has recorded in his memoirs that if Bomber Command had systematically followed up the attack on Hamburg with similar campaigns against other key cities, then Germany might not have been able to withstand the resultant damage and could not have continued.

The mainspring of self-preservation is attack and consistently Bomber Command set course for the enemy coast night after night, impregnating the enemy's stranglehold ring of steel. After the heavy raids on Britain it was imperative, for public morale, to still the uneasiness of a tired populace and show that the enemy's defences were not invincible and he was not immune from attack.

Many of the bomber raids were each the equivalent of a major battle with enormous losses. Surely no other service could have sustained such a continuous and prolonged offensive as that carried out by Bomber Command, which operated against the enemy day and night from the first to the last day of the Second World War.

The average losses were 5 per cent each night. One does not have to be a mathematician to appreciate that the equivalent of the whole of the front line operational force was wiped out every twenty trips and this could be in as little as one month. The cost in the lives of the men of Bomber Command was very high. But surely history must find a place to justify and be gratified that this sacrifice was not in vain and was the means (probably) of preventing a holocaust by a large scale land invasion on an enemy powerful and intact from within.

Let no one dare, now that the battle campaigns have coursed along to their bloody and costly end, call them wasted efforts and defeats, lest a great tumultuous cry arise from the Valhalla of the dead echoing the immortal words of Tennyson across the eons of time. 'Theirs not to reason why, Theirs but to do and die.'

As I have said, I have no wish, nor desire, to enter into controversy as to what and when Bomber Command should have attacked, but only a desire to speak on behalf of the many thousands who never returned. They were expected to take up the challenge and this they did gladly, as they impregnated, blasted and savaged the vitals of an enemy conceivably worse than any in history. They ran rings around his iron clad defences whenever and whatever time they were called upon to do so, irrevocably and irrefutably hastening his downfall and earning themselves not a grudging but an indisputable right and place amongst the immortals on the somewhat faded and dubious scrolls of history.

For some months after the war I used to wake up in a cold sweat on the floor next to my side of the bed. The dream was always much the same – my clothes were on fire and I was baling out of a burning aircraft. Marguerite would say, 'You OK Spud?' I would reply, 'Yes thanks' and she would say, 'Well get back into bed then, and stop mucking about.' And that is all the counselling I ever received. But it worked and I soon forgot about those dreams. I have never, however, forgotten my time in the RAF, or the comrades I flew with ....

Arthur R. 'Spud' Taylor

APPENDIX 1

RAF Bomber Command Operational Statistics

3 September 1939 to 7/8 May 1945

(1) Aircraft sorties and casualties

Aircraft type	Sorties	Lost (% of sorties)		Operational crashes (% of sorties)	
Lancaster	156,192	3,431	(2.20)	246	(0.16)
Halifax	82,773	1,884	(2.28)	199	(0.24)
Wellington	47,409	1,386	(2.92)	341	(0.72)
Mosquito	39,795	260	(0.65)	50	(0.13)
Stirling	18,440	625	(3.39)	59	(0.32)
Hampden	16,541	424	(2.56)	209	(1.26)
Blenheim	12,214	442	(3.62)	99	(0.81)
Whitley	9,858	317	(3.22)	141	(1.43)
Boston	1,609	42	(2.61)	4	(0.25)
Fortress	1,340	14	(1.04)	4	(0.30)
Manchester	1,269	64	(5.04)	12	(0.95)
Ventura	997	39	(3.91)	2	(0.20)
Liberator	662	3	(0.45)	nil	
Others	710	22	(3.10)	2	(0.28)
Total	389,809	8,953		1,368	(0.35)

(2) Aircrew Casualties

Approximately 125,000 aircrew served in the squadrons and the operational training and conversion units of Bomber Command during the Second World War. Nearly 60 per cent of Bomber Command aircrew became casualties. Approximately 85 per cent of these casualties were suffered on operations and 15 per cent in training and accidents.

Killed in action or died while prisoners of war	47,268
Killed in flying or ground accidents	8,195
Killed in ground-battle action	37
Prisoners of war, including many wounded	9,838
Wounded in aircraft which returned from operations	4,200
Wounded in flying or ground accidents in UK	4,203
Total aircrew casualties	73,741

(3) Aircrew casualties by nationality

Royal Air Force	38,462	(69.2%)
Royal Canadian Air Force	9,919	(17.8%)
Royal Australian Air Force	4,050	(7.3%)
Royal New Zealand Air Force	1,679	(3.0%)
Polish Air Force	929	(1.7%)
Other Allied Air Forces	473	(0.9%)
South African Air Force	34	(0.1%)
Other Dominions	27	

(4) Casualties by rank

Officers	27.6%
Warrant Officers	3.3%
Non-commissioned officers	69.1%

(5) Escapers and evaders

156 RAF men successfully escaped from German PoW camps in Western Europe.
1,975 men evaded capture after having been shot down in Western Europe.

(6) Ground crew

1,479 men and 91 WAAFs died while on duty and 52 male ground staff became PoWs.

(7) Bomber Command Victoria Cross recipients (* = Posthumous award)

	Sqdn	A/c	Action/Award
Learoyd, Acting Flight Lieutenant Roderick Alastair Brook, pilot	49	Hampden	12.8.40, 20.8.40
Hannah, Flight Sergeant John, WOp-AG	83	Hampden	15/16.9.40, 1.10.40
Edwards, Acting Wing Commander Hughie Idwal DFC	105	Blenheim	4.7.41, 22.7.41
Ward, Sergeant James Allen RNZAF, 2nd pilot	75	Wellington	7.7.41, 5.8.41
Nettleton, Acting Squadron Leader John Dering, pilot	44	Lancaster	17.4.42, 28.4.42
Manser, Flying Officer Leslie Thomas RAFVR, pilot	50	Manchester	30/31.5.42, 0.10.42*
Middleton, Flight Sergeant Rawdon Hume RAAF, pilot	149	Stirling	28/29.11.42, 15.1.43*
Newton, Flight Lieutenant William Ellis RAAF			16.3.43
Gibson, Acting Wing Commander Guy Penrose DSO DFC, pilot	617	Lancaster	16/17.5.43, 28.5.43
Aaron, Flight Sergeant Arthur Louis DFM, pilot	218	Stirling	12/13.8.43, 5.11.43*
Reid, Acting Flight Lieutenant William RAFVR, pilot	61	Lancaster	3/4.11.43, 14.12.43
Barton, Pilot Officer Cyril Joe RAFVR, pilot	578	Halifax	30/31.5.44, 27.6.44*
Cheshire, Wing Commander Geoffrey Leonard DSO DFC RAFVR, pilot	617	Lancaster	8.9.44
Thompson, Flight Sergeant George RAFVR,	9	Lancaster	1.1.45, 20.2.45*

WOp

Palmer, Acting Squadron Leader Robert Anthony Maurice DFC RAFVR, pilot	109	Lancaster	23.12.44, 23.4.45*
Swales, Captain Edwin DFC SAAF, 'master bomber'	582	Lancaster	23/24.2.45, 24.4.45*
Bazalgette, Acting Squadron Leader Ian Willoughby DFC RAFVR, 'master bomber'	635	Lancaster	4.8.44, 17.8.45*
Jackson, Sergeant (later Warrant Officer) Norman Cyril RAFVR, flight engineer	106	Lancaster	26/27.4.44, 26.10.45
Trent, Squadron Leader Leonard Henry DFC RNZAF, pilot	487	Ventura	3.5.43, 1.3.46
Scarf, Squadron Leader Arthur Stewart King, pilot	62	Blenheim	9.12.41, 21.6.46*
Mynarski, Pilot Officer Andrew Charles RCAF, mid-upper gunner	419	Lancaster	12/13.6.44, 11.10.46*

APPENDIX 2

RAF slang terms in common everyday use

A 48	A 48-hour leave of absence
Adj	Adjutant
Battle bloomers	WAAF Issue Knickers – name originally given to them by the WAAFs themselves
Bird sanctuary	WAAF quarters – usually well away from the rough airmen!
Blood wagon	Ambulance
Bods	People, bodies
Bang-on	Something very good or very accurate
Binding	Moaning, complaining
Cheesed or cheesed off	Fed up, bored
Chiefy	Head of aircraft ground crew – generally well respected
Clapped out	Worn out, well past its best
Crate	Aircraft
Best blue	Best uniform
Big City, The	Berlin
Bought it	Killed, failed to return
Cheese cutter	Peaked cap
Cookie	4,000 lb bomb
Dicey	Dangerous. A dicey do. An op when there was heavy opposition
Dicing	(Dicing with death) Mainly operational flying but sometimes, just flying. Are we dicing tonight? Are we on the Battle Order?
Ditch	To land in the drink
Drink	The sea
Duff gen	Bad information
Erks	Aircraftmen – usually reserved for the lowest
Fans	Propeller on aircraft. No fans – no engines
On a fizzer	On a charge in front of a senior
Flight	A flight sergeant
Flights	Where aircrew collected particularly on operational squadrons while waiting for the 'gen'. Cards and other games of chance were played here. More generally, any place around hangars where matters connected with flying took place.
Flight offices	Usually occupied by the CO, flight commanders and their slaves
Flying orifice	Observer's brevet – the polite versions
Fruit salad	Lots of medal ribbons particularly on Americans

Getting finger out	Extracting the digit. Originally RAF slang term now in common use. In RAF it implied sitting on ones hands – politely
Get weaving	Get a move on – from aircraft taking avoiding action from fighters
Gone for a Burton	Terms like this were always used when anyone failed to return. Killed. Failed to return. It was never said that 'old so and so was killed last night'.
Gong	Medal
Good show	Did well
Going like the clappers	Moving very fast indeed
Got the chop	Killed
Got the gen	Have got the true information
Had it	Something coming to its end. For a person – 'He's had it' – he's died or is likely to
Hairy	Dangerous or very exciting
Happy Valley	The Ruhr
Kite	Aircraft
Meat wagon	Ambulance
Milk run	Regular run (USAAF equivalent – 'easy mission')
Sprog crew	A new crew
Suffering from the twitch	(particularly pilots) To be avoided at all costs
Shaky do	Near miss or lucky escape
Scrambled egg	Gold on caps of senior officers
Snappers	Enemy fighters
Twitch	Nervy. Bags of twitch' – suffered when in danger particularly from fighters
Penguin	Non aircrew – often used for someone not popular
Poor show	Bad behaviour. Not done well
Passion bafflers	WAAF Issue Knickers – name originally given to them by the WAAFs themselves
A piece of cake	Very easy
Queen Bee	WAAF Commanding Officer
Sky pilot	Padre
Second dickie	Second pilot
A stooge	A boring flight
Stooge around	Loiter. Hang around, fly around waiting for happening
Prang	A crash, usually of aircraft. To prang – to crash or to prang a target – to hit it well
R/T	Radio telephony
Spot on	Something very good or very accurate
Sprogs	New recruits
10/10ths	Complete cloud cover
Shoot a line	To brag, enlarge, blow ones own trumpet
Stores basher	Someone who worked in Stores
Waafery	WAAF quarters – usually well away from the rough airmen!
Wimpy	Vickers Armstrong Wellington twin-engined bomber (from J. Wellington Wimpy character in 'Popeye'.)
Winco	Wing commander usually Squadron Commanding Officer
Wingless wonder	Usually very unpopular non-aircrew
Wizard prang	A good raid

APPENDIX 3

Glossary

*	(medal) and Bar
10/10ths	Complete cloud cover
AA	Anti-Aircraft
AAA	Anti-Aircraft Artillery
Ack-ack	Flak, anti-aircraft fire
ADGB	Air Defence of Great Britain
Adj	Adjutant
AFC	Air Force Cross
AOC	Air Officer Commanding
ASR	Air-Sea Rescue
ATS	Air Training Squadron
Batman	From the French *bat*, meaning pack saddle. A male or female mess steward responsible for an officer's well being on base
BBC	British Broadcasting Corporation
BFTS	British Flying Training School
Big City	Berlin
Brevet	Flying badge
BSDU	Bomber Support Development Unit
CO	Commanding Officer
CoG	Centre of Gravity
Cookie	4,000 lb bomb
Crossbow	Offensive and defensive measures against the V-1 flying bomb
CRT	Cathode Ray Tube
C-scope	CRT showing frontal elevation of target
Day Ranger	Operation to engage air and ground targets within a wide but specified area, by day
DCM	Distinguished Conduct Medal
DFC	Distinguished Flying Cross
DFM	Distinguished Flying Medal
Diver	Code name for V-1 flying bomb operation
Drem lighting	System of outer markers and runway approach lights
DSC	Distinguished Service Cross
DSO	Distinguished Service Order
e/a	Enemy Aircraft
ETA	Estimated time of arrival
FIDO	Fog Investigation and Dispersal Operation
Flak	German term for anti-aircraft fire
Flight offices	Usually occupied by the CO, flight commanders and their slaves
Flight	A flight sergeant

FNSF	Fast Night Striking Force
Freelance	Patrol with the object of picking up a chance contact or visual of the enemy
Gardening	minelaying
	Ground Control Interception (radar)
Gee	British medium-range navigational aid using ground transmitters and an airborne receiver
GP	General Purpose bomb
Gremlin	A mythical mischievous creature invented by the RAF
H2S	British 10 cm experimental airborne radar navigational and target location aid
HE	High Explosive (bomb)
HEI	High Explosive Incendiary
HRH	His Royal Highness
IAS	Indicated Air Speed
IFF	Identification friend or foe
Intruder	Offensive night operation to fixed point or specified target
IO	Intelligence Officer
LAC	Leading aircraftman/woman
LMF	Lack of Moral Fibre
LNSF	Light Night Striking Force
Loran	Long-Range Navigation
M/T	Motor Transport
Mae West	Lifejacket, named after the well-endowed American actress
Mandrel	100 Group airborne radar jamming device
Manna	Air supply mission to Holland, April/May 1945
Market Garden	Ground/airborne operations, Arnhem, September 1944
MC	Medium Capacity bomb
MCU	Mosquito Conversion Unit
Mess	Possibly from the Latin *mensa* (table) or Old French *mes* (dish of food)
Met	Meteorological
Mickey Mouse	Bomb-aiming equipment
Milk run	Regular run of operations to a particular target (US, easy mission)
Millennium	One of three 1,000-bomber raids on German cities, May to June 1942
Monica	British tail warning radar device
MTU	Mosquito Training Unit
NCO	Non-Commissioned Officer
Newhaven	Flares dropped by PFF
Nickels	Propaganda leaflets
Night Ranger	Operation to engage air and ground targets within a wide but specified area, by night
Noball	V-2 rocket and V-1 flying bomb sites
OBE	Order of the British Empire
Oboe	Ground-controlled radar system of blind bombing in which one station indicated track to be followed and another the bomb release point
Ops	Operations
OT	Operational Training

Other ranks	Ranks other than commissioned officers
OTU	Operational Training Unit
Paramatta	Flares dropped by PFF
PFF	Pathfinder Force
PoW	Prisoner of war
PR	Photographic Reconnaissance
PRU	Photographic Reconnaissance Unit
R/T	Radio telephony
RAAF	Royal Australian Air Force
RAE	Royal Aircraft Establishment
RAFVR	Royal Air Force Volunteer Reserve
RCAF	Royal Canadian Air Force
RCM	Radio countermeasures
RNZAF	Royal New Zealand Air Force
RP	Rocket Projectile
SASO	Senior Air Staff Officer
SD	Special Duties
SEAC	South-East Asia Command
Serrate	British equipment designed to home in on *Lichtenstein* AI radar
Sortie	Operational flight by a single aircraft
TI	Target indicator
TNT	TriNitroToluene
U/S	Unserviceable
UHF	Ultra-High Frequency
VC	Victoria Cross
VHF	Very High Frequency
W/T	Wireless telephony
WAAF	Women's Auxiliary Air Force (member of)
Wanganui	Skymarking a target using flares dropped blindly using H2S
Window	Thin metallic strips dropped by Bomber Command to disrupt enemy radar
WOP/AG	wireless operator/air gunner
Y-Service	British organisation monitoring German radio transmissions to and from aircraft

Index